# Issues and Trends
# in Literacy Education

# Issues and Trends in Literacy Education

**Richard D. Robinson**
*University of Missouri-Columbia*

**Michael C. McKenna**
*Georgia Southern University*

**Judy M. Wedman**
*University of Missouri-Columbia*

**Allyn and Bacon**
*Boston • London • Toronto • Sydney • Tokyo • Singapore*

*Library of Congress Cataloging-in-Publication Data*

Issues and trends in literacy education  /  [edited by]
    Richard D. Robinson, Michael C. McKenna, Judy M. Wedman.
        p.      cm.
    Includes bibliographical references and index.
    ISBN 0-205-16146-4
    1. Literacy—United States.    2. Teachers—Training of—United
States.    3. Reading—United States.    I. Robinson, Richard David
(date)    II. McKenna, Michael C.    III. Wedman, Judy M. (date)
LC151.I87    1996
372.6′044—dc20                                                                95-23601
                                                                                      C I P

Printed in the United States of America
10  9  8  7  6  5  4  3  2  1    99  98  97  96  95

*The love of books is a love which requires neither justification, apology, nor defense.*
—JOHN LANGFORD

---

*This book is dedicated to those teachers who have inspired in their students an undying love for reading and writing.*

# Contents

# *Preface*

The primary purpose of this book is to help you better study and understand the field of literacy education. What was once a rather limited discipline is today a vast and complicated body of knowledge and field of inquiry, frequently drawing on information from many diverse areas such as psychology, sociology, and linguistics. The individual wishing to investigate a question or topic in literacy today may find the experience a daunting one.

For example, a recent computer search on the subject "reading comprehension" identified over 4,000 references to this one topic. Ranging across a broad spectrum of subtopics, the results of this search clearly showed the diversity that is typical of the literacy field. These results included data-based research studies, classroom observational inquiries, theoretical research papers, as well as personal opinion articles. These references represented the work of university faculty, classroom teachers, commercial publishers, and private individuals. Complicating the situation is the fact that there is not only a great deal of information currently available, but many different opinions and perspectives as well. These viewpoints often range between a single individual's position on a topic and a national movement reflecting the philosophies and attitudes of many thousands of people.

It is with these circumstances in mind that the present textbook was written. We have attempted to identify the most significant issues and trends facing literacy educators today and to locate sources that explain principal viewpoints on these issues. Beyond selecting sources and providing textual aids to promote comprehension and engagement, our contribution has been minimal. We prefer to let the authors speak for themselves.

We have assumed that most readers of this book have had at least some introduction to the study of literacy education. The book has been developed with practicing teachers in mind—practitioners interested in extending their own thinking about the important issues they face in classrooms. We have not attempted to produce an introductory text, but assume that the foundations of literacy instruction—its purposes, concepts, and methods—have already been laid by means of prior coursework and teaching experience.

## Organization of the Text

Each chapter is made up of four parts: (1) a brief introduction to the topic, (2) the articles themselves, (3) an annotated bibliography, and (4) suggestions for further involvement.

### Chapter Introductions

Each topic is first summarized in a brief section designed both to provide necessary background and to help stimulate thinking related to the topic. Many readers of this book will have, either through previous education classes or classroom teaching experiences, developed ideas and feelings about the topics discussed in this book. We challenge you to keep an open mind about what you currently believe concerning literacy instruction. In many literacy areas, either because of recent research or relevant classroom experiences, instructional strategies that were once considered appropriate are now being challenged by new ideas and pedagogy.

Each chapter introduction concludes with a list of important questions designed to guide your reading and organize your thinking. Actively considering them should give you a better understanding of your current knowledge, beliefs, and feelings about a particular literacy issue.

### Articles

Following the introduction are the selections. Our intent is that this section will help familiarize you with important, though sometimes incompatible, views on the chapter topic. Of particular note is the presentation of differing points of view. For some topics, where there is little disagreement or controversy, you will find a general discussion of the literacy trend. You should understand that the selections are never intended to be all-inclusive but rather to introduce the topic and encourage you to pursue further study on your own.

Accompanying the selections are **Content Literacy Guides,** designed to aid you in focusing on the important issues discussed in the accompanying articles and to provide a useful review guide once completed. Some parts of the guides are designed to be completed as you read, whereas some portions are to be finished afterward. They combine literal, inferential, and critical responses to the article content. They can be used both prior to reading the articles as a purpose-setting device and following the reading as an opportunity for content review. The final portions of the guides are called **Integrating Sources** and **Classroom Implications.** These two sections follow the articles. As the headings indicate, the intent is to help you resolve differences between the articles and to consider possible implications for classroom literacy instruction. These sections are purposely designed to be open ended.

### Annotated Bibliographies

Although every article has its own reference section, we have attempted to supplement these with a careful selection of sources useful for further reading. In some cases, the material is divided into a historical and a current listing of literacy sources. In these cases, the reader can see the development and changes in thinking on a literacy topic, noting how historical issues and trends have influenced current opinions and practices.

### You Become Involved

The final section of each chapter is designed to help you formulate your own views by engaging in activities that encourage independent thought. For each chapter, a range of possibilities is presented. The ideas can be approached individually or in groups and are meant to be undertaken selectively.

## For the University Teacher

Today, colleges of education are increasingly faced with issues of accountability related to their preparation of teachers. Whereas some standards, such as those of the National Council for the Accreditation of Teacher Education (NCATE), apply across the general field of education, subject matter organizations have developed guidelines for more specialized teacher preparation. In this respect, the International Reading Association (IRA) has long been involved in the development of standards for the preparation of literacy educators at all levels. The IRA publication, *Standards for Reading Professionals* (Lunsford & Pauls, 1992), was written to guide the preparation and professional development of literacy educators. Emphasized as a fundamental principle throughout this publication is the fact that all educators, whether at the preservice or inservice level, need an extensive conceptual framework related to the field of literacy instruction.

The following specific guidelines are only part of those listed by which university and college programs of teacher education in the field of literacy will be evaluated. They include the following student outcomes:

- Has knowledge of current and historical perspectives about the nature and purposes of reading and about widely used approaches to reading instruction
- Pursues knowledge of reading and learning processes by reading professional journals and publications and participating in conferences and other professional activities
- Employs inquiry and makes thoughtful decisions during teaching and assessment
- Interprets and communicates research findings related to the improvement of instruction to colleagues and the wider community
- Initiates, participates in, or applies research on reading

- Reads or conducts research with a range of methodologies (e.g., ethnographic, descriptive, experimental, or historical)
- Promotes and facilitates teacher-based and classroom-based research

The primary purpose of this book is to assist you in helping your students meet these wide and diverse guidelines for literacy education. Chapter content is designed to encourage further exploration of certain selected topics in literacy education through the effective use of a wide variety of resources and materials. We would hope that the end product of this book and your instruction is an educator who has been made more aware of the prominent issues and trends in the field of literacy education today and who appreciates their implications for practice.

We wish to take this opportunity to thank the following reviewers for their helpful comments: Larry Andrews, University of Nebraska–Lincoln; Nancy Bacharach, St. Cloud State University; Patricia DeMay, Livingston University; Jean McWilliams, Rosemont College; and David Reinking, University of Georgia.

# Chapter 1

# Introduction to the Field of Literacy Education

*Books are yours,*
*Within whose silent chambers treasure lies*
*Preserved from age to age; more precious far*
*Than that accumulated store of gold*
*And orient gems which, for a day of need,*
*The sultan hides deep in ancestral tombs.*
*These hoards of truth you can unlock at will*
*—WILLIAM WORDSWORTH*

The study of literacy today is a vast and often complicated enterprise. In many fields, information is concentrated in a limited number of journals or produced by relatively few individuals; this is certainly not the case in literacy education, however. For example, important literacy research and writing are currently being done by individuals in fields as diverse as linguistics, cognitive psychology, sociology, computer science, anthropology, and education. Even within the general field of education, literacy materials are often indexed under a broad range of descriptors, such as emergent literacy, assessment, materials, teacher training, and so on. This information is frequently reported in a wide variety of outlets—including journals, books, and research reports—and has recently been lodged in huge computer databases. For the literacy educator, this wide spectrum of knowledge and available resources often presents a daunting challenge.

The purpose of this chapter is to facilitate your further study of literacy education. The intent here is to provide specific information that will help you learn more about the most prominent resources and current thinking in the field. You may already be familiar with some of the sources mentioned.

## As You Read

Your study of this chapter should prepare you to examine the issues that follow. As you read, keep the following objectives in mind:

1. Describe some effective strategies for literacy research and study.
2. Identify some of the current trends in literacy education.
3. Identify the major national organizations in the field of literacy study.
4. Describe some of the important journals and references in the field of literacy.

## Introduction

Edmund Huey, writing early in the twentieth century about the study of the reading process, noted that "to completely analyze what we do when we read would almost be the acme of a psychologist's achievements, for it would be to describe very many of the most intricate workings of the human mind, as well as to unravel the tangled story of the most remarkable specific performance that civilization has learned in all its history" (Huey, 1908, p. 6). This single statement, in many respects, epitomizes even today the ongoing search for a better understanding of the reading process. Although it is true that much has been done in the study of fundamental processes related to literacy as well as in the development of new instructional programs in literacy since Huey wrote, many important questions remain unanswered at the present time.

## Current Trends in Literacy Education

Today, as in the past, the literacy community often finds itself split according to philosophies, theories, and/or practical applications. Although terms may have changed, much of what is debated today is often strikingly similar to the substance of past disputes. Issues such as the most appropriate methods and materials to use in the teaching of literacy as well as how to effectively assess what is learned are, after extended controversy, still the center of much of the literacy debate today.

As you continue your study of literacy issues, it is important to be aware that you must inevitably confront divergent viewpoints and opinions. For almost any of these issues, there is a wide range of opinions and feelings. These differences are clearly evident in the available literature on most topics. Expecting them should make you better at identifying and appraising the various viewpoints on each literacy topic.

A preview of some of the most prominent issues facing literacy educators today may well convince you of the range of problems involved. A major issue is that of whole language versus more conventional philosophies to instruction. Related to it is the role of phonics instruction, spelling, and basal readers. The nature of emerging literacy in early childhood has challenged older notions of "readiness," just as research into vocabulary instruction may surprise you with its implications for day-to-day practice. In content area classrooms, new conceptualizations have arisen as to how literacy activities can help students learn. In the larger arena of education, debate over the proper approaches to assessment and the desirability of national standards has spilled over into literacy. Finally, new advances in technology challenge educators to make the best uses of it in developing literate behavior in students. Each of these topics will be covered later in this book, though their interrelatedness will frequently compel you to cross-reference your thinking!

## Organizations in Literacy Education

Many professional organizations address literacy issues as part of their programs, but the following are the most prominent.

- *International Reading Association.* The IRA is the largest organization in the literacy field, with a widespread membership that includes teachers at all levels from college and university faculty through elementary teachers. This organization is noted for its many quality literacy publications as well as a structure that invites participation at local, state, regional, national, and global levels. Its periodicals include *The Reading Teacher, Journal of Adolescent and Adult Literacy* (formerly *Journal of Reading*), *Reading Research Quarterly,* and *Lectura y Vida* (Spanish language).
- *National Council of Teachers of English.* The NCTE is a large organization representing teachers interested in language arts instruction. Like the IRA, the NCTE is noted for a variety of publications, including its two principal journals, *Language Arts* and *English Journal.*
- *National Reading Conference.* This organization is primarily comprised of college and university faculty interested in all types of literacy research. Its periodical is the *Journal of Reading Behavior* (soon to be known as the *Journal of Literacy Research*), and its yearbook also presents research on a wide variety of literacy-related topics.
- *College Reading Association.* Members of this organization are primarily college and university faculty. CRA publishes a journal, *Reading Research and Instruction,* as well as a yearbook.

## Leading Journals in the Field of Literacy

- *The Reading Teacher.* This journal, published by the International Reading Association, includes articles primarily related to the teaching of literacy in the elementary school.
- *Journal of Adolescent and Adult Literacy.* This journal, formerly titled *Journal of Reading,* is published by the International Reading Association with emphasis on literacy education in the content areas as well as on middle, high school, and adult education.

- *Reading Research and Instruction.* Formerly *Reading World,* this journal combines research reports with articles that suggest ideas. It is published by the College Reading Association.
- *Reading Research Quarterly.* This is the leading journal of literacy research. The articles published in this journal consistently represent important contributions to the field of literacy research. Often, the articles published in the *Reading Research Quarterly* include extensive bibliographies of related materials and thus are excellent sources for further study. This journal is a publication of the International Reading Association.
- *Reading Horizons.* This journal is intended primarily for classroom teachers and typically publishes articles related to classroom applications of new literacy research.
- *Journal of Literary Research.* Primarily a literacy research journal published by the National Reading Conference, this publication also presents position papers and issues-oriented commentary.
- *Reading Psychology.* This journal contains a wide variety of literacy articles, including research, opinion pieces, and suggestions for practice.
- *Language Arts.* This journal is published by the National Council of Teachers of English. Although areas of the language arts curriculum are included, there is a substantial number directly related to literacy concerns. The primary orientation of the journal is toward elementary instruction.
- *English Journal.* Published by the National Council of Teachers of English, this journal addresses the concerns of teachers serving adolescent and older populations.

## References in the Study of Literacy Education

Although a seemingly endless flow of new titles enters the field of literacy education, the following books have been selected as important sources for further study. They have been selected on the basis of their importance to the field and should be excellent starting points for further study.

### Reference Materials

Adams, M. J. (1990). *Beginning to read: Thinking and learning about print.* Cambridge, Massachusetts: MIT Press.

*This important and scholarly reference reflects the continuing interest in the study of the sound/symbol relationships related to word analysis. Comprehensive synthesis of research in the areas of cognitive and developmental psychology, instructional methodology, and related areas is included.*

Flood, J., et al. (Eds.). (1991). *Handbook of research on teaching the English language arts.* New York: Macmillan.

*This collection of research reviews focuses on topics broadly ranging across the language arts.*

Goodman, K. (1986). *What's whole in whole language?* Portsmouth, New Hampshire: Heinemann.

*A thorough discussion of the philosophical foundations of the whole language movement is provided.*

Kamil, M., & Langer, J. A. (1985). *Understanding research in reading and writing.* Boston: Allyn and Bacon.

*This book is a discussion of the uses of various research methodologies and their specific application to the study of literacy. For those interested in the development of a research design related to literacy, this is an excellent reference.*

Pearson, P. D., et al. (1984). *Handbook of reading research.* White Plains, New York: Longman.

Barr, R., et al. (1991). *Handbook of reading research, Part II.* White Plains, New York: Longman.

*Both of these volumes are important resources in the study of literacy education. They contain inclusive reviews of important issues in the field as well as extensive bibliographies of related materials. They should be excellent starting points for most studies in the field of literacy education.*

Samuels, J., & Farstrup, A. (1992). *What reading research has to say about reading instruction.* Newark, Delaware: International reading Association.

*This is a series of articles written by noted literacy authorities on how current research informs several important issues in the field.*

## Historical Materials

The following references have been selected to provide a historical perspective on the research and teaching of literacy. They should provide you with information on important past work done by noted authorities in the field.

Altick, R. D. (1963). *The art of literacy research.* New York: W. W. Norton.

*This cornerstone work on the research methods in literacy anticipates many of the present-day concerns of qualitative researchers.*

Anderson, I. H., & Dearborn, W. F. (1952). *The psychology of reading.* New York: Roland Press.

*This is an important reference in the early study of the psychology of literacy processes.*

Betts, E. A. (1946). *Foundations of reading instruction.* New York: American Book Company.

*Written for preservice teachers on the teaching of literacy in the elementary grades, this important reference is excellent for comparison with current methods texts.*

Dolch, E. W. (1939). *A manual for remedial reading.* Champaign, Illinois: Garrard Press.

> *This is one of the first references written on the topic of the remediation of reading difficulties.*

Gates, A. I. (1929). *The improvement of reading.* New York: Macmillan.

> *This is one of the first textbooks in elementary literacy instruction.*

Gray, W. S. (1948). *On their own in reading.* Chicago: Scott Foresman.

> *Written by one of the early leaders in the study of literacy, this important reference focuses on the study and classroom use of the sound/symbol relationships.*

Huey, E. B. (1908). *The psychology and pedagogy of reading.* Cambridge, Massachusetts: MIT Press.

> *This is an early exploration of cognitive processes that underlie reading. It is famed for the later substantiation through research of many of the author's premises.*

National Society for the Study of Education Yearbooks. Chicago: University of Chicago Press.

> *This series of landmark books deals with important issues in the field of education. These books contain important articles that were often instrumental in the development of later reading policies and research. The following editions deal with the study of literacy: 20th (1921), 24th (1925), 36th (1937), 47th (1948), 48th (1949), 55th (1956), 60th (1961), 67th (1968), 83rd (1984).*

Robinson, H. M. (1946). *Why pupils fail in reading.* Chicago: University of Chicago Press.

> *This is a foundation report in the clinic approach to the study of reading disabilities in children.*

Smith, N. B. (1934). *American reading instruction.* New York: Silver, Burdett.

> *This is a classic in the study of the historical foundations of the study of literacy and of reading instruction from colonial times forward.*

## Strategies for Literacy Research

For most readers of this book, the beginning of a literacy study will begin with a question about a particular concern or interest in this area. This question may arise in response to an assignment in a graduate class in literacy education or as the result of a personal interest in a literacy topic. It also might be initiated by a need to solve a classroom problem related to literacy, such as finding out more about a specific teaching technique or the background related to new commercial materials. For whatever reason, the formation of a question is a very important first step in any literacy study (Altick, 1963).

Unfortunately, it is at this point that many individuals begin to have varying degrees of difficulty. Frequently, initial questions are far too general to be answered in a realistic and effective manner. For example, questions such as the following are almost unanswerable:

- What causes literacy problems?
- What are effective literacy materials?
- What is the best method of teaching literacy skills?

These examples could be improved considerably by narrowing their scope:

- Does the home environment of a child have a lasting effect on literacy development?
- What is the influence of library books on the development of literacy skills?
- Has the use of language experience been shown to be superior to the use of the basal reader in first-grade literacy development?

The degree of specificity of any question will largely be determined by the background knowledge and purposes of each individual.

Once the question has been formulated, the investigator needs to propose a possible answer, sometimes with limited information but always on the basis of theory. Continuing with the previous examples, the projected answers might look like these:

- The home environment of a child, especially parents reading to their children, does have a positive and long-term effect on literacy development.
- Library books are best used under the direction of a professional librarian rather than the classroom teacher.
- First-grade teachers find language experience instruction to be better suited to disadvantaged students than the use of the basal reader.

Each of these statements may or may not be true. It then becomes the goal of the investigator to find information either to support or to refute these tentative conclusions. In accomplishing this objective, the literacy researcher needs to be aware of a number of potential difficulties. The first is the typically large amount of information available on almost every aspect of literacy education. In the area of literacy education, the question frequently is not "Can I find information on my topic?" but rather "How can I select from the voluminous material available?" The second problem is the wide diversity of sources. Not only are there prominent journals and references in the field but there are also many other resources that publish literacy-related information. These sources include journals, books, research and development reports, newspaper articles, and so forth. Finally, one must consider the fact that for many issues in literacy education, there are widely differing opinions. Thus, for many literacy issues, you should expect to find various personal opinions as well as research results—and differing opinions on what the results mean!

With these obstacles in mind, it may seem an almost impossible task to find an answer to any literacy question. Yet the careful and thorough process of investigation should, in most cases, prove to be successful. Altick (1963), in summarizing this approach to scholarship, noted a pair of elementary principles: "(1) collect all the evidence, internal and external, that has any connection with your hypothesis, and (2) give as much consideration to evidence that weighs against the hypothesis, or that tends to support an alternative one, as to the substantiating kind. And maintain the critical attitude to the very end; the collapsible premise and the spurious fact are always lurking in the path of the unwary" (p. 122). Hopefully, with these thoughts in mind, you should be able to successfully begin, work through, and produce an effective literacy study into a topic of particular interest to you.

## *References*

Altick, R. D. (1963). *The art of literacy research.* New York: W. W. Norton.

Huey, E. B. (1908). *The psychology and pedagogy of reading.* Cambridge, MA: MIT Press.

# Chapter *2*

# *Whole Language*

The whole language movement is unquestionably one of the most influential in recent decades. The National Assessment of Educational Progress (Mullis, Campbell, & Farstrup, 1993) reported that a significant number of fourth-grade teachers in the United States characterize their own instruction as "whole language," either completely or in part. It is important for teachers to understand the nature of whole language, and why it has become an issue as well as a trend, if they are to make intelligent decisions about their practice.

## *Philosophy versus Approach*

Defining *whole language* is not a simple task. Indeed, entire articles have been devoted to it (Bergeron, 1990; De Carlo, 1995; Watson, 1989). The lack of a clear-cut, straightforward definition is due, according to whole language advocates, to the fact that practitioners are expected to arrive at their own personalized definitions, as long as they fall within a broad set of guidelines. Many writers have listed characteristics of whole language, but Pressley (1994) has suggested that only two of these are essential. First, whole language is based on the belief that learning to read and write are natural to human development so long as opportunities to learn are provided. That is to say, direct, systematic instruction is not necessary. Second, the study of language must be undertaken for real student purposes using real examples of language.

If such beliefs do not seem very specific, it is because whole language is a philosophy and not a well-articulated approach to literacy instruction. This is why a rigid definition of the term cannot be offered, for as long as teachers use instructional techniques consistent with the philosophy, then the result is whole language. On the other hand, it is certainly possible to enumerate certain practices typical of whole language classrooms and to make a separate list of practices inconsistent with a whole language philosophy. For example, an observer is likely to see the use of predictable books (those that use rhyme and repetitive structures), trade books of all kinds, a classroom environment that is rich in examples of print, children who are encouraged to invent their own spellings of unfamiliar words, and a reliance on teachable moments to conduct skill instruction on an as-needed basis. At the same time, one is not likely to see development. In short, although whole language may be a "theory-in-practice" (Edelsky, 1990, p. 8), it must become practice. To the extent that such practice has similar elements from teacher to teacher, whole language can be characterized as an approach.

## A Place for Eclecticism?

Whole language advocates have cautioned that a mixture of whole language and traditional teaching methods is unacceptable. Since whole language is a philosophy, the use of methods inconsistent with that philosophy leads to instruction that lacks coherence. And yet most whole language teachers seem to have adopted the practices that they find useful and to have mixed them with more traditional techniques (e.g., Walmsley & Adams, 1993). It is interesting to note that a significant number of fourth-grade teachers claim to be whole language educators, yet a majority of these teachers also report using a basal reader. Some of these teachers may be confused as to the true nature of whole language, while others may have deliberately chosen to be eclectic. That is, they may have consciously selected those techniques they find useful regardless of any other considerations.

## Basals versus Trade Books

We will discuss basal readers as a separate issue, but they are inseparable from any discussion of whole language. Basals are viewed as unacceptable for a number of reasons. They have tended traditionally to provide teachers with detailed lesson plans, perhaps "deskilling" them in the process. They rely on a systematic and sequential approach to skill development, sometimes providing isolated practice in these skills. In addition, basals sometimes edit children's literature to meet space and readability requirements, and in the past stories of questionable literary merit have been produced exclusively for use in the readers. These are the major criticisms, though the list is not exhaustive. Trade books, on the other hand, lend themselves well to a whole language philosophy. They present high-quality, unedited material. They free the teacher from the confines of scripted basal lessons. They also permit student choice. Most importantly, they do not easily lend themselves to learning decoding skills in isolation.

## Skills in Context versus Skills in Isolation

An important way in which whole language is "whole" is the fact that instruction begins with entire examples of text (such as books), and skills are discussed by teachers only in this larger context and only as such discussion is needed

(Goodman, 1986). More traditional, "synthetic" approaches have sometimes attempted to teach skills one by one in the belief that children will eventually learn to integrate them. The critics of the whole language view have argued that research has strongly supported a more systematic approach to instruction, and even the occasional use of decontextualized introduction and practice of skills.

## As You Read

The following articles illustrate what we believe to be a transformation in the way whole language is viewed by U.S. teachers. Spiegel (1992) argues that skills instruction can be systematic without necessarily involving the rigid sequencing of the past. Walmsley and Adams, through their interviews with whole language teachers, conclude that they are arriving at much the same position in their own practice—a position that is clearly eclectic in nature.

Whether or not you have adopted a whole language philosophy for your own instruction, reflecting on these recent articles may help you to refine and extend your own thinking. As you read, try to arrive at answers to the following questions as they relate to your own teaching circumstances:

**1.** How would you translate whole language philosophy into a personal approach to literacy instruction?
**2.** Would you favor an eclectic approach, in which some traditional techniques are retained even though they are at odds with whole language?
**3.** Can basal readers ever be compatible with whole language?
**4.** Outline an approach to skills instruction that you believe constitutes best practice. How is it consistent with whole language philosophy? In what ways is it at variance?

## References

Bergeron, B. S. (1990). What does the term whole language mean? Constructing a definition from the literature. *Journal of Reading Behavior, 22,* 301–309.

De Carlo, J. E. (in press). Perspectives in whole language.

Edelsky, C. (1990). Whose agenda is this anyway? A response to McKenna, Robinson, and Miller. *Educational Researcher, 19*(8), 7–11.

Goodman, K. S. (1986). *What's whole in whole language?* Portsmouth, NH: Heinemann.

Mullis, I. V. S., Campbell, J. R., & Farstrup, A. E. (1993). *NAEP 1992: Reading report card for the nation and states.* Washington, DC: U.S. Department of Education.

Pressley, M. (1994). Commentary on the whole language debate. In C. B. Smith (Ed.), *Whole language: The debate* (pp. 155–178). Bloomington, IN: ERIC Clearinghouse on Reading, English, and Communication.

Spiegel, D. L. (1992). Blending whole language and systematic direct instruction. *The Reading Teacher, 46,* 38–44.

Walmsley, S. A., & Adams, E. L. (1993). Realities of "whole language." *Language Arts, 70,* 272–280.

Watson, D. (1989). Defining and describing whole language. *Elementary School Journal, 90,* 129–141.

**Blending Whole Language and Systematic Direct Instruction**
Dixie Lee Spiegel
*The Reading Teacher, 46,* 1992, 38–44

1. According to Spiegel, what two factors tend to cause some educators to "reject whole language in its entirety"?

   a.

   b.

2. Spiegel discusses many benefits of whole language without formally numbering them. See how many you can list.

3. List three of the "authentic" forms of assessment mentioned.

   a.

   b.

   c.

**4.** Restate Spiegel's definition of *systematic instruction*.

**5.** Describe how systematic instruction relates to

a. assessment

b. scope and sequence

**6.** What problems can arise in relying solely on teachable moments?

a.

b.

**7.** Summarize Spiegel's description of direct instruction.

**8.** Where do "authentic materials" enter into the direct instruction model?

**9.** (T/F)   According to Spiegel, Atwell's 5- to 10-minute lessons probably provide sufficient sustained, focused practice.

**10.** Describe Durkin's notion of "mentioning."

**11.** (T/F)   Sustained direct instruction is not complete until students can use the strategy with new, authentic materials.

**12.** (T/F)  In systematic direct instruction, the teacher makes most decisions about what is to be learned.

**13.** Spiegel lists three principal arguments whole language educators use against systematic direct instruction. State these and summarize Spiegel's counterargument(s) to each.

a.

b.

c.

**14.** (T/F)  For many affective goals, indirect instruction is more appropriate than direct instruction.

**15.** (T/F)  As a practical matter, teachers tend to draw from "both worlds."

**16.** (T/F)  Spiegel argues that whole language and systematic direct instruction can complement each other.

# BLENDING WHOLE LANGUAGE AND SYSTEMATIC DIRECT INSTRUCTION

The benefits of a whole language philosophy for teachers, children, and literacy education in general are many. However, deemphasis of systematic direct instruction within whole language classrooms often causes reservation and concern among teachers, administrators, and teacher educators. Because whole language primarily espouses indirect methods of instruction, and because whole language advocates often are perceived as assuming an all-or-nothing stance, some literacy educators may reject whole language in its entirety. I believe that this is a mistake. Concomitantly, I believe that giving systematic direct instruction a more prominent role in whole language classrooms will strengthen literacy education in those environments and enable teachers to meet the needs of more children.

In this commentary, I briefly review what I perceive to be some of the many benefits of the whole language philosophy. I then discuss the importance of systematic direct instruction, defining it and presenting arguments for including direct instruction in the classroom. Last of all, I reiterate my plea that we build bridges between whole language and more traditional approaches for the purpose of providing all children with the very best opportunities to meet their literacy potential.

## Thanks, Whole Language

Literacy educators have a great deal for which to thank whole language proponents. Many teachers who had lost their zip after years of being basal-bound, either through their own choice or through administrative fiat, are now excited again about teaching. Whole language emphases on flexibility in materials and activities, on student and teacher choice, and on viewing each child as a unique individual rather than as a third grader

*Source:* "Blending Whole Language and Systematic Direct Instruction" by Dixie Lee Spiegel, 1992, *The Reading Teacher, 46.* Copyright 1992 by the International Reading Association. Reprinted by permission.

(or even worse, a bluebird or an eagle) has given many teachers freedom to use their professional judgment, a freedom which may have been denied them in the past.

Along with liberating teachers who had felt restricted or regimented (Harste, 1989; Watson, 1989), whole language has freed many children to experiment with and explore literacy (Watson, 1989). Children are encouraged to be risk-takers, to try things out in reading and writing, and to take pride in their efforts even if their products are less than perfect (Allen, Michalove, Shockley, & West, 1991). Further, children are viewed and view themselves as members of a community of readers and writers who work together to meet genuine needs and fulfill real purposes through reading and writing (Allen et al., 1991; Goodman, 1989). As children interact with each other through and about literacy, they gain additional perspectives on how to go about becoming effective readers and writers.

Whole language has also done literacy education a great service by focusing attention on three facets of literacy: writing, children's literature, and authentic forms of assessment.

One of the most important benefits of whole language is that we are at last becoming *literacy* educators, not just reading teachers and occasionally writing teachers. Writing is increasingly viewed from the perspective of a process of communication, not as a set of mechanics to be mastered and then applied. Even very young children are being perceived as both writers and readers, not readers and then, maybe some time later, writers. And most importantly of all, children are viewing themselves as writers because they are encouraged to write, given time to write, and rewarded for writing through success in communication.

Whole language advocates have also focused our attention on the rich resources of children's literature, especially trade books. Informal conversations with teachers indicate that classrooms have been flooded with children's literature. Even teachers who continue to use basals are reading more to children, often using trade books for at least part of their instruction, and providing more time for recreational reading. And children are reading more themselves (Shulz, 1991). Through increased use of literature, especially in trade books, children may find reading more accessible and fulfilling because it is not focused on a basal that is available only in the classroom.

Whole language proponents are often adamantly opposed to standardized testing as the means of assessing student progress. In place of standardized tests, whole language teachers emphasize authentic forms of assessment that focus on students' developing literacy processes as much as on their products (Goodman, Goodman, & Hood, 1989). Further, literacy processes and products are examined through conferences, anecdotal records, work samples, and other literacy products that are part of genuine efforts at communication, rather than through tests of questionable validity taken on 1 or 2 days (Tierney, Carter, & Desai, 1991). Authentic forms of assessment can provide information about how children *use* literacy to meet communication needs. Further, portfolios, conference records, and anecdotal information allow teacher, child, and parents to view the child's progress in terms of self rather than in comparison to other children, thus emphasizing growth toward meeting a specific criterion rather than competition.

## *The Importance of Systematic Direct Instruction*

Although some whole language advocates state that direct instruction can be part of a whole language classroom (Fountas & Hannigan, 1989; Newman & Church, 1990;

Slaughter, 1988), much of the literature about whole language either implies or directly asserts that systematic direct instruction is not desirable (Doake, 1987; Goodman, 1986; Veatch, 1988). However, an extensive body of research indicates that clearly defined objectives and teacher-directed instruction are characteristics of effective reading programs (Adams, 1990; Duffy, Roehler, & Putman, 1987; Evans & Carr, 1985; Rosenshine & Stevens, 1984). This research shows that learning is more likely to occur if students know what the learning tasks are and if teachers specifically teach them.

Before proceeding further, it is important to define what systematic direct instruction is and is not. I first describe systematic instruction and then move on to direct instruction.

## *Systematic Instruction*

*Systematic* instruction is based on an identified scope of goals and objectives, and activities are designed and carried out specifically to meet these goals. Yatvin (1991) warns that without a schoolwide program "that ensures a rational and orderly distribution of content and materials over the grades" (p. 1), anarchy may result as each teacher follows his or her own curriculum.

Systematic instruction includes systematic assessment. Teachers set up opportunities for literacy interactions that will allow them to determine if children have reached identified goals and objectives. In some instances, these opportunities may be contrived and artificial, such as completing worksheets on vocabulary meanings, but they need not be. A knowledgeable teacher can follow instruction with literacy experiences in which use of a taught strategy or skill will be needed for success. For example, after teaching about the value of setting one's own purposes for reading and writing, children may design and carry out interviews of elderly friends and neighbors as part of their ongoing efforts to create a community history. As preparation, reporters identify a set of questions to ask each person.

Systematic instruction does have scope, but it does not necessarily have a prescribed *sequence*. That is, knowing what one wants children to learn does not mean that a specific order is dictated in which all children must learn. Thus, claims that systematic instruction means lock-step instruction are incorrect. Some systematic programs for teaching reading are prescriptive, but most, including basal programs, are not. Although it is convenient for some teachers to use systematic programs in a prescribed, sequential manner, that is a choice they have made and is not mandated by the nature of systematic instruction itself.

Whole language proponents often advocate the use of mini-lessons, as described by Atwell (1987). Although advocates of systematic instruction recognize the value of "seizing the teachable moment" to provide short lessons based on needs that have spontaneously arisen during authentic tasks, they suggest that relying solely on such an approach can lead to haphazard and incomplete literacy development. One problem is that teachable moments may not arise for many important literacy skills (Baumann, 1991). Further, some teachers may not always recognize these moments when they do spring up or may be unprepared to provide appropriate assistance. Fortunately, an either/or position about mini-lessons is not necessary. Durkin (1990) makes this point when she differentiates between planned and unplanned instruction and suggests that both are needed "if the reading ability of every student is to be maximally advanced" (p. 474).

## Direct Instruction

In *direct* instruction, students and teacher are focused on a goal or objective, on what is to be learned; students are aware of why it is important to learn the task at hand; and students are explicitly taught how to do a particular process through teacher modeling and explanation. This is followed by guided application as students try out their interpretations of what was taught while the teacher monitors this tryout. Then independent application takes place in authentic, whole materials (as opposed to materials created solely for the practice of the process, such as worksheets) in which utilization of the process will enhance comprehension. Durkin (1990) describes application as "giving students opportunities to experience, as soon as possible, the value of what they are being asked to do" (p. 475). Throughout direct instruction, assessment and change in instruction take place if assessment suggests that the children have not learned (Baumann, 1988; Duffy & Roehler, 1986).

Direct instruction has often been falsely equated with "skilling and drilling," in which children are taught to mindlessly apply skills in artificial situations. Of course, direct instruction *can* be skilling and drilling and often is. But direct instruction at its best teaches strategies, not skills (Duffy & Roehler, 1987) and provides children with a repertoire of strategies to meet reading needs. Children are taught to use these strategies flexibly, according to the situation at hand. Thus, direct instruction involves describing to learners situations in which a strategy might be needed, modeling how to select from alternatives which strategy to use, and modeling how one thinks when using the strategy (Duffy & Roehler, 1987). Yatvin (1991) summarizes the role of direct instruction, suggesting that "it is a teacher's job to support inductive learning by focusing children's attention on significant features of language and helping them work through the language problems they need to solve in order to achieve their purposes" (p. 80).

Direct instruction is based on providing enough sustained, focused practice to enable learners to use strategies effectively. Atwell's (1987) 5–10 minute mini-lessons do not seem to be sufficient to meet this goal. Atwell appears to take a spiral approach to learning, asserting "I don't require 'mastery' of the mini-lesson information; I don't expect every one of my students is going to take to heart every word of the mini-lesson and put it immediately into effect" (p. 78). Rather, she hopes that the mini-lesson will create a "communal frame of reference" (p. 78) to which students can be referred later in the year when a need for a particular strategy arises. Unfortunately, Atwell's description of mini-lessons comes perilously close to what Durkin (1978–79) calls "mentioning," through which the teacher provides insufficient information for children to actually learn something; the students learn only enough to be able to do the task at hand (Durkin, 1990).

Sustained direct instruction has as one of its goals that learners will indeed learn from the lesson and the job is not considered completed until transfer has occurred, that is, until the students can use the strategy with new, authentic materials for authentic purposes.

## Arguments for Direct Instruction

Some whole language advocates criticize systematic direct instruction as "teacher-centered" rather than "learner-centered." In many respects, this is a false dichotomy. Systematic direct instruction *is* teacher-centered in the sense that it is the teacher, rather than the learners, who makes informed decisions about what needs to be learned. Thus, direct instruction does not fit into Watson's (1989) description of whole language classrooms, where "nothing is set into classroom motion until it is validated by learners' interest and motivated by their needs" (p. 133). But decisions about direct instruction are also learner-centered because what is taught is determined by what children need to learn and are able to learn. The notion of a completely learner-centered curriculum may be specious anyway. At any one time a group of children will need to learn many things about literacy. What a teacher *notices* that they need to learn or *selects* to observe or *chooses* to provide experiences with is based at least in part on what the teacher thinks students of a certain age should know and should be able to do (Yatvin, 1991).

Systematic direct instruction is sometimes devalued by whole language advocates on the basis that children are preprogrammed to learn to read and "what is true for language in general is true for written language" (Altwerger, Edelsky, & Flores, 1987, p. 145). Therefore, they reason, direct instruction is not needed and may even be counterproductive. This argument is seductive in its simplicity but does not take into account two important differences between learning oral language and learning to read and write.

First, there are print-specific skills (Evans & Carr, 1985; Stanovich, 1980) that make learning to read and write different and more difficult than learning to speak. These print-specific skills (such as graphophonic relationships and reading left-to-right) are often arbitrary conventions of language, and if children are left to discover these conventions entirely on their own, they may become invested in other conventions that are logical but incorrect for their language, such as reading right to left. Further, we have evidence that not all children do naturally discover these conventions by themselves (Adams, 1990; Ehri & Wilce, 1985), especially children from lower-income families (Calfee & Piontkowski, 1981).

Second, a social imperative exists for learning to speak that does not exist for learning to read. Teale (1984) uses Feldman's (1980) work to differentiate between universal achievements, which are "eventually attained by all individuals in all cultures" (Feldman, 1980, p. 6) and cultural achievements, which involve "knowledge that all individuals within a given culture are *expected* to acquire" (Teale, 1984, p. 319). Teale identifies literacy as an example of cultural achievement, which means that "literacy is not something that everyone does achieve regardless of the environment in which he or she develops" (p. 319).

Whole language advocates often talk about "respect for the child" as a rationale against systematic direct instruction. However, "respect for the child" should not necessarily mean disrespect for the teacher, that the child knows more than the teacher about what needs to be learned and how that might best be learned. Low aptitude children and children with impoverished literacy backgrounds are especially unlikely to figure out effective strategies all by themselves, and there is evidence that high error rates correlate negatively with reading achievement (Rosenshine & Stevens, 1984), especially for young children.

Delpit (1988) offers a powerful, provocative argument that indirect or process-oriented instruction is especially inappropriate for minority children. Although Delpit agrees that there is much to be gained by having children "find their own way into literacy" (Delpit, 1991, p. 543), she suggests that such an approach is most appropriate for the development of *personal* literacy as opposed to *power code* literacy. Delpit contends that power code literacy gives readers access to the world beyond their own immediate environment and that failure to use direct, explicit instruction denies minority children the skill development they need to succeed within the majority culture, that is, power code literacy. Rather than empowering minority children, Delpit argues, instruction that is primarily or wholly process-oriented "creates situations in which students ultimately find themselves held accountable for knowing a set of rules about which no one has ever directly informed them. . . . Teachers do students no service to suggest, even implicitly, that 'product' is not important. In this country students *will* be judged on their product, regardless of the process they utilized to achieve it" (Delpit, 1988, p. 287).

Children from upper and middle classes come to school already knowing the codes and rules for participating in power; that is, they know how to operate within the "culture" of power. They have what Apple (1979) calls "cultural capital" to use. By contrast, many minority children, especially those from lower socioeconomic backgrounds, who have not had "the leisure of a lifetime of 'immersion' to learn" these rules (p. 283) find learning much easier if the rules are explicitly taught and if they are told why they need to learn that information (Delpit, 1991). Delpit (1988) quotes one Black mother: "My kids know how to be Black—you all teach them how to be successful in the White man's world" (p. 285).

Delpit (1988) says that this may not be the way we want the world to be, but it is the way the world is, and "to act as if power does not exist is to ensure that the power status quo remains the same" (p. 292). Delpit, who was initially trained as a process-oriented teacher, does not argue solely for a skills approach; she wants a range of pedagogical orientations. She does not want the teacher to be the only expert in the classroom; she wishes to acknowledge the expertise students do have. She wants children to write for real audiences and to read and write for real purposes. However, she wants children to be *taught* the codes "needed to participate fully in the mainstream of American life . . . within the context of meaningful communicative endeavors" (p. 296).

## Building Bridges

I believe that bridges can and must be built between whole language and more traditional approaches to literacy instruction to enable teachers to blend the best of both in order to help every child reach his or her full literacy potential. Above all, we must avoid either/or positions that reject out of hand the possibility of blending and blind us to the value of different perspectives. Advocacy of systematic direct instruction does not mean that indirect instruction is considered of no value. Especially for many affective goals, indirect instruction is the most appropriate form of instruction. Nor does advocacy of direct instruction necessitate a skill and drill approach where skills are taught and used in isolation. On the other hand, advocacy of whole language does not mean that children are left alone in a state of benign neglect. The whole language perspective does not mean that teachers never step in to guide children's learning. Modeling and coaching are important features of whole language classrooms. If bridges are to be built, we need to think in terms of a continuum rather than a dichotomy.

Mosenthal (1989) suggests that literacy educators focus on how traditional and whole language perspectives can complement each other rather than examining how they are incompatible. The reality of the world of schooling is that teachers *will* draw what works best for them from both worlds. Allen (1989) found that kindergarten teachers implemented a whole language program by modifying "only portions of the curriculum with which they had been dissatisfied" (p. 134).

There are voices of compromise from both perspectives. Strickland and Cullinan (1990) suggest that a whole language and integrated language arts approach be used but "with some direct instruction, in context, of spelling-to-sound correspondences" (p. 433). Heymsfeld (1989) argues for a combined approach in which aspects of traditional instruction are used to fill what she perceives as the "hole in whole language." Hillocks (1984), in a synthesis of research on writing instruction, concludes that the environmental approach, which is a structured process approach in which the teacher choreographs materials and problems in order to "engage students with each other in specifiable processes important to some particular aspects of writing" (p. 144), is most effective in teaching writing.

Systematic direct instruction and many aspects of whole language can be blended in ways that strengthen both approaches. Rather than looking for points of conflict, literacy educators will benefit children more if they look for points of compromise and opportunities to blend the best of both viewpoints.

# *References*

Adams, M. (1990). *Beginning to read: Thinking and learning about print.* Cambridge, MA: MIT Press.

Allen, J. (1989). Reading and writing development in whole language kindergartens. In J. M. Mason (Ed.), *Reading and writing connections* (pp. 121–146). Boston: Allyn & Bacon.

Allen, J., Michalove, B., Shockley, B., & West, M. (1991). "I'm really worried about Joseph": Reducing the risks of literacy learning. *The Reading Teacher, 44,* 458–472.

Altwerger, B., Edelsky, C., & Flores, B. (1987). Whole language: What's new? *The Reading Teacher, 41,* 144–154.

Apple, M. (1979). *Ideology and curriculum.* Boston: Routledge & Kegan Paul.

Atwell, N. (1987). *In the middle: Writing, reading, and learning with adolescents.* Portsmouth, NH: Heinemann.

Baumann, J. F. (1988). Direct instruction reconsidered. *Journal of Reading, 31,* 712–718.

Baumann, J. F. (1991). Of rats and pigeons: Skills and whole language. *Reading Psychology, 12,* iii–xiii.

Calfee, R. C., & Piontkowski, D. C. (1981). The reading diary: Acquisition of decoding. *Reading Research Quarterly, 16,* 346–373.

Delpit, L. D. (1988). The silenced dialogue: Power and pedagogy in educating other people's children. *Harvard Educational Review, 58,* 280–298.

Delpit, L. D. (1991). A conversation with Lisa Delpit. *Language Arts, 68,* 541–547.

Doake, D. L. (1987). Learning to read: It starts in the home. In D. R. Tovey & J. E. Kerber (Eds.), *Roles in literacy learning* (pp. 2–9). Newark, DE: International Reading Association.

Duffy, G. G., & Roehler, L. R. (1986). *Improving classroom reading instruction: A decision-making approach.* New York: Random House.

Duffy, G. G., & Roehler, L. R. (1987). Teaching reading skills as strategies. *The Reading Teacher, 40,* 414–418.

Duffy, G. G., Roehler, L. R., & Putman, J. (1987). Putting the teacher in control: Basal reading textbooks and instructional decision making. *The Elementary School Journal, 87,* 356–366.

Durkin, D. (1978–79). What classroom observations reveal about reading comprehension instruction. *Reading Research Quarterly, 14,* 481–533.

Durkin, D. (1990). Dolores Durkin speaks on instruction. *The Reading Teacher, 43,* 472–476.

Ehri, L. C., & Wilce, L. S. (1985). Movement into reading: Is the first stage of printed word learning visual or phonetic? *Reading Research Quarterly, 20,* 163–179.

Evans, M. A., & Carr, T. H. (1985). Cognitive abilities, conditions of learning, and the early development of reading skill. *Reading Research Quarterly, 20,* 327–350.

Feldman, D. H. (1980). *Beyond universals in cognitive development.* Norwood, NJ: Ablex.

Fountas, I. C., & Hannigan, I. L. (1989). Making sense of whole language: The pursuit of informed teaching. *Childhood Education, 65,* 133–137.

Goodman, K. (1986). *What's whole in whole language?* Portsmouth, NH: Heinemann.

Goodman, K. (1989). Whole-language research: Foundations and development. *The Elementary School Journal, 90,* 205–221.

Goodman, K., Goodman, Y., & Hood, W. (1989). *The whole language evaluation book.* Portsmouth, NH: Heinemann.

Harste, J. (1989). Commentary: The future of whole language. *The Elementary School Journal, 90,* 243–249.

Heymsfeld, C. (1989). Filling the hole in whole language. *Educational Leadership, 46,* 65–68.

Hillocks, G. (1984). What works in teaching composition: A meta-analysis of experimental treatment studies. *American Journal of Education, 93,* 133–170.

Mosenthal, P. B. (1989). The whole language approach: Teachers between a rock and a hard place. *The Reading Teacher, 42,* 628–629.

Newman, J. M., & Church, S. M. (1990). Myths of whole language. *The Reading Teacher, 44,* 20–26.

Rosenshine, B., & Stevens, R. (1984). Classroom instruction in reading. In P. D. Pearson (Ed.), *Handbook of reading research* (pp. 745–798). New York: Longman.

Shulz, E. (1991). Nourishing a desire to learn. *Teacher, II,* 30–34.

Slaughter, H. (1988). Indirect and direct teaching in a whole language program. *The Reading Teacher, 42,* 30–34.

Stanovich, K. E. (1980). Toward an interactive-compensatory model of individual differences in reading fluency. *Reading Research Quarterly, 16,* 32–71.

Strickland, D., & Cullinan, B. (1990). Afterword. In M. Adams, *Beginning to read: Thinking and learning about print* (pp. 425–434). Cambridge, MA: MIT Press.

Teale, W. (1984). Toward a theory of how children learn to read and write 'naturally': An update. In J. A. Niles & L. A. Harris (Eds.), *Changing perspectives on research in reading/language processing and instruction, Thirty-third Yearbook of the National Reading Conference* (pp. 317–322). Rochester, NY: National Reading Conference.

Tierney, R., Carter, M., & Desai, L. (1991). *Portfolio assessment in the reading-writing classroom.* Norwood, MA: Christopher Gordon.

Veatch, J. (1988). En garde, whole language. In J. B. Smith (Ed.), *1988 school library media annual, vol. 6* (pp. 8–14). Englewood, CO: Libraries Unlimited.

Watson, D. J. (1989). Defining and describing whole language. *Elementary School Journal, 90,* 129–141.

Yatvin, J. (1991). *Developing a whole language program.* Richmond, VA: Virginia State Reading Association.

## CONTENT LITERACY GUIDE

**Realities of "Whole Language"**
Sean A. Walmsley and Ellen L. Adams
*Language Arts, 70,* 1993, 272–280

**1.** Describe the data source used by these authors as the basis of their conclusions.

**2.** State the seven conclusions at which Walmsley and Adams arrive. (In the process, respond to the specific questions posed by this guide.)

   a. *Conclusion 1:*

- What percentage of the teachers sampled arrived at this conclusion?

- (T/F)  Whole language tends to increase self-reflection, according to these teachers.

- Contrast this sample with the one interviewed by Manning, Manning, and Long.

   b. *Conclusion 2:*

- Why did many of the teachers avoid using the term *whole language?*

- Why did some of the teachers feel uncertain about "how the day was going to go"?

- Why do the authors not find it surprising that whole language teachers often feel isolated?

- (T/F) Traditional teachers seem usually to be receptive to their whole language colleagues.

c. *Conclusion 3:*

- Summarize the four subissues described here:

1)

2)

3)

4)

- (T/F) These authors argue that teachers must rely more on themselves than on their materials and that the result is exhausting.

d. *Conclusion 4:*

- Summarize the three examples of mixed administrative messages:

1)

2)

3)

- What two forces do administrators in whole language schools often find themselves between?

1)

2)

e. *Conclusion 5:*

- What are some of the complaints voiced by whole language teachers about traditional (standardized) assessment?




- (T/F) Whole language teachers have relatively clear ideas about alternative assessment.

- (T/F) Whole language teachers enthusiastically support alternative assessment ideas offered by Brian Cambourne, Peter Johnston, and others.

f. *Conclusion 6:*



- List some of the attributes of whole language instruction mentioned by these teachers:








- (T/F) Whole language teachers in this study chose instructional activities that derived from a coherent pedagogy.

- (T/F) Whole language teachers in this study tended to be "purists."

g. *Conclusion 7:*



- What factors did these teachers identify as inhibiting the spread of whole language?

  1)

2)

3)

4)

5)

6)

- (T/F) Most whole language teachers believe that whole language will eventually gain dominance.

- (T/F) These authors conclude that virtually any teacher can become a whole language teacher.

# REALITIES OF "WHOLE LANGUAGE"

SEAN A. WALMSLEY
ELLEN L. ADAMS

*I don't think that whole language will ever be understood by a great majority of teachers. . . . I see teachers who are in the early stages of whole language who are misconstruing some of it. They think they are doing whole language, but they really aren't. I don't think that it will ever be truly understood, but I think that people who do understand it and really follow it will teach their student teachers to do it. I think there will be a small group who will continue it. It's a philosophy, but it's also a style . . . a style that fits some teachers. The student teachers are now coming out of colleges that are really promoting whole language. . . . They come well prepared, and they love it. . . . Those of us who are still doing whole language may sometimes go into hiding. . . . I think that whole language will continue, but it will be a very small movement; and I think that the majority of teachers in the United States will never know what it is, much less learn to do it. (Grade 4 teacher)*

For the past several years, large numbers of elementary school teachers have taken on the challenge of what is called a "whole language" approach to literacy instruction. As they do so, they are finding that making the transition from traditional to whole language instruction isn't quite as easy or trouble-free as they thought it might be. In many of the whole language conferences, and in much of the whole language literature, it seems that the struggles, concerns, and doubts of individual teachers are sometimes caught in the eddies of the fast-flowing whole language movement. In this article, we focus less on the ecstasy of whole language and more on the realities of becoming a whole language teacher and sustaining a whole language classroom.

To investigate the issues that teachers confront as they make the transition to whole language and attempt to sustain it, we conducted a series of confidential interviews, mostly at a whole language conference with 71 teachers in elementary and middle schools drawn from rural, urban, and suburban school districts (public and private) in upstate New York. Although we did not employ a rigorous sampling technique, the sample of teachers we interviewed represent a cross section of age and teaching experience, but they all viewed themselves as teachers with a whole language orientation. We asked how long they had been whole language teachers, how they became whole language teachers, how they defined whole language, what problems they encountered in their transition to this approach, concerns they had about sustaining it, and what they thought about the future of the whole language movement. All the interviews were tape recorded and transcribed. The data were analyzed using a contrastive analysis technique, in which repeated readings of the transcripts were made and generalizations were generated, then reverified in the transcripts.

What emerges from these educators' stories about their experiences are several concerns that relate to the amount of work involved in whole language instruction; relations with other faculty members, administrators, and parents; organization of instruction; defining what whole language is; evaluating student progress in a whole language classroom; and where respondents see themselves and the whole language movement in the next few years. From an analysis of the interviews, some generalizations about the realities of implementing whole language can be identified.

## Whole Language Instruction Is Very Demanding

The teachers were unanimous in their view that whole language instruction is tremendously demanding, greatly more so than traditional basal reading instruction. For the majority, even those who had been using a whole language approach for some time (but especially among beginners), the work wasn't getting any easier—in fact, many described it as "intensive," "exhausting," or "overwhelming":

> *I feel overwhelmed. I don't know where to start, and I don't know where to go. It's too much all at once. (Grade 2)*

> *Starting out in whole language, I used to think: Oh, it won't take me long to make those materials, so I'll just save some money and do it myself . . . but it was hard to keep up. . . . I was exhausted. . . . Sometimes I would stay until 9:00 at night . . . or come in on Saturday or Sunday. (Grade 1)*

Teachers were not only disheartened by how much there was to do (e.g., building up a library of tradebooks, individualizing instruction, building thematic units, locating or making materials) but also about how much they still had to learn:

> *I'm so overwhelmed with everything that I have learned. . . . I feel like a sponge that has absorbed so much information, and now I'm just dripping. . . . I'm wet with information. (Grade 3)*

These feelings, however, are counterbalanced for most teachers by a growing sense of comfort and confidence in themselves and their program, and a greater degree of reflectiveness in their teaching:

*Well, actually I'm very comfortable with it. It's a lot of work, but actually I'm much happier. I feel like I've come into my own in the past years, and now I am really comfortable. (Grade 4)*

*The more I become involved in whole language, the more I realize how much I have to learn and do. I find it very tough. There is always something else to do or learn . . . and yet through all of this, I find myself more at peace with myself when I think about what I do with kids. (Grade 2)*

Unlike the whole language teachers interviewed by Manning, Manning, and Long (1989), who seemed to have quickly overcome their initial difficulties making the transition to whole language, our respondents appeared to have difficulties implementing their whole language program that had yet to be resolved, even after several years of teaching from this perspective. From the almost unanimous agreement among our respondents on this issue, we are convinced that whole language advocates have underestimated the demanding nature of making the transition to whole language.

## Whole Language Alienates and Divides

We were struck by the number of respondents who felt vulnerable, isolated, alienated, or ostracized as a consequence of adopting a whole language philosophy. For some teachers, being in the minority was particularly troublesome:

*I jumped into my classroom and expected it to happen overnight, and I really became very, very depressed . . . and I was alone . . . I needed someone to talk to. . . . I had been taught a different way, and I was making a 180-degree turn . . . and my principal didn't even really know what I was doing . . . so I certainly didn't have any backing. (Grade 3)*

More unsettling to the teachers than isolation was the polarizing effect of their adopting whole language, which separates teachers into educational camps representing stereotypes of traditional (i.e., teacher-dominated instruction; children sitting passively in rows; doing dittos; being drilled, not taught; working on mindless basal stories and exercises) versus whole language (i.e., child-centered, individualized instruction; warm, colorful rooms; authentic reading of self-selected literature; journal writing; singing and chanting; project work):

*The first time I attended a whole language workshop I was told to expect daggers from other teachers. . . . To be someone different who is not using workbooks can be very threatening to other teachers. (Grade 2)*

*There are these young teachers in our school . . . and I'm at the 15th-year point now . . . and they make me feel guilty for not just jumping on the bandwagon. . . . I'm more comfortable just being me, and that's what whole language advocates—let your kids be themselves . . . but yet they don't respect me. . . . They should let me do whole language in my own way. . . . They are philosophizing a philosophy without practicing it. (Grade 1)*

*In our school, there are about 30 teachers, and 5 of us are whole language teachers. The principal likes to march visitors into the whole language classroom but not into the traditional ones. This causes a lot of hard feelings because the traditional teachers feel that they don't have anything to share or show. (Grade 3)*

Many of the teachers prefer not to use the term "whole language,'" fearful of the negative feelings it elicits:

*If you go in and say, "Oh, I'm a whole language teacher," then right away we are putting this wall around ourselves. . . . It's the label. . . . In my district you don't want to use the label because it's like a porcupine getting his bristles out. . . . They hear "whole language," and boom! the needles come out. (Grade 2)*

*I don't like the term "whole language" because there is a stigma attached. It's like waving a red flag in front of a bull for some teachers. (Grade 5)*

Several of the teachers commented on how vulnerable they felt as they left the security of traditional basal materials and ventured into the unsure waters of whole language:

*Sometimes it's kind of scary to walk into my classroom not knowing how the day is going to go. . . . The students determine this. . . . You just can't sit back and look through your lesson plans to see what worksheets come next. (Grade 1)*

*I know that some of my kids are going to end up in traditional classrooms, and their teachers will say, "What did she do with them?" It's a worry that I have. (Grade 1)*

These uncertainties also reveal themselves in teachers' comments about parents. Many parents, like fellow teachers, are either wedded to traditional notions about the elementary curriculum, or they simply do not understand what a whole language philosophy is about. Their criticisms of whole language classrooms tend to focus on the issues of grouping practices, spelling, phonics, and worksheets; and they clearly unsettle some of the teachers we interviewed:

*It's hard with the parents because they don't see all these papers coming home. . . . (Grade 1)*

*One day a parent came in and said, "What is this total language? What's this whole group teaching?" So I said, "Well, you must mean whole language." The parent then wanted to know why her daughter wasn't in the top group. When I told her that we didn't have any grouping, she said, "Well, I'm going to the administration. . . . My daughter is gifted . . . she belongs in a top group." (Grade 1)*

That whole language teachers feel isolated, alienated, or even ostracized is hardly surprising, given the challenge that whole language represents to traditional classroom practice. Whole language is not merely a new set of teaching routines that can be added to existing practices: It directly confronts and opposes practices that most teachers have become wedded to over the past 20 years. For example, it emphasizes child-centered versus teacher-dominated instruction; it strongly opposes direct teaching of isolated reading and editing "skills"; it advocates replacing the basal program with tradebooks. And it promotes these practices without providing teachers with an alternate set of materials and guides they can simply purchase and follow. What these teachers have discovered is that they are very much on their own with respect to building their new literacy programs (and it's hard work to build a program from scratch). Further, they have to contend with the political problem of how their programs will coexist with traditional ones in the same building. The very act of their adopting a whole language philosophy sets a number of opposing forces in motion. Some teachers are made to feel that they are not "progressive" if they don't join the movement, and they resent the implication that they are somehow not "with it." Other teachers who reject whole language as "soft" and lacking in "standards" and "skills coverage" are sometimes openly critical of the whole language teachers. And if they are not openly critical, there's a constant 'undertow' of criticism that can be felt throughout the building. So the whole language teachers, far from being greeted as pioneers of innovative literacy instruction, unexpectedly find themselves not only the targets of resentment and hostility but also partially responsible for an atmosphere of disharmony among colleagues. Given how difficult it is to make the transition into whole language, the intolerant atmosphere simply exacerbates their feelings of uncertainty and vulnerability. There are more consequences of adopting whole language than they ever anticipated, and these extend well beyond the classroom.

## It's Hard to Manage Whole Language Instruction

There is little doubt that managing whole language instruction was a major issue facing whole language teachers in our study. One of the reasons why teachers find it challenging is because whole language is an instructional philosophy that does not come bundled with a set of packaged materials, teacher manuals, and student workbooks. There are many routines and activities typically associated with whole language instruction (e.g., Big Books, chanting, independent reading time, reading and writing conferences, project work), but teachers are generally left on their own to figure out how to implement these activities and what they are expected to accomplish through them. Many of the teachers seemed to be still working through this issue of translating philosophy into practice:

*People are throwing out traditional materials without knowing what to do to replace them. Whole language is starting to be thrown at everyone. People are lost because they don't have the background of people like [John] Dewey and [Frank] Smith. (Remedial Reading Teacher, Primary Grades)*

*Because whole language is not a formula for teaching, you tend to get in the middle of a project, and you don't know exactly where to go with it. . . . You don't have that book to open up like a recipe for teaching, which we would all love to fall back on in the way we were taught as students . . . and trained as teachers. We may resort to (teacher-dominated methods) again, but then you feel bad the next day . . . so you just take two aspirin and try it again! (Grade 6)*

A second issue faced by these whole language teachers stems directly from the philosophy that a whole language curriculum should be child-centered, not teacher-dominated. Many teachers have struggled (and still are struggling) with this concept, and the consequences of adopting it (e.g., increased noise and movement, changes in classroom behavior).

*I had a hard time letting go and not being in charge . . . because I wanted to be the dictator of the class. . . . I didn't want to trust the children's decisions. . . . I even need to let go a little more. . . . (Grade 4)*

*The teachers have to learn how to handle the freedom, and the kids have to learn how to handle the freedom. (Grade 1)*

*That whole concept of inquiry is an important part [of whole language]. . . . Now I find as a teacher that I have a lot more questions than I have answers. I had to get to a point where I realized that it was OK. . . . That's really where I wanted to be. I kept thinking that I had to be the old model of a teacher where I knew all the answers. It changes the teacher's role entirely. (Grade 1)*

*Well, this may sound a little crazy, but I still have a traditional frame of mind in a whole language classroom. . . . I miss having a neat room . . . everything gets so messy. . . . Also, the room gets so noisy, and I can't seem to quiet the kids down. It's so unsettling. (Grade 2)*

*When you're doing traditional things like workbook pages all together, you can take comfort in the fact that everybody is doing the same thing at the same time. You know that kids aren't wasting time, and if anybody walks into your classroom, everyone is busy at work. . . . It's scary to some people letting the control go to the kids. . . . What if they all sit around wasting time? (Grade 4)*

A third issue concerns the day-to-day business of planning, organizing, and running a whole language classroom. Teachers found it difficult to find (and fund) appropriate materials and supplies; to plan for and schedule the day's activities; and to set up the physical layout of the classroom, to allow for reading and writing areas:

*You just can't give kids dittos for busy work while you sit with reading groups. . . . So much planning has to take place now. (Grade 1)*

*You can't plan a week ahead because you don't know how the kids are going to react. . . . You may plan something and have it bomb. Then you have to stop and take the direction where the kids want the lesson to go. (Grade 5)*

*Another problem is gathering the supplies. I have found this to be very difficult . . . just getting them and the money involved . . . and the time to go get the materials and the time to research . . . and even knowing what to get for all of the projects. (Grade 1)*

*Room management and time are my biggest things. I just don't know how I can possibly keep all 25 of my kindergartners writing at the same time—I'm afraid I'll wear myself out. (Kindergarten)*

Finally, teachers face the challenge of covering aspects of the traditional curriculum that either they or their school insist be taught (e.g., phonics, spelling and grammar rules, isolated reading skills such as "main idea" and "sequencing" and vocabulary lists) or skills they think students need to have mastered before they go to the next grade:

> *I've always worried about what my kids are learning. . . . Their test scores aren't tons better or anything . . . but I'm scared about when they go on. . . . At least I can say that they've learned to be writers and readers. (Grade 2)*

> *We have a generalized vocabulary list for schoolwide assessment. You hate to have those things . . . but you must meet people halfway. . . . (Grade 4)*

> *When you are into whole language and you're getting away from the textbook idea, all of a sudden you reach a point in the calendar year when you say: Oh, my God, the tests are coming up. What am I going to do? I want my kids to be prepared for the test. Then a good part of my teaching ceases, and I begin to get the kids ready for the tests. (Grade 3)*

> *I did something that was kind of taking half a step backward. . . . I found that my kids did poorly in some of the end-of-year skills tests last year, so I'm having this year's kids work in a language arts workbook . . . for only about 15 minutes per week. . . . Then at least I can say, Here it is. It was done. (Grade 6)*

A common thread running through the teachers' statements about managing their whole language programs is their need for more knowledge about how to implement a whole language philosophy, either on its own or in concert with existing literacy instruction. One of the problems teachers face is that instead of having instructional materials do the bulk of the teaching, a whole language approach places the burden of teaching on the teacher's shoulders—the program comes from her head rather than from the materials. Given the full range of language arts activities, this is an enormous task; and it clearly daunts even the experienced whole language teachers. But teachers face other challenges in translating whole language philosophy to practice. Letting go some or all of the traditional teacher's control of the classroom's activities and behaviors does not come easily to teachers, even if they subscribe to a child-centered philosophy. And the consequences of liberating oneself from traditional practice are often not easy to accept. Many of the teachers are finding it hard to adjust to a changed classroom environment, even though few of them have serious doubts about the instructional philosophy they have newly embraced. The rewards apparently outweigh the frustrations.

## *Administrators Send Mixed Messages about Whole Language*

If whole language teachers have concerns about how their programs are viewed by their colleagues, they also worry about the mixed messages being sent to them from some of their administrators. These mixed messages take a variety of forms. In some cases, administrators insist that teachers use both whole language and approaches that are philosophically incompatible with whole language:

> *I was supposed to teach Distar and process writing. I had to. I was told to use the same program as the other first-grade teachers because this is what the parents expected. . . . It was really hard. . . . It happened for 2 years. . . . So I taught Distar— the whole thing—in 4 weeks. (Grade 1)*

> *In our district what is difficult is that we are getting mixed messages. . . . They asked me to do a whole language workshop for the teachers, but they won't let go of Madeline Hunter. (Grade 4)*

> *I was teaching in a Madeline Hunter stronghold where everyone had to be put through the course. . . . I'm not a political pioneer. . . . I tried to do whole language, but the principal came in with his Madeline Hunter checklist to evaluate me. (Grade 4)*

In other cases, administrators supported whole language in principle but did not follow through when came time to fund or support the program:

> *Don't worry, there'll be plenty of money . . . but $50,000 was spent on basals, and there was only $10,000 left for our district to get the children's literature. Here they spent $50,000 for basals, and they want me to do a whole language workshop in the fall. I don't understand where they are coming from. (Grade 2)*

> *We got a lot of support from our principal. He had enough confidence in us as teachers, and he said: "In September, you can leave the basal and use the money that is normally spent on workbooks to buy your tradebooks. . . ." That's how we got started. A stumbling block was that our reading coordinator left, and someone new came. He didn't really want the two of us to be doing something different from the rest of the staff. We were told to go back to the basal and told that we could do whole language as something "extra." This daunted our enthusiasm because we had to do two reading programs at one time. (Grade 2)*

Finally, some teachers were concerned that their administrators simply did not understand what they were doing:

> *The publishers are trying to push whole language basals. . . . Every time I opened my mouth when I was on the language arts committee, my administrator would give me this "Oh no, here she goes again" look. (Grade 4)*

> *I'm supposed to be testing kids on things I'm not teaching, and this seems to fly over my administrator's head. (Grade 2)*

The mixed messages that our teachers reported receiving from their administrators may seem to them to be indicators of an inconsistent policy on curriculum reform, but perhaps we should not be surprised that a movement which advocates teacher and student empowerment is eventually bound to clash with the traditional "top-down" model of elementary school administration. Administrators often support the introduction of whole language simply as a set of new teaching techniques, unaware of the fundamental challenges that whole language poses to traditional ways of teaching, assessing, and organizing language arts. In many ways, the administrators face the same uncertainties about whole language as teachers do, and their "mixed messages" convey the same underlying uncertainties as those expressed by the teachers. Just as whole language teachers face the challenge of traditional colleagues, administrators—even if they wholeheartedly support whole language—face the pressures and challenge of traditional assessment and accountability mandated by the district or the state. As Glickman (1989) points out, administrators are caught between telling teachers to comply with district and state requirements and insisting that they do what they think is professionally appropriate for their students.

## Whole Language Is Not Compatible with Traditional Forms of Assessment

Teachers were almost unanimous in their criticism of traditional standardized measures of reading and writing, mostly because of the mismatch between what's covered in the tests and what's valued in the classroom:

*What's horrible is to watch your kids taking all of these standardized tests, using this wonderful logic and getting the answers wrong. . . . (Grade 2)*

*I feel frustrated having to give the dumb end-of-the-year tests that really emphasize phonics. . . . Our end-of-the-book tests have 100 phonics questions and only 8 on comprehension. Reading is for meaning, and it's a shame that somehow our district can't establish another way of testing. . . . (Grade 2)*

*Every year I sweat through those standardized tests. . . . I don't value them, but I know that a lot of other people do. . . . I don't want someone coming to my classroom saying, "You can't teach this way" based on a lousy test score; so I just hope that my kids are going to do O.K. (Grade 3)*

What we did not hear from these teachers was what they considered to be valid alternatives to traditional forms of assessment. Indeed, several teachers admitted to having difficulty assessing their students' growth in a whole language environment:

*I know that my students are learning, but I'm not always comfortable with the terms that I'm using to define their growth. (Grade 2)*

*In the Teacher's Manual it says that if you teach all of these skills, then you will have done a good job teaching sixth-grade English . . . but then (after I adopted a whole language approach), I had to determine where I wanted my kids to be at the end of the year; and that was a responsibility that I never had to handle before. It was scary, and it still is. (Grade 4)*

We were struck by how uncomfortable these teachers were, talking about assessment in their whole language classrooms. While they forcefully opposed traditional measures, they seemed equally frustrated by alternative assessment techniques and were not straining at the leash to tell us about new and exciting approaches they use. We sensed an air of resignation in teachers' comments about traditional assessments—they didn't like them, yet hoped their students would do well on them; and they tolerated their use as measures of their students' growth. In contrast to their exuberance about their teaching techniques, the teachers had very little to say about how they thought children's progress should be measured in a whole language program. Given the rash of recent literature on alternative techniques for assessment (Brown & Cambourne, 1987; Clay, 1985; Johnston, 1992; Tierney, Carter, & Desai, 1991), we might have expected the experienced teachers in our sample to be using some of these in their classrooms and enthusiastically endorsing them. It would seem that the teachers we interviewed are far less comfortable with these assessment techniques than those who are promoting them.

## Whole Language Is Hard to Define

We asked teachers to tell us about what counted as whole language instruction (and what didn't), and their responses reveal just how difficult it is to define the term whole language. Teachers talked about whole language in terms of attributes or features present in their class-rooms, such as its having "an abundance of books"; "lots of print"; "children making choices about what they read and write"; "children having freedom to move about the room"; "the room looking colorful, inviting, and comfortable"; "tolerating a mess"; "using literature throughout the curriculum"; and "teaching on the rug." Process reading and process writing, invented(ive) spelling, lack of worksheets, independent reading of self-selected books, shared reading of Big Books, cooperative learning, and making school enjoyable and interesting seemed to these teachers essential characteristics of a whole language classroom. Teachers focused on the practical, daily routines of whole language: What we heard was a potpourri of ideas about the classroom, not a set of instructional activities derived from a coherent peda-gogy, although, as Hargreaves (1989) points out, teachers rarely articulate underlying teaching philosophies. We were unsure whether teachers had simply picked up a set of new teaching methods but were unable to articulate how these methods fit an instructional philosophy, or whether they had a sense of the philosophy but were still working through its practical application. In either case, we had the feeling that most of the teachers were still grappling with a concept that they did not fully understand (they seemed more certain about why traditional methods were not appropriate than why whole language was); and yet they enthu-siastically embraced many of its practices (e.g., letting children decide, using literature through-out the curriculum). Certainly, many of the teachers' responses revealed a belief in the exist-ence of a "true" whole language approach, even if they themselves hadn't yet found it:

> *Right now I wonder if I am truly a whole language teacher because even though I do a lot of reading and writing, and I do a lot of projects, I still sometimes use textbooks in science and social studies. (Grade 5)*

We also learned that these teachers were not "purist" whole language teachers, in the sense that they religiously eschew the basal; textbooks for science and social studies; direct instruction of skills; workbooks; and formal, standardized testing. To one degree or another, most of the teachers compromise, either tacking on whole language activities to an existing traditional program or supplementing their whole language program with traditional materials. And yet, most of these teachers still regard themselves as whole language teachers.

> *Some teachers say they are whole language teachers, but they still pull out their basals. . . . (Grade 2)*

> *I still use a basal, so if you talk to the whole language people, they would not accept me even though I supplement my basals tremendously with the morning newspaper, literature, and response logs. (Grade 3)*

The difficulty these teachers have defining whole language parallels the debate in the professional literature, in which whole language is variously defined as "a set of beliefs about language development, language learning, and language instruction" (Altwerger, Edelsky, & Flores, 1987); a set of "conditions" for "natural learning" (Cambourne, 1988); and an educational movement that stands *for* some things (e.g., authentic reading and writing) and *against* others (e.g., basal readers, skills in isolation). We should not be surprised that teachers have difficulty defining the concept when so many different instructional practices are covered by the whole language umbrella. Further, there are many theoretical, philosophical, and practical issues surrounding whole language that have yet to be resolved (McCaslin, 1989; Watson, 1989; Willinsky, 1990).

## Whole Language Will Survive, but among the Dedicated Few

Finally, we asked teachers to look ahead and forecast what they saw as the future of the whole language movement. Paradoxically, their responses reflect both pessimism and optimism for the future of whole language. They are pessimistic about the extent to which whole language will gain widespread acceptance in schools, but they are personally optimistic about their own development as whole language teachers.

Their pessimism focuses on a number of factors that inhibit the growth of whole language, including: the validity of teachers having different (even traditional) ideas about how to teach; lack of collegial, parental, district, even state support for whole language; the widespread misconceptions about whole language held even by teachers professing to practice it; the draining, time-consuming nature of preparing and managing a whole language program; the reluctance of schools to make systemic changes in their programs; the inability of whole language to guarantee satisfactory results in traditional assessments (or at least the perception that it cannot guarantee results); and finally, the threat posed by a conservative and traditional view of schooling that singles out whole language as one more reason to "get back to basics."

Their optimism focuses on the profound changes these teachers have made in their own teaching philosophy and practice, changes which they regard as irreversible, despite the hard work and the ever-present controversy that surrounds them. This optimism extends to the movement as a whole but acknowledges that whole language will always be the philosophy of a dedicated few, rather than the orthodoxy of a entire school, district, or state. In other words, whole language will survive, but it will not dominate American public education.

> *I think that it's easy for the people involved in whole language to get so caught up in it that they don't see the bigger picture. A lot of people think that it's the answer to everyone's prayers . . . but I see a lot of people that aren't comfortable with it because they are not well read. I don't think that the majority of teachers will ever be confident enough to be whole language teachers because of the way we have all been taught. We've been taught to follow manuals. (Grade 4)*

> *Whole language really hasn't had a bigger impact than some earlier philosophies such as the Language Experience Approach; it has just had more exposure. (Grade 2)*

> *Because your goals are very different from the traditional classrooms, people like guidance counselors, building principals, and parents, and even the kids in your classroom begin to ask some real serious questions about why things are so different. We need to be able to articulate this. . . . I think whole language is going to be coming head-to-head with very traditional values about education. It's going to be scary. (Grade 2)*

> *Yes, I do think whole language will survive because those of us who are doing it won't let it go. (Grade 1)*

## Conclusion

In this paper, we have tried to articulate some of the realities of becoming and sustaining oneself as a teacher with whole language philosophy. From lengthy interviews with about 70 practicing whole language teachers drawn from a variety of school settings, grade levels, and teaching experience, we have uncovered a number of issues that whole language teachers rarely articulate but are deeply concerned about. These issues send some important messages to educators who are thinking about whole language as a viable option for reform.

One message is that whole language is not for everyone and is inappropriate for teachers who do not hold its basic instructional philosophy or have the mindset needed to run a child-centered classroom. Adopting a whole language approach involves making fundamental changes in the way teachers view children and themselves, and many teachers simply are unable or unwilling to contemplate these changes, especially without support. Another is that it may demand more of them than they are willing or able to give: It is clear from these interviews that preparing for and running a whole language classroom consumes enormous amounts of time and energy. Whole language teachers insist that it is worth the expenditure of effort and time, but they think that newcomers should not underestimate what is involved. Newcomers should also be prepared for unanticipated consequences beyond their classroom. As has been pointed out by Goodman (1988), the politics of whole language is as difficult as its practice and involves a number of issues such as being resented by traditional teachers, questioned by parents and administrators, and worrying about whether the students will do well on traditional tests or how successful students will be in the next grade. Whole language teachers will almost certainly be in a "glass bubble" (as one teacher described it), under the constant scrutiny of colleagues, parents, and administrators; they need to have confidence in their own abilities to handle these pressures. They can also expect, if our respondents' experiences are typical, occasionally to have feelings of self-doubt ("Am I really doing the right thing?") that will make them wonder if it was all worth the effort, prompting them, if only momentarily, to consider a retreat.

Another message is that educational change is a long, drawn-out process, and given the challenge of whole language to the "existing regularities" of the elementary language arts curriculum (Sarason, 1982), whole language reform will take a very long time. It is clear from accounts of teachers and programs in transition (e.g., Routman, 1991; Walmsley & Walp, 1990) that it takes not only time but also intensive support to bring about these changes. We wondered, from these interviews, whether teachers or administrators had sufficient staying power to build their whole language reforms into the school's infrastructure, not just tack them on as innovations. Also, administrators and staff need to work through the conflicts between whole language instruction and traditional assessment so that instruction and assessment are philosophically congruent, and between whole language teachers and traditional teachers in such a way that neither are devalued, ostracized, or resented. Despite its commitment to the notion of empowerment, the whole language reform movement is not particularly mindful of the importance of taking into account the legitimately different needs, expectations, philosophies, and teaching approaches of the various stakeholders in education (i.e., teachers, administrators, parents, communities); but neither are its opponents. A particularly troublesome issue is that the general thrust of federal and state reforms is in the direction of mastery of externally defined subject matter (e.g., "U.S. students will be first in the world in science and mathematics") and a focus on results as opposed to process—all of which seem to be reaffirming traditional goals (e.g., mastery of "readiness skills" before formal schooling, competency in subject areas) and traditional methods to attain them (e.g., direct teaching of a fixed rather than developmental curriculum). Despite the magnitude of the challenges facing whole language, we are encouraged by the perseverance and optimism of the teachers we interviewed. We are concerned, however, that if the issues they raise—uncomfortable as they may be to whole language advocates—are ignored, progress toward whole language may well be at risk. A better understanding of the concerns of practitioners as they make their transition to whole language will surely help ease the transition and ultimately strengthen the whole language movement.

# *References*

Altwerger, B., Edelsky, C., & Flores, B. M. (1987). Whole language: What's new? *Reading Teacher, 41,* 144–154.

Brown, H., & Cambourne, B. (1987). *Read and retell.* North Ryde, NSW (Australia): Methuen.

Cambourne, B. (1988). *The whole story: Natural learning and the acquisition of literacy in the classroom.* New York: Scholastic.

Clay, M. M. (1985). *The early detection of reading difficulties: A diagnostic survey with recovering procedures.* Exeter, NH: Heinemann.

Glickman, C. D. (1989). Has Sam and Samantha's time come at last? *Educational Leadership, 47,* 4–9.

Goodman, K. (1988). Do teachers have to suffer to become whole language teachers? Unpublished manuscript, University of Arizona, Tucson.

Hargreaves, A. (1989). *Curriculum and assessment reform.* Bristol, U.K.: Open University Press.

Johnston, P. (1992). *Constructive evaluation of literate activity.* New York: Longman.

Manning, G., Manning, M., & Long, R. (1989). In the process of becoming process teachers. In G. Manning & M. Manning (Eds.), *Whole language: Beliefs and practices, K–8* (pp. 235–240). New York: National Education Association.

McCaslin, M. M. (1989). Whole language: Theory, instruction, and future implementation. *Elementary School Journal, 90,* 223–229.

Routman, R. (1991). *Invitations.* Portsmouth, NH: Heinemann Educational Books.

Sarason, S. B. (1982). *The culture of the school and problem of change.* Boston, MA: Allyn & Bacon.

Tierney, R. J., Carter, M. A., & Desai, L. E. (1991). *Portfolio assessment in the reading-writing classroom.* Norwood, MA: Christopher Gordon Publishers.

Walmsley, S. A., & Walp, T. P. (1990). Integrating literature and composing into the language arts curriculum: Philosophy and practice. *Elementary School Journal, 90,* 251–274.

Watson, D. (1989). Defining and describing whole language. *Elementary School Journal, 90,* 129–141.

Willinsky, J. (1990). *The new literacy: Redefining reading and writing in the schools.* New York: Routledge.

## *Integrating Sources*

1. Note the comment of Walmsley and Adams (p. 39) regarding "direct teaching" made at the end of their reading. How would you predict they might respond to Spiegel's suggestions?

2. Which of the conclusions reached by Walmsley and Adams is/are most germane to the issues raised by Spiegel?

3. In what ways might the teachers in the Walmsley and Adams study react to Spiegel's suggestions?

## *Classroom Implications*

1. Is Spiegel's notion incompatible with a whole language philosophy? Why or why not?

2. What suggestions can you offer (from the perspective of your own teaching assignment) about the need to impart skills but at the same time maintain motivation and a sense of reading for meaning?

3. Can the approach you have outlined be classified as "whole language"? Why or why not?

4. What predictions can *you* offer regarding the future of whole language? Give your reasons.

## *Annotated Bibliography*

### *Whole Language*

Baumann, J. F. (1991). Of rats and pigeons: Skills and whole language. *Reading Psychology, 12*(1), iii–xiii.

*This article is a discussion of how literacy strategies, such as the use of skill instruction and the basal reader, are viewed by both those who support whole language and those who have questions about this literacy philosophy. A key question raised is whether teachable moments can be relied on to offer sufficient opportunities to conduct needed skills instruction.*

Bergeron, B. S. (1990). What does the term whole language mean? Constructing a definition from the literature. *Journal of Reading Behavior, 22,* 301–329.

*This study reviewed 64 references that defined whole language and found a wide diversity of definitions currently used in the relevant literature.*

Edelsky, C. (1990). Whose agenda is this anyway? A response to McKenna, Robinson, and Miller. *Educational Researcher, 19*(8), 7–11.

*This is the second part of a written debate on a research agenda for whole language (see McKenna, Robinson, Miller, 1990, in this listing for the first part), which defends the premise that only whole language supporters are adequately able to conduct meaningful whole language research.*

Goodman, K. S. (1967). Reading: A psycholinguistic guessing game. *Journal of the Reading Specialist, 6,* 126–135.

*This is an early paper on the development of the top-down model of reading that forms the foundation for whole language thinking, especially as it relates to the role of decoding.*

Goodman, K. S. (1969). Analysis of oral reading miscues: Applied psycholinguistics. *Reading Research Quarterly, 5,* 9–30.

*This is an important reference to the use of miscue analysis in the evaluation of oral reading behavior.*

Goodman, K. S. (1986). *What's whole in whole language?* Portsmouth, NH: Heinemann.

*This general overview of whole language places particular emphasis on the use of this philosophy in classroom settings.*

Goodman, K. S. (1989). Whole-language research: Foundations and development. *Elementary School Journal, 90,* 207–221.

*This is a discussion of whole language research and the role of classroom teachers in these practices.*

Goodman, K. S. (1992). I didn't found whole language. *The Reading Teacher, 46,* 188–199.

*This article is a discussion of Goodman's feelings about the development of whole language, its philosophical foundations, and his perspective on future developments in this movement.*

McKenna, M. C., Robinson, R. D., & Miller, J. W. (1990). Whole language: A research agenda for the nineties. *Educational Researcher, 19*(8), 3–6.

*This is the first part of a debate on whole language (see Edelsky, 1990, for the second part), which suggests a research agenda to be considered in the evaluation of the effectiveness of whole language.*

McKenna, M. C., Robinson, R. D., & Miller, J. W. (1990). Whole language and the need for open inquiry: A rejoinder to Edelsky. *Educational Researcher, 19*(8), 12–13.

*This is the third part of a debate related to whole language, calling for future research and collaboration on this literacy philosophy. (See McKenna et al., 1990, and Edelsky, 1990, for parts one and two of this debate.)*

Pearson, P. D. (1989). Reading the whole-language movement. *Elementary School Journal, 90,* 231–241.

*This important discussion of current successes and problems with whole language gives suggestions for future developments in this movement.*

Smith, C. B. (Ed.). (1994). *Whole language: The Debate.* Bloomington, IN: ERIC Clearinghouse on Reading and Communication Skills.

*This book is a collection of four essays, in a debate format, that reflect many of the current issues being discussed concerning whole language. There are also four commentaries reflecting on the written exchange. Also included in this volume is an extensive bibliography on whole language taken from the ERIC document system.*

Stahl, S. A., & Miller, P. D. (1989). Whole language and language experience approaches for beginning reading: Quantitative research. *Review of Educational Research, 59,* 87–116.

*This is an important review and evaluation of research through 1988 contrasting whole language with traditional instruction. The general conclusion is that there was little evidence to support the superiority of whole language to existing reading methodologies.*

Stanovich, K. E. (1990). A call for an end to the paradigm wars in reading research. *Journal of Reading Behavior, 22,* 221–231.

*This discussion of the whole language debate suggests that a dangerous "zero-sum game" has developed, in which research findings are inevitably characterized as for one side and against the other.*

Watson, D. (1989). Defining and describing whole language. *Elementary School Journal, 90,* 129–141.

*This article discusses the problems with adequately defining whole language and then presents a wide variety of existing definitions of this reading philosophy. It argues that each teacher arrives at whole language uniquely and that a uniform definition is neither possible nor desirable.*

## *You Become Involved*

### *Whole Language*

The following activities are designed to help you develop your own ideas related to the topic of whole language. Although there are many and varied opinions concerning whole language, the most important belief is what you develop for yourself based on your reading and interaction with classroom teachers.

**1.** Discuss the topic of whole language with different teachers, asking them what they believe about whole language. Note how these opinions are similar and different.

**2.** Observe classroom teachers who align themselves with whole language actually teaching reading. How do these classes differ from more traditional classroom literacy instruction?

**3.** Based on your reading of this chapter, begin to develop your thinking on these issues related to whole language:

    a. What is a defensible definition of whole language?
    b. What are some of the current issues being debated about whole language?
    c. What does the research say about whole language?
    d. How do classroom teachers implement whole language in their classrooms?
    e. What do you believe are the strengths and the weaknesses of whole language?

# Chapter 3

## Phonics

Perhaps no issue in literacy education has proved more durable than phonics. In 1967, Jeanne Chall called the controversy over phonics instruction "the great debate," and a quarter-century later, Frank Smith modified her phrase, calling it instead "the never-ending debate" (1992, p. 432). Understanding the sources of controversy and arriving at a coherent position with respect to phonics instruction are crucially important goals for teachers in the primary grades.

### The Phonics Pendulum

Through the years, the amount of classroom emphasis placed on phonics has varied. Rival positions have stressed teaching sight words as whole units or encouraging children to use context. These alternative emphases have had the instinctive appeal of stressing meaning. By contrast, some approaches to phonics have been atomistic, focusing on numerous subskills, each one taught to mastery before proceeding.

The evidence of research has tended to support a systematic approach to phonics (Albert, 1994; Ediger, 1994; Eldredge, 1993). Chall's landmark book (1967) in many ways launched the present-day phase of the controversy. Her conclusion that available evidence indicated that a "code emphasis" was desirable drew fire from critics who pointed to flaws in the studies. More recently, Marilyn Adams (1990) revisited the issues on the basis of much more extensive research evidence and came to essentially the same conclusion reached by Chall.

### Approaches to Phonics

Merely concluding that phonics is important says little about how it should be approached in primary classrooms. Two major issues arise with respect to phonics instruction: How such instruction should be organized and how it should be carried out.

Organizing phonics instruction obliges a teacher to make curricular decisions about what shall be taught and how. At some risk of oversimplifying the matter, we suggest that there are four basic positions on this issue. (1) Instruction in phonics is largely, if not entirely, unnecessary because children will "naturally" infer letter/sound correspondences from extensive reading. (2) Instruction should be fully contextualized within actual reading and thus involve "teachable moments." (3) Teachable moments are not sufficiently dependable, so a more systematic (though not necessarily sequential) approach is called for to ensure that appropriate instruction occurs in the most timely way. (4) Phonics instruction should be both systematic and sequential.

The second question—that of how phonics instruction should be carried out—has a long history. The two principal positions involve *synthetic* (or explicit) phonics, in which children are taught to blend individual sounds in attacking unfamiliar words, and *analytic* (or implicit) phonics, in which whole words are used to emphasize spelling patterns representing sounds reliably.

## As You Read

The three articles that follow should provide a good basis for thinking through both of the instructional issues surrounding phonics—how and how much. Goodman articulates the view that reading ability is naturally acquired. Stahl and Cunningham, on the other hand, have both concluded that systematic phonics instruction is necessary. Stahl describes the attributes of an ideal program. Cunningham, in the course of an interesting retrospective on her own teaching experience, outlines instructional strategies that have worked for her.

You will find that many of the important questions related to phonics are connected to other issues examined in this book, such as whole language and literacy materials. As you consider the following questions, your knowledge of these interrelated issues will be useful:

1. For what reasons has phonics instruction been the source of contention?
2. What are the major approaches to phonics open to teachers?
3. How does research inform the choice among these approaches?
4. Which approach do you find most acceptable? Why?
5. Are there teaching techniques for phonics that seem especially appealing? If so, which ones and why?
6. To what extent should phonics instruction allow for (a) introduction of skills in isolation? (b) practice of skills in isolation?

## References

Adams, M. J. (1990). *Beginning to read: Thinking and learning about print.* Cambridge, MA: MIT Press.

Albert, E. (1994). *Phonics for learning to read.* (ERIC Document Reproduction Service No. ED 370 078).

Chall, J. S. (1967). *Learning to read: The great debate.* New York: McGraw Hill.

Ediger, M. (1994). *The integrated reading curriculum.* (ERIC Document Reproduction Service No. ED 370 094).

Eldredge J. L. (1993). *Exploring relationships between phonics, knowledge and other reading related variables.* (ERIC Document Reproduction Service No. ED 365 942).

Smith, F. (1992). Learning to read: The never ending debate. *Phi Delta Kappan, 73,* 432–435, 438–441.

## CONTENT LITERACY GUIDE

**Saying the "p" Word: Nine Guidelines for Exemplary Phonics Instruction**
Steven A. Stahl
*The Reading Teacher, 45,* 1992, 618–625

**1.** According to Stahl, what is the primary reason the topic of phonics is so controversial?

**2.** (T/F)  Whole language involves some degree of attention to letter/sound relationships.

**3.** Describe the two extremes of the range of phonics approaches described by Stahl.

    a.

    b.

**4.** (T/F)  There is no requirement that phonics instruction use worksheets.

**5.** Identify and describe the three stages of word recognition according to Frith.

    a.

    b.

    c.

The last of these stages should be entered by the end of what grade?

**6.** (T/F)  Some children learn to decode on their own, without any instruction.

**7.** State the nine guidelines given by Stahl and respond to the specific questions that follow.

    a. *Guideline 1:*

- What does Stahl identify as the main source of the debate over phonics?

- Summarize and evaluate Stahl's baseball analogy.

- How many hours of print exposure are ideal prior to a child's learning to read?

- For the beginning reader with an impoverished background in terms of print exposure, what does Stahl recommend?

- (T/F)   Research suggests that whole language programs work better in kindergarten than in first grade.

b. *Guideline 2:*

- Define *phonemic awareness.*

- Define *phonics.*

- (T/F)   Phonemic awareness is easily taught.

c. *Guideline 3:*

- (T/F)   Stahl recommends that teachers directly point out letters *within* words together with the sounds they represent.

- (T/F)   Stahl recommends first using pictures of word concepts rather than the printed words themselves in teaching phonics.

d. *Guideline 4:*

- Stahl's rule of thumb is that _____ percent of the instructional time in beginning reading should be devoted to phonics.

- (T/F)   Basals appear to do a good job of ensuring that the selections read reflect many examples relevant to the phonics concurrently being taught.

- (T/F)   Stahl recommends selecting trade books based in part on their usefulness in teaching phonics.

- (T/F)   Phonics instruction tends to be a small but important part of Reading Recovery.

e. *Guideline 5:*

- (T/F)   Adults tend to recognize new words by comparing them, or spelling patterns within them, with words they already know.

- (T/F)   Effective decoders see words in terms of phonics rules.

- Describe Stahl's position with regard to the usefulness of rules.

f. *Guideline 6:*

- Differentiate the terms *onset* and *rhyme.*

- Compared with the 286 phonograms that appear in many primary-grade texts, a mere ____ can account for nearly 500 different words.

- Describe Gaskins's analogy-based approach to phonics instruction:

g. *Guideline 7:*

- (T/F)  Stahl believes that invented spelling is a good substitute for direct phonics instruction.

- (T/F)  Practice with invented spellings improves children's awareness of phonemes.

- (T/F)  IBM's *Writing to Read* appears to have little effect of children's reading growth when compared with traditional instruction.

- (T/F)  Invented spelling improves children's writing.

h. *Guideline 8:*

- (T/F)  According to Stahl, good phonics instruction should aim at getting children through the three stages of word recognition as quickly as possible.

i. *Guideline 9:*

- (T/F)  The real purpose of phonics instruction is to get children to the point at which their decoding is automatic enough that most of their attention can be paid to comprehension.

- The Commission on Reading has recommended that phonics instruction should be over by:

# SAYING THE "p" WORD
## NINE GUIDELINES FOR EXEMPLARY PHONICS INSTRUCTION

STEVEN A. STAHL

Phonics, like beauty, is in the eye of the beholder. For many people, "phonics" implies stacks of worksheets, with bored children mindlessly filling in the blanks. For some people, "phonics" implies children barking at print, often in unison, meaningless strings of letter sounds to be blended into words. For some people, "phonics" implies lists of skills that must be mastered, each with its own criterion-referenced test, which must be passed or the teacher is "in for it." For some people, "phonics" somehow contrasts with "meaning," implying that concentrating on phonics means that one must ignore the meaning of the text. For others, "phonics" is the solution to the reading problem, as Flesch (1955) argued and others have concurred (see Republican Party National Steering Committee, 1990), that if we just teach children the sounds of the letters, all else will fall into place.

Because "phonics" can be so many things, some people treat it as a dirty word, others as the salvation of reading. It is neither. With these strong feelings, though, extreme views have been allowed to predominate, seemingly forcing out any middle position that allows for the importance of systematic attention to decoding in the context of a program stressing comprehension and interpretation of quality literature and expository text. The truth is that some attention to the relationships between spelling patterns and their pronunciations is characteristic of all types of reading programs, including whole language. As Newman and Church (1990) explain:

> No one can read without taking into account the graphophonemic cues of written language. As readers all of us use information about the way words are written to help us make sense of what we're reading. . . . Whole language teachers do teach phonics but not as something separate from actual reading and writing. . . . Readers use graphophonic cues: whole language teachers help students orchestrate their use for reading and writing. (p. 20–21)

*Source:* "Saying the 'p' Word: Nine Guidelines for Exemplary Phonics Instruction" by Steven A. Stahl, 1992, *The Reading Teacher, 45*. Copyright 1992 by the International Reading Association. Reprinted by permission.

"Phonics" merely refers to various approaches designed to teach children about the orthographic code of the language and the relationships of spelling patterns to sound patterns. These approaches can range from direct instruction approaches through instruction that is embedded in the reading of literature. There is no requirement that phonics instruction use worksheets, that it involve having children bark at print, that it be taught as a set of discrete skills mastered in isolation, or that it preclude paying attention to the meaning of texts.

In this article, I want to discuss some principles about what effective phonics instruction should contain and describe some successful programs that meet these criteria.

## Why Teach Phonics at All?

The reading field has been racked by vociferous debates about the importance of teaching phonics, when it is to be taught, and how it is to be taught. The interested reader can get a flavor of this debate by reviewing such sources as Adams (1990), Chall (1983a, 1989), Carbo (1988), and so on. To rehash these arguments would not be useful.

The fact is that all students, regardless of the type of instruction they receive, learn about letter-sound correspondences as part of learning to read. There are a number of models of children's initial word learning showing similar stages of development (e.g., Chall, 1983b; Frith, 1985; Lomax & McGee, 1987; McCormick & Mason, 1986). Frith, for example, suggests that children go through three stages as they learn about words. The first stage is *logographic* in which words are learned as whole units, sometimes embedded in a log, such as a stop sign. This is followed by an *alphabetic* stage, in which children use individual letters and sounds to identify words. The last stage is *orthographic* in which children begin to see patterns in words, and use these patterns to identify words without sounding them out. One can see children go through these stages and begin to see words orthographically by the end of the first grade. Following the orthographic stage children grow in their ability to recognize words automatically, without having to think consciously about word structures or spelling patterns.

These stages in the development of word recognition take place while children are learning about how print functions (what a written "word" is, directionality, punctuation, etc.), that it can signify meanings, about the nature of stories, and all of the other learnings that go on in emergent literacy (see Teale, 1987). Learning about words goes hand in hand with other learnings about reading and writing.

All children appear to go through these stages on their way to becoming successful readers. Some will learn to decode on their own, without any instruction. Others will need some degree of instruction, ranging from some pointing out of common spelling patterns to intense and systematic instruction to help them through the alphabetic and orthographic stages. I want to outline some components of what exemplary instruction might look like. These components could be found in classrooms based on the shared reading of literature, as in a whole language philosophy, or in classrooms in which the basal reader is used as the core text.

## *Exemplary Phonics Instruction . . .*

   **1.** *Builds on a child's rich concepts about how print functions.* The major source of the debates on phonics is whether one should go from part to whole (begin by teaching letters and sounds and blend those into words) or from whole to part (begin with words and analyze those into letters). Actually, there should be no debate. Letter-sound instruction makes no sense to a child who does not have an overall conception of what reading is about, how print functions, what stories are, and so on, so it must build on a child's concept of the whole process of reading.

   A good analogy is baseball. For a person learning to play baseball, batting practice is an important part of learning how to play the game. However, imagine a person who has never seen a baseball game. Making that person do nothing but batting practice may lead to the misconception that baseball is about standing at the plate and repeatedly swinging at the ball. That person would miss the purpose of baseball and would think it a boring way to spend an afternoon.

   Adams (1990) points out that children from homes that are successful in preparing children for literacy have a rich idea of what "reading" is before they get to school. They are read to, play with letters on the refrigerator door, discuss print with their parents, and so on. Other children may have had only minimal or no exposure to print prior to school. The differences may add up to 1,000 hours or more of exposure to print.

   For the child who has had that 1,000 hours or more, phonics instruction is grounded in his or her experiences with words. Such a child may not need extensive phonics instruction. Good phonics instruction should help make sense of patterns noticed within words. Just "mentioning" the patterns might suffice. However, for the child with little or no exposure, phonics instruction would be an abstract and artificial task until the child has additional meaningful encounters with print.

   To develop this base of experience with reading, one might begin reading in kindergarten with activities such as sharing books with children, writing down their dictated stories, and engaging them in authentic reading and writing tasks. Predictable books work especially well for beginning word recognition (Bridge, Winograd, & Haley, 1983). Stahl and Miller (1989) found that whole language programs appeared to work effectively in kindergarten. Their effectiveness, however, diminished in first grade, where more structured, code-emphasis approaches seemed to produce better results. In short, children benefited from the experiences with reading that a whole language program gives early on, but, once they had that exposure, they benefit from more systematic study.

   **2.** *Builds on a foundation of phonemic awareness.* Phonemic awareness is not phonics. Phonemic awareness is awareness of sounds in *spoken* words: phonics is the relation between letters and sounds in *written* words. Phonemic awareness is an important precursor to success in reading. One study (Juel, 1988) found that children who were in the bottom fourth of their group in phonemic awareness in first grade remained in the bottom fourth of their class in reading four years later.

   An example is Heather, a child I saw in our clinic. As part of an overall reading assessment, I gave Heather a task involving removing a phoneme from a spoken word. For example, I had Heather say *meat* and then repeat it without saying the /m/ sound *(eat).* When Heather said *chicken* after some hesitation, I was taken aback. When I had her say *coat* with the /k/ sound, she said *jacket.* Looking over the tasks we did together, it appeared that she viewed words only in terms of their meaning. For her, a little less than *meat* was *chicken,* a little less than *coat* was *jacket.*

For most communication, focusing on meaning is necessary. But for learning to read, especially learning about sound-symbol relationships, it is desirable to view words in terms of the sounds they contain. Only by understanding that spoken words contain phonemes can one learn the relationships between letters and sounds. The alternative is learning each word as a logograph, as in Chinese. This is possible, up to a certain limit, but does not use the alphabetic nature of our language to its best advantage.

Heather was a bright child, and this was her only difficulty, but she was having specific difficulties learning to decode. Other children like Heather, or children with more complex difficulties, are going to have similar problems. We worked for a short period of time on teaching her to reflect on sounds in spoken words, and, with about 6 weeks of instruction, she took off and became an excellent reader. The moral is that phonemic awareness is easily taught, but absence of it leads to reading difficulties.

**3.** *Is clear and direct.* Good teachers explain what they mean very clearly. Yet, some phonics instruction seems to be excessively ambiguous.

Some of this ambiguity comes from trying to solve the problem of pronouncing single phonemes. One cannot pronounce the sounds represented by many of the consonants in isolation. For example, the sound made by *b* cannot be spoken by itself, without adding a vowel (such as /buh/).

To avoid having the teacher add the vowel to the consonant sound, however, some basals have come up with some terribly circuitous routes. For example, a phonics lesson from a current basal program begins with a teacher presenting a picture of a key word, such as *bear,* pronouncing the key word and two or three words with a shared phonic element (such as *boat, ball,* and *bed*). The teacher is to point out that the sound at the beginning of each is spelled with a *B.* The teacher might then say some other words and ask if they, too, have the same sound. Next, written words are introduced and may be read by the whole class or by individuals. After this brief lesson, students might complete two worksheets, which both involve circling pictures of items that start with *b* and one which includes copying upper- and lowercase *b*'s.

In this lesson, (a) nowhere is the teacher supposed to attempt to say what sound the *b* is supposed to represent and (b) nowhere is the teacher directed to tell the children that these relationships have anything to do with reading words in text. For a child with little phonemic awareness, the instructions, which require that the child segment the initial phoneme from a word, would be very confusing. Children such as Heather view the word *bear* not as a combination of sounds or letters, but identical to its meaning. For that child, the question of what *bear* begins with does not make any sense, because it is seen as a whole meaning unit, not as a series of sounds that has a beginning and an end.

Some of this confusion could be alleviated if the teacher dealt with written words. A more direct approach is to show the word *bear,* in the context of a story or in isolation, and pointing out that it begins with the letter *b,* and that the letter *b* makes the /b/ sound. This approach goes right to the basic concept, that a letter in a word represents a particular phoneme, involving fewer extraneous concepts. Going the other direction, showing the letter *b* and then showing words such as *bear* that begin with that letter, would also be clear. Each of these should be followed having children practice reading *words* that contain the letter *b,* rather than pictures. Children learn to read by reading words, in stories or in lists. This can be done in small groups or with pairs of children reading with each other independently. Circling pictures, coloring, cutting, and pasting, and so on wastes a lot of time.

**4.** *Is integrated into a total reading program.* Phonics instruction, no matter how useful it is, should never dominate reading instruction. I know of no research to guide us in deciding how much time should be spent on decoding instruction, but my rule of thumb is that at least half of the time devoted to reading (and probably more) should be spent reading connected text—stories, poems, plays, trade books, and so on. No more than 25% of the time (and possibly less) should be spent on phonics instruction and practice.

Unfortunately, I have seen too many schools in which one day the members of the reading group do the green pages (the skills instruction), the next day they read the story, and the third day they do the blue pages. The result is that, on most days, children are not reading text. Certainly, in these classes, children are going to view "reading" as filling out workbook pages, since this is what they do most of the time. Instead, they should read some text daily, preferably a complete story, with phonics instruction integrated into the text reading.

In many basals, the patterns taught in the phonics lessons appear infrequently in the text, leading students to believe that phonics is somehow unrelated to the task of reading (Adams, 1990). What is taught should be directly usable in children's reading. Juel and Roper/Schneider (1985) found that children were better able to use their phonics knowledge, for both decoding and comprehension, when the texts they read contained a higher percentage of words that conformed to the patterns they were taught. It is best to teach elements that can be used with stories the children are going to read. Teachers using a basal might rearrange the phonics lessons so that a more appropriate element is taught with each story.

Teachers using trade books might choose elements from the books they plan to use, and either preteach them or integrate the instruction into the lesson. A good procedure for doing this is described by Trachtenburg (1990). She suggests beginning by reading a quality children's story (such as *Angus and the Cat,* cited in Trachtenburg, 1990), providing instruction in a high utility phonic element appearing in that story (short *a* in this case), and using that element to help read another book (such as *The Cat in the Hat* or *Who Took the Farmer's Hat?*). Trachtenburg (1990) provides a list of trade books that contain high percentages of common phonic elements.

Reading Recovery is another example of how phonics instruction can be integrated into a total reading program. Reading Recovery lessons differ depending on the child's needs, but a typical lesson begins with the rereading of a familiar book, followed by the taking of a "running record" on a book introduced the previous session (see Pinnell, Fried, & Estice, 1990, for details). The phonics instruction occurs in the middle of the lesson and could involve directed work in phonemic awareness, letter-sound correspondences using children's spelling or magnetic letters, or even lists of words. The teacher chooses a pattern with which the child had difficulty. The "phonics" instruction is a relatively small component of the total Reading Recovery program, but it is an important one.

**5.** *Focuses on reading words, not learning rules.* When competent adults read, they do not refer to a set of rules that they store in their heads. Instead, as Adams (1990) points out, they recognize new words by comparing them or spelling patterns within them to words they already know. When an unknown word such as *Minatory* is encountered, it is not read by figuring out whether the first syllable is open or closed. Instead most people that I have asked usually say the first syllable says /min/ as in *minute* or *miniature,* comparing it to a pattern in a word they already know how to pronounce. Effective decoders see words not in terms of phonics rules, but in terms of patterns of letters that are used to aid in identification.

Effective phonics instruction helps children do this, by first drawing their attention to the order of letters in words, forcing them to examine common patterns in English through sounding out words, and showing similarities between words. As an interim step, rules can be useful in helping children see patterns. Some rules, such as the silent *e* rule, point out common patterns in English. However, rules are not useful enough to be taught as absolutes. Clymer (1963) found that only 45% of the commonly taught phonics rules worked as much as 75% of the time.

A good guideline might be that rules might be pointed out, as a way of highlighting a particular spelling pattern, but children should not be asked to memorize or recite them. And, when rules are pointed out, they should be discussed as tentative, with exceptions given at the same time as conforming patterns. Finally, only rules with reasonable utility should be used. Teaching children that *ough* has six sounds is a waste of everyone's time.

**6.** *May include onsets and rimes.* An alternative to teaching rules is using onsets and rimes. Treiman (1985) has found that breaking down syllables into onsets (or the part of the syllable before the vowel) and rimes (the part from the vowel onward) is useful to describe how we process syllables in oral language. Teaching onsets and rimes may be useful in written language as well.

Adams (1990) points out that letter-sound correspondences are more stable when one looks at rimes than when letters are looked at in isolation. For example, *ea* taken alone is thought of as irregular. However, it is very regular in all rimes, except *-ead* (bead vs. bread), *-eaf* (sheaf vs. deaf), and *-ear* (hear vs. bear). Then rime *-ean,* for example, nearly always has the long *e* sound. Of the 286 phonograms that appear in primary grade texts, 95% of them were pronounced the same in every word in which they appeared (Adams, 1990).

In addition, nearly 500 words can be derived from the following 37 rimes:

| | | | | | |
|---|---|---|---|---|---|
| -ack | -ain | -ake | -ale | -all | -ame |
| -an | -ank | -ap | -ash | -at | -ate |
| -aw | -ay | -eat | -ell | -est | -ice |
| -ick | -ide | -ight | -ill | -in | -ine |
| -ing | -ink | -ip | -ir | -ock | -oke |
| -op | -or | -ore | -uck | -ug | -ump |
| -unk | | | | | |

Rime-based instruction is used in a number of successful reading programs. In one such program, children are taught to compare an unknown word to already known words and to use context to confirm their predictions (Gaskins et al., 1988). For example, when encountering *wheat* in a sentence, such as *The little red hen gathered the wheat,* a student might be taught to compare it to *meat* and say "If m-e-a-t is *meat* then this is *wheat.*" The student would then cross-check the pronunciation by seeing if *wheat* made sense in the sentence. This approach is comprehension oriented in that students are focused on the comprehension of sentences and stories, but it does teach decoding effectively (see also Cunningham, 1991).

**7.** *May include invented spelling practice.* It has been suggested that when children work out their invented spellings, they are learning phonic principles, but learning them "naturally." For this reason, many whole language advocates suggest that practice in writing with invented spelling might be a good substitute for direct phonics instruction. Practice with invented spelling does improve children's awareness of phonemes, which, as discussed earlier, is an important precursor to learning to decode.

However, there is very little research on the effects of invented spelling. That research is positive, but I know of only one study that directly addresses the question. Clarke (1989) found that children who were encouraged to invent spelling and given additional time for writing journals were significantly better at decoding and comprehension than children in a traditional spelling program. However, the classes she studied used a synthetic phonics program as their core reading program. These results may not transfer to a whole language program or even to a more eclectic basal program. An evaluation of the Writing-to-Read program, a computer-based program incorporating writing, found that it had little effect on children's reading abilities (Slavin, 1991).

We need not wait for the research needed to evaluate the use of invented spelling. Writing stories and journal entries using invented spelling does not seem to hurt one's reading or spelling abilities and may help them, and it certainly improves children's writing.

**8.** *Develops independent word recognition strategies, focusing attention on the internal structure of words.* The object of phonics instruction is to get children to notice orthographic patterns in words and to use those patterns to recognize words. Effective strategies, whether they involve having a child sound a word out letter by letter, find a word that shares the same rime as an unknown word, or spell out the word through invented or practiced spelling, all force the child to look closely at patterns in words. It is through the learning of these patterns that children learn to recognize words efficiently.

Good phonics instruction should help children through the stages described earlier as quickly as possible. Beginning with bookhandling experiences, storybook reading and "Big Books," and other features of a whole language kindergarten support children at the logographic stage. Frith (1985) suggests that writing and spelling may aid in the development of alphabetic knowledge. This can be built upon with some direct instruction of letters and sounds, and showing students how to use that knowledge to unlock words in text. Sounding words out also forces children to examine the internal structure of words, as does rime-based instruction. These can help children make the transition to the orthographic stage. In the next stage, the child develops automatic word recognition skills, or the ability to recognize words without conscious attention.

**9.** *Develops automatic word recognition skills so that students can devote their attention to comprehension, not words.* The purpose of phonics instruction is *not* that children learn to sound out words. The purpose is that they learn to recognize words, quickly and automatically, so that they can turn their attention to comprehension of the text. If children are devoting too much energy sounding out words, they will not be able to direct enough of their attention to comprehension (Samuels, 1988).

We know that children develop automatic word recognition skills through practicing reading words. We know that reading words in context does improve children's recognition of words, an improvement which transfers to improved comprehension. There is some question about whether reading words in isolation necessarily results in improved comprehension. Fleisher, Jenkins, and Pany (1979–1980) found that increasing word recognition speed in isolation did not result in improved comprehension; Blanchard (1981) found that it did. Either way, there is ample evidence that practice reading words in text, either repeated readings of the same text (Samuels, 1988) or just reading of connected text in general (Taylor & Nosbush, 1983), improves children's comprehension.

Good phonics instruction is also over relatively quickly. Anderson, Hiebert, Wilkinson, and Scott (1985) recommends that phonics instruction be completed by the end of the second grade. This may even be too long. Stretching phonics instruction out too long, or spending time on teaching the arcane aspects of phonics—the schwa, the silent *k*, assigning accent to polysyllabic words—is at best a waste of time. Once a child begins to use orthographic patterns in recognizing words and recognizes words at an easy, fluent pace, it is time to move away from phonics instruction and to spend even more time reading and writing text.

## The "Politics" of Phonics

Given that all children do need to learn about the relationships between spelling patterns and pronunciations on route to becoming a successful reader, why all the fuss about phonics?

Part of the reason is that there is confusion about what phonics instruction is. A teacher pointing out the "short *a*" words during the reading of a Big Book in a whole language classroom is doing something different from a teacher telling her class that the short sound of the letter *a* is /a/ and having them blend in unison 12 words that contain that sound, yet both might be effective phonics instruction. The differences are not only in practice but in philosophy.

In discussions on this issue, the philosophical differences seem to predominate. These exaggerated differences often find people arguing that "phonics" proponents oppose the use of literature and writing in the primary grades, which is clearly false, or that "whole language" people oppose any sort of direct teaching, also clearly false. The truth is that there are commonalities that can be found in effective practices of widely differing philosophies, some of which are reflected in the nine guidelines discussed here.

In this article, I have proposed some characteristics of exemplary phonics instruction. Such instruction is very different from what I see in many classrooms. But because phonics is often taught badly is no reason to stop attempting to teach it well. Quality phonics instruction should be part of a reading program, integrated and relevant to the reading and writing of actual texts, based on and building upon children's experiences with texts. Such phonics instruction can and should be built into all beginning reading programs.

## References

Adams, M. J. (1990). *Beginning to read: Thinking and learning about print.* Cambridge, MA: M.I.T. Press.

Anderson, R. C., Hiebert, E. F., Wilkinson, I. A. G., & Scott, J. (1985). *Becoming a nation of readers.* Champaign, IL: National Academy of Education and Center for the Study of Reading.

Blanchard, J. S. (1981). A comprehension strategy for disabled readers in the middle school. *Journal of Reading, 24,* 331–336.

Bridge, C. A., Winograd, P. N., & Haley, D. (1983). Using predictable materials vs. preprimers to teach beginning sight words. *The Reading Teacher, 36,* 884–891.

Carbo, M. (1988). Debunking the great phonics myth. *Phi Delta Kappan, 70,* 226–240.

Chall, J. S. (1983a). Learning to read: The great debate (revised, with a new Foreword). New York, NY: McGraw-Hill.

Chall, J. S. (1983b). *Stages of reading development.* New York: McGraw-Hill.

Chall, J. S. (1989). Learning to read: The great debate twenty years later. A response to "Debunking the great phonics myth." *Phi Delta Kappan, 71,* 521–538.

Clarke, L. K. (1989). Encouraging invented spelling in first graders' writing: Effects on learning to spell and read. *Research in the Teaching of English, 22,* 281–309.

Clymer, T. (1963). The utility of phonic generalizations in the primary grades. *The Reading Teacher, 16,* 252–258.

Cunningham, P. M. (1991). *Phonics they use.* New York: HarperCollins.

Fleisher, L. S., Jenkins, J. R., & Pany, D. (1979–1980). Effects on poor readers' comprehension of training in rapid decoding. *Reading Research Quarterly, 15,* 30–48.

Flesch, R. (1955). *Why Johnny can't read.* New York: Harper & Row.

Frith, U. (1985). Beneath the surface of developmental dyslexia. In K. E. Patterson, K. C. Marshall, & M. Coltheart (Eds.), *Surface dyslexia: Neuropsychological and cognitive studies of phonological reading.* Hillsdale, NJ: Erlbaum.

Gaskins, I. W., Downer, M. A., Anderson, R. C., Cunningham, P. M., Gaskins, R. W., Schommer, M., & The Teachers of Benchmark School. (1988). A metacognitive approach to phonics: Using what you know to decode what you don't know. *Remedial and Special Education, 9,* 36–41.

Juel, C. (1988). Learning to read and write: A longitudinal study of fifty-four children from first through fourth grade. *Journal of Educational Psychology, 80,* 437–447.

Juel, C., & Roper/Schneider, D. (1985). The influence of basal readers on first grade reading. *Reading Research Quarterly, 20,* 134–152.

Lomax, R. G., & McGee, L. M. (1987). Young children's concepts about print and reading: Toward a model of reading acquisition. *Reading Research Quarterly, 22,* 237–256.

McCormick, C. E., & Mason, J. M. (1986). Intervention procedures for increasing preschool children's interest in and knowledge about reading. In W. H. Teale & E. Sulzby (Eds.), *Emergent literacy: Writing and reading* (pp. 90–115). Norwood, NJ: Ablex.

Newman, J. M., & Church, S. M. (1990). Commentary: Myths of whole language. *The Reading Teacher, 44,* 20–27.

Pinnell, G. S., Fried, M. D., & Estice, R. M. (1990). Reading Recovery: Learning how to make a difference. *The Reading Teacher, 43,* 282–295.

Republican Party National Steering Committee. (1990). *Position paper on teaching children to read.* Washington, DC: Author.

Samuels, S. J. (1988). Decoding and automaticity: Helping poor readers become automatic at word recognition. *The Reading Teacher, 41,* 756–760.

Slavin, R. E. (1991). Reading effects of IBM's "Writing to Read" program: A review of evaluations. *Educational Evaluation and Policy Analysis, 13,* 1–11.

Stahl, S. A., & Miller, P. D. (1989). Whole language and language experience approaches for beginning reading: A quantitative research synthesis. *Review of Educational Research, 59,* 87–116.

Taylor, B. M., & Nosbush, L. (1983). Oral reading for meaning: A technique for improving word identification skills. *The Reading Teacher, 37,* 234–237.

Teale, W. H. (1987). Emergent literacy: Reading and writing development in early childhood. In J. E. Readence & R. S. Baldwin (Eds.), *Research in literacy: Merging perspectives, Thirty-sixth yearbook of the National Reading Conference* (pp. 45–74). Rochester, NY: National Reading Conference.

Trachtenburg, P. (1990). Using children's literature to enhance phonics instruction. *The Reading Teacher, 43,* 648–653.

Treiman, R. (1985). Onsets and rimes as units of spoken syllables: Evidence from children. *Journal of Experimental Child Psychology, 39,* 161–181.

**CONTENT LITERACY GUIDE**

**Acquiring Literacy Is Natural: Who Skilled Cock Robin?**
Kenneth S. Goodman
*Theory Into Practice, 26,* Special Issue, 368–373

1. According to Goodman, how has research created the illusion that a skills approach to reading is research based?

2. How does achievement testing exacerbate the problem in Goodman's view?

3. (T/F) Goodman believes that a skills approach is more workable in developing countries than in industrialized nations like the United States.

4. What key does Goodman identify for literacy learning to be effective?

5. What two historical developments does Goodman identify, either of which might lead to the development of written language in a society?

   a.

   b.

6. What critical mistake does Goodman suggest we have made in literacy instruction?

7. Describe Goodman's notion of separating literacy learning from literacy use.

8. (T/F) Goodman concedes that written language is essentially harder to learn than oral language.

**9.** What two resources does Goodman attribute to the beginning reader?

a.

b.

**10.** Describe briefly the kind of classroom environment Goodman recommends.

**11.** Summarize the roles of sampling and prediction that Goodman attributes to reading.

**12.** What two types of students does Goodman describe in skills classrooms?

a.

b.

**13.** Summarize Goodman's description of the plight of the beginning reader who happens to be experiencing problems.

**14.** To what cause does Goodman attribute the widespread lack of reading for pleasure in developed countries?

**15.** (T/F)  Goodman suggests that the need to learn is more important than the quality of instruction.

**16.** What responsibility does the community have in support of the school?

**17.** Summarize Goodman's description of the typical adult illiterate in a developed country.

**18.** How, in Goodman's view, can such adult problems be prevented?

**19.** Respond to Goodman's final analogy concerning astrology and astronomy, and so on.

# ACQUIRING LITERACY IS NATURAL:
# WHO SKILLED COCK ROBIN?

### KENNETH S. GOODMAN

An old English folksong asks the question "Who Killed Cock Robin?" I've parodied that question in the title of this paper because I believe that many of the problems in literacy instruction in the world today are misunderstood because learning to read has been treated as a matter of acquiring a series of skills.

In the literate nations—particularly America—we've built a technology of reading skills. On a world basis, literacy can be easily seen to be proportionate to the need for literacy within any society or subgroup of the particular society. Even within literate societies, different ethnic, cultural and economic groups show notably different patterns of acceptance of literacy and literacy instruction.

But as we've built a technology of instruction in literate societies, we've created pathologies of failure which are independent of the need for language, the nature of language or the natural learning of language. The technology we've built treats reading as something difficult to be systematically taught skill upon skill. Though this technology has no foundation either in theory or research, it has acquired, over time, a credibility partly due to pedagogical tradition—we continue to do what others have done before us—and partly due to its arbitrary specificity. Skills are arranged sequentially and hierarchically and drills and exercises are multiplied and duplicated to teach the skills. Research fills the professional literature reporting experiments on the most effective ways of teaching the skills, creating the illusion that the skills themselves have a base in scientific research.

Achievement tests based on the skill hierarchies become the means for determining the extent of acquisition of literacy. Performance on these tests becomes synonymous with reading itself. Low scores on tests are offered as proof of failure and a new technology is created to find the pathological causes within the non-learner's failure to acquire the skills. And more drills and exercises are multiplied and duplicated to remediate the deficiencies and teach the skills.

*Source:* "Acquiring Literacy Is Natural: Who Skilled Cock Robin?" by Kenneth S. Goodman, 1977, *Theory Into Practice, 16*(5), pages 309–314. (Theme issue on "Reading and Language.") Copyright 1977 College of Education, The Ohio State University. Reprinted by permission.

Networks of professionally trained diagnosticians, clinicians and remediators are created to test, diagnose and treat the disabled learners.

The acquisition of literacy has been so obscured by equating it with the acquisition of skills that strength is mistaken for weakness and instruction is often at cross-purposes to natural language learning. The sources of problems in learning to read and even the extent of such problems are also obscured.

Furthermore, skill technologies are transferred into literacy programs in developing societies where they work even less well than in the established educational systems of highly literate societies where opportunities for natural acquisition of literacy are more abundant.

How well schemes for teaching literacy work is always a complicated issue to judge since learners are often able to overcome artificial structures to resist having literacy fractionated and to learn written language much as they learned the oral. The key seems always to be that the learner experiences functional need for written language. Language serves the communicative needs of individuals and societies and development of language including literacy can not be understood outside of the social-cultural context of learners.

In changing societies where massive literacy campaigns are conducted among people of all ages who had no prior opportunities to learn to read and write, the success of such programs is far less a result of the methods or even the quality of instruction than it is of the reality and extent of social change. If a people feel a real need to be literate because of changed roles, values, opportunities, or experiences and if written language becomes truly accessible and functional then many of them will become literate easily and well.

I'm not suggesting that instruction is either unimportant or unnecessary. I am arguing that instruction must be related to the realities of language and language learning in cultural, social contexts.

Oral language develops in all human societies. It is both a personal and social invention. It makes it possible for human societies to achieve a level of interaction unique among living species. We can truly share our problems, needs, thoughts and experiences. Oral language serves the face to face, here-and-now communicative needs common to all human societies.

For all but the deaf, oral language is the most accessible and useful form for such immediate communication. It is the form individuals develop first. Quickly, their thrust to communicate causes their personal language to move toward the forms, norms and structures of the language of the family and the community. The need to communicate becomes intertwined with the need to fully participate in society. Language is the necessary means to both. But neither the individual nor society ever lose their ability to create language to meet new need. Language remains always open, always adaptable, ever changing to represent new experiences, concepts, values or environments.

Oral language is suitable for all functions except those that require that language be preservable over time or transmittable over distance. When human societies reach a point of complexity where their ideas, concepts and experiences become too complex for preservation through the oral tradition and when society itself becomes so complex that individuals must be in regular communication with others outside the immediate community, then the societies invent the means for such communication and written language comes into being.

Sometimes the need is limited and only a small corps of literate people is needed to serve as the historians or the scribes of the society. Mass literacy represents a stage in social development in which every individual needs written language for full first class participation in the culture.

Gutenberg's invention of the printing press has been credited with making mass literacy possible. But it is probably more accurate to say that the need for widespread literacy caused the invention of the printing press. Recent developments of quick, easy, inexpensive, high-quality reproduction devices facilitate written communication but they didn't create the need they serve. They are responses to that need.

Written language is as natural as oral in human society. In fact, it is a natural extension of the human ability to create language to deal with each communicative function as it develops.

Language is universally human. The form it takes depends on the function it must perform. Deaf people cut off from sound develop a visual language, manual sign, as an alternative for face-to-face communication. Blind people, cut off from sight, use their sense of touch to read Braille.

If there are human communities which have not developed literacy they are not proof that literacy is less natural than oral language but rather than language develops as the functions for it develop.

Differences between oral and written language which will affect how they are learned, result from the differences in their use. Because of its special function, written language is more likely to be used out of the situation context in which oral language is commonly embedded. It tends to be used to express ideas which are more complex and abstract than oral language. Both language forms have some common functions too, of course. A sign that says *keep off the grass* is just as concrete and situationally embedded as the equivalent oral command. Oral discussions may become quite abstract.

Still, it is the differences and similarities in the functions of written and oral language that hold the key to understanding how acquisition of literacy is like or unlike the acquisition of oral language. We have made the critical mistake in the past of ignoring function and teaching reading and writing as the mastery of abstract form. In doing so, we have ignored the intrinsic motivation to learn to read and write that development of functional need brings about. We have ignored the lessons learned from studies of language acquisition about language development as growth in the competence to understand and be understood through language.

We made literacy something separate and apart from language and its use. We made it a set of abstract skills to be mastered sequentially as a prerequisite to use. We skilled and overskilled readers and then sought to help those who couldn't find their way to meaning with a dose of remedial skill instruction.

All language is used and learned in the context of expressing and comprehending meaning. Human infants sort out, from the sensory bombardment they receive through all their senses that which is significant and that which is not. They categorize, organize, relate as they continually seek to comprehend. They sort language out of their noisy environments and begin relating it to its functions. In the process they develop not only control over a set of symbols and a vocabulary but also a set of rules for generating and comprehending language not previously experienced.

For most people in all human societies the movement toward virtually full control of at least one form of at least one oral language is swift and easy. By age four they are highly competent.

In literate societies, children begin acquisition of literacy in much the same way. They sort out from the environment the print and its relationship to everything else within that environment. They will be most aware of the print that has functions which overlap those of oral language such as that which names and identifies—logos and brand names on cars, cereal boxes, peanut butter jars, or their own names—that which controls—signs for stop, exit, no parking. If they have a lot of experience with books and newspapers, they may become aware of the more abstract functions of providing information or entertainment through literature.

If the acquisition of literacy lags behind that of oral language at the age of school beginning, it is a demonstration of the slower development of the functions of written language and not proof that literacy is either harder or less natural to learn.

Just as in acquiring oral language, children are finding order in written language, developing control over its system as they seek to comprehend and express. They become aware of the form as they experience the function, they learn the parts from the wholes, generalize and expand their functional competence.

For most children becoming literate, they have the advantage of being already quite advanced in oral language competence. They control the rules and basic language structures as well as the terms and idioms. They can express and comprehend, through oral language, their understandings, feelings, concepts. The two most important resources that any learners bring to learning to read and write are their competence in the oral language and their undiminished ability to learn language as it is needed for new functions.

The role of literacy instruction in school is to facilitate the use by learners of these resources. To be most successful, instruction accepts and expands on the base of literacy already begun. The school's focus is on expanding awareness in the learners of the personal-social functions written language has for them. This often means enhancing and enriching the classroom making it a highly literate environment—one in which the learners are emersed in functional written language. Children must be continually in meaningful interaction with each other, with teachers, with unseen authors, with others *through print*. This is also true for those acquiring literacy at any age.

The optimally effective teacher in such a school is not the technician sequentially teaching and testing the skills assumed to be components of reading. Rather, a teacher must be knowledgable about linguistic and cognitive development, insightful in monitoring the progress of learners in acquiring the ability to get and express meaning through written language, able to plan experiences to help children to learn.

Much is now known about how language works. We understand that in producing language speakers or writers start with meaning, create an underlying or deep language structure to represent it, and then produce a surface representation either in speech or in print which must be full enough to be comprehensible to the listener or reader.

We understand that the listener or reader samples from the speech or print, predicts and assigns underlying structure and seeks meaning as efficiently as possible.

Effective language teachers need not be linguists or psycholinguists. But they must be knowledgable about language functions and processes.

There is a comfort and orderliness that appeals to teachers in sequential skill hierarchies. They particularly lend themselves to very formal and structured classrooms. But the emptiness of such hierarchies and irrelevance to actual development in reading is observable in any skill oriented classroom. In such classrooms, there always are two kinds of learners; one kind do well on the skill drills because they have enough control of the reading process to deal with the parts within the wholes. They don't need the skill instruction. The second kind have great difficulty with the sequenced skills because they are dealing with them as abstractions outside of the meaningful language process. Such learners can't profit from skill instruction unless they can transcend it and find their way to meaning on their own. Unfortunately, the difficulty they experience is often cause for more intensive instruction in skills even more removed from real functional written language. While their peers move on to more natural language with decreasing proportions of time spent on skills these learners are subjected to remedial skill instruction.

By the time they have satisfied their instructors that they can produce grunts for letters, blend sounds, sound out words, syllabicate, match words that have beginning, middle or final sounds or letters and attack, perceive, identify, recognize, analyze and synthesize words, many of them will have lost all confidence in their own ability to get sense from print. They will be the victims of overskill. Poor cock-robin!

Even if they should later overcome the fragmentation, they will have been so phonicated, so syllabified, so verbalized that they will always regard reading as dull, tedious and onerous. They will read only what they must and never of their own choice for pleasure or relaxation.

In countries with extensive literacy instruction, there are far more people who can read to some extent but don't than there are people who can't read at all. There are even people who read well enough to become highly educated who seldom read anything for their own pleasure. For them, there is no pleasure in reading.

Illiteracy in developing countries must be seen as the result of two factors: lack of functional need for literacy and lack of opportunity to acquire literacy.

Earlier, I argued that literacy campaigns in developing nations can only succeed when the conditions in the society make literacy both necessary and available.

There must be reasons for people to need to use written language—there must be signs, forms, books, newspapers, magazines, street signs and addresses to be read. Only then will substantial numbers of learners respond to instruction. If the cultural conditions are right, even nonprofessional teachers using common sense methodology will appear to be successful. Highly professional teachers can make a major difference but when the need is real many learners will transcend weaknesses in instruction.

Learning literacy is like learning a second language in that functional need and continual exposure are more important than the quality of instruction.

In many cultures some social, ethnic, occupational or economic groups may need and/or value literacy more than others. Indeed it may be possible in some countries that some people will not need to be literate to become respected members of their immediate communities while others in the same countries do need to be literate. Even within communities, it is possible that some individuals, families or social groups will attach greater value and importance to literacy than others. Response to literacy instruction will certainly be proportionate to the value and need. That doesn't mean that some groups will learn and some won't. It means that there will be significant differences in the relative degree to which literacy instruction is accepted.

I've been using the term "acceptance of literacy instruction" because I am arguing that literacy learning is not a passive response to instruction. Instruction can help to motivate and facilitate, even guide learning but it can not produce learning in a passive, disinterested or hostile learner. Even behavior modification forces active involvement of the learner through rewards or punishments.

I believe that schools can help to rebuild a sense of the functions of written language in pupils who have not yet developed such function. But there are limits on what schools and teachers can accomplish alone in this respect. The community itself must examine the uses it makes of written language and the real value that literacy has in the culture of the community. Schools can participate in changing the conditions and values of society but only as part of a much broader concentrated effort.

Illiteracy in developed nations presents a different picture. There may be sub-cultures which are very much like the developing nations within them, for example, some Native American groups in the United States. But the bulk of illiterates in countries with universal education are people who have had instruction but can't or who believe they can't get meaning from print.

These illiterates tend to have certain common characteristics. Very often, they can produce phonic approximations for virtually every word. They have the skills they've been taught but can't make them work. So they think that successful readers know some magic tricks that turn the disjointed cacophony into meaning. They tend to accept the opinion of past teachers that they can't read because they lack skills. They believe readers always know every word. So each word they meet that they don't know is one more proof of defeat. Above all, they are convinced they will never read successfully even when they are already partially successful. That's because they don't regard what they are doing as reading unless they have conscientiously used their skills to attack the words.

Deskilling reading instruction and placing greater emphasis at the beginning on building the personal-social functions of reading will help to prevent such cripples from developing. Keeping the focus of both the learner and the teacher on meaning will provide both the necessary context for learning and basic means of evaluation and self-evaluation. Readers who understand that success in reading can be easily judged by whether what is read makes sense will tend to drop non-productive strategies even if teachers advocate them.

I can't offer a neat simple sequence of testable steps in the deskilled alternative to beginning reading instruction I'm advocating. My approach starts where the learners are; it extends and establishes functional uses for written language; it employs *only* whole, real, relevant, meaningful language; it encourages risk-taking, meaning-seeking, hypothesis-testing. In other words, it treats learning to read as language learning. It treats teaching reading as helping people learn to get meaning from print. And, if you want to get back to basics, getting meaning is where it's at.

Too often in the past we tried to build technologies without a base in scientific concepts and understanding. We had alchemy before chemistry, astrology before astronomy, witch-doctors before modern medicine. Let's move on now from our reading skill technologies and relegate them to the museum of folklore and superstition in which they belong.

# CONTENT LITERACY GUIDE

**What Kind of Phonics Instruction Will We Have?**
Patricia M. Cunningham
In D. J. Leu and C. K. Kinzer (Eds.)
Forty-first Yearbook of the National Reading Conference, 1992

1. Were you surprised that the quote from Paul McKee dated from 1934? How would you compare his assessment of the debate then with now?

2. Give the general characteristics of DISTAR.

3. What problem does Cunningham identify with linguistic readers?

4. What strategy did Cunningham use to enable Todd and Eric to decode short words?

   What was the limitation of this strategy?

5. Describe Cunningham's attempt at introspection. Why do you think it failed?

6. What did Cunningham's research review reveal about teaching syllabication rules?

7. What technique did Cunningham use to help Todd and Eric with polysyllabic words?

   How did the boys like it?

   How well did it work?

**8.** What two approaches to decoding did Cunningham's research lead her to reject?

    a.

    b.

**9.** Why, according to Cunningham, does instruction in phonics rules not work very well?

**10.** Why did Cunningham's dictionary drill work?

**11.** Briefly define *parallel distributed processing.*

**12.** (T/F)  Skilled readers do not look at every word as they read.

**13.** How is the great speed of word processing by the brain explained?

**14.** (T/F)  Fluent readers rarely recode printed words into sound.

**15.** In what way does recoding printed words to sound help the reader?

**16.** (T/F)  Skillful readers use context to recognize most words.

**17.** List the three major uses of context identified by Cunningham.

    a.

    b.

    c.

When does context come into play?

**18.** (T/F)  Both good and poor readers often have problems pronouncing infrequent, phonetically regular words.

**19.** Suggest a third example of your own to complement Cunningham's pseudowords.


**20.** (T/F)  Readers use spelling patterns to decode words.

**21.** Define the following:

    a. Synthetic approach to phonics


    b. Analytic approach to phonics


    According to Cunningham, which should be used? Why?


**22.** Interletter frequencies help readers with what kind of words?


**23.** Suggest another example to complement Cunningham's *dr* versus *dn*.


**24.** Paraphrase Cunningham's summary paragraph on how words are processed.


**25.** Children from literate homes have experienced about _____ hours of print exposure.

**26.** Briefly define *phonemic awareness*.

27. (T/F)  Most children can learn to read without well-developed phonemic awareness.

28. What is Cunningham's opinion of the "I Can Read" books as tools for developing phonemic awareness?

29. List some of the techniques Cunningham recommends for K–1 development of phonemic awareness.

30. Why does Cunningham suggest that the phonics versus sight word debate "be laid to rest"?

31. Define the following:

   a. Onset

   b. Rhyme

   How has recent research confirmed McKee's instinct about onset-and-rhyme instruction?

32. In what two ways is "lots of easy reading" essential to developing readers?

   a.

   b.

33. What does Cunningham mean by a "reciprocal relationship" between reading and writing?

**34.** (T/F)  Invented spelling actually delays the development of good decoding ability.

**35.** What two areas of controversy still envelop invented spelling?

    a.

    b.

**36.** Read the sample Reading Recovery scenario and describe how phonics is handled.

**37.** What activity is missing from the Reading Recovery example (Vincent) but may be present in other examples as needed?

**38.** What is the role of fixed ability groups in Cunningham's classroom model?

**39.** List and describe each of her four time blocks:

    a.

    b.

    c.

    d.

**40.** What two elements need to be balanced, according to Cunningham, if the most effective instruction is to result?

    a.

    b.

# WHAT KIND OF PHONICS INSTRUCTION WILL WE HAVE?

PATRICIA M. CUNNINGHAM

One cold February morning, Jerry Niles called. He told me that the topic for the annual review of research was "Phonics" and that he wanted me to do it. I thought he was joking! Once he convinced me that this was not an early April Fool's joke, I tried to convince him that I was not the person to do it. "I'm not a real researcher," I protested. "All I really care about is instruction and there is a lot of process research but almost no instructional research." "But we want this to be an instructional talk," Jerry countered. "You can't review research that isn't there." I insisted. "In the last 20 years, we have learned an incredible amount about the role of mediated word identification in reading and writing but we don't have a research base for how it ought to be taught." In spite of my protests that there was nothing there to review, Jerry insisted that I was the person to review it and somehow, he convinced me!

> *The question of instruction in phonics has aroused a lot of controversy. Some educators have held to the proposition that phonetic training is not only futile and wasteful but also harmful to the best interests of a reading program. Others believe that since the child must have some means of attacking strange words, instruction in phonics is imperative. There have been disputes also relative to the amount of phonics to be taught, the time when the teaching should take place and the methods to be used. In fact, the writer knows of no problem around which more disputes have centered. (Paul McKee, 1934, p. 191)*

Clearly, the phonics question has been plaguing the field of reading for a long time. In this review, I will try to: (a) convince you that we are always going to have some phonics instruction and that *we* have a responsibility to influence the form that instruction takes, (b) share with you my own struggles as a teacher and a researcher with the

*Source:* "What Kind of Phonics Instruction Will We Have?" by Patricia M. Cunningham, In C. K. Kinzer and D. J. Leu (Eds.), *Literacy Research, Theory and Practice: Views from Many Perspectives* (pages 17–31). Chicago: National Reading Conference. Copyright 1992 by the National Reading Conference. Reprinted with permission of P. M. Cunningham and the National Reading Conference.

phonics dilemma, (c) review the major research findings of the last 20 years, and (d) describe phonics instruction which appears to be consistent with that research.

## *There Will Be Some Phonics Instruction*

Many reading experts today are opposed to any kind of phonics instruction. Some believe that decoding plays no role in meaningful reading. Others accept the notion that readers use letter-sound knowledge to decode unfamiliar words, but believe that readers will discover whatever they need to know. There is a fairly pervasive attitude which seems to translate: "Phonics happens but you can't teach it!" The reality is that teachers do teach it and parents demand that it be taught. In the week prior to NRC, as I was trying to figure out how to convince the NRC audience that there would always be some kind of phonics being taught, three persuasive events occurred.

A long article with photographs of mostly minority children headlined, "Opposed to Whole Language, Houston Schools Revert to Phonics," appeared in the November 20th issue of *Education Week:*

> *Disenchanted with or opposed to whole-language approaches to teaching reading, educators at eight Houston elementary schools have persuaded local school officials to allow them to return to a traditional phonics-based reading instruction program this year. Teachers and principals at the schools argued that their students, many of whom are from low-income families were doing poorly under the whole language method, at least in part because the students' parents were not providing the at-home support needed to make the whole language approach work. . . .*

The article goes on to explain that these schools are being given $70,000 to go back to DISTAR, "a program which is heavily structured and paces children through repetition sound drills and was dropped because its results did not meet expectations." The teachers in these Houston schools clearly thought that whole language or phonics was an either/or proposition and after trying the DISTAR approach to phonics and getting less than satisfactory results, they had tried "whole language" and were now dropping that and reverting to DISTAR.

In the same week, this item appeared on the front page of the *Greensboro News & Record* Sunday paper:

> *Mike looks at the work sheet and bears down on the five-letter word he's been asked to read. "It's got an E at the end," he tells himself, "so it must be a long I." Then he begins "sounding out" the word, letter-by-letter. "Sss. Sp. Spike?"*
>
> *"Yes," reassures his tutor.*
>
> *Mike moves down the list of words built around the letter I, the vowel he has tackled since starting the private tutoring lessons in August . . . Mike reads the words carefully.* Slide. Limp. Flirt, Flip. Rip. Bird.
>
> *"You couldn't have done that three weeks ago," his tutor tells him.*

The article goes on to explain that Mike asked for a tutor to teach him to read 3 months after graduating from Guilford Country's Northeast High. Mike's inability to read is attributed to his lack of phonics and this grueling 3-week long letter-by-letter sounding of lists of words containing the vowel I is what the public is led to think Mike should have gotten a long time ago!

The final item which caught my attention occurred on Sunday night. My teenage son likes oldies and on Sunday nights, he listens to "Cousin Brucie" on the radio. Every 15 minutes or so, the oldies are interrupted by an ad for *Hooked on Phonics.* This ad explains that there are only 44 sounds in the English language and that for $149.00, you can order a set of tapes which will teach anyone "from 4 to 44" to read. It is clear from the continuing nationwide advertising blitz that a lot of people are sending in their money to get the tapes and books with the lists of phonetically controlled words.

The kind of phonics instruction exemplified by these three examples is the worst kind of phonics. It is devoid of meaning and isolated from real reading and writing. Furthermore, the letter-by-letter sounding it teaches is not consistent with what we know about how phonics actually works. This kind of phonics instruction is selling, however, because teachers and parents know that phonics is useful, that all good readers can decode words and most poor readers cannot and because it is what is for sale. It is not, however, the kind of phonics instruction we should have.

## My Own Phonics Struggle

My fate was probably sealed in 1949 when I was a first grader at High Street School in Westerly, Rhode Island. In the morning, we were divided into reading groups and read about the adventures of Sally, Dick, Jane, Puff, and Spot. After lunch each day, we all pulled out bright blue phonics books and sounded out words. Little did I know that at 5 years old, I was thrust right into the middle of the sight-word/phonics controversy.

1965 found me teaching first grade in Key West, Florida. I taught the phonics in my basal manual and most children learned to distinguish short vowels from long vowels. The children in my top group even developed the ability to "sound out" new words, although even then I did not quite believe that what they did when they came to a new word was, in any way, related to what I was teaching them about phonics. One day, I overheard a boy remark to a friend, "the short vowels are pretty short but the long ones look pretty short, too." His friend then proceeded to explain it to him. "It's simple. The little ones are the short ones and the capital ones are the long ones!" Although I continued to teach first grade and the vowel rules for several years, my faith in them was badly shaken!

I got my master's degree in Reading from Florida State in 1968. "Linguistics" was the buzzword at that time and I thought that "linguistic readers" were going to solve the decoding problems of our poor readers. I got a chance to try this out with a whole class full of fourth grade poor readers. Armed with the Merrill Linguistic Readers and the SRA Basic Reading Series, I abandoned phonics rules for linguistic patterns. Things went pretty well for the first month. The students learned all the short *a* patterns and read about Dan in his tan van. As we moved on, however, they began to confuse the previously learned patterns with the new ones. Worse yet, I realized that the children had stopped trying to make sense of what they were reading and were simply sounding out the patterns!

"Say 'blank' and read the rest of the sentence and then go back and think about what would make sense," was my 1970 brand of decoding instruction.

In 1971, I found myself in Terre Haute, Indiana, as the special reading teacher at the Indiana State University Laboratory School. All day, I worked with poor readers. Mostly, I tried to get these students to enjoy reading and to talk about what they read. I did almost no phonics instruction but it did worry me that almost all the poor readers had little ability to decode an unfamiliar word. My "real challenges" arrived after lunch each day. Todd and Eric were sixth graders of normal intelligence who had been in remedial reading since second grade and who read at the second-grade level. Both boys were fluent with all the most-commonly occurring words and were excellent users of picture and context clues. They could understand anything they could read and most of what you read to them. They had been scheduled for 45 minutes alone with me each day because they were to go on to the junior high next year and their parents were very worried that, after all these years, they still had not "caught on to reading."

For both Todd and Eric, the problem was clear-cut. They knew what reading was and that you were to make meaning from it. They enjoyed being read to and even enjoyed reading the high-interest, low-vocabulary books I could find that they could read themselves. They simply had not learned to decode! For the first semester, I taught Todd and Eric "word families." They were very competitive and I made *Go Fish* and *Old Maid* and *Concentration* games, which they could win by matching and saying rhyming words. We also made charts of rhyming words and wrote jingles and riddles, which were awful but which appealed to their sixth-grade silliness.

In addition to rhyming games and writing rhymes, each day we read together and I reminded them of the one strategy I had taught them. Both boys knew that when you came to a short word you did not know, you should look to see if it would rhyme with a word you did know. When they could not think of a rhyming word, I prompted them with one. They used this strategy when they were reading and were amazed to discover that they could figure out even unusual names—*Tran, Zep, Kurt.*

Unfortunately, their newfound decoding ability did not transfer to bigger words. I taught them a few simple syllable division rules and they could sometimes figure out a two-syllable word, the syllables of which were familiar rhyming patterns—*zinger, target, pastor.* If a word had more than six letters, however, they could not even begin to do anything with it and would just skip it and go on!

By March, the boys were reading at a strong third-grade level—sometimes fourth—if they knew a lot about the topic. I knew that their inability and unwillingness to decode long words was the remaining hurdle but I did not know how to teach them to figure them out. I taught them some prefixes and suffixes but this did not seem to help with very many words. I would drive home in the afternoons and see a big word on a billboard and ask myself, "How did I figure out that word?" I knew that I had not applied syllabication rules and then sounded out each syllable but I did not know what I had done.

We were at 6 weeks before the end of sixth grade and Todd and Eric had begun the countdown to summer and junior high! In desperation, I searched the Ed Index for "polysyllabic word instruction." I did not find much and discounted most of what I did find. Context was what Todd and Eric were currently using. Syllabication rules were not working (and research confirmed that!). They had learned most of the common prefixes and suffixes and that was not taking them very far. Finally, one article suggested teaching students to use the dictionary respelling key. "Well, that's something I haven't tried," I thought. "But, no one is ever going to stop reading and find the word in the dictionary and use the respelling key," I argued with myself.

But I decided to do it. What did I have to lose? We had to do something useful for the last 6 weeks and at least they would know how to use the respelling key to pronounce a word if they would take the time to do it. For 2 weeks, I taught them how to use the key to figure out the pronunciation of unknown words. Then, when they understood how to do it, I gave them each a different list of five "really long" words *(conscientious, filibuster, mannequin, Phoenician, sporadically)* each day. Before we could go on to do anything interesting, they each had to find their words and use the key to figure them out and pronounce them for me!

They hated it but "it was good for them," and I was determined that they would have a big word tool to take with them to junior high, so each day, they came in and picked up their list and their dictionaries and went to work. Ten days before the end of school, Todd walked in and picked up his list of five "humongous" words and his dictionary. He began to look up the first word, then he stopped, looked at the word and then at me. "What if I already know this word? Do I still have to look it up?" he asked.

"Well no," I responded. "I am trying to give you a tool so that you can always pronounce any big word you ever come to, but if you know the word, you do not need the respelling key, do you?" Todd looked again at the first word, studying the letters. He then correctly pronounced: "spontaneous!" "That's right," I exclaimed. "Now, you only have four to look up!" "Not if I know some of the others," Todd asserted. He was able to pronounce two of the other four words and only had to look up and use the key for two of the five big words. Meanwhile, Eric was studying his five words and he managed to pronounce two of his, only having to look up three.

I was astonished! "Where had they learned those words?" I wondered. For the remaining 9 days of school, Todd and Eric competed to see how many words they could figure out and not have to look up. To my amazement, by the last day of school they had gotten quite good at figuring out words of four or more syllables. The respelling key, which I had taught them to use as a tool had taught them a system for independently figuring out big words. At the time I did not understand how this miracle had occurred but I sent Todd and Eric off to junior high more confident of their success than I had ever thought I would.

In 1972, I arrived at the University of Georgia to work on my doctorate in reading. I took my first seminar and Dr. Ira Aaron led us to do some initial thinking about a dissertation topic. I already knew what I wanted to find out: "How do we decode an unknown word, and particularly an unknown big word?" After much reading, thinking, and discussions with other doctoral students and Dr. George Mason, my advisor, I became convinced that decoding took place in what I called a compare/contrast way. Later this would be called "decoding by analogy." In addition to my dissertation (Cunningham, 1975–76), I did quite a bit of research into analogic decoding (Cunningham, 1979; 1980; Cunningham & Guthrie, 1982; Gaskins, Downer, Anderson, Cunningham, Gaskins, Schommer, & the Teachers of the Benchmark School, 1988) which confirmed for me that decoding was neither a letter-by-letter sounding process nor a rule-based, jargon-filled process. My observations of the children I had taught as well as the research I carried out convinced me that when readers come to unfamiliar words, they do a fast search through their cognitive word stores for similar words with the same letters in the same places. They then use these analogs to come up with a possible pronunciation which they try out and cross check with meaning.

I understood finally that when I complained that my first graders knew the rules but did not use them, I was right! The rules describe the system. The brain, however, is not a rule applier but a pattern detector. I also understood why teaching children linguistic patterns or "word families" was a powerful strategy if you could get them to use these spelling patterns to write and read words in meaningful texts.

By 1982, 10 years after Todd and Eric had learned to read, I had figured out how they did it. Combining word family instruction with reading and writing in which they were encouraged to use rhyming words to figure out how to pronounce or spell unknown words taught them to look for patterns in words and, most importantly that there were patterns to be found when they looked. Looking up big words in the dictionary respelling key forced them to look carefully at all the letters in the words (so that they could find them in the dictionary) and the analogs contained in the respelling key convinced them that there were patterns to be found in big words, too!

By the time I answered, to my own satisfaction, the question of how decoding happens, nobody cared! In the early 1980s, schools were still using criterion-referenced testing systems which broke decoding down into multiple rules/skills. When I tried to convince teachers, publishers, and others that these rules/skills might describe the system but that they were not what you *did* when you came to an unknown word, the response was, "But the rules/skills are what is tested!" The next wave to sweep the schools was "whole language" and then nobody really cared!

In 1989, two events occurred which re-ignited my interest in the role of decoding in beginning reading instruction. I reviewed a prepublication copy of Marilyn Jager Adams's (1990) *Beginning to read: Thinking and learning about print* and, while in the middle of reading this, I watched a Reading Recovery lesson. From reading the Adams book, I realized that there had been, mostly in the field of psychology, a huge amount of research and that we knew a lot more about how the brain functioned in identifying words. From watching the Reading Recovery lesson, I realized that the varied activities within the 30-minute lesson represented instruction compatible with what we now know about the reading process. Since 1989, I have been working with first- and second-grade teachers to try to develop compatible classroom instruction.

## What We Have Learned in the Last 20 Years

It has been 20 years since Todd and Eric propelled me off to get a doctorate in reading. In this section I shall summarize the research that had not been done yet that would have made my teaching much less of a trial-and-error process. *Beginning to Read* (Adams, 1990) is still the best overall source for this information, but there are other important sources listed with each of the major findings.

## *What We Know about How Good Readers Read Words*

We know a great deal more about how word recognition occurs than can be explained in this section. The theory that explains the incredibly fast ability of the brain to recognize words and associate them with meaning is called parallel distributed processing. This theory is complex but its most important tenets are easily understood. Information about a word is gained from its spelling (orthography), its pronunciation (phonology), its meaning (semantics) and the context in which the word occurs. The brain processes these sources of information in parallel, or simultaneously. The brain functions in word recognition, as it does in all other areas, as a pattern detector. Discussion of parallel distributed processing and its implications for word identification can be found in Seidenberg and McClelland (1989), McClelland and Rumelhart (1986), and Rumelhart and McClelland (1986). The theory is translated and explained simply and elegantly in Adams (1990). Beyond the fact that the brain responds to many sources of information in parallel and that it functions as a pattern detector, the following specific facts seem particularly pertinent to the question of what kind of phonics instruction we should have.

• *Readers look at virtually all of the words and almost all the letters in those words (Rayner & Pollatsek, 1989; McConkie, Kerr, Reddix, & Zola, 1987).* For many years, it was generally believed that sophisticated readers sampled text. Based on predictions about what words and letters they would see, readers were thought to look at the words and letters just enough to see if their predictions were confirmed. Eye-movement research carried out with computerized tracking has proven that, in reality, readers look at every word and almost every letter of each word. The amount of time spent processing each letter is incredibly small, only a few hundredths of a second. The astonishingly fast letter recognition for letters within familiar words and patterns is explained by the fact that our brains expect certain letters to occur in sequence with other letters.

• *Readers usually recode printed words into sound (Cunningham & Cunningham, 1978; Tannenhaus, Flanigan, & Seidenberg, 1980; McCutchen, Bell, France, & Perfetti, 1991).* Although it is possible to read without any internal speech, we rarely do. Most of the time as we read, we think the words in our mind. This phonological information is then checked with the information we received visually by analyzing the word for familiar spelling patterns. Saying the words aloud or thinking the words also seems to perform an important function in holding the words in auditory memory until enough words are read to create meaning.

• *Readers recognize most words immediately and automatically without using context (LaBerge & Samuels, 1974; Perfetti, 1985; Stanovich, 1980, 1986, 1991; Samuels, 1988; Nicholson, 1991).* Good readers use context to see if what they are reading makes sense. Context is also important for disambiguating the meaning of some words (I had a *ball* throwing the *ball* at the *ball*). Occasionally, readers use context to figure out what the word is. Most of the time, however, words are identified based on their familiar spelling and the association of that spelling with a pronunciation. Context comes into play after, not before, the word is identified based on the brain's processing of the letter-by-letter information it receives. Several studies have found that poor readers rely more on context than good readers.

• *Readers accurately and quickly pronounce infrequent, phonetically regular words (Perfetti & Hogoboam, 1975; Hogaboam & Perfetti, 1978; Daneman, 1991).* When presented with unfamiliar but phonetically regular words—*drite, chinique*—good readers immediately and seemingly effortlessly assign them a pronunciation. (*Drite* begins like *draw* and rhymes with *write*. It is a wonderful neologism for what 4-year-olds do when they combine drawing and writing. *Chinique* is a much needed word which combines the qualities of *chic and unique*. A jacket that is chinique is in style and uniquely you!). The ability to quickly and accurately pronounce phonetically regular words that are not sight words is a task that consistently discriminates among good and poor readers.

• *Readers use spelling patterns and analogy to decode words (Adams, 1990; Goswami & Bryant, 1990).* The answer to the question of whether phonics should be taught in a synthetic or analytic manner seems to be neither. Synthetic approaches generally teach children to go letter-by-letter, assigning a pronunciation to each letter and then blending the individual letters together. Analytic approaches teach rules and are usually filled with confusing jargon (the *e* on the end makes the vowel long). Brain research, however, suggests that the brain is a pattern detector, not a rule applier and that, although we look at single letters, we are looking at them considering all the letter patterns we know. Successfully decoding a word occurs when the brain recognizes a familiar spelling pattern or, if the pattern itself is not familiar, searches through its store of words with similar patterns.

To decode the unfamiliar word, *knob,* for example, the child who knew many words that began with *kn* would immediately assign to the *kn* the "n" sound. The initial *kn* would be stored in the brain as a spelling pattern. If the child only knew a few other words with *kn* and had not read these words very often, that child would probably not have *kn* as a known spelling pattern and thus would have to do a quick search for known words which began with *kn*. If the child found the words *know* and *knew* and then tried this same sound on the unknown word *knob,* that child would have used the analogy strategy. Likewise, the child might know the pronunciation for *ob* because of having correctly read so many words containing the *ob* spelling pattern or might have had to access some words with *ob* to use them to come up with the pronunciation. The child who had no stored spelling patterns for *kn* or *ob* and no known words to access and compare to would be unlikely to successfully pronounce the unknown word *knob.*

• *Readers divide big words as they see them based on interletter frequencies (Mewhort & Campbell, 1981; Seidenberg, 1987).* The research on syllabication rules show that it is quite possible to know the rules and still be unable to quickly and accurately pronounce novel polysyllabic words and equally possible to be able to pronounce them and not know the rules. Good readers do "chunk" or divide words into manageable units. They do this based on the brain's incredible knowledge of which letters usually go together in words. If you did not recognize the word *midnight* in print, you would divide it as you saw it, between the *d* and the *n*. For the word *Madrid*, however, you would divide after the *a,* leaving the *dr* together. Interletter frequency theory explains this neatly by pointing out that the letters *dr* often occur together in syllables in words you know *(drop, dry, Dracula)*. Words with the letters *dn* in the same syllable are almost nonexistent. This also explains why beginners might pronounce f-a-t-h-e-r as "fat her" but children who have some words from which the brain can generate interletter frequencies will leave the *th* together and pronounce "father."

To summarize what the brain does to identify words is to run the risk of oversimplification, but seems necessary before considering what we know about instruction. As we read, we look very quickly at almost all letters of each word. For most words, this visual information is recognized as a familiar pattern with which a spoken word is identified and pronounced (aloud or through internal speech). Words we have read before are instantly recognized as we see them. Words we have not read before are almost instantly pronounced based on spelling patterns the brain has seen in other words. If the word is a big word, the brain uses its interletter frequency knowledge (based on all the words it knows) to chunk the word into parts whose letter patterns can then be compared. Meaning is accessed through visual word recognition but the sound of the word supports the visual information and helps to hold the word in memory.

## What We Know about How Children Learn to Read Words

At present, we know more about how the word identification process works than we do about how children learn to do it. Here are some research-based findings which should have an impact on instruction.

• *Children from literate homes have over 1,000 hours of informal reading and writing encounters before coming to school (Adams, 1990).* We have always known that children who were read to came to school more ready, willing, and able to learn to read. In the past decade, however, findings from emergent literacy research have made it clear that the reading/writing encounters many children have include more than just a bedtime story. Estimates are that children from literate homes experience almost an hour each day of informal reading and writing encounters—being read to, trying to read a favorite book, watching someone write a thank-you letter, trying to write, manipulating magnetic letters, talking with someone about environmental print such as grocery/restaurant labels, signs, and so on. From these encounters, the children learn a tremendous amount of critical information. They know what reading and writing are really for and that you use words and letters. They know that you have to write these words and letters in a particular way, from top to bottom and left to right (though they often do not know this jargon). They also learn some words—important words like their names and the name of their pet dog and favorite fast-food restaurant. They learn the names of many of the letters of the alphabet and write these letters, usually in capital form. In addition to learning that words are made up of letters, which you can see, they somehow figure out that words are also made up of sounds, which you cannot see.

• *Phonemic awareness is critical to success in beginning reading (Bryant, Bradley, Maclean, & Crossland, 1989; Perfetti, 1991).* One of the critical understandings that many children gain from early reading and writing encounters is the understanding that words are made up of sounds. These sounds are not separate and distinct. In fact, their existence is quite abstract. Phonemic awareness has many levels and includes the ability to hear whether or not words rhyme, to know what word you would have if you removed a sound and the ability to manipulate phonemes to form different words. Phonemic awareness seems to be developed through lots of exposure to nursery rhymes and books which make word sound fun. Many of the "I can read" books *(Green Eggs and Ham, Inside, Outside, Upside Down, There's a Wocket in my Pocket, The Bernstein Bears B Book,* etc.*)* which come monthly to the homes of many preschoolers are made to order for helping children develop phonemic awareness. Although children may be able to learn some letter sounds before they develop phonemic awareness, phonemic awareness must be present before children can manipulate those sounds as they try to read and write words. Kindergarten and first-grade instruction should include lots of rhymes and chants, writing with invented spelling, and sound manipulation games which allow children to figure out the critical relationship between words and phonemes.

• *Children who can decode well learn sight words better (Jorm & Share, 1983; Stanovich & West, 1989; Ehri, 1991).* Research indicates that the sight word versus phonics debate lacks reality when you consider how children learn words. When a new word is encountered for the first time, it is usually decoded. In decoding the word, the child forms phonological access routes for that word into memory. These access routes are built using knowledge of grapheme-phoneme correspondences that connect letters in spelling to phonemes in pronunciations of the word. When the child encounters that word again, the connections between letters and phonemes is strengthened. Eventually, the spelling is represented in memory and the word is instantly recognized—but that instant recognition was based on some prior phonological processing. So words that were originally decoded come to be recognized as wholes and words originally taught as wholes must be studied letter-by-letter in order to be instantly recognized. The phonics versus sight word debate should be laid to rest.

• *The division of words into onset and rime is a psychological reality (Trieman, 1985).* In the 1934 edition of *Reading and Literature in the Elementary School,* Paul McKee discussed activities to help children decode words and indicated that opinion was mixed as to whether it was best to start with the initial letters and then add the end (sa-t) or to keep the final letters together and add the beginning (s-at). Expressing some uncertainty, he did take a stand and recommend the latter. Teachers were encouraged to do word activities in which they took a known word and then changed the initial letters—*hand, sand, band, grand, stand.* McKee also indicated that "ear training" should precede "eye training" (p. 202) and recommended oral jingles and rhymes, opinions confirmed by phonemic awareness research. Amazingly, he recommended that phonics instruction include "other tools such as analogy. . . . For example, when confronted with the strange word "meat," he may derive its pronunciation by proper associations gathered from the known words, "eat" and "met." (p. 189)

McKee's intuitive understanding of the reading process led him in 1934 to recommend what researchers confirmed 50 years later. Syllables are the most distinct sound units in English and children and adults find it much easier to divide syllables into their onsets (all letters before vowel) and rimes (vowel and what follows) than into any other units. Thus *Sam* is more easily divided into *S-am* than into *Sa-m* or *S-a-m.* It is easier and quicker for people to change *Sam* to *ham* and *jam* than it is to change *Sam* to *sat* and *sad.* The psychological reality of onset and rime confirms the age-old practice of teaching word families and spelling patterns.

• *Lots of successful reading is essential for readers to develop automaticity and rapid decoding (Samuels, 1988; Stanovich & West, 1989; Juel, 1990; Clay, 1991).* The major observable variable that separates good readers from poor readers is that good readers read a lot more and, when they are reading, they recognize most of the words instantly and automatically. If you recognize almost all the words, an unfamiliar word gets your immediate attention and you will stop and figure it out. Lots of easy reading in which most words are immediately recognized is essential for both the development of instantly recognized words and the ability and willingness to decode the occasional unfamiliar word. Many factors include topic familiarity, text and picture support, number of unfamiliar words and teacher support interact to determine how easy or difficult a particular book is for a particular child.

• *Children who write become better readers (Stosky, 1983; Tierney & Leys, 1986)*. On the face of it, this statement seems almost so obvious as to belie mentioning but in classrooms of a decade ago (and even some today), reading and writing were taught as separate entities. Research shows that the two have a reciprocal relationship and that when they are connected instructionally, children's progress in both is advanced. Young children almost always write the words they can read. As they write, they learn the conventions of reading. Children who write and read always read for meaning because they know that meaning is always what you are trying to communicate when you write. Writers make more sensitive readers and readers make more informed writers.

• *Children become better decoders when encouraged to invent spell as they write*. Children have been inventing spellings for years but, until recently, those inventions have not been valued in most classrooms. There is still controversy about how long to allow children to continue to invent spell and whether or not children will move through the stages of invented spelling if they are not given any spelling instruction. Encouraging invented spelling, however, does seem to help children develop decoding skills. Clarke (1988) compared the effectiveness of invented spelling versus an emphasis on correct spelling in first-grade classrooms. The children who had invented spellings were superior to the others on measures of word decoding at the end of the year. Furthermore, this invented spelling/decoding connection was particularly striking for the children who had been designated as having low readiness at the beginning of the year.

My own observations of young children trying to figure out how to spell a word they want to write is that they do indeed say the word slowly and try to listen for the sounds they hear. Listening for the sounds in a word you can say and want to write appears to be easier than using sounds to figure out a word during reading. Thus, children who are encouraged to invent spell as they write may have a more natural medium for applying whatever letter-sound knowledge they are learning.

## What Kind of Phonics Instruction Should We Advocate?

### The Reading Recovery Model

Earlier, I described the coincidence of reading *Beginning to Read* and viewing a Reading Recovery lesson in the same day. As I watched the Reading Recovery lesson, I saw instruction which embodied the theoretical understandings I was gaining from the research. Since then, I have watched many Reading Recovery lessons and studied Clay's (1985, 1991) works and thought about the research/instruction compatibility. I would like to describe for you a beginning Reading Recovery lesson and point out why I think this instruction demonstrates the kind of balance and variety we need:

> *Vincent enters and goes immediately to the chalkboard where he writes from memory several high-frequency words* (to my me) *his teacher dictates. He then selects, from books already read, three books he would like to reread and rereads them with high accuracy and fluency. Next, he rereads the book introduced yesterday while the teacher takes a running record, looking for at least 90% accuracy.*
>
> *Next, his teacher directs him to make words using magnetic letters. He changes letters around several times to make the rhyming words,* me, we *and* he. *He then picks up his writing notebook and rereads two previously written one-sentence stories and matches their cut-up words. He writes a new story based on a book read today. His story is:* The bear squashed the bike. *He writes the words he knows how to spell. For others, the teacher helps him to say the word slowly and write in the letters he can hear and she completes the word with other needed letters. Then, he reads his sentence to the teacher and watches as she writes it on a sentence strip and cuts it into words. He matches these cut-up words to his sentence twice and then uses the cut-up words to make the sentence without matching twice.*
>
> *The last activity in this packed 30 minutes is the introduction of a new book. The teacher reads and talks through a new predictable book with him. He then reads the new book with teacher assistance.*
>
> *Each day, Vincent leaves the lesson with an old book to take home. He also takes the cut-up words for his sentence.*
>
> *Vincent returns to his classroom. His classmates look up expectantly. "What you got today?" some ask. Proudly, Vincent takes out his book which he and his friends read together, with Vincent in the lead. Then, he puts his sentence together and reads, "The bear squashed the bike." The teacher walks over to see "what he's got!" Vincent reads his sentence to the teacher. She comments on how well he is reading and writing and Vincent proudly puts everything back into the zip-lock bag to take home and read some more!*

This description of a Reading Recovery lesson does not begin to do justice to the intricacies and complexities of the instructional decisions his teacher makes and how she moves him forward each day as he develops his "self-improving system." But, hopefully, it does demonstrate the compatibility of Reading Recovery lessons with research about how word identification abilities develop. Vincent spends most of his time reading and writing. He reads books which are easy, because he has read them many times before, because the teacher is skillful in choosing and introducing them and because the books are carefully leveled to insure a high degree of fluency. His writing is supported. He writes the words he can spell automatically and he is supported as he listens for sounds in words he wants to write. The teacher filling in letters he cannot know yet means that his sentence is written correctly and he has correct visual representations of the words to put in memory. Working with these words by matching and then using the cut-up words to make his sentence provided the practice needed for these words to become part of his automatic recognition vocabulary. Practice with high-frequency words he has read and written is also provided as he writes a few words on the chalkboard each day. The magnetic letters are used to help him learn some spelling patterns and, more importantly, to learn that there are patterns to be found if you look! (In this lesson, there was no phonemic awareness activity in which the child listened to hear sounds in words, but that is also a component of Reading Recovery, when needed.)

Vincent has many opportunities to learn how reading and writing work and all these opportunities are connected to each other and stem from a book he can read. The practice and overlearning provided by reading the book and sentence with his classmates, teacher, and presumably someone at home are also critical for developing fluency and automaticity.

## A Classroom Model

For the last several years, I have worked with first- and second-grade teachers to try to take what we know about how children develop quick, accurate word-identification systems and become readers and writers and what we know from the success of Reading Recovery and develop a classroom model. This model is a multilevel, multimethod approach because we provide in the 2-hour language arts block numerous ways (methods) for children of all different ability levels to learn to read and write. A key feature of this program is the lack of any fixed ability groups and the division of the 120 minutes of instructional time into four fairly equal blocks of instruction. We consider each block equally important and, when possible make links across the blocks. The four blocks are: Basal Block—which involves teacher-guided reading and discussion of selections from basal readers and tradebooks and children reading and working with partners; Writing Block—which follows a writing process format in which the teacher does a minilesson, the children write, using invented spelling on topics of their own choosing and the children share in an author's chair format and publish books which they are helped to revise and edit; Self-Selected Block in which the children choose what they want to read from a wide range of books and other reading materials and the Working With Words Block. The Working with Words Block includes a daily word wall chanting/writing activity designed to help children develop automatic reading and spelling of the highest frequency words and a daily Making Words activity designed to help them learn that words are made up of letters which form predictable spelling patterns (Cunningham, 1991a). Data from the first 2 years of instruction using this multilevel, multimethod approach suggests that both the most able and the least able children make better than expected progress and develop superior fluency and decoding (Cunningham, Hall, & Defee, 1991; Cunningham, 1991b; Hall & Cunningham, 1991).

Research into the word identification process supports the need for real reading and writing as well as the need for explicit instruction on how to read and write and on discovering how our alphabetic language works. Observations of the children engaged in this multilevel, multimethod approach indicate that the balance and variety of activities—some more teacher centered and some more child centered—are needed in classrooms which not only have a range of ability levels but also have children who do not all learn in exactly the same way.

# References

Adams, M. J. (1990). *Beginning to read: Thinking and learning about print.* Cambridge, MA: MIT Press.

Bryant, P. E., Bradley, L., Maclean, M., & Crossland, I. (1989). Nursery rhymes, phonological skills and reading. *Journal of Child Language, 16,* 407–428.

Clarke, L. K. (1988). Invented versus traditional spelling in first graders' writings: Effects on learning to spell and read. *Research in the Teaching of English, 22,* 281–309.

Clay, M. M. (1985). *The early detection of reading difficulties* (3rd ed.). Portsmouth, NH: Heinemann.

Clay, M. M. (1991). *Becoming literate: The construction of inner control.* Portsmouth, NH: Heinemann.

Cunningham, P. M. (1975–76). Investigating a synthesized theory of mediated word identification. *Reading Research Quarterly, 11,* 127–143.

Cunningham, P. M. (1979). A compare/contrast theory of mediated word identification. *The Reading Teacher, 32,* 774–778.

Cunningham, P. M. (1980). Applying a compare/contrast process to identifying polysyllabic words. *Journal of Reading Behavior, 12,* 213–223.

Cunningham, P. M. (1991a). Phonics they use: Words for reading and writing. New York: HarperCollins.

Cunningham, P. M. (1991b). Research Directions: Multimethod, multilevel literacy instruction in first grade. *Language Arts, 68,* 578–584.

Cunningham, P. M., & Cunningham, J. W. (1978). Investigating the "print to meaning" hypothesis. In P. D. Pearson & J. Hansen (Eds.), *Reading: Disciplined inquiry in process and practice.* Twenty-seventh Yearbook of the National Reading Conference (pp. 116–120). Clemson, SC: National Reading Conference.

Cunningham, P. M., & Guthrie, F. M. (1982). Teaching decoding skills to educable mentally handicapped children. *The Reading Teacher, 35,* February, 1982, 554–559.

Cunningham, P. M., Hall, D. P., & Defee, M. (1991). Non-ability grouped, multilevel instruction: A year in a first-grade classroom. *The Reading Teacher, 44,* 566–571.

Daneman, M. (1991). Individual differences in reading skills. In R. Barr, M. L. Kamil, P. B. Mosenthal, & P. D. Pearson (Eds.), *Handbook of Reading Research* (Vol. 2, pp. 512–538). White Plains, NY: Longman.

Ehri, L. C. (1991). Development of the ability to read words. In R. Barr, M. L. Kamil, P. B. Mosenthal, & P. D. Pearson (Eds.), *Handbook of Reading Research* (Vol. 2, pp. 383–417). White Plains, NY: Longman.

Gaskins, I. W., Downer, M. A., Anderson, R. C., Cunningham, P. M., Gaskins, R. W., Schommer, M., & Teachers of the Benchmark School. (1988). A Metacognitive Approach to Phonics: Using What You Know to Decode What You Don't Know. *Remedial and Special Education, 9,* 36–41.

Goswami, U., & Bryant, P. (1990). *Phonological skills and learning to read.* East Sussex, UK: Erlbaum.

Hall, D. P., & Cunningham, P. M. (1991). *Reading Without Ability Grouping: Issues in First Grade Reading Instruction.* Paper presented at the National Reading Conference, Palm Springs, CA.

Hogaboam, T., & Perfetti, C. A. (1978). Reading skill and the role of verbal experience in decoding. *Journal of Verbal Learning and Verbal Behavior, 70,* 717–729.

Jorm, A. F., & Share, D. L. (1983). Phonological recoding and reading acquisition. *Applied Psycholinguistics, 4,* 103–147.

Juel, C. (1990). Effects of reading group assignment on reading development in first and second grade. *Journal of Reading Behavior, 22,* 233–254.

LaBerge, D., & Samuels, S. J. (1974). Toward a theory of automatic information processing in reading. *Cognitive Psychology, 6,* 293–323.

McClelland, J. L., & Rumelhart, D. E. (Eds.). (1986). *Parallel distributed processing, vol. 2: Psychological and biological models.* Cambridge, MA: MIT Press.

McConkie, G. W., Kerr, P. W., Reddix, M. D., & Zola, D. (1987). *Eye movement control during reading: The location of initial eye fixations on words.* Technical Report No. 406. Champaign: Center for the Study of Reading, University of Illinois.

McCutchen, D., Bell, L. C., France, I. M., & Perfetti, C. A. (1991). Phoneme-specific interference in reading: The tongue-twister effect revisited. *Reading Research Quarterly, 26,* 87–103.

McKee, P. (1934). *Reading and literature in the elementary school.* Boston: Houghton Mifflin.

Mewhort, D. J. K., & Campbell, A. J. (1981). Toward a model of skilled reading: An analysis of performance in tachistoscoptic tasks. In G. E. MacKinnon & T. G. Walker (Eds.), *Reading research: Advances in theory and practice* (vol. 3, pp. 39–118). New York: Academic Press.

Nicholson, T. (1991). Do children read words better in context or in lists? A classic study revisited. *Journal of Educational Psychology, 83,* 444–450.

Perfetti, C. A. (1985). *Reading ability.* New York: Oxford University Press.

Perfetti, C. A. (1991). The psychology, pedagogy, and politics of reading. *Psychological Science, 2,* 71–76.

Perfetti, C. A., & Hogaboam, T. (1975). The relationship between single-word decoding and reading comprehension skill. *Journal of Educational Psychology, 67,* 461–469.

Rayner, K., & Pollatsek, A. (1989). *The psychology of reading.* Englewood Cliffs, NJ: Prentice Hall.

Rumelhart, D. E., & McClelland, J. L. (Eds.). (1986). *Parallel distributed processing, vol. 1: Psychological and biological models.* Cambridge, MA: MIT Press.

Samuels, S. J. (1988). Decoding and automaticity: Helping poor readers become automatic at word recognition. *The Reading Teacher, 41,* 756–760.

Seidenberg, M. S. (1987). Sublexical structures in visual word recognition: Access units or orthographic redundancy. In M. Coltheart (Ed.), *Attention and performance XII: The psychology of reading* (pp. 245–263). Hillsdale, NJ: Erlbaum.

Seidenberg, M. S., & McClerlland, J. L. (1989). A distributed, developmental model of word recognition and naming. *Psychological Review, 96,* 523–568.

Stanovich, K. E. (1980). Toward an interactive compensatory model of individual differences in the development of reading fluency. *Reading Research Quarterly, 16,* 32–71.

Stanovich, K. E. (1986). Matthew effects in reading: Some consequences of individual differences in the acquisition of literacy. *Reading Research Quarterly, 21,* 360–406.

Stanovich, K. E. (1991). Word recognition: Changing perspectives. In R. Barr, M. L. Kamil, P. B. Mosenthal, & P. D. Pearson (Eds.), *Handbook of Reading Research* (Vol. 2, pp. 418–452). White Plains, NY: Longman.

Stanovich, K. E., & West, R. F. (1989). Exposure to print and orthographic processing. *Reading Research Quarterly, 24,* 402–433.

Stosky, S. (1983). Research on reading/writing relationships: A synthesis and suggested directions. *Language Arts, 60,* 627–642.

Tannenhaus, M. K., Flanigan, H., & Seidenberg, M. S. (1980). Orthographic and phonological code activation in auditory and visual word recognition. *Memory and Cognition, 8,* 513–520.

Tierney, R. J., & Leys, M. (1986). What is the value of connecting reading and writing? In B. T. Peterson (Ed.), *Convergences: Transactions in reading and writing* (pp. 15–29). Urbana, IL: National Council of Teachers of English.

Trieman, R. (1985). Onsets and rimes as units of spoken syllables: Evidence from children. *Journal of Experimental Child Psychology, 39,* 161–181.

## *Integrating Sources*

1. Cunningham and Stahl have reached some of the same conclusions. Identify significant areas of overlap.

2. Locate and contrast key statements made by Cunningham and by Goodman regarding the role of print sampling, context, and prediction in reading. Which has the better argument? Defend your choice.

3. Which writer has the most realistic plan for contending with problem readers? Again, defend your choice.

## *Classroom Implications*

**1.** In what ways do you find the recommendations of these authors (a) feasible in real classroom settings and (b) impractical and idealistic?

a. Stahl

b. Goodman

c. Cunningham

**2.** Describe an eclectic approach to beginning reading instruction that draws on all three of these writers. Try it!

## Annotated Bibliography

### Historical References

Clymer, T. (1963). The utility of phonics generalizations in the primary grades. *The Reading Teacher, 16,* 252–258.

*This is an often quoted study in which Clymer showed that most phonics generalizations were applicable in only very limited situations and thus the extensive teaching of these rules was open to question.*

Flesch, R. (1955). *Why Johnny can't read and what you can do about it.* New York: Harper and Row.

*This book was widely read by the general public and received extensive coverage in the mass media. Flesch, a noted linguist, emphasized the fact that the ultimate answer to most reading problems, in his opinion, was simply to base all reading instruction on the heavy use of phonics. This book was criticized by many in the professional education community as being an overly simplified answer to a very complex problem.*

Gray, W. S. (1948). *On their own in reading.* Chicago: Scott, Foresman.

*This is a classic discussion of the role of word analysis in the teaching of reading. It is an excellent reference for those needing background information on how classroom teachers can use the different aspects of word analysis in an effective reading program.*

### Current References

Adams, M. J. (1990). *Beginning to read: Thinking and learning about print.* Cambridge, MA: MIT Press.

*This is a foundation book in the current thinking about the role of word analysis as a part of effective reading instruction. It reviews the past history of the debate concerning word analysis, noting that many of the current arguments about this topic have been debated in the past as well. A strong case is presented for the appropriateness of word analysis instruction in beginning reading. This book contains an excellent bibliography of related references to this topic.*

Carbo, M. (1988). Debunking the great phonics myth. *Phi Delta Kappan, 70,* 226–240.

*This article discusses the fact that in many classrooms the teaching of phonics has had little effect on students' ability to read. It makes the point that for many teachers, phonics instruction is nothing more than learning a set of rules that are seldom used. (For a response to this article, see Chall, 1989.)*

Chall, J. S. (1967). *Learning to read: The great debate.* New York: McGraw-Hill.

*This is a foundation book in the area of word analysis that had wide impact on many educators' attitudes and practices, especially in relation to the teaching of phonics. Research to that point is reviewed.*

Chall, J. S. (1989). Learning to read: The great debate twenty years later. A response to "Debunking the great phonics myth." *Phi Delta Kappan, 71,* 521–538.

This a response to Carbo's questioning (see Carbo, 1988) of the role of phonics in the classroom reading program. Chall defends the use of phonics as an integral part of an effective reading curriculum.

Cunningham, P. M. (1992). *Phonics they use: Words for reading and writing* (2nd ed.). New York: HarperCollins.

This excellent book, written for teachers, discusses the use of phonics in a classroom setting. It contains many examples of how to teach word analysis in an effective manner.

Ehri, L. C. (1991). Development of the ability to read words. In R. Barr, M. Kamil, P. B. Mosenthal, & P. D. Pearson, (Eds.), *Handbook of reading research* (Vol. II, pp. 383–417). White Plains, NY: Longman.

This is a scholarly discussion of the current research and thinking with regard to how readers identify written words. It contains an extensive bibliography of research-related articles.

Goodman, K. S. (1993). *Phonics phacts.* Portsmouth, NH: Heinemann.

This book reviews the history of the use of phonics, noting the merits and the problems associated with this aspect of literacy instruction. Of particular note is the discussion of the politics of phonics and the effects of this influence on the teaching of phonics in classrooms.

Griffith, P. L., et al. (1992). The effect of phonemic awareness on the literacy development of first grade children in a traditional or a whole language classroom. *Journal of Research in Childhood Education, 6,* 85–92.

The results of a study with first-graders receiving either whole language or traditional basal reader instruction are described. Those children who received high phonemic awareness training did better on a number of literacy assessment measures.

Grossen, B., & Carnine, D. (1993). Phonics instruction: Comparing research and practice. *Teaching Exceptional Children, 25,* 22–25.

This review of the phonics controversy presents an extended discussion of the literacy research in this area.

Smith, F. (1992). Learning to read: The never ending debate. *Phi Delta Kappan, 73,* 432–435, 438–441.

The past history of the phonics debate is reviewed, suggesting that literacy learners actually develop by being initiated into the readers' "club."

## You Become Involved

### Phonics

The value of phonics knowledge and phonics instruction is clear in research. From the reading, writing, and discussion opportunities provided during this chapter, you should have expanded your schema structures related to the phonics topic. To help you further organize those pieces of information, complete the following synthesis activities.

**1.** Use 1- to 2-word phrases to list the concepts or ideas you remember about phonics or phonics instruction. You should look back into the articles if you need to. Use a separate sheet of paper to construct your list.

**2.** Cut the phrases apart and arrange them in categories. Label the categories. Feel free to rearrange the phrases until you are satisfied with the categories.

**3.** Number the categories in some order. For example, you could number by importance, sequence for instruction, and so on.

**4.** Use your numbered categories and phrases to write a summary paper that explains what you have learned about phonics and phonics instruction.

# Chapter *4*

## *Literacy Materials*

Longstanding controversy surrounds the materials used to teach children to read. The historical development of basal readers has led, for a variety of reasons, to strong objections to their use. The 1992 National Assessment of Educational Progress (Mullis, Campbell, & Farstrup, 1993) revealed that a significant percent of fourth-grade teachers surveyed still rely on basals as the mainstay of daily instruction. But this figure represents a decline from the number who reported using basals in the 1988 NAEP survey. The reasons for this decline are complex. They include concern about what information a literacy curriculum should contain, how instruction should be organized, and who should ultimately decide such issues—publishers or teachers. These and other issues and trends must be considered by any teacher endeavoring to make informed decisions about the proper role of basals in children's literacy development.

### *Development and Rationale of Basals*

The first leveled readers were the components of Noah Webster's *American Spelling Book* (1790–1833). Only three levels were involved but this was a significant change over *The New England Primer* (1727–1776), which was not leveled at all. Webster's innovation was the precursor of still greater stratification, in the *McGuffey Readers* (1834–1907) and in twentieth-century basal series.

The rationale of a basal is the same as first used with many forms of testing. For example, in individual intelligence testing, tasks and questions are often arranged in order of difficulty and the examiner begins by estimating the student's level within the sequence. If the student performs adequately, the examiner assumes that there is no need to test at easier levels. The level of current adequate functioning is called the *basal* level. In the case of readers and their accompanying workbooks, the materials and tasks are likewise sequenced in order of difficulty and a child is placed within the sequence at the most appropriate point. As in testing, this point is the basal level, and it is assumed that the content of easier levels has been mastered. Sequencing is therefore a key to the basal's structure. Reading selections are sequenced by relative sophistication of content and by their reliance on simpler skills.

During the early twentieth century, the scientific management movement in industry further reinforced basal development by suggesting that learning to read was an additive and rather mechanical process that should be made as efficient as possible. Children were seen as passing through the basal sequence much in the way products in a factory moved along assembly lines. New skills were introduced in sequence just as parts were added and fitted in sequence.

## Objections to Basals

By the mid-twentieth century, basal use in the United States was nearly universal (Goodman et al., 1988; Shannon & Goodman, 1994). Satisfaction was not universal, however, and various criticisms emerged. One of the curious aspects of basal evolution has been that the series, as commercial products, have been sensitive to criticisms so that numerous changes have been made in response (Ediger, 1994; McCarthey et al., 1994). Basals have therefore been a moving target and critics continually are challenged to monitor each new edition to see whether specific problems have been remedied. In briefly summarizing the most frequent objections, our approach here will be to cluster them around three major components of a series: the reading selections, the skills, and the teacher's manual.

Selections have been criticized on both aesthetic and political grounds. One principle used to develop mid-century basals was that of using words that appeared often in written language. For example, the Dolch List of 220 frequent words was often used for this purpose. In each successive level, new vocabulary was introduced in limited numbers. Another principle was the frequent repetition of the words that were introduced to ensure numerous exposures. The result of using these two development principles was the occurrence of unnatural language patterns in a story text. Objections have led to increased use of unedited material borrowed from trade books, magazines, and the like.

Political objections to basal selections have concerned issues related to the multicultural representiveness of the characters portrayed. For example, stories about white middle-class families are sometimes viewed as inappropriate for inner-city minority children. Stories about traditional, two-parent families may be ill-fitted to children of divorce. Stories that portray men and women in traditional roles may perpetuate stereotypes. Stories depicting elderly citizens as infirm or passive may suggest a biased image. Again, industry responses have been reflected in far greater variety in the characters and their circumstances.

Criticism of basal skill components have centered on two issues. One is the rather rigid sequencing of skill introduction, despite the fact that some of the orderings are clearly arbitrary. The second issue is the policy of providing skill practice in isolation, in the form of expensive (and expendable) workbooks.

Children, it is argued, may fail to see the connection between completing worksheets (skill-and-drill practice) and reading for personally relevant purposes. Moreover, some critics have suggested that the psychological principles on which such practice is based are no longer viable.

Finally, the manuals accompanying each level of a series have been criticized as overly prescriptive. The manuals' tendencies to script what teachers should say and when has been viewed as preempting and subverting teachers' professional judgment. Following the manuals, it is charged, robs teachers of their rightful role and transforms them into mere "technicians."

## Objections to Literature-Based Instruction

Predictably, the alternative of using high-quality children's books as the basis of instruction has occasioned a different set of objections. Teachers must find ways of leveling the books, often a very difficult task. Also, teachers deciding on a literature-based approach to literacy instruction must decide on appropriate classroom organizational plans, such as how to organize literature groups and secure sufficient books. In addition, some children's literature authors and advocates have protested that trade books were not intended for instructional use and that building units around them violates their true nature as literature.

## As You Read

The point-counterpoint that follows develops many of these issues in more detail. Weaver and Groff take opposing sides in their reactions to *The Report Card on Basal Readers* (Goodman et al., 1988), a highly critical report on basals. In line with Weaver's negative stance is the call to action produced by the National Council of Teachers of English.

The issues surrounding basal readers and their literature-based alternative are political as well as instructional. You will need to come to terms with both the politics and the pedagogy of reading instruction in order to answer the following questions:

1. Are basals compatible with your own philosophy of instruction? In what ways?
2. Are teachers necessarily "deskilled" by using basals?
3. Are basals consistent with our current knowledge of how literacy is acquired by children?
4. If you reject basals, can you recommend changes that would make them acceptable?

## References

Ediger, M. (1994). *The reading curriculum.* (ERIC Document Reproduction Service No. ED 372 361).

Goodman, K. S., et al. (1988). *Report card on basal readers.* Katonah, NY: Richard C. Owen.

McCarthey, S. J., et al. (1994). *Engaging the new basal readers.* (ERIC Document Reproduction Service No. ED 484 801).

Mullis, I. V. S., Campbell, J. R., & Farstrup, A. E. (1993). *NAEP 1992: Reading report card for the nation and states.* Washington, DC: U.S. Department of Education.

Shannon, P., & Goodman, K. (Eds.). (1994). *Basal readers: A second look.* Katonah, NY: Richard C. Owen.

**CONTENT LITERACY GUIDE**

**Basal Readers and the State of American Reading Instruction: A Call for Action**
NCTE Commission on Reading
*Language Arts, 66,* 1989, 896–898

**1.** Summarize the current problem with basals, according to the Commission.

**2.** Describe the "gap" that involves basals.

**3.** Why does the Commission view the "comprehensiveness" of basals as a problem?

**4.** Describe the misconception about learning to read that basals promote.

**5.** How are skill sequences determined, according to the Commission?

**6.** What is the Commission's concern regarding testing programs found in basals?

7. What does the Commission point out with respect to the ratio between workbook activities and reading?

8. What is the effect of manuals on teaching, according to the Commission?

9. Describe the effect of basal use on thinking, in the Commission's view.

10. In what ways does the Commission stop short of recommending that basals be abandoned?

11. What is the Commission's prediction regarding standardized test scores if basals are abandoned?

12. Summarize the Commission's view on research and experimentation.

# BASAL READERS AND THE STATE OF AMERICAN READING INSTRUCTION

## A CALL FOR ACTION

THE COMMISSION ON READING,
NATIONAL COUNCIL OF TEACHERS OF ENGLISH

## The Problem

As various national studies suggest, the problem of illiteracy, semi-literacy, and aliteracy in the United States appears to be growing, due at least in part to escalating standards of literacy in the workplace and in the civic area. And at a time when our information-age society demands increased literacy from all citizens, reading instruction is locked into a technology that is more than half a century out-of-date.

## Basals: Part of the Problem

There is a significant gap between how reading is learned and how it is taught and assessed in the vast majority of our classrooms today. This gap is perpetuated by the basal reading series that dominate reading instruction in roughly 90 percent of the elementary classrooms in the United States. Such textbook series are often viewed as complete systems for teaching reading, for they include not only a graded series of books for the students to read but teachers' manuals telling teachers what and how to teach, workbooks and dittos for the students to complete, sets of tests to assess reading skills, and often various supplementary aids. Because of their comprehensiveness, basal reading systems leave very little room for other kinds of reading activities in the schools where

*Source:* "Basal Readers and the State of American Reading Instruction: A Call for Action" by The Commission on Reading, National Council of Teachers of English, 1989, *Language Arts, 66.* Copyright 1989 by the National Council of Teachers of English. Reprinted with permission.

they have been adopted. This is all the more unfortunate because current theory and research strongly support such conclusions as the following:

- Basal reading series typically reflect and promote the misconception that reading is necessarily learned from smaller to larger parts.
- The sequencing of skills in a basal reading series exists not because this is how children learn to read but simply because of the logistics of developing a series of lessons that can be taught sequentially, day after day, week after week, year after year.
- Students are typically tested for ability to master the bits and pieces of reading, such as phonics and other word-identification skills, and even comprehension skills. However, there is no evidence that mastering such skills in isolation guarantees the ability to comprehend connected text, or that students who cannot give evidence of such skills in isolation are necessarily unable to comprehend connected text.
- Thus for many if not most children, the typical basal reading series may actually make learning to read more difficult than it needs to be.
- So much time is typically taken up by "instructional" activities (including activities with workbooks and skill sheets) that only a very slight amount of time is spent in actual reading—despite the overwhelming evidence that extensive reading and writing are crucial to the development of literacy.
- Basal reading series typically reflect and promote the widespread misconception that the ability to verbalize an answer, orally or in writing, is evidence of understanding and learning. Thus even students who appear to be learning from a basal reading series are being severely shortchanged, for they are being systematically encouraged not to think.
- Basal reading series typically tell teachers exactly what they should do and say while teaching a lesson, thus depriving teachers of the responsibility and authority to make informed professional judgments.
- "Going through the paces" thus becomes the measure of both teaching and learning. The teachers are assumed to have taught well if and only if they have taught the lesson. Students are assumed to have learned if and only if they have given "right" answers.
- *The result of such misconceptions about learning and such rigid control of teacher and student activities is to discourage both teachers and students from thinking, and particularly to discourage students from developing and exercising critical literacy and thinking skills needed to participate fully in a technologically advanced democratic society.*

# Recommended Actions for Local Administrators and for Policymakers

## For Local Administrators:

- Provide continual district inservice for teachers to help them develop a solid understanding of how people read and how children learn to read and how reading is related to writing and learning to write.

- Provide time and opportunities for teachers to mentor with peers who are trying innovative materials and strategies.
- Support teachers in attending local, regional, state, and national conferences to improve their knowledge base, and support continued college coursework for teachers in reading and writing.
- Allow/encourage teachers to use alternatives to basal readers or to use basal readers flexibly, eliminating whatever their professional judgment deems unnecessary or inappropriate: for example,

  — encourage innovation at a school level, offering teachers a choice of basals, portions of basals, or no basal, using assessment measures that match their choice.
  — discuss at a school level which portions of the basal need not be used, and use the time saved for reading and discussion of real literature
  — provide time for teachers to work with one another to set innovative programs.

- Give teachers the opportunity to demonstrate that standardized test scores will generally not be adversely affected by using alternatives to basal readers, and may in fact be enhanced.
- Provide incentives for teachers to develop and use alternative methods of reading assessment, based upon their understanding of reading and learning to read.
- Allow/encourage teachers to take charge of their own reading instruction, according to their informed professional judgment.

## *For Policymakers:*

- Change laws and regulations that favor or require use of basals, so that

  — state funds may be used for non-basal materials
  — schools may use programs that do not have traditional basal components
  — teachers cannot be forced to use material they find professionally objectionable.

- Provide incentives to local districts to experiment with alternatives to basals, by

  — developing state-level policies that permit districts to use alternatives to basals
  — changing teacher education and certification requirements so as to require teachers to demonstrate an understanding of how people read, of how children learn to read, and of ways of developing a reading curriculum without as well as with basals
  — mandating periodic curriculum review and revision based upon current theory and research as to how people read and how children learn to read
  — developing, or encouraging local districts to develop, alternative means of testing and assessment that are supported by current theory and research in how people read and how children learn to read
  — funding experimental programs, research, and methods of assessment based upon current theory and research on reading and learning to read.

**CONTENT LITERACY GUIDE**

**The Basalization of America: A Cause for Concern**
Constance Weaver
In Arena Debate-in-Print No. 1, ERIC, 1989

**1.** According to Weaver, good readers in basal classrooms read for what purpose?

**2.** Summarize the key question the Report Card sought to address on behalf of NCTE.

**3.** Do you agree with Goodman's statement about the central premise of basals? Why or why not?

**4.** Summarize Weaver's six ways in which basals exert control.

    a.

    b.

    c.

    d.

    e.

    f.

**5.** List and summarize Thorndike's four laws:

    a.

    b.

    c.

    d.

**6.** Which laws, if any, seem plausible based on your own experience as a teacher?

**7.** Summarize Weaver's five conclusions from research:

a.

b.

c.

d.

e.

**8.** Weaver suggests what as an alternative to sequential skill instruction?

**9.** What motive does Weaver attribute to publishers that works against any hope that basals will ever improve significantly?

# THE BASALIZATION OF AMERICA
## A CAUSE FOR CONCERN

CONSTANCE WEAVER

In 1985 when the Commission on Reading of the National Council of Teachers of English (NCTE) asked Kenneth Goodman to undertake a study of basal reading programs, we were motivated not so much by the national reports on the nation's literacy as by personal observation during our day-to-day interactions with teachers and children. In traditional classrooms, most children were learning to read at least minimally, even though some were not succeeding very well in their reading programs.

We also saw, however, what others have documented: that even the "good" readers typically read for surface accuracy and details rather than for thoughtful response, and that, all too often, they read just to answer questions rather than for enjoyment or to gain information or understanding (Applebee et al., 1988). In short, we noticed that in the typical curriculum-oriented classroom, children were more likely to go mechanically through the paces of their lessons (Bloome, 1987) than to engage meaningfully in reading, writing, and thinking.

The National Assessment of Educational Progress (NAEP) studies further document what we have observed: that although the majority of our young people are learning to read at a surface level, they are not learning to reason effectively about what they read and write. Few, in fact, are able to analyze, evaluate, and extend the ideas that they encounter in print (Applebee et al., 1987; Venezky et al., 1987). As business and industry repeatedly tell us, such superficial literacy is no longer enough in our increasingly complex and technological society.

Knowing that basal reading systems are used in more than 90 percent of the nation's classrooms (Anderson et al., 1985), we on the NCTE's Commission on Reading naturally asked ourselves a question that others too have asked (e.g., Venezky et al., 1987; Anderson et al., 1985): Is there something about today's basal reading programs, or about basal programs as a genre, that might contribute to such passive and superficial reading as that documented by the NAEP reports?

*Source:* "The Basalization of America: A Cause for Concern" by Constance Weaver, in C. B. Smith (Ed.), *Two Reactions to the Report Card on Basal Readers in Print* (No. 1, pages 4–7). Bloomington, IN: ERIC. Copyright 1989, ERIC/REC (Educational Resources Information Center/Clearinghouse on Reading, English, and Communication) at Indiana University (Bloomington). Reprinted by permission.

This and other questions were explored for the Commission by Kenneth Goodman, Patrick Shannon, Yvonne Freeman, and Sharon Murphy. In addition to examining previous research on basals and the use of basals, they also undertook detailed analyses of several current basal reading programs (mostly with 1986 or 1985 copyright dates), including the six series that together account for about 80 percent of the money spent on basals (Goodman et al., 1988, p. 46). This research and analysis culminated in the *Report Card on Basal Readers* (Goodman et al., 1988).

The authors of the *Report Card* freely admit that "While we have tried to be fair in this report we have not tried to be neutral. We are concerned for what is good or bad for learners and the teachers trying to help them become literate." (Goodman et al., 1988, p. v)

Hence the authors made scant mention of recent improvements in basal reading programs, but focused instead on problems and concerns that remain. I shall do the same, for now focusing only upon the philosophy implicit in basal series, its ramifications, and its out-of-date research base.

## The Basic Premise, Promise, and Principle of the Basal Program

"The central *premise* of the basal reader is that a sequential, all-inclusive set of instructional materials can teach all children to read." (Goodman et al., 1988, p. 1) The implicit *promise* to administrators and teachers is that if the program is followed in detail, then they are not to blame if pupils fail to read easily and well; any problems must lie with the learners themselves (p. 103). Naturally, in order to deliver on this promise, the basal reading programs must *control* teaching and learning; thus control becomes the guiding *principle* of the basal programs (p. 97).

What is controlled? Virtually everything, at least in theory. For example:

**1.** The basals control the reading curriculum. The various instructional, practice and assessment activities associated with basals demand so much time that there is very little, if any, for other reading and writing.

**2.** The basals control teachers through the language used in the teachers' manuals. Instead of offering suggestions, the TMs give directions: "Do this." "Do that." While teachers can of course ignore the directions, they typically buy into the implicit promise of the basal, perhaps in part because they are intimidated by the imperative language of the teachers' manuals as well as by the fact that the basal programs appear to be "scientific" (Goodman et al., 1988, pp. 40–43). In any case, the language of the TMs suggests to both teachers and administrators that teachers are not competent to make instructional decisions, even on minutiae. Such an implication undermines the professionalism of teachers instead of enhancing it.

**3.** The basals control students in a variety of ways, one of the most insidious being through the use of questions to which a single "right" answer is expected, usually an answer based upon the text itself (p. 81). Often, "Even when the question is intended to draw on 'background knowledge' and require 'critical thinking,' a simple conformist answer is suggested as a model." (p. 77)

**4.** The basals control the sequence in which reading "skills" (and now sometimes "strategies") will be taught, if not learned. The bulk of a basal reading program consists of materials for teaching, practicing, and testing isolated reading "skills," reflecting an implicit assumption that reading is learned "a word, or sound, or a skill at a time." (p. 70) The implication is that this broad *scope* of skills is both necessary and sufficient for learning to read. The *sequence* of skills is derived by moving from smaller parts toward larger wholes, beginning with and emphasizing skills for identifying words, and moving toward skills for comprehending sentences and paragraphs.

**5.** The basals control the language of the reading selections, particularly at the earliest levels, on the assumption that simplifying the vocabulary, sentence structure, and/or the letter/sound patterns in beginning materials will make them easier to read. Thus the basals include "simple" selections like "I can go. Can you go?" "I will help you. You can go." "Help! Help! I can not go." (p. 67; from Houghton Mifflin Reading, 1986, Level B—but the selection is typical of most basals.)

**6.** Perhaps most damaging of all, the basal programs control—along with standardized and state-mandated testing—what counts as "reading." The essence of the basal program is not the pupil anthologies and their reading selections, but rather the ancillary materials for teaching, practicing, and testing reading skills. In sheer bulk, these materials far outweigh the reading selections. Examination of these materials led the authors of the *Report Card* to estimate that a basal reading program engages children in reading literary and other texts only about 10 percent to 15 percent of the time that is ostensibly devoted to "reading" (p. 73). The ultimate reduction is in the basal tests, which reduce reading to the skills which can be easily measured with paper and pencil (p. 83). So "reading is not making sense of print anymore. It is doing well on the basal tests." (p. 108)

## *Are Basal Readers Scientific?*

Such strict control of reading makes perfectly good sense according to the science of the 1920s, when basal reading programs were first being developed. Today's basals are still solidly rooted in those principles from business, industry, and science—particularly behavioral psychology—that motivated the development of the earliest basal series. These principles are reflected in the "laws of learning" articulated by Edward Thorndike (Goodman et al., 1988, pp. 12–13). The *Report Card* illustrates throughout its discussion of the contemporary basal how today's programs reflect the view of teaching and learning rooted in Thorndike's "laws." To summarize: "The *Law of Readiness* results in the readiness materials and in the tight sequence in which skill is built upon skill. The *Law of Exercise* produces drills and exercises in pupil books, workbooks, and supplemental materials. The *Law of Effect* supports the sequence of first learning words and skills and then using them in reading selections; and the *Law of Identical Elements* results in the focus on isolated skills in testing for development of reading ability and for the close match between the items in the exercises and the tests." (p. 98) Thus, from the viewpoint of the science upon which basal programs are based, strict control of teaching and learning and of what counts as "reading" is not only justifiable, but necessary.

But is this science the best that the late twentieth century has to offer? Both the authors of the *Report Card* and the members of NCTE's Commission on Reading would respond with a resounding "No!"

## The Newer Science: A Multidisciplinary Consensus

Within the past twenty or so years, a multidisciplinary consensus has developed regarding the nature of learning, the relationship between teaching and learning, the nature of the reading process, and the acquisition of literacy. (Space precludes listing most primary sources, but see such references as the following: Goodman, et al.; 1988, pp. 137–139; Weaver, 1988; Lindfors, 1987; Raphael and Reynolds, 1986; Smith, 1986; Teale and Sulzby, 1986; Crismore, 1985; Harste et al., 1984; Newman, 1985; Pearson, 1984; Shuy, 1981; and Holdaway, 1979.) Converging research from cognitive psychology and schema theory and language acquisition, from linguistics and psycholinguistics and sociolinguistics, and from reading and emergent literacy leads to conclusions such as the following:

**1.** From infancy, children actively develop, test, and refine hypotheses about their world. As preschoolers, for example, virtually all children learn to use their native language according to its basic rules, with feedback from the adults with whom they communicate but with almost no direct instruction whatsoever.

**2.** Reading is a highly complex and active process of meaning-seeking. Readers actively construct meaning as they interact with a text, and the meaning so constructed depends as much upon the prior knowledge and strategies of the reader as upon the words of the text.

**3.** Texts consisting of only a few simple words repeated in equally simple and stilted sentence patterns are typically less predictable and thus more difficult to read than texts consisting of a greater variety of words that occur in more natural sentence patterns resembling normal speech.

**4.** Both language and literacy develop best in the context of their use—that is, in situations which are functional and intrinsically motivational for learners. Children develop literacy best in an environment enriched with literature and "littered with literacy."

**5.** Learning to read is a process that develops over time, but in complex ways—not a skill or a strategy at a time, even when it is taught that way.

Such well-documented observations as these suggest that reading is not best learned when taught as if it involved mastering a sequence of skills and strategies, from simple to increasingly complex. For many and perhaps most of our youth, teaching reading one skill at a time may in fact mitigate against their developing the ability to analyze, evaluate, and extend what they read, or to read well enough to solve everyday problems in adult life (e.g., Venezky et al., 1987, pp. 28, 44–46; Applebee et al., 1987).

Although pupils may well benefit from the modeling and guided practice of certain skills and strategies, particularly strategies for getting meaning and for monitoring comprehension, they nevertheless do not need or necessarily benefit from an elaborate program that teaches isolated skills and strategies lesson-by-lesson, day-by-day, week-by-week, for seven or nine years. There is ample evidence that independent reading does considerably more to develop reading ability than all the workbooks and practice sheets children typically complete in a basal reading program (e.g., Anderson et al. 1985, pp. 75–76).

I shall risk going further than the *Report Card* and admit that I think it questionable whether basal reading systems as a genre can go very far towards meeting this basic objection to teaching reading as a long, drawn-out process of mastering a sequence of skills and strategies. After all, basals are a product of the American economy, in which profit is the bottom line. One way for basal publishers to increase profit is by enlarging their share of the market, but another and perhaps more practical way is to increase the sheer volume of materials in a basal reading program, especially the consumable materials that have to be replaced every year.

This is not to say that the authors and editors of basals are either ignorant of the newer knowledge base, or unscrupulous; typically they are neither, and in fact there is considerable truth to the argument that publishers are only providing the kinds of materials that the market demands. Furthermore, the latest series often do reflect some aspects of the newer understanding in philosophy statements in the teachers' manuals, as well as in certain other aspects of instruction. Nevertheless, it seems clear that it is in the *publishers'* best interests to *increase* the volume of materials for teaching, practicing, and assessing reading skills and strategies, not to decrease them. However, scientific evidence from a convergence of disciplines in the last two decades or more suggests that increasing the use of such materials is certainly *not* in the best interests of *children*.

# CONTENT LITERACY GUIDE

**An Attack on Basal Readers for the Wrong Reasons**
Patrick Groff
In Arena Debate-in-Print No. 1, ERIC, 1989

1. Summarize Groff's view of the biases of the Report Card authors and NCTE.

2. In what way does Groff charge that the Report Card exaggerates the claims of basals?

3. In what way do Groff and the Report Card agree on how well basals are grounded in research?

4. What question does Groff suggest in weighing the merits of the Report Card?

5. Summarize Groff's statements about teacher satisfaction with basals through the years.

6. Paraphrase Groff's "outstanding teacher" argument.

7. Summarize Groff's account of research on direct instruction in phonics.

8. Restate the quote from Berliner and Rosenshine.

9. How does Groff deal with the issue of control?

10. What practice does Groff identify as possibly the worst of those recommended by the Report Card?

11. What does Groff find puzzling about the Report Card's contention that children should behave like skilled readers?

12. What is the main conclusion of the research Groff cites on context usage?

13. How does Groff suggest that this research undermines the Report Card's goal?

# AN ATTACK ON BASAL READERS
# FOR THE WRONG REASONS

PATRICK GROFF

The *Report Card on Basal Readers* (RC) was prepared by the National Council of Teachers of English's Commission on Reading in response to its obvious dislike of what it calls "the absolute dominance of basal readers" (BRs) in today's reading instruction programs (p. iv). The report admits in its preface that it takes an "advocate's position" against the use of basal readers in our nation's classrooms. The *Report Card* thus gives an early warning that the document is not the report of a neutral-minded study of the effectiveness of BRs. To the contrary, the *Report Card* appears to be the result of comparison by its authors of their peculiar convictions about reading instruction with the methods for this purpose recommended by the BRs.

It is rightly judged by the *Report Card* that these two points of view on the teaching of reading are incompatible. The BR system stands in the way of the implementation of their conceptions about reading teaching, the authors of the RC appear to have concluded. The report was written, then, to persuade teachers, reading experts, or anyone else with influence over how reading is taught in schools, to join in the effort to eliminate basal readers from the schools.

## False Charges against Basal Readers

Expectations given readers early on by the RC that it will be a passionate endorsement of certain articles of faith about reading instruction, rather than an open-minded examination of the effectiveness of BRs, are quickly fulfilled by the document. It argues in its first chapter that the "central premise of the basal reader" is that even teachers who are otherwise incompetent will be able to teach all children to read well if they use the basal reader (p. 1). The RC maintains that BRs say that "everything" a child needs to read in

*Source:* "An Attack on Basal Readers for the Wrong Reasons" by Patrick Groff, in C. B. Smith (Ed.), *Two Reactions to the Report Card on Basal Readers in Print* (No. 1, pages 8–13). Bloomington, IN: ERIC. Copyright 1989, ERIC/RED (Educational Resources Information Center/Clearinghouse on Reading, English, and Communication) at Indiana University (Bloomington). Reprinted by permission.

order to perfect this skill is found in the readers. So students' and teachers' performances are judged entirely by basal tests, the report concludes.

None of these allegations against the typical basal reader is accurate, however. It would be patiently absurd, of course, for BRs to be so outlandishly boastful about their capabilities and influence. BRs do claim, it is true, that they can teach children at large to read better than can any other system of instruction that is presently available. This presumption is a far cry, however, from what the *Report Card* avers that BRs profess in their own behalf.

The exaggerated charges made against basals by the report in its first chapter are useful warnings for critical readers of this document, nonetheless, since they alert the critic in yet another way that the RC was conceived and written as a piece of special pleading for a peculiar opinion of how reading ability should be developed. The over-statements made about BRs in chapter one of the report thus caution anyone to read the document with his or her guard up.

## The Central Issue about the RC

The RC is correct, nonetheless, in protesting the BR's claim that everything it presents in its various books and manuals is there "for scientific reasons." (p. 1) There is other reasonable doubt, which I share, that "findings from research have not been the most compelling force behind changes that have occurred in basal reader programs." (Durkin, 1987, p. 335) Implicit in the report's statement that BRs "have not reflected the best and most up-to-date knowledge of science" (p. 31), is the claim that everything in the reading instruction program it favors is based on a preponderance of scientific evidence, however.

A more pertinent and manageable question is: Given the likelihood that basal readers can and should be improved, are their shortcomings less or more significant than are those found in the reading program, the *Report Card* advocates? This question will become the crux of my critique of the report. The vital issue for any critical reader of the RC thus is: Is it more or less likely that the reading program that it proposes will bring on greater achievement in reading for children than can the typical basal system?

## Why the RC Objects to Basal Readers

Before moving to a direct confrontation of this issue, however, it seems proper first to comment on the major reasons, other than the supposed ineffectiveness of BRs, why the RC denounces their use. The report dislikes how the ethos of business, science, and psychology of the day is reflected in the manner in which the BR is written, how in effect the basals try to maintain scientific management in the teaching of reading. As to the effectiveness of this relationship, the RC admits that "basal reading materials met the expectations of a public and profession enthralled with business, science, and psychology as they tried to find a remedy for the apparent crisis in reading instruction." (p. 19) Nonetheless, the RC castigates even the fine-turning of basal programs over the years that has been done in accordance with changes in the ethos of business, science, and psychology.

On the other hand, the continuous reformations in the content of basals have much impressed teachers—so much so, that in popularity referendums teachers are found to approve wholeheartedly of the series' self-proclaimed values (Shannon, 1983). It is clear, then, that most of today's teachers simply do not believe the senior author of the RC's contention that the use of basals results in "detrimental effects on students' desire and ability to read." (p. 24) Whether teachers truly should have such faith in the RC plan will be discussed in due course.

Having failed to document that there is any widespread lack of confidence among teachers as to the relative effectiveness of BRs versus the RC plan for teaching reading, the report maintains, nonetheless, that the favorable judgments of basals by teachers are the result of teachers' general unawareness that in so doing they are acting unprofessionally. If teachers became professional-minded, the RC bluntly contends, they would reject the use of BRs. The RC argues, then, that teachers who accept its heterodoxical point of view about reading instruction are professionals. Those who do otherwise, are not. It must be noted that this remarkable denunciation of teachers who disagree with it is made by the RC before it presents any evidence that the plan its authors recommend for teaching is actually superior to that which the BRs offer. This RC criticism of teachers also overlooks the evidence that in fact they may not be slavish adherents of basals (Durkin, 1984; Russavage et al., 1985).

It is reasonable at this point to refer to descriptions of highly successful reading programs to determine if the teachers involved in them are professional by the RC standards. It is clear that even the most eminently accomplished reading teachers in such programs (Hoffman and Rutherford, 1984) do not meet the criteria set by the RC for professionalism. Hoffman and Rutherford analyzed reports on eight reading programs that had attained relatively high pupil achievement to identify the key elements of teacher practices, instructional programming, and school environment that they had in common. The teachers in these outstanding reading programs did not conform to several of the recommendations made for instruction by the RC. Who is truly out of step in this regard, then, America's outstanding teachers or the authors of the RC? The RC cannot say it respects these teachers' "exercise of professional judgment" (p. 153), and at the same time accuse them of unprofessional practices because their teaching does not confirm the RC proposal for reading instruction. This would be a grossly inconsistent judgment.

## BRs and Teacher Effectiveness

The first part of the *Report Card* proposes, then, what it assumes is a logical syllogism about teacher effectiveness. This deduction goes like this: a) BRs persuade instructors to teach reading in a relatively ineffectual manner; b) teachers internalize the seductive rhetoric about the capacities of BRs; and c) teachers then use and defend an inferior mode of reading instruction. In this supposedly wrongful instruction, speech sounds, letters, and words are isolated. Children are taught to recognize words out of context. The RC vehemently opposes such "fracturing and narrowing" of the language (p. 82).

Is such teaching at odds with the research findings, as the RC insists? It appears not. Reviews of the research (e.g., Chall, 1967 and 1983; Johnson and Baumann, 1984; Anderson et al., 1985: Perfetti, 1985; Groff, 1987) suggest that reading programs that teach in this fashion—and which teach a controlled, carefully sequenced, hierarchical order of skills and words—produce the greatest amount of reading achievement that is possible. Drill and practice with words is carried on in such programs to the point of overlearning, so that pupils learn to decode words effortlessly and accurately (automatically). Teachers in these superior reading programs expect that pupils' learning will be a direct result of their teaching, and they are not disappointed.

The RC strenuously disapproves of this kind of teaching, however. It goes so far as to concur with Smith (1973) that one of the easy ways to make learning to read hard is to ensure that phonics skills are learned and used by children. But not so, say the many reviews of the experimental research on the value of phonics teaching. In my identification of 120 such reviews, I found they all agree that the acquisition of phonics skills by learners makes a vital contribution to their reading development (Groff, 1987). "The research is clear," says the recent *Handbook on Reading Research,* "if you want to improve word-identification ability, teach phonics." (Johnson and Baumann, 1984, p. 595) A key factor found commonly in schools with extraordinarily successful reading programs is that they all teach phonics "to a much greater degree than most." (Weber, 1983, p. 545)

Neither does the *Report Card's* proposition that children cannot be "active learners" of reading if they carry out assignments overtly directed by their teachers (p. 126) have significant corroboration from the experimental research. Typically the empirical findings about teaching support Berliner and Rosenshine's (1977, p. 393) conclusion that "the classroom behavior of the successful teacher is characterized by direct instruction, whereby students are brought into contact with the curriculum materials and are kept in contact with them until the requisite knowledge is acquired." An acceptance of the RC's notion that children learn only under their own initiatives thus cannot be a necessary condition of professionalism in teaching.

It is not altogether clear from the RC how teachers who become liberated from the BRs might express their newly acquired authority. Apparently, teachers with freshly gained dominion over reading programs firmly in hand would not be expected to do any direct instruction, teach any given set of reading skills or vocabulary, provide any individual pupil practice materials like worksheets, follow any common methodology or procedures from class to class, externally control to any significant extent the strategies children have found it useful to become consciously aware of when learning to read (metacognition), or regularly test children using normative measures. If children are given "the opportunity to learn for themselves" (p. 130), they would have teachers who "respond to what the child is trying to do" (p. 129), by encouraging him or her "to take risks in reading," that is, to guess at the identity of words by using context cues (p. 130).

## *The Unsoundness of Context Cues*

It may be, however, that the most potentially hazardous item in the list of practices that research has failed to corroborate is maintaining children at the guessing-at-words or context cue stage of word recognition. The RC makes clear its approval of the idea that "it makes sense to have children behaving like skilled readers to the fullest extent possible from the beginning." (p. 130) With this belief in focus, it is puzzling, then, why the RC persists in its denunciations of the BR's view "that learning to read is, more than anything else, learning words and skills for identifying words" (p. 66) rather than learning to use context cues.

I have surveyed the research on the facilitating effect of context cues on word recognition and comprehension (Groff and Seymour, 1987). The research findings on these topics suggest that it remains an open question (at the very best) whether context has any effect on mature reading behavior. Henderson (1982, p. 345) believes the research reveals that "there are good grounds for disputing whether any facilitatory effect of sentence context obtains if the task closely resembles normal reading." Studies show that there is no greater difference between good and poor readers' abilities to recognize words in sentence contexts than in isolation. By the time they are third graders, children do not make significantly fewer errors when reading words in contexts than as isolated items. Eye movement studies indicate that good readers normally fixate their eyes on three or four words per second. When individual words can be recognized so automatically, it is unlikely that the able reader needs to spend time guessing at their identity in context.

Teaching children to continue to use context cues runs the risk of maintaining young readers at this crude level of word recognition and thus of hindering their overall reading growth. As Gough (1981, p. 95) correctly depicts the issue: "Goodman [senior author of the RC] is dead wrong about what separates the skilled adult from the beginning reader, and hence what must be accomplished in reading acquisition. The most conspicuous difference between good and poor readers is found in the swift and accurate recognition of individual words, in decoding, and the mastery of this skill is at the heart of reading acquisition." The research, as Gough notes, devastates a main plank of the RC reading program—that it is vital to teach numerous context cues to children learning to read. With this main section of its proposed methodology reduced to shambles, the RC's goal of settling "what is good or bad for learners" (p. v) is notably frustrated.

## Summary

The *Report Card on Basal Readers* is a legitimate document in the sense that its main purpose is to create dissatisfactions on the part of teachers toward the methods of instruction they commonly use. That is, it would be foolhardy to argue that BRs now teach reading totally in accordance with what the empirical research says about this instruction. Moreover, there doubtless never will be a point in time when teachers will be able to say with confidence that a faultless or irreproachable stage in the evolution toward perfection in instruction has been reached.

Large numbers of reading professionals have devoted their efforts over the years to promoting reading reform under the assumption that the state of the art in reading instruction can be steadily improved. Change and progress in the manner in which reading instruction is customarily given, including teacher dissatisfaction with it, thus should be nourished, not suppressed. One cannot find fault, therefore, with the apparent basic motives of the authors of the RC. It should be conceded that their goal in producing this document was to improve the manner in which reading is taught in school and, through this means, reduce the degree of illiteracy in the nation. Nonetheless, as noted in the body of this discussion, serious questions can be raised about the recommendations the RC makes for teaching reading, inquiries that go beyond the fundamental objectives of its authors in writing the book.

As is admitted by its authors, the RC was conceived and written as a means of popularizing the particular approach to reading instruction that was favored, at the time of the publication of the RC, by the Commission on Reading of the National Council of Teachers of English. The analysis I have made of the contents of the RC reveals, however, that the radical plan for teaching reading that the RC advocates has basic shortcomings. By attempting to defend a predetermined point of view about reading instruction, rather than to examine, in a disinterested way, both sides of the debate over this teaching that continues to boil over, the authors of the RC also show more commitment to ideology than to the scientific method.

The prime fault of the special pleading for a particular approach to the teaching of reading found in the RC is that the document fails to provide any convincing evidence that an implementation of the RC plan for reading development will result in greater reading achievement for children than is possible with BR systems. From most accounts of research (Chall, 1967 and 1983; Johnson and Baumann, 1984; Anderson et al., 1985; Perfetti, 1985; Groff, 1987), it can be inferred that a use of the RC approach in fact would eventuate in less reading development for children than is attainable with BRs.

This is not to say that the RC has not accurately exposed some essential weaknesses of the BR system. It is true, for example, that the basal readers' claim that they scrupulously follow the research evidence when these books are written is not altogether accurate. It is also correct to charge, as the RC does, that BRs spend too much time on activities other than having children read independently. One can find basal lessons and tests that do not accomplish all their teachers' manuals claim they do. BRs do exemplify the difficulty of creating stories with high literary quality that are easy enough for beginners to read.

I recently examined how phonics is taught in grades 1 and 2 in five leading BRs. I found that pupils who used these books would not be fully prepared to decode about 60 percent of the new words presented in BR lessons (Groff, 1988). The BRs thus are also guilty of not teaching phonics intensively enough, and of using the analytic, implicit approach to word recognition which teaches about sight words and context cues. BRs present a less than desirable sequence of phonics skills, a discredited syllabication procedure, and too little practice on vowel phoneme-grapheme correspondences. They also tend to ignore the evidence that multisyllabic words are significantly more difficult to recognize than are monosyllabic ones. It was striking to realize that the errors the BRs make in teaching doubtless cause some unfortunate side effects. With BRs, children's acquisition of automatic decoding skills are delayed. Their ability, in turn, to read independently from a wide variety of sources is handicapped.

By its own admission, the RC thinks few of these faults of the BR have any consequential importance. It holds that any straightforward kind of phonics instruction will handicap the attainment by children of independent reading skills, and thus that "exercises designed to teach phonics and vocabulary directly are likely to be unnecessary and even counterproductive." (Goodman, NCTE, 1986, p. 359) The loyalty of the authors of the RC to such immoderate and unreasonable views of reading development drastically reduces the chances that the type of reading instruction it espouses will find widespread acceptance by reading teachers. In the final analysis, therefore, the RC tends to be self-defeating. It frequently battles against the BRs for wrong reasons, and thus blunts the thrust of the accurate exposé it makes of many of their shortcomings.

## *Integrating Sources*

1. Contrast Groff's quote from Berliner and Rosenshine (p. 117) with Weaver's statement about independent reading (p. 111). Are these statements really at odds?

2. Reexamine the five conclusions Weaver reaches from research. Does she deal with Groff's concern about the role of context?

3. Both Weaver and the NCTE Call for Action deal in some detail with the issue of the control basals exercise. Contrast Groff's view of this issue (p. 117).

## *Classroom Implications*

1. In what ways have these sources changed or reinforced your own views on reading instruction?

2. Can you suggest ways that basals might be modified to appeal to both Groff and Weaver, or at least to take a step in that direction?

3. What experiences have you had with basal instruction that tends to confirm or refute points made by Weaver, Groff, or the NCTE Call for Action?

## *Annotated Bibliography*

Chall, J. S., & Squire, J. R. (1991). The publishing industry and textbooks. In R. Barr, M. Kamil, P. B. Mosenthal, & P. D. Pearson (Eds.), *Handbook of reading research* (Vol. II, pp. 120–146). White Plains, NY: Longman.

*This is a detailed review of research and issues related to the commercial aspects of textbook production. It has an extensive bibliography.*

Cullinan, B. E. (Ed.). (1993). *Fact and fiction: Literature across the curriculum.* Newark, DE: International Reading Association.

*This book reviews the latest developments in trade books with an emphasis on the use of these materials in the content areas such as mathematics, science, and the social sciences. It includes a children's author and title index.*

Fox, M. (1993). *Radical reflections: Passionate opinions on teaching, learning, and living.* San Diego: Harcourt Brace.

*Mem Fox, an outspoken Australian children's author, describes her book as "ammunition, not words"—ammunition for teachers and parents who are fighting the skill-and-drill mentality of language arts instruction. Her perspective is strongly anti-basal, and she pleads for literature-based approaches in teaching young children.*

Lindeen, E., et al. (1993). Books worth teaching even though they have proven controversial. *English Journal, 82,* 86–89.

*The problem of how to select and then teach controversial literacy materials is discussed. The book is oriented toward the middle and secondary grades.*

Mudkiff, B. (1993). Stepping stones to mathematical understanding. *Arithmetic Teacher, 40,* 303–305.

*The use of trade books as an approach to connect language and mathematics is suggested. Examples are given of the types of trade books that can be used to accomplish this purpose.*

Slaughter, J. P. (1993). Stories of our past: Books for the social studies. *The Reading Teacher, 46,* 330–338.

*This review of 43 books can be used in the social studies curriculum. The article is an example of how to use trade books in a specific curriculum area.*

## *You Become Involved*

**1.** Contrast one of the current manuals of a basal series with an older version from the same publisher. What kinds of changes have been made? Do you detect trends that may be present across time? If so, list them.

**2.** Is it possible for a basal series to meet the objections of critics? Try your hand at outlining the characteristics a series would need to have in order to satisfy the objections you have read about in this chapter. Which, if any, of those characteristics would be so alien to the philosophy of basals that they might be impossible to implement within a series?

Chapter *5*

# *Emergent Literacy*

Beginning in the 1970s, early childhood educators began to question some notions such as (1) that literacy growth necessarily begins with formal schooling, (2) that reading instruction should begin in first grade, and (3) that kindergarten should be devoted largely to getting children ready for such instruction (Fields & Spangler, 1995). The realization that signs of literate behavior can be observed at much younger ages led to a new view of how children move toward literacy. The idea that reading readiness was the proper goal of any instruction received prior to first grade gave way to the view that literacy slowly develops, or emerges, if children grow up in environments where literate acts are modeled and where opportunities to use print for relevant purposes abound.

Emergent literacy is a highly complex concept (Scarborough & Dobrich, 1994). It suggests that children are developing simultaneously with respect to many dimensions crucial to eventual literate behavior. For example, a preschooler who is read to frequently begins to acquire an awareness of print, a sense of story structure, and so forth, with little or no "instruction." The same child may also experiment with writing, proceeding from pictographic representations to letter-like scribbling, and finally to letters and words. At the same time, the child's world knowledge and oral language steadily grow, providing the basis for later text comprehension. Thus, literacy emerges along many paths at the same time.

## *Instructional Issues*

This sophisticated view of children's growth toward literacy raises numerous instructional issues (Tompkins & Hoskisson, 1995). One is the proper role of direct instruction—whether it should have any place in preschool or kindergarten settings, or whether teachers should serve mainly as facilitators who help children "figure out" literacy on their own (Williams & Davis, 1994). Another issue is how long to encourage invented spelling as children use it to examine the alphabetic principle. Still another point is what to do about children whose out-of-school environment has not been conducive to the emergence of literacy (Anderson, 1994). Finally, there is the problem of efficiency, or how to balance the competing forces of limited time and the need of children to explore in a risk-free, unpressured setting.

## As You Read

The following selections provide a brief but solid introduction to the topic of emergent literacy. Teale and Sulzby give the rationale behind their preference for the term *emergent literacy* over the more traditional *readiness*. Their discussion is well seasoned with specific suggestions for teachers and parents. Adams, following the appearance of her influential and controversial book, *Beginning to Read: Thinking and Learning about Print* (1990), responds to her avoidance of the term *emergent literacy* due to confusion about its meaning.

As you examine these authors' contributions to the topic, focus on the following questions:

1. What definition of *emergent literacy* is most defensible?
2. What instructional implications does emergent literacy have for early childhood programs?
3. Which instructional practices are best aligned with the concept of emergent literacy?
4. What can be done to assist children whose home backgrounds have not been conducive to the emergence of literate behavior?

## References

Adams, M. J. (1990). *Beginning to read: Thinking and learning about print.* Cambridge, MA: MIT Press.

Anderson, J. (1994). Parents' perceptions of emergent literacy: An exploratory study. *Reading Psychology, 15,* 165–187.

Fields, M. V., & Spangler, K. L. (1995). *Let's begin reading.* (ERIC Document Reproduction Service No. ED 375 381).

Scarborough, H. S., & Dobrich, W. (1994). On the efficacy of reading to preschoolers. *Developmental Review, 14,* 245–302.

Tompkins, G. E., & Hoskisson, K. (1995). *Language arts: Content and teaching* (3rd ed.). New York: Merrill.

Williams, R. P., & Davis, J. K. (1994). Lead sprightly into literacy. *Young Children, 49,* 37–41.

# CONTENT LITERACY GUIDE

**Emergent Literacy: New Perspectives**
In D. S. Strickland and L. M. Morrow (Eds.)
*Emerging Literacy: Young Children Learn to Read and Write,* 1989, pp. 1–15
William H. Teale and Elizabeth Sulzby

1. What common elements do you see in the three examples given at the beginning of this article?


2. In what ways has research into emergent literacy broken with past methods?
   ____ Researchers have begun looking at extremely young children.
   ____ The social aspects of literacy in home and school have been deemphasized.
   ____ Researchers have attempted to see literacy growth from the child's viewpoint.

3. Summarize Conclusion 1.


   What is proved by differences in scribbling by children from different countries?


   (T/F) It appears that the beginning of literacy learning roughly coincides with a child's entry into kindergarten.

4. Summarize Conclusion 2.



5. Summarize Conclusion 3.



   Why is the word *literacy* better than *reading* for use in describing early development?



   (T/F) For young children, the language arts mutually reinforce one another.

6. Summarize Conclusion 4:


   Briefly describe how evidence supports the idea that becoming literate is developmental.

**7.** Summarize Conclusion 5.


**8.** Teale and Sulzby give two examples of "adult scaffolding" of literate behavior. Summarize these and suggest a third:

a.

b.

c.


**9.** (T/F)   According to Teale and Sulzby, the question of when to begin reading and writing instruction is absurd.

Why?


**10.** (T/F)   A good way to facilitate emergent literacy is by extending the first-grade program down to the pre-K level.

**11.** Explain how "learning should not be confused with teaching."


**12.** What are the two dimensions of storybook reading?

a.

b.


**13.** What types of books should be used for read-alouds?


**14.** What suggestions do Teale and Sulzby make for conducting a read-aloud?


**15.** In what two ways do independent reenactments of books facilitate growth in reading?

a.

b.

**16.** (T/F)   Repeatedly reading the same book should be avoided.

**17.** Summarize the four suggestions for classroom set up:

a.

b.

c.

d.

**18.** Summarize the techniques called "The Morning Message" and "The News."

a.

b.

**19.** Briefly list some of the ways Teale and Sulzby suggest for having children respond to books and extend their meaning.

**20.** Describe how a writing center would operate in a classroom.

**21.** Define *sociodramatic play* and summarize how it might be implemented in a classroom.

**22.** (T/F) The research base underlying emergent literacy is, according to Teale and Sulzby, not yet strong enough to recommend it without caution.

# EMERGENT LITERACY
## NEW PERSPECTIVES

WILLIAM H. TEALE
ELIZABETH SULZBY

In December, when he was five, Esteban presented to his parents the piece of paper shown below. He had, he told them, listed what he wanted for Christmas. As further insurance that nothing would go wrong in obtaining his presents, Esteban also numbered the items on the list and indicated who was responsible for getting what, first by writing "Mommy" or "Daddy" beside each item and also by drawing pictures of Mom and Dad atop the two columns of toys. This child was leaving nothing to chance.

*Source:* "Emergent Literacy: New Perspectives" by William H. Teale and Elizabeth Sulzby, 1989, in Dorothy S. Strickland and Lesley Mandel Morrow (Eds.), *Emerging Literacy: Young Children Learn to Read and Write.* Copyright 1989 by the International Reading Association. Reprinted by permission.

From the time Jennifer was a year old, she was read to regularly by her mother. At three years, three months of age, Jennifer was visited by a researcher (R), who asked her to read *Are You My Mother?* (Eastman, 1967), a book that had been read to her many times. In an enthusiastic manner and with a reading intonation, she read the entire book, a portion of which follows:

| *Jennifer* | **Text** |
|---|---|
| Out pop the baby birdie. | Out came the baby bird. |
| He says, "Where is my mother?" (aside to R) He's looking for it. | "Where is my mother?" he said. He looked for her. |
| Looked up; did not see her. | He looked up. He did not see her. |
| And he looked down; he didn't see it. | He looked down. He did not see her. |
| So he said he's gonna go look for her. | "I will go and look for her," he said. |
| - - - - - - - - - - - - - - - - - - - - - - - | - - - - - - - - - - - - - - - - - - - - - - - |
| Came to a kitten and he said, "Are you my mother?" | He came to a kitten. "Are you my mother?" he said to the kitten. |
| "N . . . and he didn't say anything. He just looked and looked. | The kitten just looked and looked. It did not say a thing. |
| Then he came to a hen and he said, "Are you my mother?" "No." | The kitten was not his mother, so he went on. Then he came to a hen. "Are you my mother?" he said to the hen. "No," said the hen. |

From Aaron, age fourteen months, we have data of a different sort. Aaron's mother made audio tape recordings of his vocalizations in a variety of activities. The tape recordings contain babbling, not words or sentences. But even in Aaron's babbling, one hears distinctive differences in intonation patterns between occasions when he is turning the pages of a book and those when there is no book present.

During the past decade or so, an intense interest has arisen in the early literacy behaviors of typical children like Esteban, Jennifer, and Aaron. When we observe children who have grown up with reading and writing around them, we see that they know about literacy and exhibit literate behaviors. Results of many studies of children from birth to six years of age have caused teachers and researchers to change some of their ideas about young children's reading and writing development from what was commonly believed as recently as the 1970s. A new perspective on early reading and writing has developed; it has come to be known as *emergent literacy*. In this chapter, we examine the concept of emergent literacy for the new insights it provides on young children's literacy learning. We explore what young children do with literacy, what they know about reading and writing, and how they develop literacy knowledge and literate practices. We conclude the chapter by considering what an emergent literacy perspective implies for how young children should be taught in day care, preschool, or school classrooms.

## Emergent Literacy Overview

Emergent literacy is a concept that has become prominent only recently, even though there is a long history of research in young children's reading and writing. Some of the research from past decades has contributed to an emergent literacy perspective. For example, studies of early readers (Clark, 1976; Durkin, 1966), research documenting the importance of storybook reading in early childhood literacy development (Fodor, 1966; Irwin, 1960; Templin, 1957), and pioneer work by individuals like Legrün (1932) and Clay (1967) all support an emergent literacy perspective.

It is primarily studies of the past few years, however, that have shaped the current outlook. During this period, researchers have approached their work differently. For one thing, the age range of the children studied has been extended to include children fourteen months of age and younger. Researchers also have begun to study literacy development in a fuller sense. Literacy is not regarded as simply a cognitive skill to be learned, but as a complex sociopsycholinguistic activity. Thus, the social aspects of literacy have become significant, and literacy learning is investigated not just in the researcher's laboratory, but also in home and community settings.

Perhaps the most important factor is that literacy learning has been studied in fresh ways. A concerted effort has been made to examine literacy development from the child's perspective. Researchers are now attempting to understand what is going on in the child's head and in the child's world. We have come to see that logical analyses of the task of literacy learning, such as conclusions about the literacy behaviors of young children based on adult perspectives, are not very useful in accounting for early childhood reading and writing development. Instead, studies that seek to understand literacy learning from the child's point of view have provided much more insight into the process. These studies have observed children engaged in literacy activities and interpreted what was seen from multidisciplinary perspectives grounded in cognitive psychology, anthropology, child development, and social interaction theory. As a result of employing these perspectives, we understand early childhood literacy learning in new ways. This understanding enables us to sketch a portrait of young children as literacy learners.

## Portrait of Young Children as Literacy Learners

**The first thing to recognize is that, for almost all children in a literate society, learning to read and write begins very early in life.** Even during the first few months of life, children come in contact with written language as parents place soft alphabet blocks in their environments or read them books. These early contacts with print can be thought of as the beginning of a lifelong process of learning to read and write. By the time they are two or three, many children can identify signs, labels, and logos they see in their homes and communities (Goodman, 1986; Hiebert, 1981; Kastler, Roser, & Hoffman, 1987).

Many children are fortunate enough to be read to regularly and therefore experience books and the sights and sounds of written language from an early age.

Young children also experiment with writing. Even their scribbles display characteristics of the writing system of their culture, and therefore the writings of four year olds from Saudi Arabia, Egypt, Israel, and America will look different long before the children can write conventionally (Harste & Carey, 1979). Examples like these, as well as the behaviors of Esteban, Jennifer, and Aaron (discussed earlier), clearly show that the process of learning to read and write is under way.

The more closely one looks, the more difficult it is to pinpoint a time when literacy learning begins. Certainly, it starts long before the child enters kindergarten or prekindergarten. Many would argue that even children as young as one year are processors and users of written language. The understandings and the behaviors may differ significantly from those of older children or adults. Nonetheless, young children have already begun learning to read and write.

**A second characteristic of the portrait is that the functions of literacy are an integral part of the learning process that is taking place.** Literacy develops from real life settings in which reading and writing are used to accomplish goals. Observational studies have shown that the vast majority of literacy experienced by young children is embedded in activities directed toward some goal beyond the literacy itself (Heath, 1983; Taylor, 1983; Taylor & Dorsey-Gaines, 1988; Teale, 1986). For example, children may see adults reading newspapers or greeting cards, writing checks, completing crossword puzzles, or using the TV Guide. They may find that a recipe is an integral part of helping a parent bake cookies or that written directions are used in putting a toy together. Books may be intimately involved in the religious activities of the family.

In these and other ways, young children are ushered into the world of literacy viewing reading and writing as aspects of a much larger system for accomplishing goals. The orientation to literacy as a goal directed activity is an important part of the portrait to remember because it shows that the foundation for children's growth in reading and writing rests upon viewing literacy as functional rather than as a set of abstract, isolated skills to be learned.

**The third dimension of great importance in our portrait is that reading and writing develop concurrently and interrelatedly in young children.** Since children do not first learn to read and then learn to write, we need to speak of literacy development, not of reading readiness or of prereading. [The following figure] attempts to depict how oral language, reading, and writing relate in young children's literacy learning.

Certainly, children's oral language proficiency is related to their growth in reading and to the ways in which they write. Educators have long seen that a strong oral language base facilitates literacy learning. Furthermore, it is clear that children's developing reading abilities influence their writing. However, we also must recognize that reading experiences influence oral language (e.g., reading books to children enhances vocabulary), and writing actually improves children's reading skills (e.g., allowing kindergartners to write builds decoding skills). For young children, the language arts mutually reinforce one another in development.

**The fourth major characteristic of young children as literacy learners is that they learn through active engagement, constructing their understanding of how written language works.** Young children's emergent readings of favorite storybooks

(Sulzby, 1985), for example, are not mere memorizations of books. Notice from Jennifer's reading of *Are You My Mother?* that she reconstructs the meaning of the book even though her words often deviate from the actual text.

Young children's spellings also exhibit the attempt to construct knowledge. Five year old Kayla's use of LAEYMABCODLPK to write "I like rainbows because they have so many colors" appears to be random until we add that observations of Kayla writing revealed that she used one letter to represent each syllable of the message she was encoding. The sounds conventionally associated with each of the letters bore little resemblance to the sounds of the words being written, but, nevertheless, there was a system to Kayla's writing. In other words, her emergent literacy behaviors were conceptual. The behaviors were wrong by adult standards, showing that the process of becoming literate is developmental, but Kayla was not behaving randomly. Numerous studies of invented spellings (e.g., L or LIK for like; J or JUP for jump; HRP for chirp) also provide substantial evidence of the conceptual basis of emergent writing behaviors (Henderson & Beers, 1981; Read, 1971).

Thus, the portrait shows that in a positive literacy learning environment young children grow up experiencing reading and writing in many facets of their everyday lives, primarily as purposeful, goal directed activities. As children encounter written language, they try to figure out how it works. In so doing, they form and test hypotheses, attempting to discern the differences between drawing and writing; to understand the meanings, structures, and cadences of written language; to learn the symbols of writing; and to sort out the relationships between these symbols and the sounds of oral language. The knowledge and procedures young children develop for solving the literacy puzzle often are different from adult conventions and strategies, but they are logical and understandable, once we take the children's perspectives. Furthermore, their understandings and strategies change over time, showing that literacy learning is a developmental process.

This depiction of young children as active learners, as constructors of understandings about written language, is central to the concept of emergent literacy. But the new perspectives on early childhood reading and writing development also have shown the key role parents and other literate persons play in facilitating early literacy learning. One way adults help is by demonstrating literacy. For example, as they write a shopping list, use a bus schedule, write a letter, help a school child with homework, or read the newspaper, parents demonstrate the act of literacy. From these and other demonstrations, children can discern the purposes and some of the actions involved in reading and writing.

**Even more important than the demonstrations of literacy are the times parents and children interact around print.** In these interactions, children can learn a lot because parents work with them to jointly achieve the goal of the activity. Through language and actions, parents make obvious to children what is involved in the activity because they want the children to participate.

In the example of the shopping list, the construction phase comes first. Sharita, age four years, three months, and her parents are sitting at the kitchen table. Father reminds the family that tomorrow is grocery shopping day, and together they begin to construct the shopping list. Mother and Father discuss the meals for the next week and then determine the necessary ingredients. As they note the needed items, they check the refrigerator and cupboards, and items not on hand are added to the list. Both parents talk to Sharita about the construction of the list, and Father, who is actually writing the list, consciously externalizes the process by saying things like, "Okay, parsley. Let's write that here. Parsley starts with a *p*—parsley" as Sharita sits beside him and watches. After the list is constructed, Sharita accompanies her father to the store for the shopping phase. The list is an integral part of shopping, and again the adult makes using the list a joint activity.

It is not surprising that children's independent uses of print grow out of such adult–child interactions. Sharita has written her own lists while playing by herself, and seven months after the above episode, she wrote a list using scribble at the same time her parents were constructing one. A similar phenomenon is common among children who are read to regularly. Interactive storybook readings between adults and children have powerful effects on the children's literacy development (Teale, 1987) and lead to independent reenactments of books like the one by Jennifer described earlier (Sulzby & Teale, 1987). Thus, adult scaffolding (Bruner, 1983; Cazden, 1983) of the activity is an important means of promoting literacy learning in young children (Teale, 1982, 1986) and of establishing independent reading and writing habits.

In summary, young children's literacy learning grows out of a wide variety of experiences. Children construct their knowledge about print and their strategies for reading and writing from their independent explorations of written language, from interactions with parents and other literate persons, and from their observations of others engaged in literacy activities.

## *Literacy Instruction for Young Children*

Such a perspective on young children's literacy learning carries with it significant implications for teaching reading and writing in the early childhood classroom. We begin by identifying basic principles that should guide instruction, then identify an approach to literacy learning activities suggested by classroom based investigations.

## Basic Principles

An understanding of young children as literacy learners is crucial to decisions about curriculum in school settings. When we see that legitimate literacy learning occurs during the early years, we realize that the question of when to begin reading and writing instruction is absurd. We should be teaching reading and writing to all children in day care facilities, in child development centers, in Head Start programs, in preschools, in prekindergarten programs, and in kindergartens.

But as we examine the implications just presented of the portrait of young children as literacy learners, we also should realize that the ways in which we teach reading and writing in early childhood programs must be developmentally appropriate. We cannot merely shove the first grade program down a notch or two into the kindergarten or prekindergarten and expect it to work. Traditional, formal reading instruction typical of first grade is simply inappropriate for young children. So is the worksheet dominated reading curriculum (which pays major attention to letter naming and letter sound matching) that Durkin (1987) found to be typical of the kindergarten classrooms in one state and that informal observations and reports tell us is widely practiced throughout the United States.

Priorities are out of balance and out of keeping with the nature of young children as literacy learners when kindergarten and readiness books concentrate on letter sound matching, letter discrimination, and letter names and give only scant attention to activities that involve children with stories (Hiebert & McWhorter, 1987). The early childhood literacy program must adopt as its foundation functional, meaningful activities that involve reading and writing in a wide variety of ways. A priority for the early childhood curriculum should be ensuring that all children become capable and willing participants in the literate society of the classroom, home, and community. Even before children can read and write conventionally, the curriculum can foster these knowledges and attitudes. Overall skill in reading and writing grows from this kind of start.

The curriculum also must set high priority on getting children actively involved in literacy. Children of all ages need opportunities to experiment daily with reading and writing. The classroom should provide rich demonstrations, interactions, and independent explorations. The link of literacy with experience and the active use of language must be stressed.

A final principle for the early childhood literacy curriculum is that learning should not be confused with teaching. The focus always should be on the child's learning. With zeal from administrators and state legislatures in the U.S. for direct instruction and teacher centered models of instruction, it is easy for the young child to be forgotten in the teaching process. It is especially important that the teacher understand each child's emergent literacy abilities and strategies. In this way, learning and teaching can come together. Rather than teaching reading and writing in an early childhood program, our focus should be on teaching children to read and write.

## Teaching for Literacy Learning

An emergent literacy perspective on young children's reading and writing development carries with it many implications for classroom instruction. Space permits only a general description of the emergent literacy classroom. We discuss particular activities in this section, but do not wish to give the impression that the emergent literacy classroom is merely a bag of gimmicks or a series of separate activities. In reality, the focus should not be on a literacy curriculum per se. Instead, literacy should be an integral part of the overall curriculum. Seen in this perspective, the following types of activities can be especially productive for enhancing young children's reading and writing development.

**Storybook Reading.**    Getting children to interact with books should be the key way in which children experience print in the early childhood classroom. We recommend that teachers plan two dimensions for the storybook reading programs: reading aloud daily to the children and providing opportunities for children to independently "read" books by themselves (and to one another).

Testaments to the importance of reading aloud to young children abound in the professional literature; correlational (Wells, 1985) and experimental (Feitelson, Kita, & Goldstein, 1986) research support these testaments. In other words, reading aloud to young children *teaches* them about reading.

A discussion of storybook reading raises questions such as when, what, and how to read. We recommend reading to young children at least once a day, and more often if possible. As a valued and regular part of the curriculum, storybook reading takes on great significance to the children. Children's literature—everything from folktales and fables to contemporary pieces—should be the main reading fare.

A special effort should be made to include expository books, too. Young children can learn much about how the world works from informational books, and as research has clearly shown, background knowledge and experience with processing expository text are critical to continued success in reading (Anderson et al., 1985). Predictable books (Bridge, 1986) can be profitably used for read alouds, as several authors have described (Heald-Taylor, 1987; Rhodes, 1981; Tompkins & Webeler, 1983).

There is no one best way to read to children, but several useful strategies have been widely recommended: preview the book, establish a receptive story listening context, briefly introduce the book, and read with expression. We would add two further suggestions. First, be sure to engage the children in discussion about what is being read. Talk about the characters and their motivations and responses, make predictions and then listen to confirm or disconfirm them, draw inferences, discuss the themes of books, link information in books to real life experiences, examine the author's use of language, and draw connections among various books. It is this talk about books that gives storybook reading its powerful influence on young children's literacy development (Heath, 1982; Teale, 1987). Also, read the children's favorite books again and again, just as parents who read to their children do. Repeated readings encourage indepth exploration of books, and promote children's independent, emergent readings of those books (Sulzby & Teale, 1987).

Emergent storybook readings constitute the second dimension of classroom storybook reading. Long before they are able to read conventionally, children who have been read to will "read" books on their own (Sulzby & Teale, 1987). Called emergent storybook readings or independent reenactments of books (Sulzby, 1985), these readings seem to facilitate growth in reading because they give children opportunities to practice what they learned in interactive storybook readings, and they allow children to explore new dimensions of books and reading (Holdaway, 1979; Teale & Sulzby, 1987).

Teacher practices and even the physical set up of the classroom can promote these independent reenactments. The repeated readings by the teacher are especially important. After children have heard a book read several times, they are more likely to read it themselves. Along with systematically rereading certain books, teachers also occasionally can give children "assignments" to promote emergent storybook readings. For example, children can be asked to read a book to a partner, act out a previously read book using flannel board characters, or practice in preparation to "read" a book to the class or another group of children.

The classroom set up also can encourage children's independent reading. A key aspect is the classroom library—a collection of children's trade books that provides children with immediate access to books. There are a number of design features that encourage children's use of books in a classroom library (Morrow, 1982; Morrow & Weinstein, 1982). We encourage teachers to:

- Make the classroom library a focal area of the room, partition it, making it large enough to accommodate four or five children at a time, and provide comfortable seating.
- Use open-faced book shelves.
- Provide many types of books (stories, informational books, poetry, alphabet, counting, concept, and wordless picture books).
- Use literature oriented displays (posters, bulletin boards) and props (flannel boards, taped stories).

Teacher storybook reading practices also tie in with children's use of books in the classroom library. Books used in group storybook readings are chosen by children more often than those never read aloud by the teacher, and books read repeatedly are used even more frequently than those read only once (Martinez & Teale, 1988). In summary, group storybook reading and children's independent reading of books do reinforce one another in the classroom and promote children's literacy development.

**Other Opportunities to Read.**    In addition to storybooks, environmental print, and other activities like "The Morning Message" (Crowell, Kawakami, & Wong, 1986) or "The News" offer young children valuable opportunities to read print in meaningful contexts in the classroom. Schickedanz (1986) has described how environmental print—signs, labels, charts—can be used to organize the classroom environment and also provide written language experiences. Labels and signs can indicate children's cubbies, where different classroom items belong, and directions to help the classroom run smoothly (such as how many children are allowed in a center at one time or how to operate the tape recorder). Charts can list various classroom jobs, the daily schedule, or attendance records. At first, the teacher will have to interpret and model the use of these printed materials, but the children will soon use them in their everyday activities.

The Morning Message and the News give children opportunities to see meaningful written language being constructed and to reread what has been written. A morning or afternoon message, written as the children watch, briefly tells significant things that will be happening in the classroom that day. For example:

*Good morning. It's Tuesday, February 16. We will be going on our trash walk today. Also, we have a special book about a mystery for story time today.*

Once the message is written, the children are encouraged to read aloud with the teacher and discuss the message or the kinds of things that people do when writing and reading messages. Crowell, Kawakami, & Wong (1986) and Kawakami-Arakaki, Oshiro, & Farran (1989) have discussed how the Morning Message is used in kindergarten classrooms. It also can work well with other age levels to provide yet another relatively informal way in which children can learn about literacy through meaningful activities.

The idea of reporting and recording news takes various forms in various classrooms. One teacher actually creates a newspaper on a large chart, writing headlines that capture the children's weekend experiences. In another classroom, the News is a time for examining what happened in the community, nation, or world (Martinez et al., in press). On Friday, the teacher invites children to predict weekend news, based either on their planned weekend activities or exciting events such as shuttle launchings, approaching hurricanes, or prominent sporting events. The predictions are written on chart paper. On Monday, a chart containing the weekend's actual news events is made and read. After six months of participation in the News, one kindergarten child even began to write her own news, using inventive spellings and collecting stories from classmates.

Through vehicles such as environmental print, the Morning Message, and the News, teachers provide a variety of opportunities for children to read significant, functional print in the classroom. In these and other ways, children can gain a wide understanding of the purposes and processes of reading.

**Response to Texts.**    A variety of response, or extension, activities can complement and enhance the effects of group storybook readings. Art and drama are two especially powerful techniques. For example, after reading *The Very Hungry Caterpillar* (Carle, 1981), children might make thumbprint caterpillars or water color paintings of the various items the caterpillar ate. Students can punch holes through the paintings (indicating that the items were eaten through), string them together, and attach a caterpillar face, ending up with a caterpillar composed of all the things he ate.

For dramatic activities, children can reenact stories with flannel board characters of puppets, or even play the roles themselves using simple props and costumes (perhaps ones that they have designed). One of the most successful response activities in one classroom was having the children dramatize *The Three Billy Goats Gruff* on the clatter bridge in the school playground. Another class made stick puppets of Mr. Gumpy, his motor car, and all the characters who accompanied him on his ride in *Mr. Gumpy's Motor Car* (Burningham, 1973). The children reenacted the book, placing the characters in the car one by one, getting everyone out to push the car out of the mud after it rains, and finally having a swim together.

Books can also be extended through activities such as cooking and even eating. There's nothing quite like making and sampling stone soup after reading Marcia Brown's (1947) version of the story. Moreover, her rendition can be neatly tied into a nutrition lesson or unit because she includes all of the major food groups in the book.

Many expository books for young children like those from the Lets-Read-and-Find-Out Book™ series contain experiments illustrating concepts discussed in the books. For example, an excellent way to make *Air Is All Around You* (Bradley, 1986) have an even greater impact is to invert a glass containing a napkin crumbled in the bottom and place it into a bowl of water to see what happens, just as described in the book. Another effective tactic is to have children draw and write "learning logs" about what they learned from an informational book. As part of a unit on rodeos, one kindergarten teacher read the National Geographic book *Cowboys* (Filcott, 1979). The children enthusiastically produced drawings of chaps, spurs, and other things relating to cowboys. It was apparent when they reread what they had written about their drawings (often writing in scribble or random letters) that they had learned a lot.

**Writing.**   In this section, we focus on the composing and spelling aspects of writing development. Research cited earlier shows that these facts of writing development begin early in a child's life and that reading and writing develop concurrently. Furthermore, research confirms what has often been stated: Children learn to write by writing. Therefore, the early childhood curriculum should encourage children to write often and to write for a wide variety of purposes and audiences. Much has already been written about how to establish writing as part of the early childhood program (e.g., Kawakami-Arakaki, Oshiro, & Farran, 1989; Martinez & Teale, 1987; Salinger, 1988; Schickedanz, 1986; Teale & Martinez, 1989). Here are some general ways in which writing may be incorporated into the curriculum in preschool, prekindergarten, and kindergarten.

First, we recommend that a writing center be an integral part of every classroom. The writing center is a place where children can experiment with writing, collaborate with others through writing, and have an audience to whom they can read their writing and get responses. A writing center should contain a variety of writing instruments and materials: chalkboard; magnetic letters; unlined, lined, and story paper; typewriter; computer; markers; crayons; pens; and pencils. Children can visit the writing center frequently and write on topics they choose and topics assigned by the teacher that fit into the themes of the curriculum units. Of course, young children will use a variety of forms (scribbling, drawing, random letters, inventive spelling) in their writing. The writing center is the key necessary for building a community of writers in the early childhood classroom. It makes writing a visible part of the curriculum and serves as a place where children can write for a wide variety of reasons.

Martinez & Teale (1987) have described how to introduce a writing center in a kindergarten classroom, and Schickedanz (1986) provides guidelines for using writing in a preschool setting. Children will write many types of stories, ranging from personal narratives to takeoffs on familiar books or television shows to fanciful, original creations. Also, the utility of other types of writing should not be overlooked. Children may write letters, make lists, create signs, write invitations, and do many other things.

Once writing becomes established in the classroom, it will carry over into a variety of activities, such as becoming an integral part of children's dramatic play. Also children will engage in self-sponsored writing at home. After the first few weeks of school in the classroom of one kindergarten teacher who emphasized writing, the children literally lined up each morning to give the teacher (and read to her) personal notes they had written the night before.

Other ways in which the teacher can promote writing is by establishing a postal system in the classroom or organizing a pen pals program (Teale & Martinez, 1989).

Also, writing can be an excellent way of responding to books (see previous section). For instance, after reading *Go and Hush the Baby* (Byars, 1973), the children could write about how they would hush the baby. A response activity to *King Bidgood's in the Bathtub* (Wood, 1985) that incorporates art, drama, and writing is to have children write what they would do if they were king and then make crowns for themselves and act out their scenarios.

**Literacy and Play.**    As a final and related topic, we highlight the importance of integrating literacy into children's play activities in the early childhood classroom. Filling children's play with reading and writing is a primary means of ensuring that literacy instruction is developmentally appropriate. We already have discussed one kind of play in talking about dramatization as a response activity. In addition to thematic fantasy play like that, sociodramatic play can be profitably incorporated into the curriculum.

Sociodramatic play involves two or more children adopting roles and acting out a situation. To promote children's knowledge of the functions and uses of literacy, real life situations can be especially useful. For example, the teacher might set up the dramatic play area of the classroom as an airport or travel agency. Included in such a setting could be a great deal of print—travel posters and brochures, a schedule board indicating destinations, times and numbers of flights, airline tickets, and magazines. Of course, writing materials would be present so that children could write phone messages, tickets, boarding passes, and itineraries, and make signs for the area.

A dramatic play area can be set up in any number of ways, depending upon the theme being stressed in the curriculum. For a nutrition unit, it could become a restaurant, bakery, or supermarket. A dinosaur museum would complement the study of dinosaurs. A fire or police station, doctor's office, or post office could be used for a unit on community helpers. Written language can be made an integral part of all these settings. The teacher provides the props and models the use of print or writing if necessary, but basically allows children to create their own scripts and scenarios. With such preparation, and with occasional praise and suggestions from the teacher, the extent to which literacy becomes a part of this sociodramatic play can be remarkable.

## Conclusion

Although this chapter is designed to provide new perspectives on young children's reading and writing development, readers no doubt will recognize much familiar information. Many early childhood educators, especially those acting from a child centered, holistic perspective on learning and teaching, have proposed similar views and advocated similar practices since the late 1800s. We have learned a great deal in the past decade that supports these educators. We also have gained new understandings that help refine and extend such ideas.

There is much yet to be learned, but an emergent literacy perspective rests on a solid research foundation. It certainly challenges the current status quo in early childhood education, as revealed in studies of the way reading is typically taught in the kindergarten (Durkin, 1987; Hiebert & McWhorter, 1987). The goal now is to make this new perspective the way in which teachers and publishers think about young children's literacy development. Then we can have early childhood programs that are indeed developmentally appropriate.

## References

Anderson, R. C., Hiebert, E. H., Scott, J. A., and Wilkinson, I. A. G. *Becoming a nation of readers.* Champaign, IL: Center for the Study of Reading, National Institute of Education, and National Academy of Education, 1985.

Branley, F. M. *Air is all around you.* New York: Thomas Y. Crowell, 1986.

Bridge, C. Predictable books for beginning readers and writers. In M. Sampson (Ed.), *The pursuit of literacy: Early reading and writing.* Dubuque, IA: Kendall/Hunt, 1986, 81–96.

Brown, M. *Stone soup.* New York: Macmillan, 1947.

Bruner, J. S. *Child's talk.* New York: Norton, 1983.

Burningham, J. *Mr. Gumpy's motor car.* New York: Thomas Y. Crowell, 1973.

Byars, B. *Go and hush the baby.* New York: Viking, 1971.

Carle, E. *The very hungry caterpillar.* New York: Philomel Books, 1981.

Cazden, C. B. Adult assistance to language development: Scaffolds, models, and direct instruction. In R. P. Parker and F. A. Davis (Eds.), *Developing literacy: Young children's use of language.* Newark, DE: International Reading Association, 1983.

Clark, M. M. *Young fluent readers.* London: Heinemann, 1976.

Clay, M. M. The reading behavior of five year old children: A research report. *New Zealand Journal of Education Studies,* 1967, *2,* 11–31.

Crowell, D. C., Kawakami, A., and Wong, J. Emerging literacy: Reading-writing experiences in a kindergarten classroom. *The Reading Teacher,* 1986, *40,* 144–151.

Durkin, D. *Children who read early.* New York: Teachers College Press, 1966.

Durkin, D. A classroom-observation study of reading instruction in kindergarten. *Early Childhood Research Quarterly,* 1987, *2,* 275–300.

Eastman, P. *Are you my mother?* New York: Random House, 1967.

Feitelson, D., Kita, B., and Goldstein, Z. Effects of listening to stories on first graders' comprehension and use of language. *Research in the Teaching of English,* 1986, *20,* 339–356.

Filcott, P. *Cowboys.* Washington, DC: National Geographic, 1979.

Fodor, M. *The effect of systematic reading of stories on the language development of culturally deprived children.* Unpublished doctoral dissertation, Cornell University, 1966.

Goodman, Y. M. Children coming to know literacy. In W. H. Teale and E. Sulzby (Eds.) *Emergent literacy: Writing and reading.* Norwood, NJ: Ablex, 1986, 1–14.

Harste, J. C., and Carey, R. F. Comprehension as setting. In J. C. Harste and R. F. Carey (Eds.), *New perspectives in comprehension.* Bloomington, IN: Indiana University School of Education, 1979.

Heald-Taylor, G. Predictable literature selections and activities for language arts instruction. *The Reading Teacher,* 1987, *41,* 6–12.

Heath, S. B. *Ways with words: Language, life, and work in communities and classrooms.* New York: Cambridge University Press, 1983.

Heath, S. B. What no bedtime story means: Narrative skills at home and school. *Language in Society,* 1982, *11,* 49–76.

Henderson, E. H., and Beers, J. (Eds.). *Developmental and cognitive aspects of learning to spell.* Newark, DE: International Reading Association, 1980.

Hiebert, E. H. Developmental patterns and interrelationships of preschool children's print awareness. *Reading Research Quarterly,* 1981, *16,* 236–260.

Hiebert, E. H., and McWhorter, L. *The content of kindergarten and readiness books in four basal reading programs.* Paper presented at the annual meeting of the American Educational Research Association. Washington, DC, 1987.

Holdaway, D. *The foundations of literacy.* Sydney, Australia: Ashton Scholastic, 1979.

Irwin, O. Infant speech: Effect of systematic reading of stories. *Journal of Speech and Hearing Research,* 1960, *3,* 187–190.

Kastler, L. A., Roser, N. L., and Hoffman, J. V. Understanding of the forms and functions of written language: Insights from children and parents. In J. E. Readance and R. S. Baldwin (Eds.), *Research in literacy: Merging perspectives.* Rochester, NY: National Reading Conference, 1987.

Kawakami-Arakaki, A., Oshiro, M. I., and Farran, D. C. Research into practice: Integrating reading and writing in a kindergarten curriculum. In J. Mason (Ed.), *Reading and writing connections.* Newton, MA: Allyn & Bacon, 1989.

Legrün, A. Wie und was "schrieben" kindergartenzoglinge? *Zeitschrift fur Padogogische,* 1932, *33,* 322–331.

Martinez, M. G., and Teale, W. H. The ins and outs of a kindergarten writing program. *The Reading Teacher,* 1987, *40,* 444–451.

Martinez, M. G., and Teale, W. H. Reading in a kindergarten classroom library. *The Reading Teacher,* 1988, *41,* 568–573.

Martinez, M. G., Cheyney, M., McBroom, C., Hemmeter, A., and Teale, W. H. No risk kindergarten literacy environments for at risk children. In J. Allen and J. Mason (Eds.), *Reducing the risks for young learners: Literacy practices and policies.* Portsmouth, NH: Heinemann, in press.

Morrow, L. M. Relationships between literature programs, library corner designs, and children's use of literature. *Journal of Educational Research,* 1982, *75,* 339–344.

Morrow, L. M., and Weinstein, C. S. Increasing children's use of literature through program and physical design changes. *Elementary School Journal,* 1982, *83,* 131–137.

Preston, E. M. *The temper tantrum book.* New York: Viking, 1969.

Read, C. Preschool children's knowledge of English phonology. *Harvard Educational Review,* 1971, *41,* 1–4.

Rhodes, L. K. I can read! Predictable books as resources for reading and writing instruction. *The Reading Teacher,* 1981, *34,* 511–518.

Salinger, T. *Language arts and literacy for young children.* Columbus, OH: Merrill, 1988.

Schickedanz, J. A. *More than the ABCs: The early stages of reading and writing.* Washington, DC: NAEC, 1986.

Sulzby, E. Children's emergent reading of favorite storybooks: A developmental study. *Reading Research Quarterly,* 1985, *20,* 458–481.

Sulzby, E., and Teale, W. H. *Young children's storybook reading: Longitudinal study of parent–child interaction and children's independent functioning.* Final Report to the Spencer Foundation. Ann Arbor, MI: University of Michigan, 1987.

Taylor, D. *Family literacy: Young children learning to read and write.* Portsmouth, NH: Heinemann, 1983.

Taylor, D., and Dorsey-Gaines, C. *Growing up literate: Learning from innercity families.* Portsmouth, NH: Heinemann, 1988.

Teale, W. H. Emergent literacy: Reading and writing development in early childhood. In J. Readance and R. S. Baldwin (Eds.), *Research in literacy: Merging perspectives.* Rochester, NY: National Reading Conference, 1987.

Teale, W. H. Home background and young children's literacy learning. In W. H. Teale and E. Sulzby (Eds.), *Emergent literacy: Writing and reading.* Norwood, NJ: Ablex, 1986.

Teale, W. H. Toward a theory of how children learn to read and write naturally. *Language Arts,* 1982, *59,* 555–570.

Teale, W. H., and Martinez, M. G. Connecting writing: Fostering emergent literacy in kindergarten children. In J. Mason (Ed.), *Reading and writing connections.* Newton, MA: Allyn & Bacon, 1989.

Teale, W. H., and Sulzby, E. Literacy acquisition in early childhood: The roles of access and mediation in storybook reading. In D. A. Wagner (Ed.), *The future of literacy in a changing world.* New York: Pergamon Press, 1987, 111–130.

Templin, M. *Certain language skills in children.* Minneapolis: University of Minnesota Press, 1957.

Tompkins, G. E., and Webeler, M. What will happen next? Using predictable books with young children. *The Reading Teacher,* 1983, *36,* 498–502.

Wood, A. *King Bidgood's in the bathtub.* San Diego, CA: Harcourt Brace Jovanovich, 1985.

# CONTENT LITERACY GUIDE

**From "A Talk with Marilyn Adams"**
*Language Arts, 68, 1991, 210–211*

*Note:* In this excerpt, Adams defends her avoidance of the term *emergent literacy* in her 1990 book, *Beginning to Read: Thinking and Learning about Print.*

1. Summarize the three definitions of the term *emergent literacy* to which Adams alludes.

   a.

   b.

   c.

2. Which one does she most fully endorse?

3. Which one does she reject?

4. (T/F)  Adams believes some children need specific guidance during the emergent literacy period.

5. Use the following chart to categorize the predictors of reading success given by Adams.

| *Strong Predictors of Success* | *Weak Predictors of Success* |
| --- | --- |
|  |  |

6. (T/F)  According to Adams, the best thing a teacher can do for young children who are at risk of not succeeding is simply to wait for literate behaviors to emerge.

7. Summarize Adams's view that a teacher should be partly an "interventionist."

# FROM: A TALK WITH MARILYN ADAMS

*Language Arts:* Let's talk about emergent literacy. Some people have said, in print or in conversations, that Marilyn Adams doesn't care and doesn't know anything about emergent literacy. She never refers to that literature, they say or they contend, or she only gives lip service to it but doesn't really take it into account. What do you say to that?

*Marilyn Adams:* I read deeply in the literature on emergent literacy. Much of the book is principally about the concepts and principles of emergent literacy. I didn't use the term because it is associated with several very different definitions in the literature. For some people, the term emergent literacy alludes to the notion that literacy development is an enormously complex process—that only as its many components mature and merge together can literacy in any real sense "emerge." That is the meaning that I used in the book and tried to develop in depth. But then there are the other interpretations of the term. Don Holdaway defines it as a stage that occurs when the child has begun to recognize letters but still can't sound out words. That's very different. And in a third usage, which is one that I cannot endorse, emergent literacy is linked to the idea that literacy will naturally blossom forth if only the child is surrounded by a rich and joyful world of print.

*Language Arts:* So teachers should not take a hands-off, let-it-blossom role in early literacy instruction?

*Marilyn Adams:* There are certain insights and observations on which reading and comprehension depend critically. For many children, these insights and observations are just not forthcoming without some special guidance.

*Language Arts:* And that's why you can't endorse this third position, why the teacher needs to take more of an "interventionist" position with certain kids at certain times?

*Marilyn Adams:* What's the alternative? To wait? To sit comfy with the notion that when they're ready, they'll learn? In this spirit, we're beginning to hear the word "developmental" slung around in much the way that the term "reading readiness" was sometimes used around the turn of the century. In fact, the research on reading readiness, for which I have also been criticized for reviewing, contains some very useful information. In particular, the traditional indicators—which include, for example, IQ, mental age, chronological age, gender, perceptual-motor skills or styles, handedness, and affluence—have been shown at best to be weak or remote predictors of how well a child will take to reading.

In contrast, the strong predictors of how well a child will learn to read correspond to how much she or he already knows about what text is for and how it works. The strong predictors are directly tied to the child's knowledge and experience with print and print concepts. This means, incontrovertibly, that just to wait is to put that child at an increasing disadvantage. For children who have not gotten—either at home or at school—the experience to enable them to read at 6 years, what makes anybody think that by leaving them alone they will read by the time they are 7?

Meanwhile, children are the most merciless critics of themselves. They have their own standards and expectations. They keenly observe how well their buddies are doing; and, heart and soul, they want to do well themselves. If a child feels embarrassed or self-conscious, if a child is not progressing to her or his own satisfaction, then the challenge of learning to read is not a joyful experience—regardless of how many prize-winning picture books there are in the classroom.

I admit that I don't like the sound of the word "interventionist," but in some sense that's what teaching is about. You want to understand that child and the nature of literacy as deeply as possible. You want to figure out that child's strengths and confidences; you want to identify the ways in which her or his experience or understanding mismatch the demands of the task; you want to use those strengths and confidences to build to the child's needs; and you want to begin immediately so that hurt feelings never develop.

## *Integrating Sources*

1. Of the three definitions of emergent literacy supplied by Adams, to which would Teale and Sulzby be most likely to subscribe? Defend your answer.

2. How do you think Teale and Sulzby would react to Adams's claim that "special guidance" is sometimes necessary for children? That a teacher must therefore intervene in cases where literacy is not emerging properly?

3. How do you think Adams would react to the statement of Teale and Sulzby that "the question of when to begin reading and writing instruction is absurd"?

## Classroom Implications

1. It is now clear that the parent plays a crucial role in a child's early progress toward literacy. What are some ways educators can encourage parents to act purposefully?

2. Given what you know about emergent literacy, do you still think there is a place for "readiness" books in a kindergarten classroom? Explain.

3. The concept of emergent literacy has major implications for the way children are assessed in the primary grades. Describe a few of them.

## *Annotated Bibliography*

### Emergent Literacy

Clay, M. M. (1991). *Becoming literate: The construction of inner control.* Portsmouth, NH: Heinemann.

> *This text traces the changes that occur over time in young children's literacy development. The emphasis in this reference is on the role the individual child plays in these literacy changes.*

Clay, M. M. (1993). *An observational survey of early literacy achievement.* Portsmouth, NH: Heinemann.

> *Reflecting current thinking in emergent literacy instruction, this book details classroom activities that enhance effective literacy learning.*

Clay, M. M. (1979). *What did I write? Beginning writing behavior.* Portsmouth, NH: Heinemann.

> *The early development of children's writing as a significant aspect of literacy development in young children is emphasized.*

Halliday, M. A. K. (1973). *Exploration in the function of language.* London: Edward Arnold.

> *This important reference in the study of early literacy development in young children is based on the belief that literacy learning for children is basically a process of learning how to mean.*

Jackson, N. E., et al. (1993). Components of reading skill in postkindergarten precocious readers and level-matched second graders. *Journal of Reading Behavior, 25,* 181–208.

> *This article describes the reading behavior of a group of precocious postkindergarten students, noting their literacy strengths and weaknesses.*

Mason, J. M., et al. (1992). *Toward an integrated model of early reading development. Technical report No. 566.* Urbana, IL: Center for the Study of Reading.

> *Reports are made on the results of a study of 127 children from the beginning of kindergarten to the end of third grade, noting the critical influences in the development of literacy abilities. Included with this reference is an extensive review of relevant research.*

McMackin, M. C. (1993). The parent's role in literacy development: Fostering reading strategies at home. *Childhood Education, 69,* 142–145.

> *This article summarizes the traditional and current beliefs related to literacy development in young children and the role of parents in this process. Specific suggestions are given as to how parents can become more effective in helping their children's literacy growth.*

Morrow, L. M. (1993). *Literacy development in the early years: Helping children read and write* (2nd ed.). Boston: Allyn and Bacon.

*Current research and practices related to emergent literacy are reviewed. This reference stresses the importance of literature as a basis for literacy instruction.*

Morrow, L. M., et al. (1992). *Resources in early literacy development. An annotated bibliography.* Newark, DE: International Reading Association.

*This reviews 125 references related to early literacy development in young children. The bibliography is divided into the following areas: (1) General Issues, (2) The Home Environment, (3) Oral Language, (4) Writing and Drawing, (5) Children's Literature, (6) Developing Comprehension, (7) Learning About Print, (8) Play, (9) Television, (10) Computers, and (11) Assessment.*

Neuman, S. B., & Roskos, K. (1993). *Language and literacy learning in the early years: An integrated approach.* Orlando, FL: Harcourt Brace.

*This book supports an integrated approach to literacy learning in younger children. It details specific classroom applications of an integrated literacy curriculum.*

Pellegrini, A. D., & Galda, L. (1993). Ten years after: A reexamination of symbolic play and literacy research. *Reading Research Quarterly, 28,* 162–175.

*The roles of Piagetian and Vygotskyan theories of literacy development and their effects on symbolic play in young children are examined. There is an extensive bibliography in this area of emergent literacy.*

Rhodes, L. K., & Shanklin, N. L. (1993). *Windows into literacy: Assessing learners, K–8.* Portsmouth, NH: Heinemann.

*This book discusses the importance of literacy assessment, in its many forms, as being part of all instruction. It contains many classroom examples of the effective use of literacy assessment.*

Strickland, D. S., & Morrow, L. M. (Eds.). (1989). *Emerging literacy: Young children learn to read and write.* Newark, DE: International Reading Association.

*The development of early literacy as it relates to both oral and written language is discussed. Issues such as theoretical perspectives in early literacy development, literature and early literacy, writing and organizing literacy learning are presented.*

Sulzby, E., & Teale, W. (1991). Emergent literacy. In R. Barr, M. Kamil, P. B. Mosenthal, & P. D. Pearson (Eds.), *Handbook of reading research* (Vol. II, pp. 727–757). White Plains, NY: Longman.

*This is an extensive review of investigations into emergent literacy. Many dimensions of this broad topic are included.*

Yaden, D. B., et al. (1993). A psychogenetic perspective on children's understanding about letter associations during alphabet book readings. *Journal of Reading Behavior, 25,* 43–68.

*An important reference in the study of young children's letter associations with their sound representations, this article contains an excellent bibliography related to literacy development in young children.*

## *You Become Involved*

**1.** Reflect on what you remember about your own personal experiences in learning to read and write. What specifically do you recall about emergent literacy activities and your family? What memories do you have of your first experiences in school with literacy? Are they generally positive or negative? Commit your remembrance to writing and consider sharing it with a colleague.

**2.** Talk with colleagues about how they encourage parents to help their children's development of a variety of literacy abilities. What are some of the problems you have faced in developing a positive home/school relationship?

**3.** Review a commercial reading program and note how it encourages students to develop early literacy abilities. What are some specific activities that are included to help with this process? Are there ways in which the program falls short?

**4.** During conferences, ask parents what they are doing in their homes to foster literacy development. Document both their successes and problems. See if you can discern patterns related to socioeconomic status.

*C h a p t e r* **6**

*Spelling*

How important is correct spelling? Centuries ago, the spellings of many words were not fixed, and writers tended to vary the way they spelled certain words from one instance to the next—including their own names! The development of dictionaries as standard references after the English Renaissance changed all that, however. Today, only a small number of words have more than one acceptable spelling, and people who regularly fail to use established spellings generally make a poor impression on those with whom they attempt to communicate through writing. Because of the standardization of spelling in English, educators tend to agree that children must ultimately learn the correct spellings of those words they are likely to use on a frequent basis. Tradition suggests that the best way to foster good spelling is by systematically introducing a prescribed curriculum of words, each to be learned to the point of mastery. Historically, the extensive use of a carefully prescribed list of spelling words has been the foundation on which teachers have taught this subject. It has only been within recent years that deviation from a specific list of spelling words has been encouraged. As we will see, however, there are other issues involved.

## Invented versus Formal Spelling

Many educators believe that a good way of introducing children to the alphabetic principle (the idea that letters are used to represent sounds on a systematic basis) is by encouraging them to spell *phonetically* whenever they write (Manning & Manning, 1994; Powell & Hornsby, 1993). Children's efforts to invent spellings have been carefully studied and tend to progress through identifiable stages toward formal standardized spelling of words. Teachers who favor invented spelling often find themselves in a quandary, however, because of the delayed development of correct spelling. Parents and administrators tend to raise questions, not to mention more traditional colleagues.

A compromise position of encouraging invented spellings and then correcting them before the papers are returned may risk stifling the inventive and exploratory process. Moreover, some students seem to demand a knowledge of correct spellings from the outset, and they are hard to persuade to take chances. As Adams (1990) has pointed out, research has done little to enlighten the issue of when and how to introduce correct spellings. There is evidence that children's decoding ability improves when they study orthographic elements of words, as in techniques that stress phonogram families and word analogies. But such study is possible without a traditional, word-by-word approach to spelling mastery (Stanovich, 1994).

## Contextualized versus Leveled Approaches

Traditional approaches to spelling present children with a small number of words, generally on a weekly basis. Children learn these words to the point of mastery, often by writing them in isolation repeatedly. Although generally effective, this approach is clearly at odds with a whole language philosophy, since it does not begin with books and other textual materials but rather moves from part to whole.

A contextual, or embedded, approach is more consistent with whole language teaching. From actual reading (and/or writing) (Scott, 1994), in which the children are engaged, clusters of words are singled out for additional study. The notion of proceeding from the whole to the part is intended to reinforce for children the true purpose of studying spelling in the first place.

How these two approaches compare is not well understood. Each seems to offer specific advantages and drawbacks. A leveled approach tends to be efficient, clear-cut, and easy to manage. Its organization from simple to more complex words makes sense and a fair body of research supports its effectiveness. On the other hand, it tends to be tedious and may risk disinteresting students and overly fragmenting their growth toward literacy. The contextualized approach, on the other hand, has the advantage of moving from whole to part and of linking other elements of word study, such as word meanings and phonics. It also introduces an element of student choice that may contribute to interest and motivation. But relying on student choice and on chance as well (in terms of which words may occur in a given piece of writing) means that this approach will almost inevitably lack the efficiency and dependability of the leveled approach. As in the case of invented spelling, each teacher will need to resolve the issue through classroom trial.

## As You Read

The selections that follow develop these issues in detail. O'Flahavan and Blassberg describe and advocate the contextual approach, whereas Henderson writes from the traditional perspective. Adams attempts to find common ground in approaching the issues from the viewpoint of what research suggests.

Regardless of the grade level you teach, you may well have found it necessary to deal with these issues on a practical basis already. The selections that follow may reinforce your decisions—or cause you to reconsider them. As you read, focus your thinking on the following questions:

1. Should invented spellings be corrected? If so, when and how?
2. Weigh the plusses and minuses of contextualized and leveled approaches to a spelling curriculum. Which do you favor? Are they really mutually exclusive? That is, would it be possible, or desirable, to combine elements of the two?

## *References*

Adams, M. J. (1990). *Beginning to read: Thinking and learning about print.* Cambridge, MA: MIT Press.

Manning, M., & Manning, G. (1994). Writing: Spelling and handwriting. *Teaching Pre K–8, 25,* 103–104.

Powell, D., & Hornsby, D. (1993). *Learning phonics and spelling in a whole language classroom. Teaching strategies.* (ERIC Document Reproduction Service No. ED 371 338).

Scott, J. E. (1994). Spelling for readers and writers. *The Reading Teacher, 48,* 188–190.

Stanovich, K. (1994). Romance and reality. *The Reading Teacher, 47,* 280–291.

## CONTENT LITERACY GUIDE

**Toward an Embedded Model of Spelling Instruction for Emergent Literates**
John F. O'Flahavan and Renée Blassberg
*Language Arts, 69,* 1993, 409–417

1. (T/F) O'Flahavan and Blassberg subscribe to a separate, stand-alone spelling program to complement reading and writing.

2. What two abilities do O'Flahavan and Blassberg see as symbiotically related?

   a.

   b.

3. The view of O'Flahavan and Blassberg is that

   a. the content of spelling instruction should depend on two sources:

      1)

      2)

   b. instruction should occur in a setting that

4. List the three dimensions of orthographic knowledge that students must develop:

   a.

   b.

   c.

5. How do formal and informal approaches to spelling instruction differ?

**6.** O'Flahavan and Blassberg suggest another distinction—that between insulated and embedded programs. Using both the text of the article and Table 1, enumerate the characteristics that you feel are most important to each:

  a. Insulated spelling approaches

  b. Embedded spelling approaches

**7.** Can you identify with some of the practices used by Ms. Butler? If you have found some of these practices productive, which are they?

**8.** What is the chief problem with insulated approaches, according to O'Flahavan and Blassberg?

**9.** What two activities overlap to allow children to construct spelling knowledge?

**10.** Differentiate children's word recognition attempts in the logographic versus alphabetic stages.

**11.** React to the suggestion of O'Flahavan and Blassberg that this development strengthens the case for embedded instruction.

**12.** Summarize what O'Flahavan and Blassberg identify as the first step toward embedded spelling instruction.

**13.** (T/F)  O'Flahavan and Blassberg recommend making a list of those words a child can already spell correctly.

**14.** Summarize the four conditions O'Flahavan and Blassberg give for selected words  to work on for spelling instruction:

  a.

  b.

  c.

  d.

**15.** In what way is a traditional (insulated) approach to spelling *normative?*

**16.** (T/F)  Word families offer a good means of organizing spelling instruction.

**17.** Words included in a family for instruction should have three characteristics:

  a.

  b.

  c.

**18.** (T/F)  According to O'Flahavan and Blassberg, the groups formed for word study should be homogeneous, consisting of students who have reached the same need.

**19.** Based on the conclusion section, what do you think is the basis for O'Flahavan and Blassberg's recommendation regarding the makeup of word study groups?

# TOWARD AN EMBEDDED MODEL OF SPELLING INSTRUCTION FOR EMERGENT LITERATES

JOHN F. O'FLAHAVAN
RENÉE BLASSBERG

Few educators would argue with the notion that a deep and thorough knowledge of spelling enables fluent decoding during reading and accurate spelling in writing. However, the variety of instructional conclusions emanating from these apparent truths spark contentious debate (see Adams, 1990, and Strickland & Cullinan, 1990). Should phonics instruction buoy the reading program? Should a formal spelling program exist apart from the writing program? Is it appropriate to insulate instruction in sound-symbol correspondence from children's attempts to read and write?

We argue that orthographic knowledge develops amidst cultural activity for which reading and writing are social and intellectual tools. A child's orthographic knowledge develops as a product of overlapping reading and writing activities: The ability to read words and to represent words in writing evolves symbiotically.

Consequently, we advocate school-based spelling instruction that promotes a deep and thorough understanding of orthography at the same time that children develop as full-fledged members of literate communities. In some ways, our view is consistent with the ideas put forth by Morris (1989):

**1.** Learning to spell is a developmental process influenced by language and memory variables coupled with the opportunity to practice spelling in purposeful writing activity.

**2.** Knowing how students fall along the developmental continuum enables teachers to assess students' spelling knowledge and to design appropriate instruction.

**3.** Delivering appropriate instruction involves students in comparing and contrasting individual words across structural and semantic features.

**4.** Reforming spelling instruction does not imply that educators need to "reinvent the wheel."

Our view extends these broad goals by (a) using students' spelling attempts in writing as the primary source and decoding efforts in reading as the secondary source for decisions about what spelling content to teach and (b) anchoring individual and group instructional activities within a constructivist paradigm (e.g., Guba & Lincoln, 1989; MacGoon, 1977) so that students and teachers construct and refine generalizations about orthography in social contexts.

## Insulated versus Embedded Spelling Programs

In order to spell, write, and read well, students must develop an understanding of three dimensions of orthography: relations between letters and sounds, relations between letter sequences and sounds, and relations between letter sequences and meaning (Henderson, 1990). Knowledge of these relations evolves through a combination of inductive learning, scaffolding, and explicit teaching (Ehri, 1991; Mason & McCormick, 1981).

Most spelling programs today are characterized as formal or informal. Formal approaches are organized around a predetermined scope and sequence of generalizations and exemplars that are based upon normative notions of spelling development. Words are "met head on" (Henderson, 1990, p. 167) and their features compared, contrasted, and memorized. Informal programs are improvised as students engage in the complementary acts of reading and writing. Informal programs respond to developmental changes in students' spelling knowledge (see Henderson, 1990).

While these distinctions are useful, we prefer descriptions that emphasize the degree to which spelling instruction is guided by the learner's developing sense of orthography and is integrated within the total language program. Thus, spelling programs are either insulated from or embedded within the learner's development and the language program. Table 1 highlights the differences between these program orientations.

*Insulated* spelling programs are steeped in formal traditions. Such programs teach spelling from a normative orientation. The objective is to teach orthographic generalizations to students within an explicit teaching paradigm, using words from graded series or students' reading texts. Word lists are organized according to generalizations (e.g., accented syllables) or orthographic structure (e.g., final *-r* words) and sequenced according to perceived difficulty. Consequently, insulated spelling programs engage students in memorizing word spellings within the context of broad generalizations or structural patterns.

The bulk of spelling instruction occurs in a separate time slot, apart from the reading and writing time slots, thus elevating spelling to the same status as reading and writing. A linear routine of the test-study-test approach, managed by the teacher, sequences the teaching and learning activities in the following manner: The teacher introduces a list of words weekly, conducts a pretest, prepares instructional and follow-up activities, encourages correct spelling, conducts a posttest, and documents development. Students participate in a variety of instructional activities such as filling in crossword puzzles, writing definitions and sentences, crafting stories composed from the spelling list, copying words, sorting words, and taking dictation.

**TABLE 1   Insulated and Embedded Approaches to Spelling Instruction**

|  | INSULATED | EMBEDDED |
|---|---|---|
| *Objective* | develop orthographic knowledge by teaching prescribed rules explicitly | develop orthographic knowledge and the reader/writer simultaneously within constructivist paradigm |
| *Orientation to Learner* | normative | developmental |
| *Orientation to Assessment, Teaching, and Learning* | introduction, pretest, repeated exposure, memorization, practice, and posttest | assessment of spelling in writing, constructivist small group activity, ongoing documentation, and self-assessment |
| *Schedule* | occurs within separate time slot | subsumed within total language program |
| *Unit of Instruction* | school week | variable |
| *Source of Spelling Words* | graded or leveled series students' reading | students' writing environmental print (reading and writing) |
| *Common Instructional Activities* | worksheets, sentences, stories, copying, sorting, dictation | construct word families, spelling logs, personal dictionaries, class dictionaries |

In our view, *embedded* spelling approaches may actually prove to be more systematic in nature and more direct in delivery than traditional, insulated programs. Embedded approaches begin with careful teacher and student assessments of students' attempts to craft words in their writing and to decode words in their reading. These collaborative assessments enable the teacher to dovetail constructivistic learning activities into students' emerging theories about orthography. Rather than engaging students in independent memorization activities, teachers invite students to generate theories collaboratively about particular sound-symbol and meaning-symbol relations. These theories are refined over time as generalizations and exemplified as word families that students create to be compiled in personal and class archives.

## An Illustration of an Insulated Program

To illustrate how insulated spelling programs operate, we describe a second-grade language program in the following section. We return to this case later to provide suggestions, by way of example, as to how this teacher could move to an embedded approach.

Ms. Butler has taught second grade for many years. She is open to new ideas about language and literacy instruction but is reticent to alter her program totally every time a new idea surfaces in the field. However, she willingly experiments with those innovations she finds compelling; consequently, her reading and writing program is a tapestry of past and current approaches.

At times, she convenes three reading groups on a regular basis to read from a basal text. Students write their answers to teacher-generated questions that are designed to assess their comprehension of a story. Students complete skills worksheets. Book reports and formulaic paragraph writing are frequent writing assignments.

In other moments, she exhibits the desire to create a community of authors and readers by patterning her program after the approaches described by such literacy educators as Graves (1983, 1991), Calkins (1986), and Atwell (1987). Students choose the topics they write about and the texts they read. She provides instruction in the writing process and textual conventions (e.g., punctuation and grammar) during a writing workshop scheduled three times a week. Students spell inventively when they craft texts. They respond to their reading in journals and share their interpretations in small groups. Overall, students sample and produce a variety of genres. Also, Ms. Butler reads to her students and chooses texts that fit into student interests.

Despite her willingness to innovate, Ms. Butler remains perplexed about how to alter the way she teaches spelling. Her spelling program is anchored by activities that promote memorization and multiple exposure to conventionally spelled words. On a weekly basis, students focus on a predetermined list of words from the district's mandated spelling curriculum. On Mondays new words are written on the blackboard with two additional words the teacher selects from students' content area readings. Each list is organized around a particular sound-symbol correspondence (e.g., *c* in the initial position) or structural pattern common to many words (e.g., final *-r* words).

Typically, in a whole-class session, Ms. Butler points out the target pattern in each word, articulates the generalization that governs the spelling pattern, and adds words that the students contribute orally. Students copy this list into their spelling notebooks. Spelling homework consists of copying each word three times in their spelling notebooks.

On Wednesdays, students work on a page in their spelling textbooks that corresponds to the list of words. These worksheets engage students in sorting, identifying, copying, and fill-in-the-blank activities. At home, students are required to use the words in a sentence or a story and study for a spelling test to be given on Friday. For the spelling test, students number their papers from 1 to 10. Ms. Butler pronounces each word alone and in a sentence, and the students write it. Students grade their own papers as a class, and Ms. Butler records the number correct in her grade book.

## Key Principles Guiding Embedded Spelling Instruction

Insulated spelling programs such as Ms. Butler's neutralize the constructive nature of students' thinking and may also inhibit students' sense of self-determination. Instead, language instruction should strive to cultivate the child's motivational, social, orthographic, and strategic abilities as a reader/writer, and spelling instruction should be embedded within the language program. In support of these goals, spelling instruction should emanate from and at the same time extend an individual's understanding of orthography in the context of ongoing, student-directed reading and writing experiences.

Embedded spelling instruction is guided by the complementary notions that children's developing word knowledge is primarily self-directed (Temple, Nathan, Burris, & Temple, 1988) and that instructional contexts that foster a sense of student self-determination

(Deci, Vallerand, Pelletier, & Ryan, 1991) better enable the teacher to guide spelling development. Children's developing word knowledge reflects predictable growth as they adapt to the conventions in the English orthographic system (e.g., Henderson & Beers, 1980; Templeton, 1979; Zutell, 1979). This knowledge is constructed by the individual in social contexts as a result of overlapping reading and writing activity.

Research on the development of word reading and spelling competence sheds light on how orthographic knowledge evolves (e.g., Ehri, 1991; Temple, Nathan, Burris, & Temple, 1988). This research suggests that reading and writing experiences contribute to a child's understanding of the structural and semantic features of words. In order to develop the sophistication needed to read fluently and write conventionally, a child must construct and reconstruct a system of generalizations that govern spelling (e.g., Bissex, 1975; Read, 1971). If a child knows how letters are formed and that they represent language (and if given the opportunity to experiment with written language), she uses this knowledge to spell prephonemically (Temple, Nathan, Burris, & Temple, 1988) and to read logographically (Ehri, 1991). In writing prephonemically, she composes letter strings to represent words and sentences; however, since her knowledge of letter-sound correspondence is in its infancy, the letters do not correspond to the sounds she intends to represent. As a logographic reader, she keys on the visual features of the letters, identifying the word *dog* by the vertical stem of a *d,* for example (Ehri, 1991), instead of keying on the phonemic and/or semantic cues available in spelling patterns.

Because the sound-symbol associations that prephonemic and logographic readers make rarely conform to the underlying sound-symbol conventions of English orthography, a child discovers the need to spell and read alphabetically. The alphabetic reader applies knowledge about letter names, letter sounds, and sounds of letters in combination to recode words into phonological representations. As a writer, the child breaks words into constituent phonemes and represents the sounds with letters of the alphabet (e.g., *LEFNT* for *elephant*).

As the child displays increasingly fluent decoding prowess when reading, his spellings employ many of the features of conventional spelling with occasional reversions to alphabetic strategies, resulting in a kind of transitional spelling (e.g., *MITE* for *might,* when the child spells *light* conventionally). However, when he begins to generate conventional spellings of words he has never seen before, his ability to decode words has usually become automatic (Ehri, 1991).

Thus, high quality language instruction should embed a study of orthography within the broader concern for developing other literate competencies (see also Wilde, 1990) such as developing a flexible, self-improving cueing system for decoding (Clay, 1985) and building a repertoire of writing strategies for planning, revising, and the like (Atwell, 1987; Calkins, 1986; Graves, 1983; Harste, Short, & Burke, 1988). Further, the social context of instruction should contribute to students' sense of self-determination by including students in the decision-making process related to what spelling content is important to learn next and from whom.

## *Programmatic Suggestions for Ms. Butler*

Ms. Butler may find challenging the suggestion to deepen the integration between the reading and writing programs in her classroom; she may also wonder how she might include her students in decisions related to the evolving spelling program. However, given the fact that her writing program is already couched in a workshop model (e.g., Calkins, 1986) and that she addresses important skills through the use of mini-lessons and encourages her students to use invented spelling, she may already be headed in this direction. These instructional events afford Ms. Butler possible connecting points between reading and writing, and they can function as sources of information about students' developing theories about orthography as well as venues for instruction.

Nonetheless, she could begin to reflect upon changes that could be made in her language program as a precursor to embedding spelling instruction. She could explore the difference between her instructional stance that favors reading for reading's sake and writing for writing's sake and a stance that promotes active participation in a literate community. She could organize her language curriculum around oral language opportunities (e.g., Author's Chair; Reader's Theater; Literature Circles) so that reading and writing activities have socially functional outlets. Lastly, she could integrate the time blocks now set aside for separate reading, writing, and spelling instructional activities.

The authoring cycle (Harste, Short, & Burke, 1988) could prove to be a viable model with which to frame her language program. This model would allow Ms. Butler's second graders to use their nonacademic and academic experiences as fodder for uninterrupted reading and writing activities that lead to recursive engagements involving reading, drafting, sharing, discussing, revising, editing, and publishing. Ms. Butler could provide mini-lessons at any point in this authoring cycle to promote specific types of literate development. In our view, since spelling is part of the larger concern for written convention, spelling instruction would occur in mini-lesson settings roughly around the time students edit texts.

Creating an integrated language program requires attention to space and time considerations. Integrated language activity demands open and timely access to varying contexts and resources in the classroom. The room must be designed to afford students the opportunity to determine their own movements from one literate engagement to another (O'Flahavan & Tierney, 1990). For example, if two or more writers wish to discuss their evolving drafts, they know to sign up for a time to meet with other writers in a conference area. If a group of students wish to discuss texts they have read, they may choose to explore their thoughts in a peer discussion (Raphael, McMahon, Goatley, Bentley, Boyd, Pardo, & Woodman, 1992). Some students may wish to commit their drafts to the computer or use desktop publishing software in a computing area. Some students may wish to read quietly in a reading loft or browse through the collection in the classroom library. Another student may convene a group of actors to act out a rough draft of a skit she is preparing. Some students may be involved in creating a multimedia display of an author's major works in the shelves/display area. Any time a student needs materials for authorship, he can find them in a supply area. An editorial board (see Harste, Short, & Burke, 1988) may meet once a day to edit peer work. An observant teacher can glean important information about students' developing notions of spelling in many of these literate contexts.

All language activity would occur within one monolithic time period. Imagine the following scenario that could evolve in Ms. Butler's class. The language period opens with a status-of-the-class check (Atwell, 1987), during which students make public their plans for the period. The class breaks into collaborative or individual activity. The editorial board meets in the beginning of the period to address manuscripts that have already been revised by the authors and placed in an "in box." Other groups convene in the conference, discussion, or performance areas, depending upon the literate functions such participation would serve. The remaining students choose to work at their desks, at the computer, or in the library or loft areas.

Movement into and out of these areas is facilitated by students reserving the space on a sign-up sheet near each area at the close of the language period the day before. Ms. Butler also made plans the day before as to who would participate in a mini-lesson the following day. She convenes these groups based upon common need and often constitutes groups that are heterogeneous in target ability or skill to maximize the benefits gained from peer tutoring and modeling.

In this new scenario, Ms. Butler's second graders move constantly from topic choice to going public within the context of the authoring cycle. This allows her to track students' development as readers, group participants, and writers, using anecdotal records or more systematic checklists. This integrated activity allows Ms. Butler the opportunity to track the state of students' orthographic generalizations in writing—and reading-related activity—the crucial first step in embedded spelling instruction.

## Embedded Spelling Instruction Occurs within a Generative Cycle of Contextualized Assessment, Teaching, and Learning

Contextualized assessments of students' orthographic theories lead naturally into socially constructed orthographic generalizations. These assessments enable instructional decisions that are closely aligned with students' developing literacy abilities (Lucas, 1988a, 1988b; Valencia, McGinley, & Pearson, 1988). While reading provides students optimal exposure to new and correct spellings (Henderson, 1990), students' writing serves the teacher best as insight into students' generalizations about sound-symbol correspondence.

Young children's writing is often a rich combination of conventionally and inventively spelled words. Some invented spellings are better approximations of conventional spellings than others. It would be folly to have students create lists of words they can spell conventionally with some constancy; likewise, it would also be a waste of instructional time to teach students the words they represent only cryptically (e.g., *G* for *girl*). A more sensible approach suggests that words or spelling patterns chosen for the basis of instruction by the teacher from students' writing need to conform to four conditions:

1. The word or spelling pattern must be an approximation of the conventional spelling.
2. The student must recognize this as so (i.e., the student must be confident that the word is not spelled conventionally).
3. All phonemes must be represented sufficiently through symbol use (e.g., *OHVORE* for *over*).
4. The student plays a role in choosing words or patterns for further study. Selected patterns then become the content of instructional activities that engage students in constructing generalizations and word families which illustrate the generalizations.

Embedded approaches enable teachers and students to negotiate the scope and sequence of the spelling curriculum as students produce and respond to environmental print and make known which words they think they need to learn next. Traditional approaches, on the other hand, predetermine the scope and sequence of abstract generalizations for all children and treat learning explicitly, providing procedures for learning generalizations and practicing their application. However, unlike an embedded approach, normative orientations to spelling instruction may be the most indirect means through which to evoke individual change. Instruction must be dovetailed into the ongoing literate and orthographic development of the individual (Wilde, 1990).

Tailoring spelling instruction to individual development in the context of ongoing literacy activity requires the recognition of what to teach and when to attend to it. Consider Wesley's story in [this figure] as an example. Wesley, a second grader, tells his story using 16 words. If we include the reversal in *and,* 6 of the words are spelled conventionally. According to our criteria above, 5 words are candidates for spelling instruction *(CAM, OHVORE, HUOS, SICKR, FOTBALL).* These words can serve as the genesis for word families in mini-lesson settings, as we illustrate later. Once an assessment is made, the teacher solicits from Wesley which of these words he would like to study further. These words become part of an ongoing record for Wesley, as well as a class

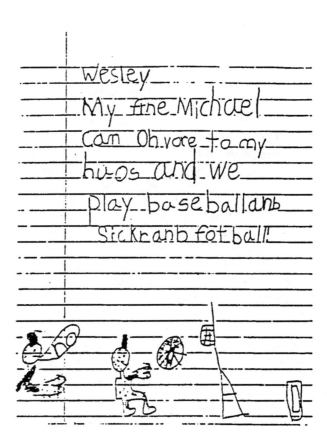

record that also includes words students voiced an interest in learning more about. These archives help the teacher design learning activities that are social and constructivistic.

Just as the botanist studies and classifies physical phenomena, teachers who embed their spelling instruction in the total language program invite students to view the words they read and compose as linguistic, cultural, and historical phenomena to be selected, studied, and classified. Driven by their subjective perspectives on orthographic generalizations, students make other wise internalized theories public in direct ways such as decoding attempts, invented spellings, and small group discussion of novel spelling patterns encountered in reading. The kaleidoscope of public renderings, coupled with reflective activities and responsive teacher guidance, establishes a dialogue between students through which individual change becomes possible (Vygotsky, 1978).

While the variation of social activity is unlimited, we see the social construction of word families as a powerful tool in spelling instruction. Developing these families is a theory-driven enterprise, especially when families take on the following characteristics:

1. Families illustrate specific orthographic generalizations.
2. Families are composed of words that are in the realm of students' oral language use.
3. Families are flexible in composition (i.e., some words fall within more than one family).

Let us offer an example of how constructing word families may follow from contextualized assessments.

## A Mini-Lesson in Ms. Butler's New Language Program

A quick assessment of student manuscripts placed in the "in box" of the editorial board alerts Ms. Butler to authors who are motivated to have their texts published for wider circulation. Ms. Butler uses this opportunity to teach spelling content to most or all of these authors, depending upon the students' ongoing development and the approximations that surface in the manuscripts awaiting publication.

Returning to Wesley's manuscript as an example, Ms. Butler might decide to focus on "vowel sounds controlled by the final-*e*" because she notices that Wesley consistently misrepresents the long vowel sound with conventional spelling patterns that cue short vowel sounds (e.g., *CAM*) in his daily journal writing and in the text ready to be edited. Since she has two other students in class who exhibit the same tendency and two who have learned the conventions, she convenes a heterogeneous mini-lesson group. Armed with their personalized spelling logs and writing journals, these students gather at a time specified by Ms. Butler.

As the mini-lesson gets underway, Ms. Butler solicits a short list of words that rhyme with *CAM* in Wesley's text. This yields *same, blame, shame, lame,* and *name.* The students generate the list and provide the conventional spellings of these words when they can; Ms. Butler provides conventional spellings when the students cannot. The students and teacher together theorize about orthographic regularities, coming to the conclusion that the final-*e* is a common structural feature.

Ms. Butler then mediates the construction of contrasting cases with a list of words that are verbalized frequently by her students and that contain spelling patterns that cue for the short *a* sound (e.g., *cap, tap, lap*). She pronounces each word, emphasizing the short vowel sound, and provides a contrast by using the long vowel sound. She asks the group to comb their texts and minds for words that they think fit the same pattern. Realizing that she already has a word family in her spelling log that is based on the same generalization, one student turns to the correct page and reads from the short vowel list those words which include the short *a: tap, rat, map, zap,* and *dad*.

The group deliberates over the proper description of the differences in the sound/symbol correspondences, settling on a tentative, "When you add an *e* on the end of a word, it gives the *a* a long sound." As time goes on, Ms. Butler leads the group through contrasting cases of long and short vowel constructions for all vowels, using the final *-e* as a visual cue. She emphasizes that these cues are for readers. Words are classified, grouped, and regrouped, and then documented in the students' spelling logs. With Ms. Butler's informed guidance, the group settles on, "A final *-e* tells the reader to say the long vowel sound," and its antithesis, "No final *-e* tells the reader to say the short vowel sound." Corrections are made to the students' texts, and the group disperses to engage in other activities.

In the future, students will add to these families when they encounter new words in their reading or as a result of a mini-lesson activity, or use them as a reminder when they edit their own and other students' texts. Generalizations will continue to be refined and new generalizations created to account for more complex spelling patterns. Students will learn that some spellings simply defy logic (e.g., *pterodactyl*), and these must simply be memorized until some other explanation surfaces around which a new family may evolve (e.g., historical explanation: that the spelling derives from the Greek roots, *pteron* and *daktylos*). For the most part, however, these young readers and writers will actively search the visual features of words for clues to pronounciation and meaning and begin to use this emergent knowledge to build bridges to new words.

## Conclusion

The alphabet is arguably the most efficient system of all writing systems for proficient literates (Gelb, 1952); however, since so few symbols account for so many sounds and combinations of sounds, learning how the alphabet works can be a tremendous challenge for emergent literates. The conventions that govern English orthography evolved over centuries of social and cultural development; the rationale underlying these "decisions" is no longer evident. Learning to use the alphabet as a social and intellectual tool requires tremendous amounts of inductively generated approximations, exposure to conventional forms, and contextual support.

Theories of social cognition place an enormous amount of influence upon the role of an adult or more capable peer in the socialization and learning of the young (e.g., Rogoff, 1990; Vygotsky, 1978); this responsibility holds true for socializing children into literate culture. In our view of embedded spelling instruction, students' approximations determine a significant amount of the content of spelling instruction. However, teachers play a critical, interpersonal role in students' development. In embedded approaches to spelling instruction, teachers are the orthographic insiders for their students. Teachers dovetail instruction into the ongoing literate and orthographic development of the individual when:

1. Teachers have the capability and opportunity to observe and assess students as students decode words when they read and produce spellings when they write.
2. Teachers have a flexible grasp of English orthography.
3. Teachers provide students access to word families that are relevant to students' emerging knowledge.
4. Teachers know how to exploit integrated reading and writing activity as the basis for assessment and instruction.
5. Students are given the opportunity to construct theories about orthography, individually and collectively.

As is true for Ms. Butler, educators must learn more about their personal theories of orthography to suppress the desire to teach didactically, to integrate the language modes so that language opportunities follow the natural course of development, and to subsume spelling instruction within the total language program.

## *References*

Adams, M. J. (1990). *Beginning to read: Thinking and learning about print.* Cambridge, MA: MIT Press.

Atwell, N. (1987). *In the middle.* Portsmouth, NH: Heinemann.

Bissex, G. (1985). *GNYS AT WRK: A child learns to read and write.* Cambridge, MA: Harvard University Press.

Calkins, L. (1986). *The art of teaching writing.* Portsmouth, NH: Heinemann.

Clay, M. (1985). *The early detection of reading difficulties.* Portsmouth, NH: Heinemann.

Deci, E. L., Vallerand, R. J., Pelletier, L. G., & Ryan, R. M. (1991). Motivation and education: The self-determination perspective. *Educational Psychologist, 26,* 325–346.

Ehri, L. (1991). Development of the ability to read words. In R. Barr, M. Kamil, P. Mosenthal, & P. D. Pearson (Eds.), *The handbook of reading research* (Vol. 2) (pp. 383–417). New York: Longman.

Gelb, I. J. (1952). *A study of writing.* Chicago, IL: University of Chicago Press.

Graves, D. (1983). *Writing: Teachers and children at work.* Portsmouth, NH: Heinemann.

Graves, D. (1991). *Building a literate classroom.* Portsmouth, NH: Heinemann.

Guba, E., & Lincoln, Y. S. (1989). *Fourth generation evaluation.* Newbury Park, CA: Sage.

Harste, J., Short, K., & Burke, C. (1988). *Creating classrooms for authors.* Portsmouth, NH: Heinemann.

Henderson, E. (1990). *Teaching spelling* (2nd ed.). Boston, MA: Houghton Mifflin.

Henderson, E., & Beers, J. W. (Eds.). (1980). *Developmental and cognitive aspects of learning to spell: A reflection of word knowledge.* Newark, DE: International Reading Association.

Lucas, C. K. (1988a). Toward ecological evaluation. *The Quarterly Newsletter of the National Writing Project and the Center for the Study of Writing, 10* (1), 1–17.

Lucas, C. K. (1988b). Toward ecological evaluation, Part 2. *The Quarterly Newsletter of the National Writing Project and the Center for the Study of Writing, 10* (2), 4–20.

MacGoon, A. J. (1977). Constructivist approaches in educational research. *Review of Educational research, 47,* 651–693.

Mason, J., & McCormick, C. (1981). *An investigation of prereading instruction from a developmental perspective: Foundations for literacy* (Tech. Rep. No. 224). Urbana, IL: University of Illinois, Center for the Study of Reading.

Morris, D. (1989). Editorial comment: A developmental perspective on spelling instruction. *Reading Psychology, 10,* iii–v.

O'Flahavan, J. F., & Tierney, R. J. (1990). Reading, writing, and critical thinking. In L. Idol & B. Jones (Eds.), *Educational values and cognitive instruction: Implications for reform* (pp. 41–64). Hillsdale, NJ: Lawrence Erlbaum.

Raphael, T. E., McMahon, S. I., Goatley, V. J., Bentley, J. L., Boyd, F. B., Pardo, L. S., & Woodman, D. A. (1992). Literature and discussion in the reading program. *Language Arts, 69,* 54–61.

Read, C. (1971). Preschool children's knowledge of English phonology. *Harvard Educational Review, 41,* 1–34.

Rogoff, B. (1990). *Apprenticeship in thinking.* New York: Oxford University Press.

Strickland, D., & Cullinan, B. (1990). Afterword. In M. Adams, *Beginning to read: Thinking and learning about print* (pp. 425–434). Cambridge, MA: MIT Press.

Temple, C., Nathan, R., Burris, N., & Temple, F. (1988). *The beginnings of writing* (2nd ed.). Boston, MA: Allyn & Bacon.

Templeton, S. (1979). The relationship between orthography and higher order phonological knowledge in older students. *Research in the Teaching of English, 13,* 255–264.

Valencia, S., McGinley, W., & Pearson, P. D. (1988). Assessing reading and writing. In G. Duffy (Ed.), *Reading in the middle school* (2nd ed.) (pp. 124–153). Newark, DE: International Reading Association.

Vygotsky, L. (1978). *Mind in society.* Cambridge, MA: Harvard University Press.

Wilde, S. (1990). A proposal for a new spelling curriculum. *The Elementary School Journal, 90,* 265–282.

Zutell, J. (1979). Spelling strategies of primary school children and their relationships to Piaget's concept of decentration. *Research in the Teaching of English, 13,* 69–80.

## CONTENT LITERACY GUIDE

**From: Teaching Spelling (2nd ed.)**
Edmund H. Henderson

1. About how long is a traditional spelling lesson?

2. What class of words occur most frequently in the English language?

3. How many words account for about 95 percent of everyday writing?

4. (T/F)  According to Henderson, a child must be able to read a word (not just sound it out) in order to study its spelling successfully.

   Why?

5. On what basis are traditional spelling lists "a true sample of natural language"?

6. (T/F)  Using a list approach to spelling means deemphasizing word meanings.

7. (T/F)  In formal spelling instruction, spelling principles are directly taught.

8. (T/F)  According to Henderson, some children need formal spelling instruction.

9. Describe what Henderson views as the potential of basal spelling programs.

10. (T/F)  Research has tended to support traditional notions of how formal spelling instruction should be sequenced.

# *FROM:* TEACHING SPELLING

EDMUND H. HENDERSON

## Spelling Instruction Today

In the majority of school systems today, a basal spelling program is adopted and a single grade-level speller is issued to each child. Formal spelling instruction is administered by the teacher in accordance with the directions given in the teacher's manual. These lessons are designed to fill about a fifteen-minute period in the teaching day, but much of the work is expected to be carried out by pupils independently. Typically, the teacher administers a pretest of list words on Monday and a post-test on Friday. Assigned study activities are carried out by the pupils during the week, and the teacher monitors the final evaluation and the grading-period tests.

## Core Vocabulary and Spelling Lists

One very helpful product of language research has been the careful documentation of words according to their frequency of occurrence in texts of various kinds (Thorndike and Lorge, 1944). Frequency counts are also available based on samples of children's writing (E. Horn, 1926; Jacobson, 1974). Still other assessments show the likelihood of a particular word's occurrence in basal readers across a grade-level progression (Harris and Jacobson, 1972). In addition, researchers have been able to show the probability of selected words being spelled correctly at varied grade levels (Green, 1955) and the most probable specific misspelling for selected words at grade-level progressions (Gates, 1937).

These statistical records serve a useful and common sense role for the preparation of a core list of spelling words for children to study. Because of the way that language works, certain words are bound to occur more frequently than others. Function words, those that declare the relationships among meanings, are by far the most frequently occurring. Words that are more homely and concrete often occur more frequently and certainly occur earlier in children's writing than do the words that are exotic or abstract.

It has been shown that a core of about five thousand words accounts for about 95 percent of the running words in everyday adult writing. Few would question the importance

*Source:* Edmund Henderson, *Teaching Spelling,* Second Edition. Copyright © 1990 by Houghton Mifflin Company. Reprinted with permission.

of knowing how to spell correctly words of such impressive utility. Quite obviously, children must be able to spell more words than just these, but if, in the course of study, these basic words can be sensibly included, one would certainly think that they should be.

From the point of view of development, the frequency configuration of English words is a happy one. High-frequency function words are largely Old English in origin, and though these are by now quite irregular phonetically, frequency supports them powerfully. The next large band of frequently occurring words serves to exemplify precisely the pattern-to-meaning relationship that applies to modern English spelling. Classically derived English words entered the language much later and are little used by beginners in either reading or writing. Thus, frequency tables can safely direct inclusion of words for study in a natural developmental hierarchy and predict as well their utility in pupils' writing.

The more detailed statistical accountings of words by reading level and by spelling attainment are also useful. To study a word for spelling, it is necessary that the pupil be able to read that word. This is true because learning to spell, at least beyond its most primitive stage, has little to do with sounding a word out. One must be able to speak the word naturally and then discern how this particular letter pattern goes beyond a one-to-one phonetic code. Accordingly, the authors of most spelling programs have chosen list words that pupils *can* read and that they *do* need to learn to spell.

Altogether, then, the core vocabulary from which modern spelling lists are made has a direct relation to language development. These lists have a high utility for the learner in their own right, and they are suitably representative of the underlying word-knowledge principles that require mastery. On these grounds it may be held that properly derived spelling lists today are not at all artificial but a true sample of natural language.

## Learning Spelling Words from Lists

Still, it may be asked, should spelling words be learned in lists or should they be acquired only in the context of reading and writing? Some educators are convinced that a contextual setting is the only admissible one for word study. The very strong feeling that motivates this anti-list position stems from the belief that meaning is the key to an understanding of English spelling. A concern for this principle is valid and deserves respect.

On the other hand, spelling does involve dealing with words one at a time. Meaning is important, but it is meaning in relation to alphabetic patterns. The context of this relationship is word, not sentence. If meaning were not emphasized as an important factor in the study of listed words, then a serious fault would be committed. There is, however, no reason why meaning may not be emphasized in list presentations—indeed, lists can be composed to highlight the particular meaning relationship to be taught, as with the spelling of roots, prefixes, inflectional endings, and homophones specifically.

Formal spelling instruction means that a plan for instruction is adopted and applied on a systematic and regular basis. Words to be learned are selected, spelling principles are taught directly, and practice is provided and maintained until pupils have an automatic control of what is taught. Mastery of English spelling is attained by some children without formal instruction. For most children, however, formal spelling instruction is absolutely necessary. No elementary or junior high curriculum can be considered adequate or responsible without such a plan, and the plan should be administered by teachers who understand its place and purpose.

Experienced teachers who thoroughly understand spelling development and word-study techniques can structure such a formal program, making use of the words that children meet in reading and writing. Indeed, such a design is often applied to children who are progressing rapidly and who have already mastered the basic spelling vocabulary usually studied by their peers. Similarly, children who are radically behind in spelling knowledge may require a teacher-designed plan of study that exceeds the scope of a typical basal spelling program. A good number of the ideas about pacing and planning for follow-up study in this chapter will be found useful in designing this kind of formal spelling instruction.

Most experienced teachers also make use of one or another of the commercially published spelling series, and there is good reason that they should. Basal spellers are adaptable to a wide range of language achievement and have the potential to deliver systematic, efficient, and correctly sequenced study across the grades. The adoption of such a series is thus a reasonable first step toward instituting formal spelling study within the school curriculum. These materials, however, do not work all by themselves. Teachers must fit them to their pupils and both pace and supplement practice as required by individuals and groups. The major objective of this chapter and the rest of the book is to describe the content of a sound basal spelling program grade by grade and to present the information needed in order to adjust and supplement such a program.

One important contribution of developmental spelling research has been to clarify the word-knowledge progression that normal children follow and so make it possible for teachers to know both what the content of a basal spelling program should be and when and how to follow up such study with individuals and groups. In the past the placement and pacing of word-study skills was based upon guesswork—common sense, tradition, and hunch. Today we have hard data against which to validate the scope and sequence of a formal instructional plan. Curiously, and I think not surprisingly, these data tend to support the general sequencing plan that has evolved traditionally. Radical programs have almost invariably failed; conservative programs have tended to succeed.

## CONTENT LITERACY GUIDE

**From: Beginning to Read: Thinking and Learning about Print**
Marilyn J. Adams
A Summary by Steven A. Stahl, Jean Osborn, and Fran Lehr
*From Spelling and Writing to Reading,* pp. 95–104

1. (T/F)  Emphasizing early writing tends to improve reading skills.

2. (T/F)  Montessori believed in teaching reading prior to writing.

3. Summarize the six common features of invented spelling:

   a.

   b.

   c.

   d.

   e.

   f.

4. What sort of spellings may warrant direct instruction due to children's difficulty at hearing them?

5. What forms the early "centerpiece" of students' self-expression on paper?

6. (T/F)  Clarke's study found that encouraging invented spelling tended to help the word recognition ability of low-readiness students more than did traditional spelling instruction.

7. (T/F)  High-readiness students were clearly at a disadvantage in the invented spelling environment.

8. Summarize the "tempting conclusion" about why invented spelling tended to be better for low-readiness readers.

9. (T/F)  Spelling development where invented spelling is encouraged is apt to be very gradual.

10. Why is the success of invented spelling in developing phonemic awareness and knowledge of the alphabetic principle especially promising?

**11.** (T/F)  Work with writing may well take the place of instruction and practice in reading.

**12.** Identify two positions taken by teachers of invented spelling concerning giving students correct spellings when they ask.

    a.

    b.

**13.** Why did Noah Webster advocate teaching reading through spelling?

**14.** (T/F)  Spelling-to-sound rules work better for pronouncing words seen in print than for spelling words known only in their spoken form.

**15.** Why is there more uncertainty in going from sound to spelling than from spelling to sound?

**16.** (T/F)  Spelling skills are highly correlated with reading ability.

**17.** (T/F)  Good spelling depends on being sensitive to *patterns* of letters, not individual sound-letter correspondences.

**18.** (T/F)  Poor spellers tend to rely on the initial letters of words when reading.

**19.** (T/F)  Knowledge of correct spelling assists in word recognition during reading.

**20.** On what does successful spelling improvement depend?

**21.** (T/F)  Spelling the word orally for students is more effective than showing it in print.

**22.** (T/F)  Teachers should habitually encourage students to look at the spelling of words.

**23.** How does time pressure limit reading as a way to improve spelling?

**24.** Why can most readers read more words than they can spell?

**25.** (T/F)  Copying words in isolation does not result in lasting spelling knowledge.

**26.** (T/F)  Reading is more beneficial to writing than is grammar study.

**27.** (T/F)  Children tend to incorporate content from what they read into their writing.

**28.** Summarize how early writing helps children conceptualize the nature of reading.

# *FROM:* BEGINNING TO READ
## THINKING AND LEARNING ABOUT PRINT

MARILYN J. ADAMS
A Summary by Steven A. Stahl, Jean Osborn, and Fran Lehr
*From Spelling and Writing to Reading*

Across evaluations of beginning reading programs, emphasis on writing activities is repeatedly shown to result in special gains in early reading achievement.[1] Although the supportive relations between reading and writing surely run in both directions, this chapter concentrates on those that run *from* spelling and writing *to* reading.

## *Early Spelling and Phonemic Awareness*

In an increasing number of American classrooms, children are encouraged to write even before they receive much instruction in reading. Although the idea of "write first, read later" was long promoted by Maria Montessori,[2] writing instruction, until recently, was generally postponed until after reading was well underway.

In a classic study of children who learned to read well before entering school, it was observed that, for many of these children, writing came first. Indeed, the "ability to read seemed almost like a by-product of [the] ability to print and spell."[3]

The spellings that young children produce are, of course, often incorrect by conventional standards. Using their knowledge of letter names and sounds, children spell the words as they sound to them. And, as shown by their spellings, the children quickly develop an impressive appreciation of the phonemic structure of the English language.

The educational interest in such children centers on the prospect that their phonemic awareness develops through their efforts to spell. Does such awareness grow through the process of having children figure out sound-to-spelling translations on their own? Research evidence is scant. However, examining the spellings that children produce suggests that it does. The invented spellings of different children have long been recognized to exhibit a number of common features.

These common features have been summarized as follows:[4]

- Often, children will incorporate whole letter names into their spellings: *YL* (while), *THAQ* (thank you), *NR* (nature), *PPL* (people).
- More generally, the consonants tend to contribute part of their names—though sometimes unconventionally: *KAN* (can), *JRIV* (drive).
- Long vowels generally speak for themselves: *BOT* (boat), *STA* (stay), *AGRE* (angry).
- Short vowels come as close as they can: *BAD* (bed), *COL* (call), *LUKS* (looks), or are omitted altogether: *TST* (test).
- Letters such as *l* and *r* tend to lose their vowels: *GRL* (girl), *KLR* (color), *PKN* (picking).
- And *n* and *m* before stop consonants often go unrepresented: *WOT* (won't), *PLAT* (plant).

Thus we have one explanation for the peculiarities of children's invented spellings. In deciding how to represent a word, they tend to exploit the names of the letters, rather than a direct image of the sounds they formally represent. Over time, children's writing gradually but clearly reflects increasing knowledge of the spellings of particular words and of general orthographic conventions. In addition, it reflects increasing sensitivity to the phonemic structures of words. Of particular interest, young writers have special difficulty in hearing the separate phonemes of consonant clusters, suggesting that the spellings of consonant blends warrant explicit instruction attention.

## Instructional Issues

In the classroom, invented spelling is generally encouraged in simple ways. Students are given regular opportunities to express themselves on paper. Initially, at least, the centerpieces of their products are typically illustrations. With encouragement from their teachers and from watching their classmates, students begin, first to caption, then to write stories about the pictures they have drawn. In such classrooms, teachers report providing little explicit instruction on exactly how to go about invented spellings—"Just spell it the way it sounds. I'll be able to read it."

The major reservation to promoting invented spelling in the classroom is the concern that students' invented spellings might interfere with their ability to recognize the correct spellings of words. A recent study focused precisely on this issue.[5]

All of the students in the study received reading instruction through a basal reading program along with supplementary phonics activities. In addition, all were regularly engaged in creative writing sessions each week. The students in two of the four classrooms were encouraged to invent their spellings while writing; the students in the other two classrooms were encouraged to spell correctly.

During writing sessions in the classrooms in which invented spellings were encouraged, teachers circulated, encouraging effort and discussing ideas that might be developed.

The teachers discouraged erasing ("just cross it out"), and they did not spell words for students, telling them that, instead, they should sound out the words and print the letters thus heard. In addition, the teachers told students that their letter choices were not always going to be correct, and emphasized that that did not matter at the moment.

In contrast, when students in the classrooms emphasizing traditional spellings were ready to write, they got out their dictionaries or personal word lists, which they used when they wanted to write a word they were not sure how to spell. The students often consulted friends for help in finding a word in the dictionary or for confirmation on how a word should be spelled. Teachers printed words on the chalkboard or on the students' papers, and spelled words aloud while students printed the letters. Teachers also circulated to see that students having difficulty were able to write something. In the beginning months, this involved having some students dictate their stories and then copy the teacher's printing.

Examinations of writing samples collected between November and March indicated that the students using traditional spelling wrote with slightly more sophisticated vocabulary and more complex syntax and committed far fewer spelling errors (6%) than those using invented spellings (34%). But the students using traditional spelling tended to write much shorter stories.

Given the difference in the classroom emphases for these two groups, did the students' spelling accuracy reflect real differences in their knowledge? Both groups displayed considerable but comparable difficulty in spelling high-frequency but orthographically irregular words. However, in contrast to the evidence obtained from the writing samples, the children in the invented spelling group were significantly more successful with both a list of lower frequency, regularly spelled words and with the words on a standardized spelling test.

While the performance of the two groups was quite comparable on a reading comprehension test, it differed significantly on several tests of word recognition skill. Children in the classrooms that relied on invented spelling significantly outperformed the others on reading regularly spelled nonsense words and on untimed reading of lists of high-frequency irregular and lower frequency regular words.[6]

On balance, the results seem to indicate a definite advantage for the invented over the traditional spelling groups. Yet one wonders why. True, the children in the invented spelling group wrote more, but their evident attentiveness to correct spelling during writing seemed so much less. For example, in the writing samples analyzed, spelling accuracy increased from 88% to 95% for the traditional spellers between November and March; for the inventive spellers it decreased from 66% to 58%.

A closer look at the results of the study showed that though the performance of the traditional spellers was often lower than that of the inventive spellers, the range of scores was often greater. For the high-readiness students, the invented spelling and the traditional spelling groups performed similarly on spelling and word recognition posttests. *For the low-readiness students, however, those in the invented spelling group significantly outperformed their traditionally instructed peers on the majority of the measures.*

Could the difference between the performance of the low-readiness students come from the ways they were encouraged to confront holes in their knowledge? The traditional spellers dictated their earliest stories. The inventive spellers were on their own from the start. The traditional spellers were given correct "models" to follow. The inventive spellers had to figure the system out by themselves. The tempting conclusion is, in other words, that the advantage of the low-readiness inventive spellers reflected a better developed sense of the relations between spoken and written words, a sense that had grown from their own necessarily thoughtful and active efforts to spell.

Another study of the written products of children who had been encouraged to write and spell creatively in class showed that spelling development is often quite gradual.[7] The earliest "spellings" of many children often captured but a sampling of the phonemes of the word of interest, and not always correctly.

In overview, classroom encouragement of invented spellings and independent writing from the start seems a very promising approach toward the development of phonemic awareness and orthographic skills. Beyond this, early writing seems an incomparable means of developing children's abilities to reflect on their own thoughts, to elaborate and organize their ideas, and to express themselves in print. Moreover, such challenges require children to think actively about print.[8]

## Invented Spelling and Phonics

Restricting concern to the issue of learning to read words, note that the process of inventing spellings is essentially a process of phonics. Not surprisingly, then, how well sounds are represented in prereaders' invented spellings is found to be predicted by their level of phonemic awareness[9] and to predict their later success in learning to read words.[10] In addition, there is evidence that invented spelling activity simultaneously develops phonemic awareness and promotes understanding of the alphabetic principle. This is extremely promising, especially in view of the difficulty with which children are found to acquire these insights through other teaching methods.

Equally inspiring are the reports that early writing activities promote children's interest in learning about what words say and how they are spelled. Yet these are only starting points. Exercise in writing and invented spelling may significantly enhance children's attitudes toward and their linguistic readiness for reading. As such, it may invaluably complement instruction in reading.

But exercise in writing cannot take the place of instruction and practice in reading and word recognition. Note that all of the children discussed above were receiving instruction in reading and word recognition alongside their exercises in writing, and that their effects cannot be separated. Further, for children's interest in how words actually are spelled to be functional, they must be exposed to properly written text. For children to learn how words actually are spelled, they must also learn to read. But this raises one of the sticky points among advocates of invented spelling.

## Learning How to Spell Correctly

When or how should children be taught about correct spellings? Some advocates suggest that parents and teachers should take care to provide correct spellings whenever a child asks.[11] In contrast, the invented spelling teachers in the study just reviewed not only refused to answer when students asked for correct spellings, but actively discouraged such questions.[12] Going one more step, it might be argued that in the coming world of word processors, letter perfect spelling will be as obsolete a skill as using logarithmic tables to multiply. But let's not be hasty.

Prior to this century—in fact, for thousands of years prior to this century—spelling drill was the principal means of teaching children to read. The reasons for this emphasis on spelling surely included many that are of little interest to us now—the relative availability of chalk tablets versus books, the appropriateness within other eras of drill and rote recitation, the classroom structure of the one room school . . . or, try this: Noah Webster is said to have held that spelling was the proper way to teach reading because at the earliest instructional levels, the child's mind was not ready to deal with word meanings.[13] However remote these reasons may be from today's widely held educational philosophies and processes, there must also have been one more: For the method to have prevailed for thousands of years, people must have felt that it worked.

## The Relation Between Reading and Spelling Skills

Good spelling cannot be a direct derivative of phonological knowledge. First, people with different dialects still can and do learn standard spellings. Second, and more persuasively, spelling-to-sound rules just plain do not work in reverse. In one study, 166 spelling-to-sound correspondences were found successfully to generate pronunciations for 90% of the one- and two-syllable words known by six to nine year olds.[14] Applying those rules in reverse, however, resulted in correct sound-to-spelling translations for fewer than half of these words.[15] In another study, 300 spelling rules correctly predicted the spelling of fewer than 50% of the 17,000 words studied.[16]

Even if they worked better, 300 is probably more rules than one could expect the average fourth grader to have usefully learned. Yet, in a spelling bee between fourth graders and a computer that had been programmed with these rules, the fourth graders won handily.[17]

The problem, more specifically, seems to be that there is considerably more uncertainty in sound-to-spelling than in spelling-to-sound translations. For example, the letter *f* quite reliably symbolizes the phoneme /f/. In contrast, the phoneme /f/ can be spelled as *f, ff, ph,* or *gh.*

Some spellings may help the reader to perceive the relations between word cousins, as in *sign/signature,bomb/bombard,* and *muscle/muscular.*[18] But they are not terribly helpful for the speller. Further, spelling skills appear not to be associated with receptive and productive language capacities, nor with reading ability. Still more provocative, however, are the contrasting patterns of behaviors found among normal children who are good spellers as opposed to poor ones.

Just as in good reading, good spelling seems to depend on sensitivity to patterns of letters, rather than individual letter-sound correspondences.[19] Good spellers tend to use their knowledge of patterns in their spelling of pseudowords, spelling *jation* in analogy to *nation*—instead of *jashun,* as would be produced by a letter-by-letter translation.[20] Poor spellers, in contrast, do tend to produce such letter-by-letter translations, relying more on simpler spelling-to-sound rules.

Good spellers also seem more sensitive to whether a spelling "looks right." [21] Yet researchers have shown this to reflect their greater knowledge of which letters typically go together, the orthographic knowledge discussed earlier, rather than any superiority in visual imagery.

Think about what you have to do to spell a never-seen word independently. First you must analyze the sounds in the spoken word and then produce the spelling patterns associated with those sounds. Difficulty in either phonemic analysis or knowledge of spelling patterns, or both, will interfere with good spelling.

The reading behavior of good and poor spellers similarly reflects differences in knowledge of spelling patterns. During reading, poor spellers tend to rely on the initial letters of words and to make substitution errors that make sense but do not contain the same sounds as the text word. [22]

Remember that efficient reading of a word proceeds through the complete recognition of individual letters. To the extent that the spelling patterns of the word are familiar, recognition of the pattern will be accompanied by phonological translation. To the extent that the word is also familiar, the meaning also will be stimulated.

If students have not learned a complete representation of a spelling pattern, they cannot process the word rapidly without glossing over the unfamiliar parts of its spelling. On the other hand, when students gloss over the complete spelling of a word as they read, they miss the opportunity to learn its spelling more thoroughly. To release them from this dilemma, their spelling knowledge must be improved.

## Directing Students' Attention to Spellings

Successful spelling improvement depends on getting children to attend to unfamiliar patterns. One may figure out the correct spelling of a word either by having somebody else spell it aloud or by looking at it in print. Research indicates that the experience of seeing a word in print is not only superior to hearing it spelled but, further, is an extremely powerful and effective means of acquiring its spelling. [23] In addition, the experience of seeing or imagining a word's spelling, as contrasted with repeatedly hearing the word or even rehearsing it aloud, has been shown to be a superior means toward remembering its pronunciation, even among first graders. [24] One obvious instructional implication of this evidence is that teachers should habitually encourage students to look at the spellings of words. Teachers should write the words of interest on the board or point to them on the page. Merely spelling words aloud, relatively speaking, is a waste of time.

Reading, because it requires children to look at words in print, should be a superlative means of learning the spellings of words. But as quickly as we recognize this point, we realize its limitations.

Where the purpose of reading is to comprehend, the process of word recognition is under considerable time pressure. Readers can invest extra time in identifying or sounding out letter sequences only at the expense of losing the meaning of the surrounding text. Yet unless the word is already familiar, readers can fully process its letter sequences only through the time-consuming application of conscious effort and attention.

The only way to process a troublesome word fully and comprehend the sentence to which it belongs is by working out the word and then rereading the sentence. Although, for purposes of learning, this is an excellent strategy,[25] an easier alternative exists. Specifically, readers can finesse their difficulties with the word. Relying on whatever fragments of its spelling pattern they have perceived, along with contextual cues, they can just gloss over the fuzzier visual details. To a greater or lesser extent, this option is probably used by all readers. The result is that virtually all readers can read more words than they can spell.

In contrast, if students are given isolated words to spell, there is no comprehension pressure to divert their attention. Moreover, research demonstrates that the process of copying new words strengthens students' memory for those words and does so rather enduringly.[26] Perhaps this should not be surprising—the writing of a word forces attention to its full sequence of letters. For students, the thought that somebody else might evaluate their products may encourage such attention all the more.

In summary, the arguments for including spelling instruction as a major component of the reading program are strong. Learning about spelling reinforces children's knowledge about common letter sequences. It also reinforces their knowledge about spelling-sound relationships and may help children become aware of word parts. Because of this, spelling practice enhances reading proficiency.

## The Influence of Spelling on the Perception of Sounds and Meaning

The connections between sound and spelling are so strong that even adults, when they hear a nonsense word that violates common spelling patterns (such as /sbal/) tend to think they heard a familiar pattern (such as /spal/).[27] Even when encouraged to listen harder and try something different, many adults have trouble—indeed, cannot—hear the actual sounds as they are spoken. They know how such syllables should be spelled, and that knowledge prevails. In contrast to the adults, kindergarten and first-grade listeners tend to hear and spell the sounds as spoken.[28]

Clearly, the connections between sound patterns and spelling patterns must enhance our ability to remember or figure out how a new word is spelled. They must enhance our ability to recognize a printed rendition of a word once having heard it. And they must enhance our ability to recognize a spoken rendition of a word once having seen it in print.

## Beyond Spelling: Writing

Even among older students, the strongest measurable links between reading and writing abilities tend to cluster at the level of spelling and word recognition skills. But just as there is more to reading than word recognition, there is more to writing than spelling. And there is much more to the reading-writing connection than just reading and spelling individual words.

Indeed, children's writing is strongly influenced by their reading. One review of the literature on the reading-writing relationship makes the point that better writers tend to read more than poorer writers.[29] Moreover, the reading experiences in which children are engaged are more beneficial to their writing abilities than either grammar study or extra writing practice.[30] Finally, children tend to incorporate into their writing not only the content of material they have just previously read, but also its syntactic patterns and themes.

Nevertheless, for young or uncertain readers, the potential contribution of writing to reading runs much deeper than any concern of form or style. In particular, as children become authors, as they struggle to express, refine, and reach audiences through their own writing, they actively come to grips with the most important reading insights of all.

Through writing, children learn that text is not preordained or immutable truth. It is human voice. It is produced by people—people with their own personal and sometimes inappropriate sets of information and points of view; people with their own prior assumptions about who their readers will be and what those readers will already know and think; people who themselves struggled, and not always more fruitfully, to find clear ways of expressing the ideas and information in their texts. Through writing, children learn that the purpose of text is not to be read, but to be understood.

They learn that text does not contain meaning, but is meaningful only to the extent that it is understood by the reader. They learn that different readers respond differently to the same text. They also learn that sometimes understanding comes only through hard work even for the best of readers. They learn that cogent writing may depend on consulting other sources, inviting the insight that cogent reading may do this too. They learn that text is written about an underlying organization, inviting the insight that it may be read that way too.

They learn, in short, that reading is about thinking, and that lesson is essential. For the beginner, as we have seen, learning to read depends critically on thinking and understanding. Yet more. The ultimate power of text is not from its understanding but from its broader interpretation, its critique, its extension through the reader's own knowledge and thought and to the reader's own needs and interests. It is this power, most of all, that we want to give all of our children.

# Endnotes

1. See: Aukerman, R. C. (1971). *Approaches to beginning reading*. New York: Wiley.

   Aukerman, R. C. (1984). *Approaches to beginning reading* (2nd ed.). New York: Wiley.

   Bond, G. L., & Dykstra, R. (1967). The cooperative research program in first-grade reading instruction. *Reading Research Quarterly, 2*, 5–142.

   Chall, J. S. (1967). *Learning to read: The great debate*. New York: McGraw-Hill.

   Evans, M. A., & Carr, T. H. (1985). Cognitive abilities, conditions of learning, and the early development of reading skill. *Reading Research Quarterly, 20*, pp. 327–350.
2. Montessori, M. (1966). *The secret of childhood*. New York: Ballantine Books.
3. Durkin, D. (1966). *Children who read early: Two longitudinal studies* (p. 137). New York: Teachers College Press.
4. Chomsky, C. (1979) op. cit. Chomsky attributes these observations to Read, C. (1975). *Children's categorization of speech sounds in English*. Urbana, IL: National Council of Teachers of English.

5. Clarke, L. K. (1988). Invented versus traditional spelling in first graders' writing: Effects on learning to spell and read. *Research in the Teaching of English, 22,* pp. 281–309.

6. Baron, J., & Treiman, R. (1980). Use of orthography in reading and learning to read. In J. Kavanaugh & R. Venezky (Eds.), *Orthography, reading and dyslexia.* Baltimore, MD: University Park Press.

7. Ehri, L. C. (1988). Movement into word reading and spelling: How spelling contributes to reading. In J. Mason (Ed.), *Reading and writing connections* (pp. 65–81). Boston, MA: Allyn & Bacon.

8. Adams, M. J. (1989). Thinking skills curricula: Their promise and progress. *Educational Psychologist, 24,* 25–77.

9. Liberman, I. Y., Rubin, H., Duques, S., & Carlisle, J. (1989). Linguistic abilities and spelling proficiency in kindergartners and adult poor spellers. In D. B. Gray and J. F. Kavanagh (Eds.), *Biobehavioral measures of dyslexia* (pp. 163–176). Parkton, MD: New York Press.

Morris, D. (1981). Concept of word: A developmental phenomenon in beginning reading and writing processes. *Language Arts, 58,* pp. 659–668.

10. Mann, V. A., Tobin, P., & Wilson, R. (1987). Measuring phonological awareness through the invented spelling of kindergartners. *Merrill-Palmer Quarterly, 33,* pp. 365–391.

Morris, D., & Perney, J. (1984). Developmental spelling as a predictor of first-grade reading achievement. *Elementary School Journal, 84,* pp. 440–457.

11. Chomsky, C. (1979) op. cit.

Clay, M. M. (1975). *What did I write? Beginning writing behaviour.* Portsmouth, NH: Heinemann.

12. Clarke (1988) op. cit.

13. Venezky, R. L. (1980). From Webster to Rice to Roosevelt. In U. Frith (Ed.), *Cognitive processes in spelling* (pp. 9–30). New York Academic Press.

14. Berdiansky, B., Cronnell, B., & Koehler, J. (1969). *Spelling-sound relations and primary form-class descriptions for speech comprehension vocabularies of 6–9 year olds.* Southwest Regional Laboratory for Educational Research and Development, Technical Report No. 15. Cited in Smith, F., *Psycholinguistics and reading.* New York: Holt, Rinehart, & Winston.

15. Cronnell, B. A. (1970). *Spelling-to-sound correspondences for reading vs. sound-to-spelling correspondences.* Tech. Note TN2-70-15. Los Alamitos, CA: Southwest Regional Laboratory. Cited in Desberg, P., Elliott, D. E., & Marsh, G. (1980). American Black English and spelling. In U. Frith (Ed.), *Cognitive processes in spelling.* New York: Academic Press.

16. Hanna, P. R., et al. (1966). *Phoneme-grapheme correspondences as cues to spelling improvement.* Washington, DC: USOE Publication No. 32008.

Cronnell (1970) op. cit.

17. Simon, D. P., & Simon, H. A. (1973). Alternative uses of phonemic information in spelling. *Review of Educational Research, 43,* pp. 115–137. Cited in Desberg, P., Elliott, D. E., & Marsh, G. (1980). American Black English and spelling. In U. Frith (Ed.), *Cognitive processes in spelling.* New York: Academic Press.

18. See Chomsky, N., & Halle, M. (1968). *The sound pattern of English.* New York: Harper & Row.

19. Baron, J., Treiman, R., Wilf, J. F., & Kellman, P. (1980). Spelling and reading by rules. In U. Frith (Ed.), *Cognitive processes in spelling* (pp. 159–194). New York: Academic Press.

Barron, R. W. (1980). Visual and phonological strategies in reading and spelling. In U. Frith (Ed.), *Cognitive processes in spelling* (pp. 195–214). New York: Academic Press.

Sloboda, J. A. (1980). Visual imagery and individual differences in spelling. In U. Frith (Ed.), *Cognitive processes in spelling* (pp. 231–250). New York: Academic Press.

20. Marsh, G., Friedman, M., Welch, V., & Desberg, P. (1980). The development of strategies in spelling. In U. Frith (Ed.), *Cognitive processes in spelling* (pp. 339–353). New York: Academic Press.
21. Sloboda (1980) op. cit.
22. Baron, Treiman, Wilf, & Kellman (1980) op. cit.
23. Henderson, L., & Chard, J. (1980). The readers' implicit knowledge of orthographic structure. In U. Frith (Ed.), *Cognitive processes in spelling* (pp. 85–116). New York: Academic Press.
24. Ehri & Wilce (1979) op. cit.
25. Dahl, P. R., & Samuels, S. J. (1979). An experimental program for teaching high speed word recognition and comprehension skills. In J. E. Button, T. C. Lovitt, & T. D. Rowland (Eds.), *Communications research in learning disabilities and mental retardation.* Baltimore, MD: University Park Press.

    Herman, P. A. (1985). The effect of repeated readings on reading rate, speech pauses, and word recognition accuracy. *Reading Research Quarterly, 20,* pp. 553–565.

    Samuels, S. J. (1985). Automaticity and repeated reading. In J. Osborn, P. T. Wilson, & R. C. Anderson (Eds.), *Reading education: Foundations for a literate America* (pp. 215–230). Lexington, MA: Lexington Books.
26. Whittlesea, B. W. A. (1987). Preservation of specific experiences in the representation of general knowledge. *Journal of Experimental Psychology: Learning, Memory, & Cognition, 13,* pp. 3–17.
27. Treiman, R. (1985d). Spelling of stop consonants after /s/ by children and adults. *Applied Psycholinguistics, 6,* pp. 262–282.
28. See Treiman, R. (1985c). Phonemic awareness and spelling: Children's judgments do not always agree with adults'. *Journal of Experimental Child Psychology, 39,* pp. 182–201.
29. Stotsky, S. (1984). Research on reading/writing relationships: A synthesis and suggested directions. In J. M. Jensen (Ed.), *Composing and comprehending* (pp. 7–22). Urbana, IL: ERIC Clearinghouse on Reading and Communication Skills; Urbana, IL: National Council of Teachers of English.
30. Ibid.

## *Integrating Sources*

1. Can Adams's recommendation to occasionally copy words in isolation be reconciled with the notion of embedded instruction?

2. Locate and contrast the advice given by these sources for contending with the problem of delays in acquiring correct spelling.

3. With respect to spelling instruction, do the views of Adams align more closely with those of Henderson or with those of O'Flahavan and Blassberg? Give your reasons.

## *Classroom Implications*

**1.** Discuss embedded spelling instruction in terms of practicality.

**2.** Do you think the case for embedded spelling instruction varies with grade level? Explain your answer.

## *Annotated Bibliography*

### Spelling

Allred, R. A. (1993). Integrating proven spelling content and methods with emerging literacy programs. *Reading Psychology, 14,* 15–31.

*This article recommends blending techniques popular in whole language programs with direct instruction in core spelling words.*

Barone, D. (1992). Whatever happened to spelling? The role of spelling instruction in process-oriented classrooms. *Reading Psychology, 13,* 1–17.

*Practitioners are surveyed on common approaches to spelling. Four research-based recommendations are provided.*

Glazer, S. M. (1994). A meaningful way to assess spelling. *Teaching Pre K–8, 24*(7), 87–88.

*A "Spelling Trend Assessment Sheet," useful in assessing spelling problems and noting trends within a student's development, is described.*

Gordon, J., et al. (1993). Spelling interventions: A review of literature and implications for instruction for students with learning disabilities. *Learning Disabilities Research and Practice, 8,* 175–181.

*This reviews 17 intervention studies for students with learning disabilities and provides implications for practice relative to the size of spelling units, computer-assisted instruction, peer tutoring, modeling, modality, and study techniques.*

Opitz, M. F. (1993). Adapting the spelling basal for spelling workshop. *Reading Teacher, 47,* 106–113.

*A workshop approach to the use of spelling basals is described as a modification that leads to greater engagement and interest.*

Routmen, R. (1993). The uses and abuses of invented spelling. *Instructor, 102*(9), 36–39.

*This describes how elementary teachers can get good results by striking a balance between writing and spelling. The use of core word lists and conferences are recommended.*

## *You Become Involved*

### Spelling

1. The following story was written by a six-year-old girl:

   *Ounce ther was a lone lee fraf and all his old frends did was make fasise at him but he onlee smild be kuos he was alive. But one he got home he notiste*

*that they were all cwiit to hav a porte for him and he was so supriste that day they all so had dringks to. And that was his brth day porte and he was six years old all of the livd haple ever aftr*
*the end*

### Translation:

*Once there was a lonely giraffe, and all his old friends did was make faces at him, but he only smiled because he was alive. But one day [when] he got home he noticed that they were quiet to have a party for him, and he was so surprised that day. They also had drinks too. And that was his birthday party and he was six years old. All of them lived happily ever after.*
*The End*

Examine the invented and conventional spellings to determine appropriate actions a teacher might take with this child.

2. Compare your conclusions with the four conditions O'Flahavan and Blassberg identified in their article. Would they have agreed with your approach?

3. Identify a school (perhaps your own) in which invented spelling is strongly encouraged in the primary grades. Talk with several teachers in the intermediate grades and ask if they have encountered spelling problems they attribute to the invented spelling policy. If they have noticed problems, what measures have they taken to contend with them? Do you agree with their approaches? Has the invented spelling policy caused dissention between primary and intermediate teachers? Explain.

# Chapter 7

# *Assessment*

The issue of reading assessment has led to pointed debate in a range of educational forums (Greene, 1994; McLain & Mayer, 1994; Valencia et al., 1994). Perhaps not surprisingly, the issue is complex and involves a number of specific questions—debates within the debate. In our opinion, five of these are especially important in defining the overall issue of reading assessment.

Historically, students' assessment data have been used for making instructional decisions, such as student placement, class grouping, materials selection, and so on. In addition, assessment procedures have been used to measure literacy program effectiveness and to track student achievement over time. More recently, school districts and government leaders have utilized assessment results to support various types of school reform, most notably in the areas of teacher accountability and curricular change (Pearson & Stallman, 1993).

## *Administrative versus Instructional Uses of Assessment Results*

There seems to be little argument that administrators and governmental units are entitled to information regarding student growth (Bruce et al., 1993; White & Kapinus, 1994). Standardized tests have traditionally served this function, but they have occasioned sharp criticisms. Some educators now recommend that the administrative "need to know" be satisfied by compiling much less formal classroom assessment data. For example, portfolios for individual students can be quantified and the results accumulated across large groups. Major logistical problems are involved with such a recommendation, although statewide initiatives have provided instructive first steps.

Recently, initiatives have developed to establish national standards for literacy programs and instructional practices (*Standards,* 1994). These plans are in the early stages of development, but the ramifications will undoubtedly have important effects on future directions for many literacy programs.

## *Process versus Product Assessment*

Any test designed to measure a child's ability in a given area at a given time is primarily concerned with the *product* of learning. On the other hand, measures such as observation and miscue analysis, designed to provide information about the processes of reading, tend to be more qualitative in nature. Quantitative product measures include standardized tests but also tests devised to measure the mastery of specific skills. Whether a teacher's practice is better informed by specific-skill product tests or by continuously compiled process measures will depend largely on the teacher's instructional philosophy. Much of the controversy in this area is a direct result of conflicting literacy philosophies concerning the role of the teacher, the effective use of literacy materials, and the type of assessment being used.

## *Traditional versus Progressive Standardized Comprehension Formats*

Traditionally, standardized tests of reading comprehension have relied on short passages followed by a combination of literal and inferential comprehension questions. Sometimes, the troublesome task of composing good questions has been circumvented by using a multiple-choice cloze format, which requires the reader to choose the best word for completing sentences. These approaches have been challenged in recent years on several grounds. First, they fail to assess a student's ability to integrate information across large samples of text. Second, they fail to account for prior knowledge. Present-day initiatives to bring comprehension test formats into line with reading theory have led to longer selections (for example, entire short stories or textbook chapters), to prior knowledge tests administered before the students begin to read, and to the use of questions that draw on information located at more than one point in the selection. Whether such test reforms can satisfy critics is inevitably related to a question that is essentially political: What should be expected of students in terms of comprehension?

## *Constructive versus Reconstructive Assessment of Reading*

If you believe that comprehension is largely a matter of discerning what an author has intended to convey, then you have taken a reconstructive view. That is, you probably see the goal of the reader to be "reconstructing" the author's meaning that has been encoded in print. If so, you probably have little objection to using traditional assessment formats to determine the extent to which students have been successful in their effort to reconstruct meaning. On the other hand, you may view the reading process as a "transaction" between what a reader *wishes* to derive from a text and what the text offers the reader. A reader's personal desires, cultural background, language distinctions, and so forth will all determine what is actually "constructed" from a given reading experience. If you take this view, then a traditional comprehension assessment format will have serious shortcomings in that it will have been constructed by someone removed from the immediate learning environment, who has specific ideas about what meaning a reader should derive, which answers to questions are "correct," and so on.

## Situated versus Decontextualized Assessment

Standardized tests, and for that matter other types of paper-and-pencil tests, may produce misleading results because they require students to apply skills in artificial, contrived settings. Critics of such measures have argued that it is more valid to observe how students perform "authentic" tasks undertaken for reasons the students value. That is to say, the assessment should be situated within the learning context (Farr & Greene, 1993). This view has great appeal but poses serious logistical problems. It might prove especially difficult to use truly situated assessment for administrative purposes given the lack of uniformity among the techniques used by various teachers. One of the outcomes of the drive toward situated assessment has been the development of portfolios. These provide collections of records of performance during authentic tasks. Whether the benefits of portfolios outweigh their inherent disadvantages (e.g., size, subjectivity, lack of uniformity, etc.) is a decision that individual teachers must ultimately make.

## As You Read

Roger Farr attempts the difficult task of building a consensus between opposing views of reading assessment. You must judge for yourself whether he succeeds. Marie M. Clay is noted for less conventional approaches to assessment and at present may represent a midpoint between the extreme views associated with this issue.

We suggest that you attempt to clarify your own position with regard to the following questions as you study the broad and complex issue of reading assessment:

1. How can a district's need to monitor literacy growth best be met by classroom teachers?
2. To what extent have reforms in the design of standardized tests made them more valid measures?
3. Are process or product measures better suited to the ongoing assessment needs of classroom teachers? Is there a place for both?
4. Is comprehension better seen as the construction or the reconstruction of meaning? Again, is there a place for both views?
5. Is situated, performance-based assessment significantly more valid than traditional paper-and-pencil measures?

# *References*

Bruce, B. C., et al. (1993). *The content and curricular validity of the 1992 national assessment of educational progress in reading.* Urbana, IL: Center for the Study of Reading.

Farr, R., & Greene, B. (1993). Improving reading assessment: Understanding the social and political agenda for testing. *Educational Horizons, 72,* 20–27.

Greene, B. G. (1994). Writing models, portfolios, and performances. *Reading Research and Instruction, 33,* 257–262.

McLain, K., & Mayer, V. (1994). *Informal assessment: An organized meld of evaluative information.* (ERIC Document Reproduction Service No. ED 366 936).

Pearson, D., & Stallman, A. C. (1993). *Approaches to the future of reading assessment: Resistance, complacency, reform. Technical report no. 575.* Urbana, IL: Center for the Study of Reading.

*Standards for the assessment of reading and writing.* (1994). Newark, DE: International Reading Association.

Valencia, S. W., et al. (1994). *Authentic reading assessment: Practices and possibilities.* Newark, DE: International Reading Association.

White, S., & Kapinus, B. (1994). 1994 NAEP assessment in reading. *Focus on NAEP.* (ERIC Document Reproduction Service No. ED 366 915).

**Putting It All Together: Solving the Reading Assessment Puzzle**
Roger Farr
*The Reading Teacher,* September 1992, 26–37

1. Describe the "truly puzzling" irony identified by Farr.

2. What factors led to the increase in standardized, norm-referenced testing and state mini-mum competency testing?

3. How well have standardized test results confirmed the public's belief that reading ability is declining?

4. How has analysis of ACT and SAT score declines supported the public view that poor schools are to blame?

5. Do you think Farr would support Finn's call for national achievement tests? Why or why not?

6. What distinction does Farr make between *show* portfolios and *working* portfolios?

**7.** To what two causes does Farr attribute the increase in the amount of testing?

a.

b.

**8.** What is Farr's "bottom line" with respect to the acceptability of any assessment?

**9.** (T/F)   Recent public/federal initiatives seem to be moving toward performance-based assessment.

(T/F)   Administrators, in Farr's view, need both normative and criterion-referenced information.

**10.** How do the information needs of parents differ from those of the public?

**11.** (T/F)   Farr intimates that normative assessment is best suited to instructional decision making.

**12.** (T/F)   Students' assessment needs are, according to Farr, largely metacognitive.

**13.** On which side of "the wall" (page 202) would a standardized, norm-referenced reading achievement test fall?

**14.** What trend among many standardized tests has added to the confusion over assessment?

**15.** What four potential problems have arisen, according to Farr? Briefly describe each.

a.

b.

c.

d.

**16.** Briefly define the following terms discussed by Farr:

    a. authentic assessment

    b. performance assessment

    c. observation

    d. portfolios

**17.** Describe how a rubric with anchors is used to evaluate student writing.

**18.** Which type of assessment does Farr argue is the single solution to the testing puzzle?

**19.** List and describe the "three major types of assessment" discussed by Farr (see page 205).

    a.

    b.

    c.

**20.** Summarize Farr's advice to:

    a. critics of schools

    b. test producers

**21.** List two innovations developed in the Michigan and Illinois statewide testing programs.

    a.

    b.

**22.** Check the following norm-referenced testing policies with which Farr would agree:

— linking accountability assessment and instructional assessment
— reporting a global comprehension score
— incorporating subtests of word recognition and vocabulary
— longer passages
— scores broken down according to thinking subskills
— matrix sampling

**23.** What is "the long-standing primary purpose of large-scale testing"?

**24.** What is the key type of assessment linking various groups interested in assessment results?

**25.** Farr recommends which of the following practices in using portfolios (check all that apply):

— stressing student ownership of the portfolio
— frequently adding student products
— conducting at least four student-teacher conferences per semester
— never showing the portfolio to parents
— encouraging self-assessment on the part of the student

**26.** Who does Farr suggest present inservice workshops on assessment?

**27.** Do you think Farr's idea of assembling representatives of the various interest groups (parents, administrators, etc.) is viable? Explain.

# PUTTING IT ALL TOGETHER
## SOLVING THE READING
## ASSESSMENT PUZZLE

ROGER FARR

Reading assessment has become a genuine puzzle. Confusion and debate continue about what the goals of school assessment of reading should be and about what types of tests and other assessments are needed to achieve those goals. That debate should focus on the purposes for assessment and whether current tests achieve those purposes. Too often, however, the focus of the debate is on the latest testing panacea. In this article, I first examine the complex components of the assessment puzzle. Next I propose a solution to the puzzle that involves linkages among various assessment audiences and approaches. I conclude with a few remarks about how school districts in the United States might pull together all the pieces and solve the assessment puzzle for themselves.

## *Examining the Pieces of the Assessment Puzzle*

The pieces of the puzzle represent many types of assessments, critical attitudes about them, and attempts to challenge or improve them. One of the truly puzzling aspects of reading assessment to many educators is that the amount of testing appears to increase at the same time that criticism of it intensifies (Farr & Carey, 1986; McClellan, 1988; Salganik, 1985; Valencia & Pearson, 1987).

### *Criticism of Schools Has Led to More Assessment*

Public disappointment with student achievement has led to extensive criticism of U.S. schools. This disapproval intensified in the 1950s with a focus on reading. Reading assessment conducted to prove or disprove the criticism has received a great deal of attention ever since. Could Johnny read or not, and how well or how poorly? By the 1960s,

*Source:* "Putting It All Together: Solving the Reading Assessment Puzzle" by Roger Farr, 1992, *The Reading Teacher, 46.* Copyright 1992 by the International Reading Association. Reprinted by permission.

and beyond, score declines on tests used to predict how well high schoolers would do in college compounded public concern and criticism (The National Commission on Excellence in Education, 1983).

The conviction that many students were receiving high school diplomas and yet were almost totally illiterate became firmly established in the public's mind (Purves & Niles, 1984). The Peter Doe case in California exemplified that concern (Saretsky, 1973). The case concerned a high school student who sued the school district for graduating him without teaching him to read. As a result of this kind of dissatisfaction with educational outcomes, the use of standardized, norm-referenced assessment intensified, and state minimum competency testing programs proliferated (Madaus, 1985; Salmon-Cox, 1981).

The data to determine whether scores on reading tests were deteriorating over time is sketchy at best and tends not to substantiate dramatic declines in the reading performance of U.S. students over the years (Farr & Fay, 1982; Farr, Fay, Myers, & Ginsberg, 1987; Stedman & Kaestle, 1987). Nonetheless, the public has remained convinced that performance has dropped rather dramatically. Further, the prevalence of minimum competency programs has not significantly altered the conviction of the public and press that student achievement, particularly in reading, continues to deteriorate.

This unabated critical concern was at least partly responsible for the establishment of the National Assessment of Educational Progress (NAEP), an ongoing federally mandated study that now provides some reading performance data over time. Any declines it has depicted are small compared to the public's determined assumptions (Mullis, Owen, & Phillips, 1990). And although careful analyses of the ACT and SAT score declines has cited several reasonable causes other than poor schools, that phenomenon did much to sustain and cement public conviction and the demand for accountability testing (Popham, 1987; Resnick, 1982).

The continuing debate about the quality of U.S. schools has now given rise to a new focus on standards and assessment. At the same time that they reaffirm their conviction that children are not learning in school, critics like Chester Finn (1992) echo the call from the White House "for new American achievement tests" that compare student performance to "world class standards" that would be set as criterion references. President Bush (1991) has called for "voluntary national tests for 4th, 8th, and 12th graders in the five core subjects" to "tell parents and educators, politicians and employers, just how well our schools are doing."

## The Search for Alternative Assessments Has Also Led to More Assessment

In addition to dissatisfaction with the schools, there has been a quest for assessments that are closely aligned with more holistic views of language development. Some curriculum theorists concerned with the mismatch between curriculum and assessment have determined that if curriculum is to change, the reading tests must change. This has brought about a proliferation of new assessments—both formal and informal (Brown, 1986; Burstall, 1986; Priestley, 1982; Stiggins, Conklin, & Bridgeford, 1986).

Included in this mix have been modifications of conventional tests with new item formats and the addition of the assessment of behaviors not often included on traditional tests, such as background knowledge, student interests and attitudes, and metacognition. Other assessments in reading have taken an entirely different approach to assessment, relying entirely on student work samples collected in portfolios (Jongsma, 1989; Valencia, 1990; Wolf, 1989). Portfolios have themselves taken many different forms from *show portfolios,* which include only a few carefully selected samples, to *working portfolios,* which include a broad sample of work and which are used to guide and organize daily instruction. In addition, numerous professional publications have published articles calling for the use of a broader range of teacher observations and informal assessment techniques (Cambourne & Turbill, 1990; Goodman, 1991).

## Different Audiences Need Different Information

Thus, it seems that the increased amount of testing has resulted from greater accountability demands as well as from attempts to find alternatives to traditional assessments. In order to bring some sense to this proliferation of assessment, we need to understand that tests have only one general purpose: Tests should be considered as nothing more than attempts to systematically gather information. The information is used to help children learn about their own literacy development and to give teachers and others concerned with students' literacy the information they need for curriculum planning. *The bottom line in selecting and using any assessment should be whether it helps students.*

A book that I first authored more than 20 years ago regarding the assessment of reading was entitled *Reading: What Can Be Measured?* (Farr, 1970; Farr & Carey, 1986). I have always felt that the title gave the wrong focus to the review of assessment issues. That book should have been entitled, *Reading: Why Should It Be Measured?* We need to consider who needs information about reading, what kind of information is needed, and when it is needed. Only then can we begin to plan for more sensible assessment.

In order to think more clearly about overall assessment plans, we need to know why we want to test. There are, of course, different groups that need information. Without considering these groups and their information needs, the assessment program in any school system will remain as a set of jumbled puzzle pieces. The general distinctions between audiences are covered in Figure 1.

### The Public

Members of the general public, who make decisions through their elected officials, including school boards, have a vested interest in the future of children and in their effective and cost-efficient instruction. It is recognized as vital to Americans' and their nation's future that schools produce educated students. Indeed, the most recent federally supported efforts to improve education have been on establishing standards that presumably will result in the development of assessments related to those standards. At the present time, those involved with establishing the standards are moving in the direction of holistic kinds of performance assessment.

### Administrators

Ideally school administrators would rely most heavily on performance assessments that are criterion-referenced. These performance measures should compare student performance against a clearly defined curriculum. But since we live in a complex world where

**FIGURE 1**  **Assessment Audiences**

| Audiences | The information is needed to: | The information is related to: | Type of information | When information is needed: |
|---|---|---|---|---|
| General public (and the press) | Judge if schools are accountable and effective | Groups of students | Related to broad goals; norm- & criterion-referenced | Annually |
| School administrators/ staff | Judge effectiveness of curriculum, materials, teachers | Groups of students & individuals | Related to broad goals; criterion- & norm-referenced | Annually or by term/semester |
| Parents | Monitor progress of child, effectiveness of school | Individual student | Usually related to broader goals; both criterion- & norm-referenced | Periodically; 5 or 6 times a year |
| Teachers | Plan instruction, strategies, activities | Individual student; small groups | Related to specific goals: primarily criterion-referenced | Daily, or as often as possible |
| Students | Identify strengths, areas to emphasize | Individual (self) | Related to specific goals; criterion-referenced | Daily, or as often as possible |

mobility and diversity are the reality, administrators also need norm-referenced comparisons of their students' performance.

### Parents

While parents share the public's interests, they have a vested interest in their own individual children. In order to monitor their children's progress and to be active in their education, parents want criterion-referenced reports; additionally parents are also typically interested in how their children perform on normed tests in comparison to children from across the United States.

### Teachers

A teacher's primary concern is helping students learn. While teachers are necessarily aware of normed assessment's comparative reports as a kind of bottom-line accountability, they are primarily interested in the kind of information that will support the daily instructional decisions they need to make. This kind of information has been generated by criterion-referenced tests and by other types of assessment that can be utilized more effectively in the classroom as a part of instruction.

### Students

Students need to become good self-assessors if they are to improve their literacy skills. They need to select, review, and think about the reading and writing they are doing.

They need to be able to revise their own writing and to revise their comprehension as they read. If students understand their own needs, they will improve. Students should, in fact, be the primary assessors of their own literacy development.

## The Wall between Understanding

It is important for each of these audiences to recognize, understand, and respect the needs of the others if we are to pull the assessment puzzle together. Audience needs cluster around those of teachers and students on the one hand and those of other decision-makers on the other.

The assessment needs of these two general groups tend to be dramatically different and even contradictory, and if the users of assessment do not recognize one another's needs, it is because these distinctions create a kind of wall depicted in Figure 2. It is essential that we breach that wall if we are to get our assessment act together!

## Some Tests Attempt to Do It All

No single assessment can serve all the audiences in need of educational performance information. Yet developments in standardized tests have attempted to do so. The tests have added criterion-referenced interpretations, special interpretations for teachers, special reports for parents, individual score reports, and instructional support materials of various kinds. These developments have made the tests longer, more expensive, more time-consuming, and more confusing. Consequently, teachers are expected to justify these investments by making more instructional use of the test results.

At the same time, the increased investment in assessment time and money has tended to give these tests even more importance in determining school accountability and in making high-stakes educational decisions. Specifically, four potential problems have arisen.

**FIGURE 2** **Opposing Views of Assessment**

| A teacher's view of assessment | A lack of understanding/acceptance | Other decision-makers' views of assessment |
|---|---|---|
| *Assessment is for*: Nurturing | | *Assessment is for*: Gate keeping |
| Guiding the development of students | | Judging the success of students, teachers, and schools |
| Promoting student self-reflection | | Finding relatively singular correct answers |
| Enabling the teacher to teach flexibly | | Exercising control over school behavior |
| Comparing student performance to a task to be completed | | Comparing student performance to that of other students |
| Making decisions based on multiple samples, including student-selected activities | | Making decisions based on single test scores |

## Teaching to the Test

As accountability became more and more of a concern, teachers have felt pressured to place emphasis on what the standardized tests covered, regardless of what the school curriculum called for. Over time, reading curricula have begun to reflect the skill breakdown of many tests, and reading textbooks have tended to emphasize the skills tests cover as well.

## Contaminating the Evidence

Standardized reading tests used to mean something. They were genuine indications that a student who performed adequately on them could read. This was so because they *sampled* reading behavior. But now that indication is contaminated. If teachers are deliberately stressing the sub-behaviors that they know are on the tests, the assessments are no longer sampling reading behavior—they are, in effect, covering a very limited definition of it. A good score on a standardized reading test no longer indicates that the student can read in general. It means only the student can do those limited things the test covers.

## Crunching Objectives

Attempts to make reading assessment tests more encompassing have tended to make them much longer. Even so, tests are forced to cover the numerous subskills they contain with only a few items each. "What does it mean," a teacher may legitimately ask, "if a student misses one of three items that report on comprehending cause-and-effect?"

## The Potential for a Mismatch

Teachers have long noted that nationally normed tests do not reflect particular emphases in their classrooms. How can a standardized reading test, they have correctly argued, tell them much about a particular curriculum they are following? What can it tell the public about how well the teacher has done using the curriculum?

The more a teacher adheres to instruction related directly to the needs, interests, and backgrounds of his or her particular students, the less assured is the match of that instruction to standardized test content—and the less likely the test's scores will serve that instruction.

# Good Reading Theory Recommends Authentic Performance Assessment

Most published tests have not adequately responded to emerging reading theory, which explains reading comprehension as a meaning-constructing process. Any subskills factored out of the process are not discrete; if they actually exist as behaviors, they appear to operate in such an intricate fashion that it is difficult if not impossible to isolate them.

## Authentic Assessment

Relatively wide acceptance of a constructivist, context-specific definition of reading has promoted a careful analysis of current reading and language arts test content and format to see how authentic the testing experience is. This analysis has led to the conclusion that the reading required on most tests is not much like the reading behavior that our new understanding describes. How valid is the content of a reading test in terms of reader purpose, interests, and background, which we now believe are primary influences on reading behavior?

## Performance Assessment

Attention to authenticity has accompanied and helped generate the development and use of performance assessment. A student's language behaviors need to be assessed, it is contended, as they are used in real-life situations. Students don't comprehend something read, for example, as a multiple-choice response, and marking those answers has nothing to do with the way reading is actually used, except in taking tests. Reading performance assessment must look at the reading act in process or judge comprehension of a text as it is applied in some realistic way.

## Observation

Observation is one way to do this and can lead teachers to meaningful insights about the progress and needs of individual students. Yet teachers need to be trained in regard to what they can look for and what those signs suggest. They need to develop useful ways to make discrete notes about observations and to synthesize what they find. Observation generates many details in relatively random order, and they seldom become clearly useful until they are gathered into patterns that can direct instruction.

## Portfolios

Another highly valuable form of performance assessment is the portfolio. For these collections, students and teachers select numerous samples from drafts and final versions of various kinds of a student's writing. The idea is to demonstrate the student's progress and development in the combined process of reading, thinking, and writing. Thus many of the samples in the portfolio are responses to reading. The portfolio is reviewed and discussed regularly by the teacher and student, who may arrange it for others to examine.

## Integrated Assessment

Assessments in which thinking, reading, and writing are integrated have been developed in recent years. Such assessments have been developed by classroom teachers, school districts, and publishers in an attempt to integrate reading and writing and to assess reading and writing with more realistic activities. These vary widely, but for most of them the student is given a writing task related to a text that is supplied. The task has been deemed to be authentic because it is typical of something the student might do in real life, including the kinds of activities often used for learning in the classroom. It is designed to emphasize the use of information in the reading selection in a realistic and interesting writing task.

For example, one such test asks students to read a nonfiction article that categorically discusses and describes how insect-eating plants lure, capture, and digest their victims. The task is to write a fictional piece telling what a mother bug might say to her children in cautioning them about these plants. Teachers use what the students write to assess students' understanding of the text. They rate other integrated behaviors as well, such as the students' organization and application of the text's content to the task and factors related to writing.

Such reading/writing assessments encourage students to develop a variety of responses based on their interpretation of the reading selection, their background knowledge, and the direction they choose to take in constructing a realistic response. These kinds of performance assessments provide teachers with valuable insights regarding a student's ability to read, write, and construct a meaningful response to an interesting task. Prewriting notes, first drafts, and teacher observation notes all make the assessment a valuable source of information.

In addition, the final drafts can be scored to serve as information that can help determine accountability. The responses can be scored following a "rubric," a list of criteria that describes several levels of performance in each of the categories to be analyzed. Samples of actual student papers ("anchors") that represent each score level described the rubrics can also be used in scoring. Thus these tests are criterion-referenced. Yet the guides to scoring are somewhat equivalent to normed scores in the sense that the anchor papers were taken from many gathered in field-testing and were judged to be typical of the range of responses described in the rubric.

## *A Combined Solution to the Assessment Puzzle*

None of the preceding types of assessment should be argued to be the single solution to the testing puzzle. Figure 3 depicts how performance assessments can provide direct linkage among the main users of assessment and how the three major types of assessment are linked. The chart is a plan for pulling the pieces of the assessment puzzle together into a solution that can inform all the decision makers involved in a student's development into an effective reader and language user.

**FIGURE 3   The Solution-Linkage**

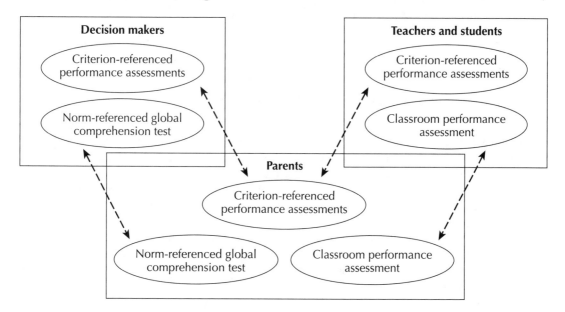

## Solving the Puzzle Will Require Cooperation

Pulling the assessment puzzle together will require tolerance and compromise on the part of many critics of particular types of assessment. The process would be facilitated if:

- Critics of the schools would become aware that assessment must serve more than school accountability. Ideally, critics will inform their concerns with a better understanding of what schools are trying to accomplish.
- Decision makers would understand that assessment is more than numbers on a test paper. They would begin to understand and use the kinds of assessments that are based on real classroom activities and that represent the types of activities in which students who are effective readers and writers should become proficient.
- The most idealistic of the critics of assessment would become more realistic and flexible, tempering their insistence on authentic performance assessment. It seems fruitless, in particular, for some critics to insist that all assessment revolve around observation of activities that are apt not to involve all children and that reveal language use in highly varying degrees.
- Producers of assessments would acknowledge that no one assessment is going to suffice as a school's examination of reading. This would mean that they would no longer promote any of their products as such a test. It would also mean that future revisions of standardized reading tests would undo much of the complexity they now contain.

None of this is to suggest that critical analysis of reading assessment should stop, nor should attempts to improve tests in response to criticism cease. Efforts to develop and institute the new accountability assessments in Illinois (Pearson & Valencia, 1987), where the assessment allows for multiple correct responses within each multiple-choice item, and in Michigan (Michigan State Board of Education, 1987), where the assessment relies on longer passages followed by more numerous items, have been interesting, if not conclusive, efforts to contribute to a solution to the assessment puzzle. So have attempts to construct items that will reveal students' awareness of how they are processing texts. Although longer reading test passages, different question formats, etc. will not solve the assessment puzzle, they can certainly shape the parts we pull together for a better fit.

## Norm-Referenced Tests Need to Change

To solve the assessment puzzle, it will be necessary for teachers and other educators to admit that norm-referenced test results can be of some value to the public and other decision makers, including parents. But these standardized tests should not be of the form that has evolved in response to criticism.

Test authors and publishers should begin to plan assessment *programs* that address the multiple audiences. Teachers and schools will need assistance in developing portfolios, planning performance assessments, and integrating assessment information. What is not needed are large single test batteries that promise to meet all of a school's assessment needs from classroom diagnosis to accountability. That attempt, especially linking accountability assessment and instructional assessment, has led to a narrowing of the curriculum.

For the large-scale assessments, this suggests the elimination of the designation of items by subskills and reporting on those subbehaviors as if they truly are separable and distinct. More publisher efforts should go into the development of a variety of creative and useful curriculum assessments in which students have to actually perform the behaviors the school is attempting to teach.

What large-scale assessment can and should do is to report a global comprehension score, with no special subtests on traditional focuses like word recognition and vocabulary. Without the time-consuming battery of accompanying tests, reading tests can be shorter while using longer passages of a variety of types. These passages must evoke different purposes for reading that reflect the real reasons students read in and out of school. Thus, the reading test will be more authentic.

Without the burden of reporting on a host of specific reading and thinking subskills, test makers can write items that truly reflect the balance of a passage, the students' probable purpose for reading such a text, and the aspects of the writing that make the text one of quality and worth the students' time.

It should also be remembered that the long-standing primary purpose of large-scale testing has been to provide a general assessment as to how groups of students are progressing in a school district. Such information, if it does not become the focus of instruction, can be one piece of information used to contribute to a broad base of information for planning, supporting, and evaluating school- and system-wide curricula and instruction.

This approach strongly suggests that *matrix sampling* be used for large-scale assessment, thus eliminating the need to administer to all students the same test items or tasks. Testing time can be considerably shorter if carefully selected samples of students take different parts of a test instead of the whole thing. Good sampling should yield results similar to those obtained when all students take the entire test. Nothing is lost in reporting, since individual scores are of little concern. In addition, matrix sampling provides a general indication of the progress of groups of students, not a blueprint for instruction of individual students.

## Performance Assessments Can Provide the Key Linkage

Figure 3 illustrates the linkages across three general audience types that will be essential to solving the assessment puzzle. Norm-referenced information provides a link between parents and decision makers other than teachers. However, the key linkage across all three general audiences is criterion-referenced performance assessments. Various approaches to performance assessment are being developed and tried out in school district assessment programs. Such assessments can be designed by teachers themselves. In fact, this has been done in several local school districts around the United States by teachers cooperating and interacting in order to meet their assessment needs. The same procedures are being tried at the state level in Maryland, Arizona, California, and Utah, and other states are sure to move in this direction.

The teachers who have been most successful in using this approach have had the support of administrators who could see over the assessment wall. Their support generated public interest and support. In some school systems, published or teacher-created integrated language performance assessment has already become a primary source of information for judging school accountability.

While teachers can create integrated language performance activities on a classroom basis, using them for accountability will require carefully developed or prepared programs that have been made congruent system-wide. This was done in River Forest, Illinois, where teachers developed their own rubrics, anchor papers, and inservice training. This kind of structuring will be necessary if the public, the press, and administrators are to be expected to value these tests as the key indicators of accountability and sources of directions for key decisions, such as curriculum development.

At the same time, of course, these tests can reflect authentic student performance. Not only are they very closely related to instructional activities and thus of high utility to teachers, they are actually instructional activities in and of themselves so the class time they require is doubly well invested.

## The Portfolio Is the Flagship of Performance Assessment

Most developers of integrated language assessment programs highly recommend putting the student products into portfolios, a direct acknowledgment that the roots of language performance assessment lie in a portfolio approach to assessment and instruction. So integral is the portfolio performance assessment in good classrooms today that it is vital to note the qualities that make the portfolio approach a successful one.

A successful portfolio approach to assessment must revolve around regular and frequent attention to the portfolio by the student and the teacher. It does minimal good just to store a student's papers in a big folder and let them gather dust for lengthy periods of time. Papers must be added frequently; others can be weeded out in an ongoing rearrangement and selection process; most importantly, the whole process should involve frequent self-analysis by the student and regular conversations between the teacher and the student.

Too many teachers who contend that they are using portfolios do not do these things. Here are a few requirements if portfolios are to provide good assessment:

- The portfolio *belongs* to the student. It is his or her work and property, not some classroom requirement. Students should have choice about what goes in, and they should be encouraged to decorate and personalize their portfolios in unique ways.
- Portfolios are not primarily a display, although students may help arrange them for their parents and administrators to see. They are a shifting, growing repository of developing processes and ideas—a rather personal melting pot that the student uses to reflect on his or her own literacy development and to discuss interesting reading and writing activities with the teacher.
- The teacher's role in portfolio development is that of a consultant who helps convince the student that the work should show a variety of materials reflecting the reading-writing-thinking process as well as examples of responses to common classroom tasks and the student's favorite creations.
- The portfolio should contain numerous and varied pieces written and revised in response to reading. Reading logs reporting ongoing responses to books and articles make valuable contributions to portfolios.

- Portfolios should be reflective collections, revealing genuinely individual and personal responses to classroom activities and to ideas.
- At an absolute minimum, there should be four one-on-one, teacher/student discussions and analyses each semester of a student's developing portfolio. These sessions should not be short and perfunctory. If this requirement is not met, the assessment potential of the portfolio process is forfeited.
- Keeping the portfolio is an ongoing process. Its real value as an assessment tool materializes as the student can analyze his or her progress and development over time.

## New Emphases in Assessment Have Common Qualities

Portfolios are part of a group of classroom performance assessments, some of them quite informal, that link the assessment interests of teachers, students, and parents. Portfolios can also be highly revealing to school specialists and administrators who, with the students' permission, take the time to examine them. All of these emerging strategies are both authentic and involve performance assessment. They are:

- Highly individualized, even though they may take place during activities that involve groups of students.
- A part of classroom activities and instruction designed to match an individual student's interests and needs and to use a student's strengths to develop more incisive and creative use of language.
- Activities that integrate several language behaviors.
- Chances to use critical thinking and to express unique and emerging reactions and responses to ideas encountered in text.
- Models that encourage and develop self-assessment by the student, making him or her aware of the language-related strengths that are developing.

## How School Districts Can Begin to Solve the Assessment Puzzle

Too often school district testing programs are nothing more than test-and-file procedures. The tests are administered; when the scores are available, they are reported in some way; and teachers are admonished to peruse and use the test results. Yet many educators across the U.S. already embrace the suggestions made here for solving the assessment puzzle. Administrators are aware that testing programs can and do divide educators. Superintendents do not want to abandon their accountability responsibilities, yet they want to support effective ongoing classroom assessment that provides teachers with information that is congruent with current knowledge about reading/writing processes. Teachers want to be more involved in developing an assessment program that serves and matches their instructional needs. They all sense that what is needed is an integrated system that is effective in fostering better teaching and learning.

Many of these school districts need help with developing an assessment program that links audiences instead of dividing them—one that supplies broad-based accountability information yet is customized to the particular system, its teachers, and its students. One way for school districts to begin is to discuss the pieces of the assessment puzzle in their system. Representatives of all the audiences with assessment needs should take part. As this process develops, the discussions need to be recorded in some way and synthesized. Out of all this can come other brainstorming sessions and ultimately inservice workshops to help all teachers understand how a broad-based assessment program can be pulled together. Equally important, many teachers will welcome inservice training on using different types of informal assessments.

These kinds of workshops can be started within school districts right away. For instance, teachers who are exceptionally good observers or use the portfolio approach with great success are almost always easily identified. They could be enlisted and supported by administrators to run workshops that can be conducted while the discussions about broader reading assessment are helping representative groups define the assessment problems and their district's needs.

The assessment puzzle can be solved. The solution, however, is not as simple as identifying a nonexistent test that will do the whole job nor as arbitrary as eliminating most reading assessment. Rather it takes a vision that focuses on what real literacy means and the awareness that various groups have a stake in helping students to develop as literate citizens. Such a vision must not use assessment to isolate. It must respect the complex nature of literacy, it must serve students and help them to become reflective self-assessors, and it must create links that bring instruction and assessment together.

## *References*

Brown, R. (1986). Evaluation and learning. In A. R. Petrosky & D. Bartholomae (Eds.), *The teaching of writing: Eighty-fifth yearbook of the National Society for the Study of Education* (pp. 114–130). Chicago, IL: University of Chicago Press.

Burstall, C. (1986). Innovative forms of assessment: A United Kingdom perspective. *Educational Measurement: Issues and Practice, 5,* 17–22.

Bush, G. (1991). *America 2000: An education strategy.* Washington, DC: U.S. Department of Education.

Cambourne, B., & Turbill, J. (1990). Assessment in whole language classrooms: Theory into practice. *The Elementary School Journal, 90,* 337–349.

Farr, R. (1970). *Reading: What can be measured?* Newark, DE: International Reading Association.

Farr, R., & Carey, R. (1986). *Reading: What can be measured?* (2nd ed.). Newark, DE: International Reading Association.

Farr, R., & Fay, L. (1982). Reading trend data in the United States: A mandatre for caveats and caution. In G. Austin & H. Garber (Eds.), *The rise and fall of national test scores* (pp. 83–141). New York: The Academic Press.

Farr, R., Fay, L., Myers, R., & Ginsberg, M. (1987). *Reading achievement in the United States: 1944–45, 1976, and 1986.* Bloomington, IN: Indiana University.

Finn, C. E., Jr. (1992, January 12). Turn on the lights. *The New York Times,* Sect. 4, p. 19.

Goodman, Y. (1991). Evaluating language growth: Informal methods of evaluation. In J. Flood, J. Jensen, D. Lapp, & J. Squire (Eds.), *Handbook of research on teaching the English language arts* (pp. 502–509). New York: Macmillan.

Jongsma, K. (1989). Portfolio assessment. *The Reading Teacher, 43,* 264–265.

Madaus, G. F. (1985). Public policy and the testing profession: You've never had it so good? *Educational Measurement: Issues and Practice, 4,* 5–11.

McClellan, M. C. (1988). Testing and reform. *Phi Delta Kappan, 69,* 766–771.

Michigan State Board of Education. (1987). *Blueprint for the new MEAP reading test.* Lansing, MI: Author.

Mullis, V. S., Owen, E. H., & Phillips, G. W. (1990). *Accelerating academic achievement: A summary of the findings from '20 years of NAEP.* Princeton, NJ: Educational Testing Service.

National Commission on Excellence in Education. (1983). *A nation at risk.* Washington, DC: U.S. Department of Education.

Pearson, P. D., & Valencia, S. (1987). *The Illinois State Board of Education census assessment in reading: An historical reflection.* Springfield, IL: Illinois State Department of Education.

Popham, W. J. (1987). The merits of measurement-driven instruction. *Phi Delta Kappan, 68,* 679–682.

Priestley, M. (1982). *Performance assessment in education and training: Alternate techniques.* Englewood Cliffs, NJ: Educational Technology Publications.

Purves, A., & Niles, O. (1984). The challenge to education to produce literate citizens. In A. Purves & O. Niles (Eds.), *Becoming readers in a complex society: Eighty-third yearbook of the National Society for the Study of Education* (pp. 1–15). Chicago, IL: University of Chicago Press.

Resnick, D. (1982). History of educational testing. In A. K. Widgor & W. R. Garner (Eds.), *Ability testing: Uses, consequences, and controversies,* Part 2 (pp. 173–194). Washington, DC: National Academy Press.

Salganik, L. H. (1985). Why testing reforms are so popular and how they are changing education. *Phi Delta Kappan, 66,* 628–634.

Salmon-Cox, L. (1981). Teachers and tests: What's really happening? *Phi Delta Kappan, 62,* 631–634.

Saretsky, G. (1973). The strangely significant case of Peter Doe. *Phi Delta Kappan, 54,* 589–592.

Stedman, L. C., & Kaestle, C. F. (1987). Literacy and reading performance in the United States from 1880 to the present. *Reading Research Quarterly, 22,* 8–46.

Stiggins, R. J., Conklin, N. F., & Bridgeford, N. J. (1986). Classroom assessment: A key to effective education. *Educational Measurement: Issues and Practice, 5,* 5–17.

Valencia, S. (1990). A portfolio approach to classroom reading assessment: The whys, whats, and hows. *The Reading Teacher, 43,* 338–339.

Valencia, S., & Pearson, P. (1987). Reading assessment: Time for a change. *The Reading Teacher, 40,* 726–732.

Wolf, D. P. (1989). Portfolio assessment: Sampling student work. *Educational Leadership, 46,* 35–39.

## CONTENT LITERACY GUIDE

**Research Currents: What Is and What Might Be in Evaluation**
Marie M. Clay
*Language Arts,* March 1990, 288–298

**1.** What reason does Clay give for the inability of standardized tests to inform instruction?

**2.** Clay recommends three separate evaluations of:

  a.

  b.

  c.

**3.** According to Clay, standardized tests have one important and acceptable purpose. What is it?

**4.** Summarize the "three big problems" of standardized reading tests:

  a.

  b.

  c.

**5.** When do New Zealand children enter school for the first time?

**6.** Describe how the New Zealand teacher begins with a newly arrived five-year-old student.

**7.** Clay does not use the word *portfolio* to describe how writing evaluation occurs. Does what she does describe amount to a portfolio?

**8.** Does Clay's notion of the "running record" differ much from miscue coding and analysis? Discuss any differences you perceive.

**9.** Which of the following techniques does Clay recommend for assessing comprehension?
— giving children multiple-choice tests
— asking children questions
— asking children to make predictions
— asking children to retell what they've read

**10.** Why are New Zealand's teachers skeptical about their standardized word test?

**11.** Standardized tests at the upper-elementary level (check all correct answers):
— are used to compare schools and teachers
— are used for pre-post measurement
— are used to group or place children

**12.** Nicholson's program was designed to help high school teachers do what?

**13.** What "distinction" must reading assessment address, according to Clay?

**14.** Is Clay's analogy to math assessment applicable to reading? Explain.

**15.** Does Clay convince you that informal evaluation can be reliable? What argument is effective?

**16.** Why is validity not usually a problem in process measures? Do you accept this argument?

**17.** Summarize Clay's view on having separate reading measures for use by teachers and administrators.

**18.** Clay suggests that "careful records" in a "standard format" can satisfy administrators and the public. Do you agree? Explain.

**19.** When is a follow-up assessment generally conducted for a young child?

**20.** Is this assessment based on a standardized test?

**21.** What is the primary purpose of this assessment?

**22.** What does Clay suggest about teachers' exploring and discussing informal assessment? What is your opinion of her suggestion?

# RESEARCH CURRENTS
## WHAT IS AND WHAT MIGHT BE
## IN EVALUATION

### MARIE M. CLAY

*Department editors' note:* In this column we've been privileged to be able to feature contributors who exemplify varied aspects of language arts research. This month Marie Clay brings to life the well-worn phrase, *theory and research into practice,* which encapsulates her work in literacy education. Before *emergent reading,* a term she introduced in 1966, became an accepted part of our views of early literacy, Clay was carrying out research in New Zealand that led to the development of a many-faceted program called Reading Recovery. This is a tutorial intervention program for first-grade children who in their classes or schools are having the greatest difficulties with beginning reading. A unique feature of the program is that its teachers take part in a year-long training program, revolving around careful observation and work with individual children. Though it's true that the program succeeds in helping most children who participate in it to become literate, it is also remarkable for changing the ways that teachers look at children. They learn to take cues from the child as he develops strategies for reading and writing. The program is optimistic about teacher and child; both are learners who together can make sense of print. Clay's research and writing have been uniquely persuasive in illustrating this view of learning.

The same optimism and willingness to inform a theory of learning with research and practice underlie the article that follows. In his call for manuscripts for this issue, Editor David Dillon accurately said that "we have done little work to develop, try out, document, and disseminate information on alternative means of evaluation of language and learning." Here Professor Clay demonstrates that she is an exception to this claim as she responds to our request for her personal view of evaluation as it is in New Zealand, as well as how it might be. She writes with the assurance and sense of one engaged in a down-to-earth dialogue with countless children, teachers, administrators, and researchers as she works toward the improvement of teaching and evaluation practices.

Marie Clay is the author of numerous articles and books, including, *What Did I Write?* (1975), *The Early Detection of Reading Difficulties,* third edition (1985), and *Reading: The Patterning of Complex Behavior,* revised edition (in press). Among the many honors that she has received are the NCTE David H. Russell Research Award and the IRA International Citation of Merit. She has been adviser and collaborator in the Ohio Reading Recovery Program and is Professor of Education, the University of Auckland, Auckland, New Zealand.

C. G.

A. H. D.

New Zealand has fifty thousand children entering its schools each year for ten years of compulsory schooling, followed by three more optional years in the senior classes of high school. The structure of the system is six years in an elementary school, two in an intermediate school, and five in a high school, with many variants to deal with rural education in a mountainous country.

Recent moves to reform educational administration in Britain, Australia, and New Zealand have been accompanied by calls for more testing. There is an assumption that giving tests will, ipso facto, improve teaching and learning. However, standardized test scores are only outcome measures. They do not tell us what kinds of teaching to engage in to change those outcomes. Administrators can expect knowledge of test scores to be useful for classification and comparison of children, classes, or schools, but classifying and comparing children is several steps removed from teaching them effectively. To do that we need information on the day-to-day learning of two groups, the successful children and the poor performers. That way we learn from the successful children what it is we have to teach the poorer children to do on the way to the outcome assessment.

If we want to have the poor performers do much better, then we have to upset the high correlations between children's achievement at the time they enter a program and the outcome test. This calls for three different kinds of evaluations. Low student outcome scores do not distinguish between three things which might have been responsible: low prior achievement of the students, or poor program delivery, or ineffective education policies. Thus, administrators need separate and different evaluations of: a) students in the process of learning, b) teachers teaching, and c) the effectiveness of policies.

I do not reject standardized measures. They are elegantly designed for the comparison task. However, such tests have three big problems:

Firstly, they never measure well at the earliest stages of learning (onset ages) nor at the point where most children are competent.

Secondly, they do not allow the study of the processes which contribute to better learning, and one can only guess at how to go about interventions which might bring about improvements.

Thirdly, they have to made up of items that are relatively simple and quantifiable, involving only perfected responding, and ignoring the partial successes of children in the process of learning.

## *Brief Overview of New Zealand Practice*

### *Coming Ready or Not (Escape from Readiness Testing)*

In New Zealand we developed the tradition of letting children enter school on their fifth birthday on any day of the year (Birch and Birch 1970). The Metropolitan Readiness Test was standardized for New Zealand in the 1940s, but it was rarely used in the 1960s when I included it in a research study. I found that as children learned to read and write they got much higher scores on readiness tests! Before long the tests were dropped from the publishers' listings as their scores served no practical purpose in New Zealand classrooms.

Why was this so? A teacher in New Zealand observes the adjustment of each new pupil to various activities in her classroom. Then she places them with a group of children who seem to be working at approximately the same level. Children have opportunities to work at whatever level they can manage with teacher assistance. Comparing what the child does today with what he did last month and with what she has learned from all the children she has ever taught, the teacher judges what each child can do and what he next needs to learn to do. She groups and regroups her pupils throughout the year according to the kind of new things they learn to do. She knows how fast they are moving and whether they need extra help. She continually adapts her teaching to meet those needs. Within a few weeks children move at different rates beyond their initial readiness test scores, and then teachers need other kinds of information to guide their teaching for the rest of that first year of school.

### *Writing*

In the first three years of instruction, writing means writing one's own composed story, and it tends to be a daily affair. Often the writing will arise from drawing, a shared book or craft activity, or some theme for the week. Sooner or later there will be an invitation to write about it. Teachers support and stimulate the composition through interaction but do not do the composing. Help is given but independence is expected so that self-evaluation by the student emerges.

Writing is usually taken home, but from time to time the teacher keeps a sample. Reviewing a child's dated writing samples (each one different from every other child's), it is easy to see the progression in what the child is able to control or needs more assistance with. Extra evidence is easily gained from a quick check on Writing Vocabulary (all the words a child can write) or Dictation (a check on letter-sound relationships) (Clay, 1985).

Having captured changes over time in how the child writes, the teacher needs to be able to demonstrate the progress to parents or principal perhaps by presenting samples of work for comparison. This teacher's record of one child's achievements in writing could be compared with progress at a later time to demonstrate the changes, gains, and new learning needs.

### Writing

Chose to write 'Little Red Riding Hood'—and to illustrate with map (inspired by Karl's map of The Three Bears).

Wrote on her own—said it was her favorite story.

### Type of Writing

Story: She wrote only the first part of the story and extended and elaborated it in the map she made.

Interesting beginning—'One day Little Riding Hood came down the stairs.'

Uses written language well—makes events explicit: 'I want you to go to Grandma's house for me because she is not well.'

In the conference she revealed interesting images and knowledge of the story—gave glimpses of the way it 'goes together' for her.

### Conventions—Spelling—Punctuation

Her writing is now readable—early transitional spelling. Can spell a number of words, makes good attempts to construct others. Still sorting out words like *little, came* and the medial vowel in R*e*d and R*i*ding. Still using upper and lower case letters indiscriminately.

### Needs

To begin to sort out upper and lower case letters, to pay attention to medial vowels and gradually sort them out. (McKenzie 1986)

## Reading

Teachers can take a lasting record of how the child reads short, whole stories, making notes of strengths and challenges as they occur. They can return to these to analyze or think about what the child is doing and how best the teaching can interact with what a child can do. (I have called these 'running records' of what occurs; Clay 1985; McKenzie 1986; Andreae 1988; Department of Education 1985; the ERIC and ELIC inservice training programs.) Most often a running record would show the child's reading of a text which has been introduced in some way and which the child is now ready to read independently. The records can also be quantified to plot individual progress. Having selected some gradient of difficulty in reading materials the teacher can record the child's path of progress through texts of increasing difficulty. These observations give the teacher information about how the child works with texts: the developing strategies are captured.

(Checks show correct responses; a dash shows an omission in a running record.)

✔   ✔   ✔   ✔ ✔   ✔

"My master wanted to cook me

✔   _   ✔✔✔   ✔

for dinner, so I ran away,"

✔   ✔   ✔

said the rooster.

*Child* (working it out): Oh! Dinner!

The understanding a child is gaining about books, how they work, and how print carries the messages, is probably a kind of window through which the child gains access to the reading process. This can be tested with a booksharing task in the Concepts About Print test (Clay 1985, 1989; Andreae 1988), which gives teachers insight into what the young reader is attending to.

## *And What of Comprehension?*

Teachers expect understanding to be the purpose of every encounter with text for beginning readers. Little stories read as a whole allow the child to work with and understand the narrative. Teachers sharing books with large or small groups of children teach for response to the story, linking to prior knowledge, and understanding what is happening. They question, call for predictions, ask for checking of those predictions, for alternatives and self-corrections. Children expect to read with understanding and to ask themselves questions as they read a text, from their first days in school: "If it doesn't make sense, it isn't reading."

The retelling of a story is an easy way for the teachers of young children to check on understanding (Morrow 1989; McKenzie 1986).

### *Comprehension*

(Seen in manner of reading and story retelling, and in follow-up discussion.)

Retelling indicated James's clear understanding of the story:

• noted details, names of characters.
• recalled events, related them sequentially, related the beginning and end of the story, aware that Muffles's and Percy's comment was no longer right.
• made inferences about Freddy's feelings when his flying attempt failed.
• seemed to bring a good deal of personal association to the story—demonstrated in his use of language:
  e.g. 'Want a go Percy?'
       'Hop on. This ride's on me.'
• showed sensitivity to the characters, their feelings and relationships.

### *Comprehension*

Her general reading—miscues, phrasing, intonation, comments—all indicated comprehension. Retelling and discussion confirmed this.

Took a while to understand the point at the end where the clown's fall was accidental.

### Comprehension

(Gleaned from her retelling of the story and follow-up discussion and comments.) Retelling indicates Fatima's overall understanding of the story:

- noted details—names of characters, how the three attempts were made to catch the cloud.
- recalled events, related them sequentially.
- made inferences about events and actions of the characters, e.g., Stan was cleverer than the others because he understood there was only one way to 'catch' a cloud.
- used mostly 'written language' (but gestures used, too, to make meanings clear to audience), e.g. 'We must try again to get the cloud.'
- related what she read to her own knowledge and understanding of people and concepts, e.g. clouds and rain. (McKenzie 1986)

## A Quick Check with a Word Test

In New Zealand there is only one standardized test in the literacy area in the first three years of school, a word reading test given individually. Teachers know that such tests do not measure competent children's progress well until after eighteen months at school and less competent children's progress until after thirty months at school. It provides a check on the school's program and is useful to researchers, but teachers regard its results with skepticism because knowledge of words is not seen as a very good indicator of the reading of texts with understanding.

## Beyond the Junior School Level

In the upper elementary level the picture is less clear. Nationally-normed group tests prepared by the New Zealand Council for Educational Research were free to schools for many years. Although schools might choose not to use these tests, administrators were likely to ask what information the school had on the progress of children. So 'Progressive Achievement Tests' of various kinds (word knowledge, comprehension, proofreading for spelling, study skills) are used and tend to be administered *early in the school year.* They are used to group or place children and sometimes for diagnostic information.

Note that these have not been used as outcome measures or before and after checks. They provide a distribution of scores for a class or school, a baseline from which to achieve change during the school year. They are not used for public comparison of schools except that principals might use them as an argument for extra resources.

Informal inventories, book conferences, running records, miscue analyses, and cloze tests are some of the other assessments used by particular teachers, supported by an inservice training program for reading in the upper elementary school available on videotape. It is my suspicion that a legacy of talking about books before or after reading in the primary school has become less systematic in the upper elementary school and it is an "if-I-can" and "when-I-can" occurrence rather than a deliberate plan to introduce texts and develop particular strategies in older readers.

At entry to high school, achievement tests of various kinds are used to place children in classes or curricular tracks, and then testing becomes very much a subject teacher's responsibility until the national examination at the end of compulsory education. Two years later there is a further national examination for entry to universities.

A remarkable floodlight on the problem of reading texts in the high school came from Nicholson's (1984) widely reported study which showed how high school teachers could be trained to watch and question pupils to reveal the extraordinary difficulties they were having with reading their textbooks. I think this is a breakthrough technique, showing where teachers can help their students with the comprehension of different kinds of texts. It provides high school teachers with observational techniques which, like running records, greatly enhance the effectiveness of their teaching. The widely reported research on reciprocal teaching (Palincsar and Brown 1984, 1986) also provides teachers with the means of observing the process of comprehension in older readers while at the same time acting to improve comprehension strategies.

## Some Tensions to Consider

### Who Designs the Answer?
### The Student or the Teacher?

> *"What do you want us to do, Miss?" asked one child. "Choose the right words and draw circles around them," was the answer.*

In this task every child should have the same answer because the task has been set to find out which children have learned what the teacher taught.

> *"What do you want us to do, Miss?" asked another child. "Write me a story and then come and read it to me."*

In this task all the products are different, because the teacher has asked the children to use what they know in a constructive activity.

Are we teaching children to store information so it can be recalled, or is learning how to use what we know our real goal? The former does not ensure that the child knows how to work with information, while the latter demonstrates the generative power of the learning. Teaching the child how to learn will empower the child to learn independently and leave the teacher less work to do. Assessment must address this distinction.

### Product or Process?

Standardized testing aims to capture perfected performing, which yields little information about how the learning process is shaping up. For reasons of efficiency, reliability, and validity, it requires test items for which the answers can be clearly indicated by the testee and objectively marked by the tester.

A teacher seeking maximum information for teaching will wish to see the student working and observe the process of arriving at the final product. In mathematics this has been acknowledged by marking not only the correct answer but also the "working" which has been recorded. This calls for observing the production process in two ways: firstly, recording how individuals or a group working cooperatively go about an activity, watching the partially correct moves as well as the perfect responses, and secondly, keeping a record of how a child's learning changes over time from partial success to a perfect performance. Perhaps we need a new surge of research on the qualitative rating of products and processes which reflect individual differences.

As a teacher at what point are you interested in assessment? Probably it is pointless to try to measure this thing if the child has not yet started to learn it. Probably it is equally silly to take time out to assess it if the child can already complete the task perfectly. That leaves the period in between as a time that might be very interesting to the teacher. It could be the time when support or a hint about direction to move next might have the most effect. So, for the purposes of teaching we might want to be able to capture the half-right, half-wrong responding of our students and gain the maximum information on how to guide their next attempts or what opportunities we might provide to help them.

## Integrating Competencies or Separating Subskills?

One of the problems with quantifiable test results is that they force us, in the interests of reliability or validity, to single out specific competencies for evaluation when a large part of education should be concerned with how we coordinate our information, bringing things together.

# Challenges in Search of Solutions

## Reliable and Valid

Informal evaluations can be designed to give reliable results. If teachers are going to compare children or compare one child at two points of time, then their measuring tape should not be elastic. It should be doing the same measuring task each time it is used. Two or ten teachers should theoretically get the same result from using the observation task. We can be systematic about such assessments, and we need to be if we want administrators to accept our assessments (Farr and Carey 1986).

Validity is a question of whether a test measures what it purports to measure. As reading theories have demonstrated, the strategic nature of reading the validity of traditional reading tests has been questioned (Valencia and Pearson 1987). Validity is not usually in question with process measures because the measure is usually part of the learning task or a product of it. There is little question that these task-involved assessments are real ones. Informal measures are not necessarily loose measures that cannot be trusted, and administrators would want to be assured of their reliability and validity and of the ease and consistency with which they can be used by teachers.

## Making Change Over Time Visible

An apparently simple division into assessments made for administrators and assessments which improve teaching is not the answer. There is work to be done in finding assessments which can be part of teaching interactions from which we can present visible evidence of progress to parents and administrators.

Administrators and teachers are both looking at change over time in learning—one in a sophisticated quantification of group trends and the other in highly individual patterns of progress. The assessments need to be reliable and easily administered and monitor change over time.

It is my experience with classroom evaluation and with the Reading Recovery program that administrators, parents, and the lay public can be very impressed by Johnny-the-Individual's records of learning over time. When careful records (writing samples, reading book graphs, art samples, or constructions) are presented in some standard format, each child's progress can be viewed and 'no progress' is not masked in a class average. One of the strengths of the Reading Recovery program is that it can demonstrate the progress or change over time to members of the public in a number of ways which have been convincing.

## Assessments of Individuals and Schools

To meet administrators' needs, some of the procedures which individual teachers choose to use need to be presented in ways which provide a record of what is happening in a school or across schools in a district. This is the status of running records in New Zealand. They are likely to be found in most schools in the country. As well as day-to-day evaluations of strategies the child is learning and using, there is likely to be an appraisal of most children on their sixth birthday, one year into school. This aims to locate children making the least progress so they can be offered supplementary programs. Nationally, administrators accept the observation tasks of my Diagnostic Survey for this purpose, perhaps because they have stood up as well as standardized tests in research studies and appear to have some of the qualities of normative tests in terms of standard administrations, scoring, reliability, and validity. Like many informal assessments they are most useful at particular times of acquisition and do not have the general application across wide age bands that "vocabulary" and "comprehension" have had.

## The Challenge to Teachers

Teachers are coming to know how gross standardized tests are as estimates of progress or achievement and are favoring the validity of process measures to help them in the day-to-day business of lifting their students' achievements. They are now more aware of how tests affect those who administer them as well as those who respond to them (Teale, Hiebert, and Chittenden 1987). Teachers have a challenge to demonstrate to administrators how such measures can be reliable indicators of successful teaching and successful educational policies. It will take ingenuity, cooperation among teachers, and good communication.

## A Conclusion and a Starting Point

If I had to design an intervention to massively and rapidly change educational performance in schools, I would not spend much money on standardized tests. Instead I would run inservice programs at three levels. I would train teachers of children up to nine years of age to use running records in their day-to-day work with children, upper elementary teachers to engage in reciprocal teaching, and high school teachers to work alongside children as Nicholson's teachers did, watching, listening, and questioning to uncover children's problems in understanding their tasks and texts.

I would encourage teachers to explore and discuss informal assessments with administrators, working out how these could be used to meet the administrator's needs in the school or district. I know that teachers who are empowered by checking their own assumptions against what they find out in systematic observations, can be fired by "intelligent unrest" (Johnston 1987) to search for explanations of what they find out. This leads teachers to be active constructors of their own programs and their own evaluations. And I would ask assessment researchers to help me to solve some of the challenges I have identified in this paper.

## References

Andreae, J. *Early Literacy Project: A Framework for Assessment.* Manchester: Education Department, 1988.

Birch, J. W., and Birch, J. R. *Preschool Education and School Admission Practices in New Zealand.* Pittsburgh: University Center for International Studies, 1970.

Clay, M. M. *The Early Detection of Reading Difficulties.* Auckland and Portsmouth, N.H.: Heinemann Publishers, 1985.

Clay, M. M. "Concepts About Print in English and Other Languages." *the Reading Teacher,* 42(1989): 268–275.

Farr, R., and Carey, R. F. *Reading: What Can Be Measured?* Newark, Delaware: International Reading Association, 1986.

Johnston, P. "Teachers as Evaluation Experts." *The Reading Teacher,* 40(1987): 744–748.

McKenzie, M. *Journeys Into Literacy.* Huddersfield: Schofield and Sims, 1986.

Morrow, Lesley M. *Literacy Development in the Early Years.* Englewood Cliffs, New Jersey: Prentice-Hall, 1989.

New Zealand Department of Education. *ERIC: The Early Reading Inservice Programme.* Wellington, 1974.

New Zealand Department of Education. *Reading in the Junior Classes.* New York: Richard Owen, 1985.

Nicholson, T. "Experts and Novices: A Study of Reading in the High School Classroom." *Reading Research Quarterly* 19(1984): 436–451.

Palinscar, A. S., and Brown, A. "Interactive Teaching to Promote Independent Learning from Text." *The Reading Teacher,* 39(1986): 771–777.

Palincsar, A. S., and Brown, A. "Reciprocal Teaching on Comprehension-fostering and Comprehension-monitoring Activities." *Cognition and Instruction,* 1(1984): 117–175.

*Progressive Achievement Tests.* Wellington: New Zealand Council for Educational Research, (Dates various).

South Australian Department of Education. *ELIC: Early Literacy Inservice Course.* Adelaide, 1984.

Teale, W. H., Hiebert, E. H., and Chittenden, E. A. "Assessing Young Children's Literacy Development." *The Reading Teacher* 40(1987): 772–777.

Valencia, S., and Pearson, D. P. "Reading Assessment: Time for a Change." *The Reading Teacher* 40(1987): 726–732.

## *Integrating Sources*

1. Clay and Farr appear to disagree on the matter of whether multiple types of assessments are desirable. Restate their positions. With which do you tend to agree?

   Farr:

   Clay:

2. Contrast Farr's ideas of what portfolio assessment should entail with those of Clay.

   Farr:

   Clay:

3. Compare the views of Farr and Clay as to whether standardized literacy tests are useful in comparing groups of children. Locate quotes that summarize their views.

   Farr:

   Clay:

## *Classroom Implications*

1. How can classroom teachers effectively use literacy assessment results in their teaching? Suggest some specific problems that must be overcome in this area as well as appropriate solutions.

   a.

   b.

   c.

2. Describe what you believe is an effective classroom program of literacy assessment. What types of tests would you use, including both formal and informal tests? How would you use the results of these assessment procedures both in terms of designing the total literacy curriculum as well as teaching individual students?

## *Annotated Bibliography*

### *Assessment*

Calfee, R., & Hiebert, E. (1991). Classroom assessment of reading. In R. Barr, M. Kamil, P. B. Mosenthal, & C. D. Pearson (Eds.), *Handbook of reading research* (Vol. II, pp. 281–309). White Plains, NY: Longman.

*This chapter provides an excellent grounding in the models, methods, purposes, and issues of assessment. The view that assessment is best viewed as a kind of applied research is discussed.*

Five, C. (1993). Tracking writing and reading progress. Portfolios: Windows on learning. *Learning, 21,* 48–51.

*The use of portfolios in the assessment of literacy skills is described. Information on student self-evaluation through the use of portfolios is also included.*

MacGinitie, W. H. (1993). Some limits of assessment. *Journal of Reading, 36,* 556–560.

*An argument concerning the inherent limitations of human judgment as it relates to literacy assessment is presented. The article cautions that there need to be more tentative decisions made concerning such assessment.*

McKenna, M. C. (1993). Computerized reading assessment: Its emerging potential. *The Reading Teacher, 44,* 692–693.

*This article discusses the use of expert systems and interactive computer assessment in helping classroom teachers make decisions about the literacy needs of their students.*

O'Neal, S. (1991). Leadership in the language arts: Student assessment: Present and future. *Language Arts, 68,* 67–73.

*This is an excellent discussion of the current field of reading assessment with particular emphasis on suggestions for future development in this area. An excellent bibliography is included.*

Pikulski, J. J. (1990). The role of tests in a literacy assessment program. *The Reading Teacher, 44,* 686–687.

*This article discusses many of the misuses of standardized reading tests and suggests alternatives.*

Valencia, S. (1991). Portfolio assessment for young readers. *The Reading Teacher, 44,* 680–682.

*This a good discussion of how to create and use portfolios to assess literacy development.*

Valencia, S., et al. (1992). Theory and practice in statewide reading assessment: Closing the gap. *Educational Leadership, 70,* 57–63.

*The innovative statewide reading assessment programs underway in Illinois and Michigan are described.*

## *You Become Involved*

### *Assessment*

Prior to the 1980s and 1990s, assessment and evaluation practices had not undergone extensive reevaluation in schools. Students' learning was generally evaluated using standardized achievement tests and alternative-choice classroom tests. Since that time, educators, government leaders, and communities have begun to question and seek alternative measures for examining individual student's progress, making program and instructional decisions, and evaluating school effectiveness from a global perspective. Using your reading, experience, and discussion with others, complete the following activities.

**1.** How do assessment and evaluation differ? Who should have a role in assessment practices and what should that role be? Who should have a role in evaluation? What should that role be?

**2.** Make three concentric time lines of factors and events that relate to assessment/evaluation. Time line 1 should reflect *school* issues and trends, time line 2 should reflect *societal* issues and trends, and time line 3 should reflect *global* issues and trends. Use the chart provided to complete the time line. When you have completed the time lines, analyze for the following purposes:

- What story does each time line tell about our history?
- Look at each time line in relation to the other two. What patterns and connections do you see?

### Assessment/Evaluation Time Lines

|          | 1960 | 1970 | 1980 | 1990 |
|----------|------|------|------|------|
| Schools  |      |      |      |      |
| Societal |      |      |      |      |
| Global   |      |      |      |      |

# Chapter 8

## Content Literacy

The realization that students in the middle and secondary grades may experience difficulty with assigned materials is hardly new. Historically, teachers associated the problem with a need for remediation on the part of some students. Their difficulties, it was assumed, were the result of deficiencies in basic reading skills. Clearly, this has been the case for some students. A more modern appraisal of the situation, however, involves an awareness that content classrooms present unique demands that may place even good readers at risk. Content reading assignments tend to rely on prior knowledge of content and on reading skills specific to certain areas (for example, the ability to interpret charts in the social studies). Teachers who do not take these factors into account and simply assign materials to be read without adequate preparation of students are often unhappy with the results. Not surprisingly, a large majority of states now require a course in content area reading of those seeking certification at the middle and secondary levels.

### Misconceptions about Content Literacy

Certification regulations have not been universally applauded by teachers (Misulis, 1994). Many continue to view with suspicion the suggestion that they take into account the reading needs of their students. Stewart and O'Brien (1989) surveyed high school teachers to find out why their reactions tend to be so negative. They identified three principal reasons given by these teachers for resisting what they perceived to be "content area reading":

1. Many teachers feel inadequate to contend with the reading problems they face in their classes.
2. Many believe that literacy activities would infringe on subject matter time.
3. Many deny the need for content area literacy techniques.

We suspect that a large number of elementary teachers would offer an additional reason: Literacy needs can be addressed at other times during the day (in a language arts block, for example). These arguments miss two important points about the nature of content literacy techniques. First, such techniques are always integrated with content; they are not taught separately. The use of graphic organizers to teach a cluster of technical vocabulary is one example; the use of a reading guide covering a textbook chapter is another. This means they require no *extra* time. Rather, they represent alternative ways of presenting content in the first place. Second, they are designed to enhance content learning and not to improve general reading ability. If the latter occurs, it is a by-product (Hadaway & Young, 1994; McAloon, 1994).

## As You Read

Martha Rapp Ruddell provides an excellent and succinct history of the movement toward content literacy that originated early in the twentieth century. We have used our own article (McKenna and Robinson) to complement Ruddell's historical perspective because we believe that it summarizes current views of content literacy. The definition it presents has been used to ground two texts devoted to content area reading and writing. Together, these sources should enable you to develop answers to the following questions:

**1.** What is the subtle distinction between the catch phrases "Every teacher a teacher of reading" and "Reading across the curriculum"? With which are you more comfortable?
**2.** How is content literacy much more than the basic ability to read?
**3.** In what way is writing helpful to students as they seek to understand content?
**4.** In your own teaching situation, what are ways you can improve the content literacy of students?

## References

Hadaway, N. L., & Young, T. A. (1994). Content literacy and language learning: Instructional decisions. *The Reading Teacher, 47,* 522–527.
McAloon, N. M. (1994). It's not my job! *Journal of Reading, 37,* 322–334.
Misulis, K. E. (1994). Nurturing the growth of content teachers in content area reading instruction. *Reading Improvement, 31,* 125–128.
Stewart, R. A., & O'Brien, D. G. (1989). Resistance to content area reading: A focus on preservice teachers. *Journal of Reading, 32,* 396–401.

# CONTENT LITERACY GUIDE

**From: Teaching Content Reading and Writing, pp. 5–12**
Martha Rapp Ruddell

1. (T/F) Attention to reading development past the beginning reading stage goes back to the mid-1600s.

2. (T/F) In the twentieth century, secondary reading started as a remedial program rather than a developmental one.

3. Summarize key events in secondary reading during the four decades (1930s–1960s). Use the following time line to organize your notes:

    1930s

    1940s

    1950s

    1960s

4. Why do you think the phrase "developmental reading" is placed in quotation marks?

5. Why did many secondary teachers balk at the saying "Every teacher a teacher of reading"?

6. What two developments characterized increasing concern with secondary reading during the 1970s?

    a.

    b.

**7.** (T/F)  The 1970s saw a decline in state and university requirements that secondary teachers take reading courses.

**8.** List the five emphases of the Bay Area Writing Project (later the National Writing Project):

   a.

   b.

   c.

   d.

   e.

**9.** (T/F)  During the 1980s, accelerated reading courses became as prevalent as remedial courses in high schools and junior highs.

**10.** Do you think the changed "slogan" for secondary reading was more persuasive for content teachers? Why or why not?

**11.** Briefly summarize how the middle school movement affected secondary reading.

**12.** Calls for reform during the 1980s led to (or reinforced) what two major shifts in middle and secondary literacy movements?

   a.

   b.

**13.** Summarize the four reasons given by Ruddell for increasing attention to reading and writing in the middle and secondary grades.

   a.

   b.

   c.

   d.

# FROM: TEACHING CONTENT READING AND WRITING

## MARTHA RAPP RUDDELL

## Middle and Secondary Literacy Instruction in Perspective*

Literacy issues in middle and secondary schools are relative newcomers in the history of education in the United States. The reason is, in part, because U.S. reading instruction began in the mid-1600s as burgeoning communities organized to provide education for young children. Reading instruction was the nucleus of that education and was *developmental* in nature. That is, the major purpose for instruction was to move children from nonreading or prereading stages into beginning reading; from there, individuals advanced more or less independently toward mature reading.

Attention and emphasis on reading instruction beyond early grades, on the other hand, extends back only to about the late 1920s/early 1930s. At that time, various educators and educational movements began to acknowledge differences between literary and technical reading and to promote the practice of providing organized reading instruction for middle-grade and secondary students (Moore et al., 1992). Concurrent with this movement were revelations that many adolescents and adults were unable to perform well on newly developed reading tests, along with concerns regarding the literacy demands for soldiers during World War I and World War II. The major focus of secondary reading instruction in its earliest years was therefore *remedial* in nature, rather than developmental. This difference accounts for the nature and format of contemporary middle school and secondary reading instruction, and it assists us in understanding how this instruction evolved.

### The 1930s

This decade could be characterized as the incubation period for secondary reading instruction. It was a time when professional interest and concern about secondary reading, growing from issues raised in the late 1920s, led to the initiation of research efforts to

* Much of the information for the first three-and-a-half decades of this discussion is taken from Nila Banton Smith's classic study, *American Reading Instruction* (1965).

determine the nature and extent of adolescent and adult reading problems. A major impetus for this research was the combined effect of the discovery, more than a decade earlier, that thousands of soldiers could not read well enough to do their jobs in the army and the availability of newly refined, standardized tests for identification and analysis of reading problems. Although few, if any, instructional programs were established during the 1930s, the interest and study during this period provided the foundation for much of the subsequent research and program development.

## The 1940s

At the beginning of this decade, once again we were involved in a world war, and once again we discovered that many soldiers could not read. This discovery served as a final catalyst for the implementation of remedial reading programs in junior and senior high schools. Although not widespread, such programs were our first attempt to provide systematic reading instruction to even one segment of the secondary school population. By the mid to late 1940s, leaders in the field of reading were recommending—not for the first time but with growing strength—that systematic reading instruction for all students continue into the middle grades and secondary school (Bond, 1941; Gray, 1948) and called for the establishment of developmental reading programs for this purpose.

## The 1950s

During the 1950s, considerable expansion of secondary remedial programs occurred. In this period, reading instruction in general, and reading disability specifically, were receiving intense professional and public scrutiny. With the publication of Rudolph Flesch's *Why Johnny Can't Read* (1955) and with the launching of the Soviet rocket *Sputnik* in 1957, serious questions were raised concerning the quality of American education, with specific attention directed toward reading and reading instruction (science and mathematics were similarly examined). Increased interest in developmental secondary reading programs and content area reading instruction resulted. In 1958, the National Defense Education Act (NDEA) provided massive federal funds for research, teacher training, school programs, and curriculum projects, much of which was allocated for both elementary and secondary reading.

## The 1960s

Secondary remedial reading programs continued to grow during this period. Most programs were funded wholly or in part by the Title I section of the Elementary and Secondary Education Act (ESEA) of 1956 and were subject to strict federal guidelines concerning testing, student selection, and teacher certification. One of the most immediate problems was staffing these programs with certified secondary reading specialists at a time when few, if any, were available. Consequently, many programs, especially in junior high schools, were taught by relocated elementary reading teachers. Newly organized "developmental" reading classes appeared in greater numbers, usually designated as "Basic English" or "Remedial English" classes, and were taught by willing and courageous, but untrained, English teachers who went on to become the secondary reading specialists of the 1970s and 1980s. Rarely did these developmental programs reach all of the students in a junior or senior high school. For the most part, they were intended to provide additional instruction for students who did not qualify for Title I programs or those who had mild reading problems. In some schools, accelerated reading classes were established for college-bound seniors, either as separate courses or as units of study in senior English classes. By the mid- to late 1960s, content area reading instruction was receiving increasingly widespread recognition and support. Its proponents made a clear distinction between their instructional approaches and traditional developmental reading instruction (Herber, 1970, 1978); however, this distinction was not always fully understood or practiced.

## The 1970s

Wide expansion and growth of remedial reading programs occurred during the 1970s. Emerging programs in learning disabilities, English as a Second Language (ESL), and other special education fields were frequently combined with the reading program to form Learning Resource Centers that served an ever-expanding population. Developmental programs also grew, especially in junior high schools, and were still generally intended for students identified as "reading below grade level." By the end of this decade, every major publisher of elementary reading textbooks had added, or was in the process of adding, seventh- and eighth-grade books to their reading series to meet the demands of newly extended developmental reading programs. Even with this expansion, however, "developmental reading" was almost universally interpreted as something that goes on outside the regular classroom. So, some junior high schools supplemented English classes with an additional hour of developmental reading class; others replaced English with a reading class for some students.

### Right to Read and Minimum Competency Movements

During this same period, the Right to Read and minimum competency movements were launched. Right to Read was a campaign aimed at achieving universal national literacy by 1980. The slogan "Every Teacher a Teacher of Reading" (Early, 1957) was adopted as its rallying cry, causing no small amount of frustration and anger among junior and senior high school teachers. The general feeling was that secondary teachers were being asked to replace subject area instruction with reading instruction—to teach phonics instead of physics—a task for which they felt no sympathy and had little, if any, training. Subject area teachers were not happy about this turn of events and made absolutely no effort to disguise their feelings. Because of this negative reaction, and it was substantial, many secondary reading people felt that "Every Teacher a Teacher of Reading" had done more harm than good for secondary reading programs (Herber, 1978).

Certainly, during this time, the reading teacher was often *not* the most popular person among secondary school faculties (remember, many of them were relocated elementary teachers to begin with!). Few of their efforts to convince subject area teachers to incorporate reading instruction into content teaching met with much success. To remedy this situation, schools and districts began sponsoring in-service meetings in which college and university professors in secondary reading met with junior and senior high school faculties to convince teachers of their responsibility and to demonstrate ways to incorporate reading instruction into content classes. I have faced many a tight-lipped, arms-crossed faculty under such circumstances, and I'm certainly not alone in that experience. The success of these efforts varied widely (just as it does today).

Concomitant with Right to Read was the growing impetus of the minimum competency movement. As with Right to Read, the goal was universal literacy, with much of the minimum competency emphasis placed on testing to determine who would pass or graduate from junior high and senior high school, and on a highly publicized "back-to-basics" approach to teaching the so-called basic skills of literacy. By the end of the decade, most schools were doing some type of minimum competency testing, either voluntarily or in compliance with state legislative mandate, and providing compensatory programs for students who did not meet the test standards. These testing programs created many new problems: They required educators to examine such issues as the fine-line distinction between "teaching students how to take the test" and "teaching the test," what to do about students who repeatedly fail the tests (or, How many times can one repeat the eighth grade?), and what to do about the alarming increase in dropout rates (clearly, the students *already knew* what to do when faced with repeated failure). Easy answers to these and other problems were not found, and in fact, the problems still exist.

In spite of disgruntled faculties and new problems, however, the combined impact of Right to Read and the minimum competency movement served to focus attention on the reading needs of secondary students. For all the negative effects, the result was further expansion of secondary school reading programs, increased university and state requirements for secondary teachers to take one or more reading education classes, and growing acceptance of instruction advocated by content area reading proponents.

### Writing Instruction

Significant innovation in writing instruction occurred on a small scale in the 1970s that would have enormous impact in the following decades. In 1973, the Bay Area Writing Project (affectionately called BAWP) was introduced at the University of California at Berkeley with James Gray at its helm (Gray, personal communication, 1989). This project—with its emphasis on writing as a medium of understanding and learning, the teacher as writer, writing for different purposes, extension of classroom writing opportunities, and teachers teaching teachers—formed the nucleus for sweeping reforms in writing instruction. Initially, the project served English and elementary teachers in northern California classrooms, but it has exerted increasing national and international influence since 1976, when it expanded to become the National Writing Project.

## The 1980s

By the beginning of the 1980s, reading programs of one type or another were well established in most secondary schools. While the emphasis was still remedial, developmental programs, accelerated programs, and attention to content reading instruction were growing. Greenlaw and Moore (1982), in a survey of junior and senior high schools, found that over 75 percent of the schools reporting had separate reading courses available to their students. Of these courses, 74 percent were remedial, 44 percent were developmental, and 36 percent were accelerated (many schools reported two or more types of courses). Schools without separate reading courses reported that reading was taught as part of

English, social studies, mathematics, and science courses. Although based on a fairly small sample of schools, this survey is probably indicative of national trends at that time.

Most, if not all, of the remedial reading programs in schools were funded through Chapter I of the Education Consolidation and Improvement Act of 1981 (ECIA), which superseded Title I of the old Elementary and Secondary Education Act of 1965. "Reading Across the Curriculum" replaced "Every Teacher a Teacher of Reading" as the slogan for secondary reading in-service programs and became the rationale for increasingly widespread requirements for all secondary teachers to have at least one course in reading methods.

In the mid-1980s, the middle school movement gained increasing attention and momentum. Rooted in the 1960s, the ideals of the movement grew from educators' beliefs that junior high schools did not adequately meet the needs of the students they served (Moore & Stefanich, 1990). Embedded in the goals of the middle school movement was to provide instruction focused on ". . . higher literacy and thinking strategies . . ." (Moore & Stefanich, 1990, p. 8), and throughout the 1980s, growing numbers of school districts converted junior high schools or formed new middle schools to begin implementing these ideals.

### Criticism and Reform

Midway through the 1980s decade, the nation experienced a major wave of educational reform triggered by the report *A Nation at Risk: The Imperative for Educational Reform,* sponsored by the National Commission on Excellence in Education (1983). This report was followed in rapid succession by (among others) *High School: A Report on Secondary Education in America* (Boyer, 1983), which was commissioned by the Carnegie Foundation for the Advancement of Teaching; *Horace's Compromise: The Dilemma of the American High School* (Sizer, 1984); *A Place Called School* (Goodlad, 1984), and *Becoming a Nation of Readers: The Report of the Commission on Reading* (Anderson et al., 1985). In each, literacy was a focal point, and in each, teachers, schools, textbook publishers, teacher education programs, and any others even remotely responsible for schooling were severely taken to task for the failure of some students to become literate and of other students to achieve beyond the most basic, minimal literacy levels.

This great storm of criticism led to much discussion, more than a little finger-pointing, and legislative as well as other types of reform. The Hawkins-Stafford School Improvement Amendments Act of 1988 repealed the Education Consolidation and Improvement Act of 1981 and brought with it much more stringent educational accountability, but fewer fiscal regulations, for Chapter I reading programs. A major reform emphasis was movement away from "basics" and toward a "critical thinking" and "critical reading" focus. Prominent also was discussion regarding the importance of connecting reading and writing processes, and, by the end of the decade, "Writing Across the Curriculum" had joined "Reading Across the Curriculum" as a major goal of secondary schools (the most telling picture of pre-reform movement writing practices in secondary schools is Applebee's 1981 study, *Writing in the Secondary School*).

The National Writing Project was, by now, well established. Its influence had spread within schools as well as geographically among them, so that Writing Across the Curriculum projects were involving teachers in all subject areas and at all levels of middle, junior, and senior high schools. Thus, writing instruction in middle and secondary schools began to change, bringing into more common practice literacy instruction, planned and taught by classroom teachers, that reflects a view of reading and writing as different sides of the same coin, each of which contributes substantially to learning and cognitive growth.

## The 1990s and Beyond

By the end of the 1980s, then, not only had reading instruction expanded in middle and secondary schools, but writing instruction was gaining acceptance at an increasingly rapid rate. This trend continues today. Some critics view such efforts as yet another indication that schools have been remiss, that we have failed to teach youngsters how to read and write, and because of this failure, now have to establish more and larger second-ary programs to "take care of the problem." A growing number of educators, however, think just the opposite; we understand "the problem" to be one in which fundamental changes are needed in how middle and secondary school students are taught (Atwell, 1987, 1990; M. Ruddell, in press; Sizer, 1992). We believe that expansion of reading and writing instruction into middle schools and junior/senior high schools—with emphasis both in content area literacy instruction and in special reading and writing programs—is a *positive* factor in contemporary education for all of the following reasons.

**1.** Expanded reading and writing instruction acknowledges the fact that literacy growth is continuous and does not stop at the end of fourth or sixth grade. Neither should instruction. All students can and should have the opportunity to experience continued growth as readers and writers, and in order for them to do so, various types of instruction must be available.

**2.** Expanded reading and writing instruction provides for diversity of student literacy abilities and needs. Middle school and secondary classrooms are filled with students who represent wide variation in literacy achievement and English language fluency. This diversity in no way suggests that there is anything "wrong" with any students or casts aspersions on students' previous classroom learning or life experience; nor does it mean that only the bilingual/bicultural students require assistance with English language flu-ency and literacy. Rather it recognizes and celebrates human differences. Middle school and secondary reading and writing instruction provides for all students: those who are achieving satisfactorily, those who simply need more time to arrive at expected achieve-ment levels, those who are in the process of becoming fluent and literate in a second language, and those whose achievement goes well beyond the norm.

**3.** Expanded reading and writing instruction allows students to learn new, more diffi-cult reading/writing/study skills *as they are needed* to complete school tasks (Herber, 1978). Many students find that the skills that served them well in elementary school simply are not adequate for success with the more difficult texts, heavier assignment load, and generally less personalized atmosphere of middle and secondary school. Read-ing and writing instruction in content area classrooms assist students in extending and adapting their skills to meet these new conditions.

**4.** Expanded reading and writing instruction place remedial reading and writing pro-grams into a perspective that more accurately reflects reality. When the *only* literacy instruction in middle and secondary schools was remedial, all discussion of reading, writing and literacy was negative, and all attention and concern were focused on the relatively small percentage of the school population with literacy problems. Certainly that population did and does exist; it would be foolish and irresponsible to suggest otherwise. The net effect, however, was that students, teachers, administrators, and parents alike saw reading and writing instruction as appropriate only for students who were experiencing serious difficulty. Very little effort was made to acknowledge and provide for the many, many students who were progressing well. Negative attitudes linger, but expanded efforts to address reading and writing in all classes have done much to reduce this disparity.

Contemporary middle and secondary reading and writing instruction thus appears to be moving toward the goals and ideals first voiced by reading educators in the 1920s: continued, systematic literacy instruction for all students throughout their school years. As such instruction becomes more and more a part of middle, junior high, and senior high schools, we will be able to turn our attention from literacy *problems* to address more adequately the literacy *processes* of the students we teach.

## *References*

Anderson, R. C., Heibert, E. H., Scott, J. A., & Wilkinson, I. A. G. (1985). *Becoming a nation of readers: The report of the Commission on Reading.* Washington, DC: National Institute of Education.

Applebee, A. N. (1981). *Writing in the secondary school.* Urbana, IL: NCTE.

Atwell, N. (1987). *In the middle: Writing, reading and learning with adolescents.* Portsmouth, NH: Boynton/Cook.

Atwell, N. (1990). *Coming to know: Writing to learn in the intermediate grades.* Portsmouth, NH: Heinemann.

Bond, G. L., & Bond, E. (1941). *Developmental reading in high school.* New York: Macmillan.

Boyer, E. L. (1983). *High school: A report on secondary education in America.* New York: Harper and Row.

Early, M. J. (1957). What does research reveal about successful reading programs? In M. A. Gunn et al. (Eds.), *What we know about high school reading.* Champaign, IL: National Council of Teachers of English.

Flesch, R. (1955). *Why Johnny can't read.* New York: Harper and Row.

Goodlad, J. I. (1984). *A place called school.* New York: McGraw-Hill.

Gray, W. S. (1948). *Reading in the high school and college,* Forty-Seventh Yearbook, Part II, of the National Society for the Study of Education.

Greenlaw, J., & Moore, D. (1982). *Reading programs in secondary schools.* Paper presented at the National Reading Conference, St. Petersburg, FL.

Herber, H. L. (1970). *Teaching reading in content areas.* Englewood Cliffs, NJ: Prentice-Hall.

Herber, H. L. (1978). *Teaching reading in content areas* (2nd ed.). Englewood Cliffs, NJ: Prentice-Hall.

Moore, D. W., Readence, J. E., & Rickelman, R. J. (1992). An historical exploration of content reading instruction. In E. K. Dishner, T. W. Bean, J. E. Readence, & D. W. Moore (Eds.), *Reading in the content areas* (3rd ed.), (pp. 5–29). Dubuque, IA: Kendall/Hunt.

Moore, D. W., & Stefanich, G. P. (1990). Middle school reading: A historical perspective. In G. G. Duffy (Ed.), *Reading in the Middle School* (2nd ed.), (pp. 3–15). Newark, DE: IRA.

National Commission on Excellence in Education. (1983). *A nation at risk: The imperative for educational reform.* Washington, DC: U.S. Government Printing Office.

Ruddell, M. R. (In press). Instructional strategies for developing student interest in content area subjects. In D. Lapp, J. Flood, & N. Farnan (Eds.), *Content area reading/learning: Instructional strategies.* (2nd ed.). Boston: Allyn and Bacon.

Sizer, T. R. (1984). *Horace's compromise: The dilemma of the American high school today.* Boston: Houghton Mifflin.

Sizer, T. R. (1992). *Horace's school: Redesigning the American high school.* Boston: Houghton Mifflin.

Smith, N. B. (1965). *American reading instruction.* Newark, DE: International Reading Association.

# CONTENT LITERACY GUIDE

**Content Literacy: A Definition and Implications**
Michael C. McKenna and Richard D. Robinson
*Journal of Reading,* November 1990, pp. 185–186

**1.** McKenna and Robinson argue against what extension of the term *literacy?*

**2.** In what way can writing help in acquiring new content knowledge?

**3.** State the definition of *content literacy* given by McKenna and Robinson.

**4.** Write *Implication 1:* _____

_____

**5.** (T/F) Content literacy is a prerequisite for content knowledge.

**6.** (T/F) Content knowledge is a prerequisite for content literacy.

**7.** Write *Implication 2:* _____

_____

**8.** Explain this implication in your own words.

**9.** Write *Implication 3:* _____

_____

**10.** (T/F) One's literacy level may vary from one subject to another.

**11.** Write *Implication 4:* _____

_____

**12.** How are reading and writing complementary?

**13.** Write *Implication 5:* _____

_____

**14.** How could content literacy be useful in a course in which no reading or writing is typically done?

**15.** Write *Implication 6:* _____

_____

**16.** (T/F)  Content literacy implies that some of the time traditionally devoted to subject matter instruction be spent in developing decoding skills and writing mechanics.

**17.** Write *Implication 7:* _____

_____

**18.** (T/F)  Students at a rudimentary level of general literacy are not in a position to profit from content literacy activities.

**19.** Write *Implication 8:* _____

_____

**20.** Summarize the four arguments given by McKenna and Robinson against relying totally on direct instruction:

a.

b.

c.

d.

# CONTENT LITERACY
## A DEFINITION AND IMPLICATIONS

MICHAEL C. McKENNA
RICHARD D. ROBINSON

In the past century, the word *literacy* has undergone numerous changes in the broad array of concepts it has denoted (e.g., see Purves, 1984; Stedman & Kaestle, 1987; Venezky, 1990). Some changes, such as the generalization of the term to denote mere knowledgeability of a specific subject (as in *computer literacy, cultural literacy,* etc.), have been unfortunate and continue to make consistent usage difficult. Other changes, such as a multidimensional conceptualization of literacy (Guthrie & Kirsch, 1984; Taylor, 1989) and the necessity that it embrace both situational demands (Guthrie, 1983; Mikulecky, 1990) and cultural considerations (Kazemek, 1988; Levine, 1982) have reflected a growing appreciation for the complexity of literacy processes.

One especially important advance in our understanding has been the recognition that both reading and writing are constructive processes in which information is organized and accommodated into memory structures (see Squire, 1983). Accordingly, the writing-to-learn movement has stressed that writing, like reading, is a means of clarifying, refining, and extending one's internalization of content (Myers, 1984). Writing as well as reading therefore becomes a tool for acquiring content. These realizations together suggest the following further expansion of the concept of literacy.

*Content literacy* can be defined as the ability to use reading and writing for the acquisition of new content in a given discipline. Such ability includes three principal cognitive components: general literacy skills, content-specific literacy skills (such as map reading in the social studies), and prior knowledge of content.

This definition has significant implications for content area teachers—implications that may add to the arguments used to encourage these educators to view matters of literacy with an open mind.

- **Content literacy is not the same as content knowledge.** Content literacy represents skills needed to acquire knowledge of content; the terms are in no way synonymous, as popular usage might suggest. Nor is content literacy a prerequisite of content knowledge, for it is certainly possible to acquire knowledge of content without recourse to reading or writing. On the other hand, content knowledge is a prerequisite of content literacy. In a cyclical pattern, the more prior knowledge one possesses, the more such knowledge will facilitate reading and writing as activities leading to the integration of still more knowledge, and so forth.

• **Teaching content automatically makes students more content literate.**   Whether they know it or not, content area teachers enhance the ability of their students to read and write about content simply by teaching it. There is an irony in this notion, for even those teachers refusing to embrace the ideas of "reading in the content areas" and "writing to learn" have nevertheless improved their students' ability to read and write within their disciplines whenever their instruction has been successful. This is because enhanced knowledge enhances any subsequent reading and writing germane to that knowledge. What is unfortunate is that many teachers, by providing high-quality direct instruction, set the stage for even greater levels of content acquisition—through reading and writing—but never realize this potential with appropriate assignments.

• **Content literacy is content specific.** To be literate in, say, mathematics is not to know mathematics per se but to be able to read and write about the subject as effective means of knowing still more about it. While the general ability to read and write obviously bears on one's success in this process, prior knowledge of the specific topics involved is a vital variable of content literacy. Thus, an individual who is highly literate in math may have a far lower level of literacy in history or economics. This circumstance is largely the result of differences in prior knowledge and is true even though the individual brings the same general literacy skills to all reading and writing tasks.

• **In content literacy, reading and writing are complementary tasks.** While reading and writing can serve well enough as alternative means of enhancing content learning, the greatest gains can be expected when the two are used in tandem. When printed materials are assigned to be read and when written responses are also required, students are placed in the position first of constructing an internal representation of the content they encounter in print and next of refining that representation through such processes as synthesis, evaluation, and summarization.

• **Content literacy is germane to all subject areas, not just those relying heavily on printed materials.** Teachers of subjects such as art, music, physical education, and other fields tending to involve little use of prose materials have frequently objected that content area reading coursework, now compulsory for teachers in at least 36 U.S. states (Farrell & Cirrincione, 1986), does not apply to their instructional situations. Certain states have in fact excluded such groups from these course requirements. The notion of content literacy, however, suggests that students' understanding of the content presented in all subjects could be substantially enhanced through appropriate writing assignments or through supplemental reading.

While the primary presentation may comprise lecture and demonstration rather than reading, and while the principal domain involved may be psychomotor rather than cognitive, content acquisition nevertheless invariably includes an understanding of key concepts and their interrelationships. Such understanding can always be fostered through literacy activities.

• **Content literacy does not require content area teachers to instruct students in the mechanics of writing.** A longstanding misinterpretation has hampered the effort to encourage content area reading techniques. It is that such techniques call for subject matter specialists to teach the minutiae of decoding, requiring them in consequence to master a new and very different curriculum and, worse, to take class time away from subject matter instruction. This false notion has lingered tenaciously despite widespread efforts to overcome it. It is therefore important in elaborating the idea of content literacy, which embraces writing as well as reading, to make clear that it includes no responsibility for developing the mechanical skills of writing.

As Myers puts it, "Writing to learn is not learning to write" (1984, p. 7). It is true that mechanical aberrations severe enough to distort meaning may require a teacher's attention, especially in disciplines like mathematics, where precise usage is an absolute necessity (Orr, 1987). However, the focus of such follow-up should be meaning, not mechanics.

• **Content literacy is relative to the tasks expected of students.** The literacy requirements of a classroom, like those of a workplace or of an entire culture, readily define who is literate and who is not (Guthrie, 1983; Mikulecky, 1990; Wedman & Robinson, in press). In an effort to reduce or eliminate the "illiterate" subpopulation in their classes, teachers all too frequently resort to slashing literacy requirements. Reading assignments may be circumvented or minimized while writing may never be seriously considered. Although students consequently meet the literacy demands of the instructional setting—so that all are technically literate—the opportunity to enhance content learning through reading and writing is in effect waived. Students at even a rudimentary level of general literacy are equipped to advance their understanding through literacy activities, provided that reading materials are commensurate with ability (or steps are taken to facilitate comprehension of more difficult material) and writing assignments are within the range of student sophistication.

• **Content literacy has the potential to maximize content acquisition.** While reading content materials may introduce new ideas into a student's knowledge base and while writing about content may help the student to organize and store that information more effectively, it can be argued that similar results can be accomplished without resort to reading or writing. Instructors may indeed spoon feed new content in carefully organized curricular designs using direct oral instruction. This argument has been strong enough to permit the aliterate environments, mentioned earlier, that have been deliberately established by some teachers.

There are, however, at least four persuasive reasons for not depending exclusively on direct instruction. One is the fact that the products of literacy activities will never precisely match those of oral instruction. They therefore serve to complement such instruction and broaden student perspectives. Another is the individualized extension made possible through such activities as a natural follow-up to direct instruction. Students are in a position to pursue content on their own, following in some measure their personal predilections, needs, and interests.

A further reason is that present models of direct instruction incorporate practice phases that follow up the presentation of content for the purpose of reinforcing it (e.g., Rosenshine, 1986). Such practice could certainly incorporate literacy activities, which seem ideally suited to these models. Finally, students who have been afforded opportunities to become content literate will be better able to use content literacy as a means of extending their knowledge of a discipline even after they have completed a given course.

## New Potential

Little more than a decade ago, the principal message of content area reading courses was a simple one: Because students may find assigned materials difficult, teachers should take steps in advance to facilitate reading. Improved understanding of how literacy processes operate in content classrooms now suggests a constructive role for writing and a more complex view of reading. The potential of these processes for improving content acquisition is actually increased by the knowledge-building effects of day-to-day instruction.

Consequently, the message to content teachers is being revised, and the considerations discussed here, when properly described and advocated, should make the incorporation of content literacy activities a possibility to be pursued rather than shunned.

## References

Farrell, R. T., & Cirrincione, J. M. (1986). The introductory developmental reading course for content area teachers: A state of the art survey. *Journal of Reading, 29,* 717–723.

Guthrie, J. T. (1983). Equilibrium of literacy. *Journal of Reading, 26,* 668–670.

Guthrie, J. T., & Kirsch, I. S. (1984). The emergent perspective on literacy. *Phi Delta Kappan, 66,* 351–355.

Kazemek, F. E. (1988). Necessary changes: Professional involvement in adult literacy programs. *Harvard Educational Review, 58,* 484–487.

Levine, K. (1982). Functional literacy: Found illusions and false economies. *Harvard Educational Review, 52,* 249–266.

Mikulecky, L. (1990). Literacy for what purpose? In R. L. Venezky, D. A. Wagner, & B. S. Ciliberti (Eds.), *Toward defining literacy* (pp. 24–34). Newark, DE: International Reading Association.

Myers, J. W. (1984). *Writing to learn across the curriculum.* Bloomington, IN: Phi Delta Kappa.

Orr, E. W. (1987). *Twice as less: Black English and the performance of Black students in mathematics and science.* New York: Norton.

Purves, A. C. (1984). The potential and real achievement of U.S. students in school reading. *American Journal of Education, 93,* 82–106.

Rosenshine, B. V. (1986). Synthesis of research on explicit teaching. *Educational Leadership, 43,* 60–69.

Squire, J. R. (1983). Composing and comprehending: Two sides of the same basic process. *Language Arts, 60,* 581–589.

Stedman, L. C., & Kaestle, C. F. (1987). Literacy and reading performance in the United States, from 1880 to the present. *Reading Research Quarterly, 22,* 8–46.

Taylor, D. (1989). Toward a unified theory of literacy learning and instructional practices. *Phi Delta Kappan, 71,* 184–193.

Wedman, J., & Robinson, R. D. (in press). Workplace literacy: A perspective. *Adult Literacy and Basic Education.*

Verezky, R. L. (1990). Definitions of literacy. In R. L. Venezky, D. A. Wagner, & B. S. Ciliberti (Eds.), *Toward defining literacy* (pp. 2–16). Newark, DE: International Reading Association.

## *Integrating Sources*

**1.** The authors of both selections argue for increased attention to literacy in content classrooms. The reasons vary somewhat, however. Complete the chart below in an effort to uncover common arguments made in the two selections.

| Ruddell | McKenna and Robinson |
|---|---|
|  |  |

**2.** Now examine the arguments made in one selection but not the other. Are there any inconsistencies or contradictions? Could a single, comprehensive list of reasons be formed? Explain.

## *Classroom Implications*

1. Describe three ways you might incorporate more reading and writing into content instruction.

   a.



   b.



   c.



2. Describe an action research study that might convince a resistant content teacher (not you, of course) that content literacy activities can improve content learning.

## *Annotated Bibliography*

### *Content Literacy*

Alvermann, D. E., & Moore, D. W. (1991). Secondary school reading. In R. Barr, M. Kamil, P. B. Mosenthal, & P. D. Pearson (Eds.), *Handbook of reading research* (Vol. II, pp. 951–983). White Plains, NY: Longman.

*This is an extensive research review of effective practice in content area settings, with additional focus on actual practice.*

Armbuster, B. B. (1993). Readings about reading to learn. *The Reading Teacher, 46,* 598–600.

*An annotated list of references related to content literacy instruction for elementary classroom teachers is included.*

Cooter, R. B. (1993). A think aloud on secondary reading assessment. *Journal of Reading, 36,* 584–586.

*The current role of literacy assessment in secondary content classes is discussed, and suggestions are made for effective changes in these procedures.*

Daisey, P., & Shoryer, M. G. (1993). Perceptions and attitudes of content and methods instructors toward a required reading course. *Journal of Reading, 36,* 624–629.

*This reviews the results of a survey of university student attitudes in relation to a content area reading course. Results are divided into seven categories based on changing ideas of the purpose for content literacy instruction.*

Feathers, K. M. (1993). *Infotext: Reading and learning.* Portsmouth, NH: Heinemann.

*This text describes students who have difficulty learning from information text and suggests specific strategies for help with these problems. An excellent bibliography of related references is included.*

Flood, N., et al. (1993). Teaching the whole enchilada: Enhancing multiculturalism through children's literature in the content areas. *Reading Horizons, 33,* 359–365.

*This article suggests that the integration of content disciplines (social studies, mathematics, art, etc.) can best be accomplished through the use of thematic units. This article includes examples of various types of thematic units based on the theme of Mexico. It also includes a current bibliography.*

Frager, A. M. (1993). Affective dimensions of content area reading. *Journal of Reading, 36,* 616–622.

*The importance of the affective element in the development of content literacy is discussed. Also suggested are classroom strategies to enhance the affective behavior of students' reading in content classes.*

Mosenthal, P., & Kirsch, I. S. (1993). Profiling students' quantitative literacy abilities: An approach with precision. *Journal of Reading, 36,* 668–674.

*An approach to helping content area students improve their quantitative literacy ability is discussed.*

Reinking, D., et al. (1993). Developing preservice teachers' conditional knowledge of content area reading strategies. *Journal of Reading, 36,* 458–469.

*A model for preservice teachers' implementation of effective literacy strategies is presented.*

Schumm, J. S., et al. (1992). What teachers do when the textbook is tough: Students speak out. *Journal of Reading Behavior, 24,* 481–503.

*This article reviews the opinions of a group of middle and high school students on what content literacy teachers do when the textbooks are difficult to read. Suggestions are given to facilitate the effective reading of these literacy materials.*

## You Become Involved

**1.** Locate a content textbook at any grade level published more than 25 years ago. Contrast it with a present-day text in the same area designed to be used at the same level. As you contrast the two, you might use the following questions as guidelines:

- Does the reading level of the material seem appropriate for the intended readers?
- How well is the content of the material likely to reflect the background of the students?
- Is the material well organized? What devices have the authors used to make the organization visible to students?
- What devices appear as comprehension aids? In which text is there better use of charts, marginalia, diagrams, boldface and italics, and other aids?

**2.** Recall your own personal experiences with literacy in the content areas. Were they positive or negative? What do you think made the difference in your reaction to your past experiences? Some possible reasons include the instructional activities of your content teachers, the materials that were used, or perhaps your individual background of experiences related to a particular content subject.

**3.** Visit a high school content classroom and note the literacy activities taking place. In what ways are reading and writing incorporated in the students' learning activities? If you note few examples, ask the teacher why literacy activities are not used more often. Do you agree with the answer(s)?

# Chapter 9

## Vocabulary Instruction

It is clear that children need to know the meanings of a great many words if they are to be effective readers (Anderson & Nagy, 1993). Less clear is what role the teacher should play in helping them acquire word meanings. It would be unusual to find a teacher who never provides instruction in vocabulary, for the simple reason that words are used to symbolize the concepts that constitute knowledge. It would be virtually impossible to teach most subjects without the introduction of new terms.

Many situations present themselves during which introducing new words is appropriate. Words a teacher suspects are unfamiliar might be presented prior to a reading assignment. Word meanings might also be taught with no particular reading assignment in mind, as when a tennis coach demonstrates what the word *volley* means. Technical terms might be logically clustered together and discussed in lecture format, such as the parts of an engine or the stages of mitosis. Last, and most controversially, words might be systematically introduced in an effort to broaden children's vocabulary in a general way. It is on this issue—the best method of accomplishing general vocabulary growth—that this chapter will focus.

### Types of Vocabulary

The word *vocabulary* is usually used in the singular, but it may be more accurate to speak of different sorts of vocabularies. A given individual, for example, not only has a comprehensive vocabulary but a great many specific ones as well. The following are the major types usually discussed among educators:

| | |
|---|---|
| Receptive vocabulary | all of the words an individual can understand when the words are seen or heard (includes reading and listening vocabularies) |

| | |
|---|---|
| Sight vocabulary | all of the words immediately pronounceable when seen |
| Reading vocabulary | all of the words recognizable in their printed form (includes sight vocabulary plus decodable words) |
| Listening vocabulary | all of the words known in their auditory form |
| Expressive vocabulary | all of the words that can be used appropriately in speech or writing |
| Speaking vocabulary | all of the words that can be used appropriately in spoken form |
| Writing vocabulary | all of the words that can be used appropriately in written form |
| Technical vocabulary | all of the words associated with a specific field of study |
| General vocabulary | all of the words not specifically associated with a specific field of study |

It is sometimes useful to think of these vocabulary types in contrasting pairs—for example, expressive versus receptive vocabulary, technical versus general vocabulary, reading versus listening vocabulary, and so on.

## Two Approaches to Instruction

This chapter is concerned primarily with the issue of expanding general vocabulary. Two major positions have arisen with respect to how this goal might best be accomplished. One view advocates an *incidental* approach, in which the teacher ensures that children have numerous and varied opportunities to read widely (Anderson & Nagy, 1993). According to this view, the number of words an individual must acquire is too great for systematic instruction so that repeated exposures in context must be relied on. The second view holds that a *direct* approach is preferable to haphazard reliance on contextual exposure. A systematic introduction to important new words is, according to this view, an essential ingredient of a good vocabulary program (Buikema & Graves, 1993; Medo & Ryder, 1993). It is unlikely that very many educators hold either of these views exclusively. The real issue is one of emphasis.

## As You Read

The Anglo-Saxons had no word for vocabulary. Instead, they used the phrase "word horde" to describe the accumulation of words a person had learned—an expression that suggests an individual's ownership of words once their meanings have been acquired. Adding significantly to the general "word hordes" of today's students is a daunting task that requires some strategic decisions about how the best results are likely to be achieved.

The two approaches—incidental and direct—are well discussed in the following articles. Nagy and Herman argue for the former but concede that there are many occasions when direct instruction is important. Blachowicz and Lee acknowledge the usefulness of wide reading but advocate some direct instruction in vocabulary situated within a whole language environment. It will become clear that none of these authors is recommending an all-or-nothing stance, but it will be up to you to decide what kind of mix is likely to be most effective. These questions might be useful in guiding your thinking:

**1.** What arguments support an incidental approach to vocabulary acquisition?
**2.** Under what circumstances is it preferable to provide direct instruction in word meanings?
**3.** Is a combination of incidental and direct approaches possible and/or desirable?
**4.** If so, how would the two components complement each other?

## References

Anderson, R. C., & Nagy, W. E. (1993). *The vocabulary conundrum. Technical report no. 570.* Urbana, IL: Center for the Study of Reading.

Buikema, J. L., & Graves, M. F. (1993). Teaching students to use context cues to infer word meanings. *Journal of Reading, 36,* 450–457.

Medo, M. A., & Ryder, R. J. (1993). Effects of vocabulary instruction on readers' ability to make causal connections. *Reading Research and Instruction, 8,* 97–105.

## CONTENT LITERACY GUIDE

**Incidental vs. Instructional Approaches to Increasing Reading Vocabulary**
William E. Nagy and Patricia A. Herman
*Educational Perspectives, 23,* 1985, 16–21

1. In your own words, restate the authors' thesis with regard to incidental vocabulary instruction.

2. Summarize their rationale for the position they take.

3. At what rate does a child's vocabulary typically grow from grades 3 to 12?

4. Each year, children in grades 3–12 probably encounter

   ____ hundreds of unfamiliar words.

   ____ thousands of unfamiliar words.

   ____ tens of thousands of unfamiliar words.

   ____ hundreds of thousands of unfamiliar words.

5. (T/F)  Very little vocabulary instruction occurs in elementary classrooms.

6. Summarize the authors' position with respect to the need to teach individual word meanings.

7. Why do Nagy and Herman describe learning words from reading as a "default" argument?

8. Why are written contexts apt not to be as useful as oral contexts in learning words?

9. Briefly, how do the studies cited tend to explain away the fact that written contexts are often not very useful in providing the meaning of an unfamiliar word?

**10.** What are the approximate chances of adequately learning a new word's meaning after one exposure in context?


**11.** Summarize the effects on word exposure of asking children to read for 25 minutes per day.


**12.** State the two complementary approaches to increasing incidental word learning:

a.

b.


**13.** (T/F)  Research has established that vocabulary and comprehension are related.

**14.** (T/F)  Preteaching vocabulary contained within a reading selection, by providing definitions, is a dependable means of increasing students' comprehension of that selection.

**15.** What attributes are needed to ensure that vocabulary instruction translates into improved comprehension?

a.

b.

c.

d.

e.


**16.** (T/F)  Teaching individual word meanings tends to increase general comprehension ability substantially.

**17.** Summarize what Nagy and Herman mean by "less intensive approaches" to vocabulary instruction.


**18.** What is their view of such approaches?

# INCIDENTAL VS. INSTRUCTIONAL APPROACHES TO INCREASING READING VOCABULARY

WILLIAM E. NAGY
PATRICIA A. HERMAN

Our concern is with the effectiveness of different approaches to vocabulary, relative to two major, related educational goals: Increasing the overall size of students' reading vocabulary and increasing students' ability to comprehend text. Educators and basal publishers rightly recognize the importance of vocabulary knowledge in reading and, therefore, include some form of vocabulary instruction in most current reading programs. Our thesis, however, is that explicit vocabulary instruction, even at its best, is not very effective at producing substantial gains in overall vocabulary size or in reading comprehension. Major progress towards these goals can only be attained by increasing incidental vocabulary learning.

In the first section of this article we consider the size of the task: that is, the number of words students would have to learn to make any substantial gains in overall vocabulary size. We feel that the size of the task is almost universally underestimated, or else simply not taken into account. Teaching the meanings of individual words may be effective for a specific reading lesson but it cannot result in any substantial increase in overall vocabulary size.

In the short run, incidental learning looks ineffective compared to almost any other instructional approach to vocabulary growth. But when the size of the task is accurately assessed, it is seen that the bulk of children's vocabulary growth necessarily comes through incidental learning. We will argue that regular and sustained reading can lead to substantial gains in vocabulary size.

In the second section we will consider the nature of the task: that is, the type of word knowledge that is necessary to facilitate reading comprehension. Evidence from a number of studies[1] shows that reliable gains in reading comprehension can be produced through instruction of words from a given passage only if the instruction provides multiple encounters that supply a variety of information about the instructed words. Since vocabulary instruction can supply multiple, rich encounters for only a small number of words (or a small number of encounters for a slightly larger number of words), students must have additional opportunities to encounter large numbers of words repeatedly.

## The Size of the Task

What would count as a reasonable yardstick for measuring the size of the task? That is, how can we decide how many words would be "a lot" to learn, and how many words would be "far to few?" One such measure is the number of words children are actually learning. According to our estimates,[2] the reading vocabulary of the average child grows at a rate of 3,000 words per year between grades three and 12.

Another possible measure of the size of the task is in terms of individual differences. According to figures reported by M. K. Smith[3] for grades four through 12, there is about a 6,000-word gap in vocabulary size between a child at the 25th percentile in vocabulary and a child at the 50th percentile. While Smith's figures for absolute vocabulary size are probably inflated, it still appears that bringing a low-vocabulary student up to the median would involve a gain of 4,000–5,000 words or more—not to mention keeping up with the yearly 3,000-word vocabulary growth of the average student.

Another measure of the size of the task is the number of unknown words a student encounters in reading. Unfortunately, there is little information available on the number of unfamiliar words students find in-text. However, additional analyses of data reported in part by Anderson and Freebody[4] indicate that reading 25 minutes per school day an average student in the fifth grade would encounter tens of thousands of different words a year which he or she did not know, even by a lenient criterion of word knowledge. For a student with a smaller-than-average vocabulary, the number of unfamiliar words would be even higher.

### Implications of the Size of the Task

No matter how one measures the task, then, it is extremely large. Most children encounter new words by the tens of thousands per year, and learn thousands of them. Given this yardstick, what is the role of vocabulary instruction in children's vocabulary growth? Surveys of classrooms[5] reveal that very little explicit vocabulary instruction occurs. The number of words covered in such instruction is, at best, a few hundred a year. Thus, it is evident that most children must be acquiring the vast bulk of their vocabulary knowledge apart from instruction specifically devoted to vocabulary learning. It also follows that children who acquire a larger-than-average vocabulary—who may be learning 1,000 words per year more than the average student—are not doing so simply through better vocabulary lessons.

Should one take this as an indication of the sorry state of current vocabulary instruction in our schools and call for more time spent teaching words? There is room for improvement in the area of vocabulary instruction, but the size of the task is such that just teaching more words cannot be seen as the answer. With very few exceptions,[6] even extremely ambitious vocabulary programs do not cover more than a few hundred words per year.[7] While there are good reasons for teaching children the meanings of individual words, it is important to recognize the limitations of such instruction. Teaching children specific words will not, in itself, contribute substantially to their overall vocabulary size. Even an ambitious and systematic approach to vocabulary will not cover enough words to bring a low-vocabulary student up to average.

## Promoting Large-Scale Vocabulary Growth

Given the size of the task, it is clear that teaching individual word meanings cannot, in itself, produce large-scale vocabulary growth in school children, or make up for the deficiencies of students with inadequate vocabularies. However, this fact should not lead to a fatalistic or *laissez-faire* attitude about vocabulary. On the contrary, the size of average annual vocabulary growth shows that most children are capable of learning new words rapidly and effectively. Therefore, it is very important to determine *where* and *how* children are learning so many words, and to determine how maximum use can be made of all these avenues of vocabulary acquisition. It is also important to find out why some children fail to utilize them effectively.

## Learning Word Meanings from Context

If only a few hundred of the 3,000 words the average child learns in a year are learned in instruction specifically aimed at vocabulary, where are all the other words learned? A number of sources are possible: The speech of parents and peers, classroom lectures and discussions, school reading, free reading, and television. Speech of parents and peers may well be the most significant source of vocabulary for many children, but this factor is the least under the teacher's control. We want to focus on the possible contribution to vocabulary growth of a factor that is, to large extent, under the teacher's control: Reading.

Many believe that incidental learning of words from context while reading is, or at least can be, the major mode of vocabulary growth once children have really begun to read. This is our position also. It is not, however, held universally. There are a number of grounds on which one can question the effectiveness of learning from written context as an avenue of vocabulary growth.

For the most part, arguments for learning from context have been largely "default" arguments.[8] That is, learning from context is assumed to be effective because nobody can figure out where else children could be learning all those words.

Even if one accepts the "default" argument for learning from context, this does not establish that learning from *written* context is an effective means of vocabulary acquisition; much of the incidental word learning that makes up the bulk of children's vocabulary growth might be from *oral* context.

Learning word meanings from *oral* context is obviously a major mode of vocabulary acquisition, especially in the preschool years. Many, if not most, of the thousands of words that children learn before they enter school are learned without any explicit definition or explanation. However, there is good reason to believe that written context will not be as helpful as oral context in illuminating the meanings of unfamiliar words. When a child learns a word from oral context, there is also a rich extralinguistic context—in the easiest case, the object named might be physically present. There are also clues from intonation and gesture that can make the context richer. In addition, the speaker will usually have some sensibility to gaps in the listener's knowledge, and the listener can always ask questions if something isn't understood. Written context will, therefore, usually not be as rich or helpful as oral context in providing information about the meanings of new words.

Some studies have, in fact, found written context ineffective at providing information about the meanings of new words.[9] Written contexts usually supply only limited information about the meaning of unfamiliar words, and are sometimes even misleading.[10] Also, experimental studies have generally found inferring meanings from context to be less effective than more intensive or explicit forms of instruction.[11]

Such results pose a problem for those who would like to believe that inferring meanings from written context is an effective means of learning new words. We believe that the discrepancy can be resolved by specifying more precisely how incidental learning of word meanings from written context takes place.

Two recent studies[12] have attempted to assess the volume of incidental word learning from context under as natural conditions as possible. Subjects were asked to read silently, without any information about the nature of the experiment. Texts were taken from school materials at the grade level of the subjects and represented narratives and expositions. Word knowledge was assessed after reading (in one study, a week later) without the text present. Target words were real words, selected by teachers as being the most difficult words in the text.

In most learning-from-context experiments, prior knowledge of the target words is controlled for by using either nonsense words or real words for which it can be demonstrated or assumed that subjects have no prior knowledge. In the two studies by Nagy et al., on the other hand, it was assumed that subjects would have at least partial prior knowledge of some of the target words. Degree of prior knowledge was controlled for statistically through pre-testing and control groups.

A basic presupposition of these studies was that learning word meanings from context proceeds in small increments. Any single encounter with a word in context is likely to provide only a small gain in knowledge of that word.[13] If one starts with words about which nothing is known, a single encounter in context is not likely to produce a measurable degree of word knowledge, especially if the test of word knowledge used requires a fairly complete knowledge of the meanings of the words tested. This, it is argued, accounts for the failure of some experiments to find a significant amount of learning from context.

Using real words from grade-level text insures that for any given subject, there will be target words at various points along a continuum of word knowledge. Even a single encounter with the word in context should move most of these words a little bit higher on the scale of knowledge. For any given criterion of word knowledge, it is likely that some words not previously known to that criterion will be known to that criterion after reading.

The results of the studies by Nagy et al., indicate that reading grade-level texts does produce a small but statistically reliable increase in word knowledge. This effect was found in all grades tested (three, five, seven, and eight). While different texts produced differing amounts of learning from context, there was no indication that the younger or less-able readers were not able to learn new word meanings through reading.

The absolute amount of learning found was small; the chance of learning a word to any given criterion from one exposure in-text is somewhat around one in twenty. This low figure shows why learning from natural context appears ineffective compared to any other type of instruction on word meanings.

However, learning from context must be evaluated in terms of its long-term effectiveness. The long-term effectiveness of learning from written context depends on how many unfamiliar words are encountered over a period of time. If students were to spend 25 minutes a day reading at a rate of 200 words per minute for 200 days out of a year, they would read a million words of text annually. According to our estimates, in this amount of reading children will encounter between 15,000 and 30,000 unfamiliar words. If one in twenty of these words are learned, the yearly gain in vocabulary will be between 750 and 1,500 words.

Such a gain is substantial, considering the proportion of yearly vocabulary growth that is covered and the fact that it would be extremely difficult, if not impossible, for any word-by-word approach to vocabulary instruction to cover the same number of words in the same amount of time. The amount of reading required—25 minutes per school day—may involve more reading than many students actually do, but could hardly be called excessive.

Incidental learning of word meanings from written context may, therefore, account for a large proportion of the annual vocabulary growth of those students who do read regularly. A period of sustained and silent reading could lead to substantial yearly gains in vocabulary, probably much larger than could be achieved by spending the same amount of time on instruction specifically devoted to vocabulary.

Given the size of the task—the number of words children should be learning in a year—an effective approach to vocabulary development has to take advantage of all avenues of word learning. Since the bulk of children's vocabulary growth occurs incidentally, that is, outside of situations specifically devoted to word learning, the most important goal of vocabulary instruction should be to increase the amount of incidental word learning by students. There are two complementary approaches to increasing incidental word learning: First, increasing children's *ability* to profit from potential word-learning situations outside of vocabulary instruction, and, second, increasing children's *opportunities* to learn.

There are a number of ways in which children's ability to learn words independently might be increased. Reasonable arguments can be made for teaching affixes, for the use of context clues, and for finding ways of increasing children's motivation to learn new words. All of these are undoubtedly of some value, but we are not aware of any published research demonstrating a successful method for making students into better independent word learners. However, it is clear how children's opportunity to learn words independently can be increased: By increasing the amount of time they spend reading. Incidental learning of words during reading may be the easiest means of promoting large-scale vocabulary growth.

## The Nature of the Task

So far, we have presented evidence that the *size* of the vocabulary-learning task is larger than is often recognized. The large number of words to be learned shows the limitations of any form of vocabulary instruction taking words one at a time, and shows the need for maximizing students' abilities and opportunities for learning words on their own. Now we want to consider the *nature* of the task: What kind of word knowledge one hopes to produce in students and how different labels of word knowledge affect comprehension.

## Vocabulary Knowledge and Reading Comprehension

Educators and researchers have long known that a strong correlational relationship exists between vocabulary knowledge and reading comprehension: Children who know more words understand text better.[14]

This relationship is the motivation for what is done in vocabulary instruction. There are, of course, other reasons for teaching words—increasing students' speaking and writing vocabularies, improving scores on standardized tests, or teaching specific concepts in content areas. Much of the time, however, words are taught to enable students to understand what they read. Even if the words are taught for another purpose—for example, for use in writing—the instruction would be suspect if it did not also enable students to understand sentences containing the instructed words. An appropriate measure of the effectiveness of most vocabulary instruction, then, is its effectiveness in increasing comprehension.

The strong correlational relationship between vocabulary knowledge and reading comprehension would seem to imply that teaching words should automatically increase reading comprehension. This is not the case, however, as surveys of attempts to increase reading comprehension through vocabulary instruction[15] reveal that approaches to vocabulary instruction differ widely in their ability to increase the comprehension of texts containing the instructed words. Stahl and Fairbanks report that "methods which provided only definitional information about each to-be-learned word did not produce a significant effect on comprehension, nor did the methods which gave only one or two exposures to meaningful information about each word."[16] Pearson and Gallagher found that studies which were successful in increasing passage comprehension through pre-teaching vocabulary were the exception rather than the rule.[17] The exceptional studies were those in which the vocabulary instruction was richer than a simple definitional approach.

It appears that the following are attributes which can make vocabulary instruction effective at increasing reading comprehension: Multiple exposures to words, exposure to words in meaningful contexts, rich or varied information about each word, establishment of ties between instructed words and students' own experience and prior knowledge, and an active role by students in the word-learning process.

## The Difficulty of Producing Overall Gains in Reading Comprehension through Vocabulary Instruction

Some types of vocabulary instruction have been shown to increase reading comprehension for passages containing the instructed words, although much of current practice does not seem to fall into this category of instruction. But can vocabulary instruction produce overall gains in comprehension for passages which have not specifically been targeted for instruction?

Stahl and Fairbanks found that vocabulary instruction did, in fact, produce significant, although small, gains in general reading comprehension.[18] We find it surprising, not that the gain is small, but that it occurs at all. The number of words in print is so great that even an extensive program of vocabulary instruction is unlikely to cover much more than a minute percentage of the words in a text selected at random. Stahl and Fairbanks hypothesize that the general increase in reading comprehension produced by vocabulary instruction may be the result, not of the words specifically covered in the instruction, but in increased incidental learning that the instruction may also produce.[19]

It is highly unlikely that teaching individual word meanings could ever produce more than a very slight increase in general reading comprehension. Overall improvement in reading comprehension requires improvement in skills and strategies. In fact, explicit training in comprehension strategies has generally produced measurable gains in comprehension.[20]

## Reading and Reading Comprehension

Although hard experimental evidence is not at hand, one can make a well-reasoned argument that reading itself can be an effective way of increasing reading comprehension. First, as we have already argued, wide reading seems to be an effective way of producing truly large-scale vocabulary growth. There is also reason to believe that the type of word knowledge gained through wide reading would be the type that is effective at facilitating comprehension. Wide reading will lead to multiple encounters with words in a variety of meaningful contexts. To the extent that the rest of the text is comprehensible, these encounters will help the reader establish ties between the new word and prior knowledge. Pearson and Gallagher, in reviewing the effects of pre-teaching vocabulary on passage comprehension, conclude that "knowledge acquired gradually over time in whatever manner appears more helpful to comprehension than knowledge acquired in a school-like context for the purpose of aiding specific passage comprehension."[21] This description certainly fits the type of knowledge gained through wide reading.

Increased vocabulary knowledge is not the only benefit of wide reading that might increase comprehension. There is also the increase in general knowledge. Crafton found that reading one article on a topic strongly improved comprehension of a second article on the same topic.[22] In addition, practice in reading would lead to improvement or automatization of a wide range of reading skills that contribute to comprehension.

Improving reading comprehension is certainly an important instructional goal. However, vocabulary instruction as such is of limited usefulness in this regard. Teaching the meanings of individual words appears to be an efficient means of increasing comprehension only with specific passages and with a relatively small number of words. To produce general gains in comprehension, the most profitable use of instructional time would appear to be a focus on comprehension skills and strategies. Reading itself should also increase comprehension through the accumulation of background knowledge and practice in various reading subskills.

## In Defense of "Superficial" Vocabulary Instruction

It has been argued[23] that the benefits of even definitional methods of vocabulary instruction have been underestimated in the following sense: We have shown so far that the level of word knowledge required to improve reading comprehension can only be gained by multiple exposures to a word which provide a variety of information about that word. Learning definitions alone does not produce this level of word knowledge and, therefore, does not enhance reading comprehension. However, just as we have already argued in the case of learning from written context, one should not underestimate the value of any meaningful encounter with a word even if the information gained from that one encounter is relatively small.

A single encounter with a word in a definitional approach to vocabulary will not produce very deep word knowledge; but it is very likely to provide more information than a reader's initial encounter with that word in context, which, in fact, is likely to be rather uninformative, and, at worst, possibly misleading.[24] This initial definitional encounter may provide a good foundation for learning from additional exposures to the word in context.[25]

This line of reasoning is plausible enough. If demonstrated to be valid, such definitional encounters might provide grounds for the use of less-intensive methods as one component of a comprehensive approach to vocabulary, even though these methods by themselves cannot reliably increase reading comprehension. Less-intensive methods would allow a larger number of words to be covered. However, the value of such methods depends on later multiple exposures to the instructed words in meaningful context. Therefore, such an approach to vocabulary would still require a large volume of reading to produce the kind of word knowledge that is actually the proper goal of vocabulary instruction.

## Conclusion

The purpose of this article has been to make a case for the importance of incidental vocabulary learning. We do not want to overstate our case and imply that no words should be explicitly taught. But reports of new effective methods of vocabulary instruction seldom contain any warnings about their limitations. We feel that methods of vocabulary instruction can be effectively developed and implemented only if their limitations as well as their strengths are clearly understood. The major limitation of any approach to vocabulary development which takes words one at a time is that it can only cover a small fraction of the words that students should be learning.

The ultimate test of a comprehensive approach to vocabulary must be whether it results in large and long-term gains in reading vocabulary and reading comprehension. Success in these terms cannot be attained without increasing students' incidental word learning. It is important to determine what types of vocabulary instruction can effectively increase students' ability to learn independently. Attention must be given to affixes, context clues, awareness of words and their meanings, and motivation to learn them. But any attempt to increase incidental learning substantially must include an increase in the opportunity to learn new words, and this will occur primarily through regular, sustained reading.

# *Footnotes*

1. Pearson, P. and M. Gallagher. "The Instruction of Reading Comprehension," in *Contemporary Educational Psychology, 8,* 317–334, 1984. Also, S. Stahl and M. Fairbanks, "The Effects of Vocabulary Instruction: A Model-Based Meta-Analysis," unpublished manuscript, Western Illinois University, 1984.

2. Nagy, W., P. Herman and R. Anderson. "Grade and Reading Ability Effects on Learning Words From Context," paper presented at the National Reading Conference, St. Petersburg, Florida, December 1984.

3. Smith, M. K. "Measurement of the Size of General English Vocabulary Through the Elementary Grades and High School," in *General Psychological Monographs, 24,* 311–345, 1941.

4. Anderson, R. and P. Freebody. "Reading Comprehension and The Assessment and Acquisition of Word Knowledge," in B. Hutson, ed., *Advances in Reading/Language Research,* 231–256, Greenwich, Connecticut: JAI Press, 1983.

5. Durkin, D. "What Classroom Observations Reveal About Reading Comprehension Instruction," in *Reading Research Quarterly, 14,* 481–533. 1979. Also, N. Roser and C. Juel, "Effects of Vocabulary Instruction on Reading Comprehension," in J. Niles and L. Harris, eds., *New Inquiries in Reading Research and Instruction,* Rochester, New York: National Reading Conference, 1982.

6. Draper, A. and G. Moeller. "We Think With Words (Therefore, To Improve Thinking, Teach Vocabulary), in *Phi Delta Kappan, 52,* 482–484, 1971.

7. Beck, L., C. Perfetti and M. McKeown. "The Effects of Long-Term Vocabulary Instruction on Lexical Access and Reading Comprehension," in *Journal of Educational Psychology, 74,* 506–521, 1982.

8. Jenkins, J., and R. Dixon. "Vocabulary Learning," in *Contemporary Educational Psychology, 8,* 237–260, 1983.

9. Sachs, H. "The Reading Method of Acquiring Vocabulary," in *Journal of Educational Research, 36,* 457–464, 1943. Also, R. Baldwin and E. Schatz, "Are Context Clues Effective With Low-Frequency Words in Naturally Occurring Prose?", paper presented at the National Reading Conference, St. Petersburg, Florida, December 1984.

10. Beck, I., M. McKeown and E. McCaslin. "All Contexts Are Not Created Equal," in *Elementary School Journal, 83,* 177–181, 1983. Also, L. Deighton, *Vocabulary Development in the Classroom,* New York: Bureau of Publications, Teacher's College, Columbia Univesity, 1959.

11. Margosein, C., E. Pascarella and S. Pflaum. "The Effects of Instruction Using Semantic Mapping on Vocabulary and Comprehension," paper presented at the annual meeting of the American Educational Research Association, New York, April 1982. See also, M. Pressley, J. Levin and H. Delaney, "The Mnemonic Keyboard Method," in *Review of Educational Research, 52,* 61–91, 1982.

12. Nagy, et al. *op. cit.,* see Footnote 2.

13. Deighton, *op. cit.,* see Footnote 11.

14. Anderson, R. and P. Freebody. "Vocabulary Knowledge," in J. Guthrie, ed., *Comprehension and Teaching: Research Reviews,* 77–117, Newark, Delaware: International Reading Association, 1981. Also, F. Davis, "Fundamental Factors of Comprehension in Reading," in *Psychometrika, 9,* 185–197, 1944, and "Research in Comprehension in Reading," in *Reading Research Quarterly, 3,* 499–545, 1968. And, L. Thurstone, "A Note on a Reanalysis of Davis' Reading Tests," in *Psychometrika, 11,* 185–188, 1946.

15. Pearson, et al., *op. cit.,* see Footnote. 1.

16. Stahl, et al., *op. cit.,* see Footnote 1.

17. Pearson, et al., *op. cit.,* see Footnote 1.

18. Stahl, et al., *op. cit.,* see Footnote 1.

19. *Ibid.*

20. Pearson, et al., *op. cit.,* see Footnote 1.

21. *Ibid.*

22. Crafton, L. "The Reading Process as a Transactional Learning Experience," unpublished doctoral dissertation, Indiana University; also cited in Pearson, et al., see Footnote 1.

23. Personal communication between authors and Isabel Beck, November 30, 1984.

24. Beck, et al., *op. cit.,* see Footnote 10. Also, Baldwin, et al., *op. cit.,* see Footnote 9.

25. Jenkins, J. R., M. L. Stein and K. Wysocki. "Learning Vocabulary Through Reading," in *American Educational Research Journal, 21,* 767–787, 1984.

# *References*

J. Jenkins, D. Pany and J. Schreck, *Vocabulary and Reading Comprehension: Instructional Effects.* Tech Rep No. 100, Urbana: University of Illinois Center for the Study of Reading, 1978.

W. Nagy and R. Anderson. "The Number of Words in Printed School English," in *Reading Research Quarterly, 19,* 304–330, 1984.

W. Nagy, P. Herman and R. Anderson. "Learning Words From Context," in *Reading Research Quarterly,* in press.

# CONTENT LITERACY GUIDE

**Vocabulary Development in the Whole Literacy Classroom**
Camille L. Z. Blachowicz and John J. Lee
*The Reading Teacher, 45,* 1991, 188–195

1. (T/F) Blachowicz and Lee contend that their suggestions come from "shared principles" (i.e., ideas common to otherwise differing viewpoints).

2. Summarize the three characteristics of whole literacy instruction identified by Blachowicz and Lee.

   a.

   b.

   c.

3. Summarize the sports metaphor for the place of direct instruction in whole literacy.

4. Summarize the "dimmer" analogy to describe word knowledge.

5. (T/F) Blachowicz and Lee, while acknowledging the usefulness of wide reading, still maintain that "small instructional interventions" can be helpful.

6. Why does wide reading, by itself, often not work well for poor readers as a means of increasing vocabulary size?

7. List six instructional methods that encourage "deeper processing" of word meanings.

   a.

   b.

   c.

   d.

   e.

   f.

**8.** Restate, in your own words, the six guidelines for classroom vocabulary instruction:

a.

b.

c.

d.

e.

f.

**9.** (T/F)  Most vocabulary instruction occurs *prior* to reading.

# VOCABULARY DEVELOPMENT IN THE WHOLE LITERACY CLASSROOM

CAMILLE L. Z. BLACHOWICZ
JOHN J. LEE

Currently there is an active and productive dialogue about what constitutes appropriate literacy instruction (e.g., Aaron, Chall, Durkin, Goodman, & Strickland, 1990; Hoffman, 1989) which is resulting in attempts to structure more holistic literacy instructional approaches. These approaches are many and varied and include programs such as whole language programs, literature-based instruction, and content reading programs. At the same time, teachers and researchers are rethinking many of the components of traditional instruction, such as that of vocabulary instruction (Baumann & Kameenui, 1991; Beck & McKeown, 1991; Nagy & Herman, 1987) in the light of these new perspectives.

How to use the information generated by these dialogues to make sensible change while continuing to offer effective instruction is every teacher's challenge. One way to approach this task is to extract shared principles from different proposals for change and to test them in instruction. The first purpose of this article is to describe three characteristics of what will be termed whole literacy instruction, an umbrella term used for current holistic trends in literacy instruction. The second goal will be to relate these characteristics to current perspectives on vocabulary instruction. Included are examples designed by middle-grade teachers who were interested in using these ideas to shape classroom instruction.

## Defining Whole Literacy Instruction

Though not exhaustive, there are three characteristics we believe to be essential to whole literacy instruction and relevant to making sense of current perspectives on vocabulary instruction.

**1.** *Time is spent on real reading.* Both early and more recent research emphasize that instructional time is often squandered on isolated drill, management, and other activities of questionable instructional effectiveness (Fisher et al., 1980). A significant trend in whole literacy instruction has been toward allocating more in-school time to the reading and writing of longer, natural texts. This is a general recommendation in the literature from educators whose theoretical perspectives might place them at different spots along the whole literacy continuum (Durkin, 1987; Smith, 1982) and is consistent with classroom initiatives calling for literature-based curricula.

**2.** *Learners are actively engaged with meaningful, language-rich tasks.* Any instructional tasks surrounding authentic reading must engage learners in active, meaningful ways. Whether the task is student initiated, teacher directed, or cooperatively defined, it is a task that makes sense to all involved and is one in which students are personally involved. This occurs when students read and respond, write and share, as active participants, rather than passive receivers of information.

**3.** *Problem-solving strategies are utilized and developed.* Whole literacy instruction emphasizes the development of student problem-solving strategies and metacognition within the context of larger communicative tasks, such as predictive reading or process writing. Specific instruction is given when it is needed to accomplish the larger task. Further, the instruction is scaffolded to promote the development of the student's own problem-solving abilities. The teacher can help a student develop a personal question, provide clues or models for its solution, and help the student consolidate new processes or knowledge for future learning (Pearson & Gallagher, 1983).

A good metaphor for this characteristic is that provided by learning a sport, for example, tennis. A general ability to play tennis is best developed by game play, but it is sometimes helpful to have an expert help you locate a problem, to take you aside and show you how to hit a more effective backhand, for example. However, such instruction is truly helpful only when the expert gets you right back into a game where you can try out new instruction integrated into a real game situation.

## Whole Literacy and Vocabulary Development

These three characteristics—emphasizing real reading in classrooms, engaging learners in active ways in instruction, and developing independent problem-solving strategies— are hallmarks of current best practice in literacy instruction (Alvermann & Moore, 1991; Pearson & Fielding, 1991; Sulzby & Teale, 1991). Further, these same three assumptions are also critical to understanding current perspectives on vocabulary instruction.

Wide reading is agreed to be an important contributor to general vocabulary development by researchers and theorists who might disagree on the shape of appropriate school vocabulary instruction (cf. Baumann & Kameenui, 1991; Beck & McKeown, 1991; Nagy, 1988). Knowledge of a word is not an all-or-nothing proposition, like a light switch that is in an "off" or "on" position. A better metaphor is that of a light *dimmer* switch that gradually supplies an increasingly richer supply of light. Learners move from not knowing a word, to being somewhat acquainted with it, to a deeper, richer, more flexible word knowledge that they can use in many modalities of expression (Carey,

1978; Dale, 1965). Repeated encounters with a word, in oral and written language, provide experiences with and clues to the word's meaning that accrue over time and help build and change our mental structures for the word's meaning (Eller, Pappas, & Brown, 1988; Nagy, 1988; Vosniadou & Ortony, 1983).

Wide reading also helps readers develop and retain meaningful personal contexts for words (Whittelsea, 1987). For example, the word *wardrobe* becomes meaningful in *The Lion, the Witch and the Wardrobe* (Lewis, 1950) in a way it never could in its dictionary definition or in an isolated sentence. Specific events in the novel help the learner note that a wardrobe is a piece of furniture that can be located in a bedroom, that has a front door, and that is big enough to walk through; it is a term that is critical to the setting and action of this novel. The setting, problems, and actions of stories; the structure and content of exposition; and the imagery and affective appeal of literature all provide situational contexts to build and retain word knowledge.

The principles of effective vocabulary learning are also consistent with the remaining two assumptions of whole literacy instruction: active engagement with meaningful, language-rich tasks and the development of problem-solving strategies. Surveys of effective instruction conclude that vocabulary must be learned in meaningful contexts with wide reading, that the learner must be active in solving the problem of a word's meanings, and that meaning-focused use and manipulation of the word in many modalities give the learner ownership of the new terms (Beck, Perfetti, & McKeown, 1982; Mezynski, 1983; Nagy, 1988; Stahl & Fairbanks, 1986).

## The Need for Vocabulary Instruction

Though it is clear that wide reading provides students with many rich and meaningful contexts for word learning, there is still a place for vocabulary instruction. Contextual reading does not automatically result in word learning (Jenkins, Stein, & Wysocki, 1984), nor does context always give clear clues to word meaning (Schatz & Baldwin, 1986). Small instructional interventions, such as priming students to notice new words, can increase the likelihood that students will learn from context (Elley, 1989; Jenkins et al., 1984). This may be of special importance for readers who begin school knowing fewer school-type words (Becker, 1977) and those who have limited networks of meaning for the words that are familiar to them (Graves & Slater, 1987).

Poorer readers know less about fewer words than do more able readers, and poor readers are frequently unmotivated or unable to do the amount of contextual reading required to extend their vocabularies. Further, McKeown (1985) found that disabled readers lagged behind able readers in the use of strategies that allow readers to gain new word meanings from context. Research suggests that judicious attention to vocabulary can build knowledge of specific vocabulary and can have a positive, though modest, impact on comprehension. Specifically, interventions that call for deeper, more meaningful uses of words result in learning that is more durable and that affects comprehension (Mezynski, 1983; Stahl & Fairbanks, 1986). This deeper processing can be achieved through discussion (Stahl & Vancil, 1986) by establishing rich semantic networks (Beck et al., 1982), through mapping of semantic features (Johnson, Toms-Bronowski, & Pittleman, 1982), and from examination of context and production of new uses (Gipe,

1979). Engagement can also be brought about by playful activities such as word collection contests (Beck et al., 1982) and dramatization (Duffelmeyer, 1980). All of these studies provide useful insights for generating guidelines for classroom instruction. But what should the shape of vocabulary instruction be like to concur with the research, the needs of the students, and the other assumptions of whole literacy instruction?

## Guidelines for Classroom Vocabulary Instruction

Based on the preceding insights, the following guidelines for vocabulary instruction in the whole literacy classroom can be drawn:

**FIGURE 1**  **Map of** *No One Is Going to Nashville* **with Target Vocabulary Italicized**

Characters:

1. Sonia, loves animals so much; dresses like a *vet;* asks people to call her "Dr. Ackley"
2. Richard = dad
3. Annette = *stepmother*
4. Max, *abandoned, stray* dog

Setting:

Sonia lives with mom during week, dad and *stepmother* during weekend

Problem:

— Sonia wants to keep dog
— Richard doesn't want *responsibility* of dog during week and feels all pets *abuse* him.
— Wants to send dog to *pound*
— Annette is empathetic with Sonia but doesn't feel she has much to say in *decision*

Resolution:

Annette asserts herself as someone who has *responsibility* for Sonia and can be part of *decision*

Note: Phrase *hopped a freight* is important to Annette's story and her feelings

Possible "big ideas":

1. What is a stepmother and stepmother's relationship to stepchildren?
2. How do decisions get made in a family?
3. Genre—reverses stereotype of stepmother

**1.** *Choose all vocabulary for instruction from contextual reading to be done in the classroom, both literary and content material.* By focusing on words that students will encounter within the regular curriculum, the teacher integrates vocabulary instruction with wider areas of learning to emphasize word meanings as they relate to reading comprehension.

**2.** *Use maps or organizers of the reading material to help identify the words for study, in contrast to more traditional frequency-based selection processes.* If words are important in explaining, summarizing, using, or responding to the material, they are appropriate for consideration. For example, for the book *No One Is Going to Nashville* (Jukes, 1983) used in a fourth-grade classroom, the teacher chose the vocabulary from a map she constructed (see Figure 1).

**3.** *Plan prereading knowledge activation activities for the selection or chapter.* Where appropriate, use vocabulary in this process, being sure to highlight the focal terms by having the students, at the minimum, see and hear the words before reading (Elley, 1989). For *No One Is Going to Nashville,* the teacher decided to focus on the concept *stepmother* (in this story the stepmother aids her stepchild). The teacher used a technique called "Connect-2" (Blachowicz, 1985) where the students made prereading predictive connections among the vocabulary words centered around *stepmother* (see Figure 2). This also set the purpose for reading which was to focus on finding out what the stepmother was like and to evaluate the students' predictions about how the words might be connected.

Alternatively, if the teacher felt many of the important words were familiar to her class, the teacher might have chosen to place the words on the board, pronounce them with the students, ask them to watch for the words as they read, and then discuss them after reading as needed.

**4.** *Involve vocabulary in postreading discussion.* If vocabulary is chosen properly, it is difficult *not* to use it in postreading discussion. The italicized words in Figure 1 naturally emerge in retellings, question responses, or other comprehension activities. For example, when asked to summarize *No One Is Going to Nashville,* a fourth grader responded with the following:

> Sonia wanted to be a *veterinarian* and loved animals. Max was her *stray* dog and she wanted to keep Max. Her dad didn't like animals as much 'cuz they always *abused* him. He wanted to send Max to the dog *pound.* Her *stepmother* helped her dad make the *decision* to let her keep Max.

As is frequently the case when words are chosen to reflect the story line in narratives or key concepts in expository text, students must use them when responding after reading.

Another teacher planned postreading questions using the vocabulary. She asked: "Who was the *stray*? Why wouldn't Sonia want Max to go to the *pound*? Would Sonia be a good *vet*?" In asking students to answer specific questions using these words, she could assess their knowledge of the words, ask them to go back to the text to gather clues, or provide more direct instruction.

**5.** *Use contextual reinspection and semantic manipulation for words that are still unclear after reading and discussion.* Research has suggested that most vocabulary instruc-

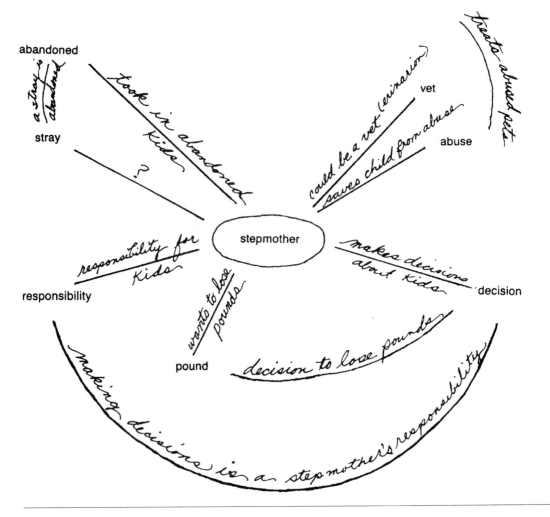

**FIGURE 2    Connect-2 Chart for *No One Is Going to Nashville***

tion occurs before reading, with little attention to vocabulary after reading (Blachowicz, 1986). Since whole literacy classrooms focus on developing *students'* problem-solving abilities, it is necessary that postreading time be allocated to help students locate information to flesh out their knowledge of words and experiment with using words in situations where they receive feedback on their attempts.

Many ways of further analyzing the vocabulary are possible. For example, the teacher who did the Connect-2 chart returned to the words *stray, pound,* and *vet* after reading. She asked the students if they knew what the words meant and had them locate and read text sections which gave clues to their meanings. For the word *pound,* the students located the following sentences in the text and extracted some information:

Richard wanted to send Max to the pound.

(*pound* is a place)

"We'll keep the dog as long as the pound would . . ."

(*pound* keeps animals)

Richard called the pound. They only keep dogs 5 days.

(*pound* only keeps animals 5 days)

From these examples, the teacher had the students conclude that the pound is a place that keeps unwanted animals but only for a limited time. They then discussed why this was so distressful to Sonia.

Alternatively, the teacher could pose, or have students pose, a series of questions that would have the readers respond on the basis of their understanding of the semantic features of the word. For example, a teacher might ask, "Does a pound need walls? Explain. Would a dog want to go to the pound? Explain."

**6.** *Use vocabulary in an integrated way.* By this point in the lesson, the readers would have seen, heard, read, and used the vocabulary in many ways. If needed, further response activities could also require use of the words in retelling, response, artistic, dramatic, or aesthetic ways. Because the selection integrates what would otherwise be a somewhat unrelated set of words, a teacher might let the use of the words emerge in response activities. For example, one teacher's group dramatized the selection. Some of the vocabulary was utilized in the character descriptions; other vocabulary emerged in dialogue, such as when Richard, the father, explains: "Those animals all *abuse* me. One bit my foot. The other tore up my best slippers. They know I am afraid of them and they take advantage of me, especially that *stray,* Max."

Another teacher had students do the illustrations to the book in their own style, writing descriptive phrases labeling each. A third teacher had students rewrite the ending when the *decision* was made in a different way. In each of these extensions, words were used in new, student-created contexts, all of which were related to the selection.

## A Final Word

Teachers employing appropriate vocabulary instructional techniques select words from contextual reading situations and involve the students in some or all of the steps in problem solving. They require that the students activate what they know about the vocabulary; make predictions about how words will be used; gather data; and later reformulate, refine, or clarify what they know about a term. In some instances, this process is modeled by the teacher; in other instances, the teacher provides explicit instruction in the process. Providing readers broad, rich experiences with words within a framework of contextual reading, discussion, and response is the goal of vocabulary instruction in a whole literacy classroom.

## References

Aaron, I. E., Chall, J. S., Durkin, D., Goodman, K., & Strickland, D. S. (1990). The past, present, and future of literacy education: Comments from a panel of distinguished educators,

Parts I and II. *The Reading Teacher, 43,* 302–311, 370–380.

Alvermann, D. E., & Moore, D. W. (1991). Secondary school reading. In R. Barr, M. Kamil, P. Mosenthal, & P. D. Pearson (Eds.), *Handbook of reading research: Vol. II* (pp. 951–983). White Plains, NY: Longman.

Baumann, J. F., & Kameenui, E. J. (1991). Research on vocabulary instruction: Ode to Voltaire. In J. Flood, J. M. Jensen, D. Lapp, & J. R. Squire (Eds.), *Handbook on teaching the English language arts* (pp. 604–632). New York: Macmillan.

Beck, I., & McKeown, M. (1991). Conditions of vocabulary acquisition. In R. Barr, M. Kamil, P. Mosenthal, & P. D. Pearson (Eds.), *Handbook of reading research: Vol. II* (pp. 789–814). White Plains, NY: Longman.

Beck, I., Perfetti, C., & McKeown, M. (1982). Effects of long term vocabulary instruction on lexical access and reading comprehension. *Journal of Educational Psychology, 74,* 506–521.

Becker, W. C. (1977). Teaching reading and language to the disadvantaged—What we have learned from field research. *Harvard Educational Review, 47,* 518–543.

Blachowicz, C. L. Z. (1985). Vocabulary development and reading: From research to instruction. *The Reading Teacher, 38,* 876–881.

Blachowicz, C. L. Z. (1986). Making connections: Alternatives to the vocabulary notebook. *Journal of Reading, 29,* 643–649.

Carey, S. (1978). Semantic development: The state of the art. In E. Warner & L. R. Gleitman (Eds.), *Language acquisition: The state of the art* (pp. 345–489). Cambridge, England: Cambridge University Press.

Dale, E. (1965). Vocabulary measurement: Techniques and major findings. *Elementary English, 42,* 895–901, 948.

Duffelmeyer, F. A. (1980). The influence of experience-based vocabulary instruction on learning word meanings. *The Reading Teacher, 34,* 35–40.

Durkin, D. (1987). *Teaching young children to read* (3rd ed.). Boston: Allyn and Bacon.

Eller, R. G., Pappas, C. C., & Brown, E. (1988). The lexical development of kindergarteners: Learning from written context. *Journal of Reading Behavior, 20,* 5–24.

Elley, W. B. (1989). Vocabulary acquisition from listening to stories. *Reading Research Quarterly, 24,* 174–187.

Fisher, C., Berliner, D., Filby, N., Marliave, R., Cahen, L., & Dishaw, M. (1980). Teaching behaviors, academic learning time, and student achievement: An overview. In C. Denham & A. Lieberman (Eds.), *Time to learn.* Washington, DC: National Institute of Education.

Gipe, J. (1979). Investigating techniques for teaching new word meanings. *Reading Research Quarterly, 14,* 624–644.

Graves, M. F., & Slater, W. H. (April 1987). *The development of reading vocabularies of rural disadvantaged students, inner-city disadvantaged students, and middle-class suburban students.* Paper presented at the meeting of the American Educational Research Association, Washington, D.C.

Hoffman, J. V. (Ed.). (1989). Whole language [Special issue]. *Elementary School Journal, 90*(2).

Jenkins, J. R., Stein, M. L., & Wysocki, K. (1984). Learning vocabulary through reading. *American Educational Research Journal, 21,* 667–687.

Johnson, D., Toms-Bronowski, S., & Pittleman, S. D. (1982). *An investigation of the effectiveness of semantic mapping and semantic feature analysis with intermediate grade level students* (Program Rep. No. 83-3). Madison, WI: Wisconsin Center for Education Research, University of Wisconsin.

Jukes, M. (1983). *No one is going to Nashville.* New York: Knopf.

Lewis, C. S. (1950). *The lion, the witch and the wardrobe.* New York: Macmillan.

McKeown, M. G. (1985). The acquisition of word meaning from context by children of high and low ability. *Reading Research Quarterly, 20,* 482–496.

Mezynski, K. (1983). Issues concerning the acquisition of knowledge: Effects of vocabulary training on reading comprehension. *Review of Educational Research, 53,* 253–279.

Nagy, E. (1988). *Teaching vocabulary to improve reading comprehension.* Newark, DE: International Reading Association.

Nagy, W. E., & Herman, P. (1987). Breadth and depth of vocabulary knowledge: Implications for acquisition and instruction. In M. McKeown & M. Curtis (Eds.), *The nature of vocabulary acquisition* (pp. 19–36). Hillsdale, NJ: Erlbaum.

Pearson, P. D., & Fielding, L. (1991). Comprehension instruction. In R. Barr, M. Kamil, P. Mosenthal, & P. D. Pearson (Eds.), *Handbook of reading research: Vol. II* (pp. 815–860). White Plains, NY: Longman.

Pearson, P. D., & Gallagher, M. C. (1983). The instruction of reading comprehension. *Contemporary Educational Psychology, 8,* 317–344.

Schatz, E. K., & Baldwin, R. S. (1986). Context clues are unreliable predictors of word meanings. *Reading Research Quarterly, 21,* 439–453.

Smith, F. (1982). *Understanding reading* (3rd ed.). New York: Holt, Rinehart & Winston.

Stahl, S., & Fairbanks, M. (1986). The effects of vocabulary instruction: A model-based meta-analysis. *Review of Educational Research, 56,* 72–110.

Stahl, S., & Vancil, S. (1986). Discussion is what makes semantic maps work in vocabulary instruction. *The Reading Teacher, 40,* 62–67.

Sulzby, E., & Teale, W. (1991). Emergent literacy. In R. Barr, M. Kamil, P. Mosenthal, & P. D. Pearson (Eds.), *Handbook of reading research: Vol. II* (pp. 727–758). White Plains, NY: Longman.

Vosniadou, S., & Ortony, A. (1983). The influence of analogy in children's acquisition of new information from text: An exploratory study. In J. Niles (Ed.), *Searches for meaning in reading/language processing and instruction* (pp. 27–39). Rochester, NY: National Reading Conference.

Whittelsea, B. W. (1987). Preservation of specific experience in the representation of general knowledge. *Journal of Experimental Psychology: Learning, Memory and Cognition, 13*(1), 3–17.

## Integrating Sources

1. Nagy and Herman suggest that direct instruction cannot possibly account for the size of students' vocabularies. Blachowicz and Lee, while acknowledging the usefulness of wide reading, still maintain that "small instructional interventions" can be helpful. If children learn so many words without such interventions, however, are they worth the trouble? Explain your position.

2. Locate the statement by Blachowicz and Lee on the source of words used in classroom vocabulary instruction. Jot it down here:

3. Given this view, are Blachowicz and Lee apt to differ or agree with Nagy and Herman as to the value of a preset general vocabulary curriculum? Explain, supporting your response with one or more citations from Nagy and Herman.

## *Classroom Implications*

It's time to take a stand! Describe your own position with respect to vocabulary instruction. Relate your answer to the two basic positions described in this chapter. If your approach is a combination, explain how you arrived at the elements you pulled from each viewpoint.

## *Annotated Bibliography*

### *Vocabulary*

Anderson, R. C., & Nagy, W. E. (1991). Word meanings. In R. Barr, M. Kamil, P. B. Mosenthal, & P. D. Pearson (Eds.), *Handbook of reading research* (Vol. II, pp. 690–724). White Plains, NY: Longman.

*This is an extensive discussion of psychological models of how word meanings are processed.*

Anderson, R. C., & Nagy, W. E. (1991). *The vocabulary conundrum.* Technical Report No. 570. Urbana, IL: Center for the Study of Reading.

*This report reviews research in vocabulary development, noting that students' knowledge of words has often been vastly underestimated. It includes a description of a program of vocabulary instruction that promotes word consciousness, a sense of curiosity about word meaning, appreciation of nuances of meaning, independence in word analysis, and wide regular reading.*

Beck, I., & McKeown, M. (1991). Conditions of vocabulary acquisition. In R. Barr, M. Kamil, P. B. Mosenthal, & P. D. Pearson (Eds.), *Handbook of reading research* (Vol. II, pp. 789–814). White Plains, NY: Longman.

*This extensive research review is organized around various approaches to acquiring knowledge of word meanings. Effective assessment is also addressed.*

Klesius, J., & Searls, E. (1991). Vocabulary instruction. *Reading Psychology, 12,* 165–171.

*Both direct and indirect vocabulary instruction are examined, along with how each can be used effectively in the classroom.*

McKeown, M. G., & Curtis, M. E. (Eds.). (1987). *The nature of vocabulary acquisition.* Hillsdale, NJ: Erlbaum.

*This collection of articles addresses, first, the research and theory underlying vocabulary development and, second, instructional approaches.*

Medro, M. A., & Ryder, R. J. (1993). The effects of vocabulary instruction on readers' ability to make causal connections. *Reading Research and Instruction, 33,* 119–134.

*The results of teaching text-specific vocabulary on readers' comprehension of expository text are discussed. This article also suggests that an important result of this type of teaching is improvement in the ability to make causal connections.*

Johnson, D. D., & Pearson, P. D. (1984). *Teaching reading vocabulary* (2nd ed.). Fort Worth: Holt, Rinehart and Winston.

*This is an extensive compendium of instructional approaches. It especially focuses on techniques useful for teaching groups of related words.*

Shand, M. (1993). *The role of vocabulary in developmental reading disabilities.* Technical Report No. 576. Urbana, IL: Center for the Study of Reading.

*Suggested here is that problems with vocabulary knowledge are one of the principal reasons for reading failure, especially in students from grades 3 through 7. A program is presented for remedying this problem through classroom instruction in vocabulary. This article also contains an excellent bibliography of related references.*

Wheatley, E. A. (1993). Computer-assisted vocabulary instruction. *Journal of Reading, 37,* 92–102.

*Three teachers' classroom experiences using computer technology for the development of vocabulary knowledge are described. Program design, software, and the effectiveness of these efforts are also discussed.*

## *You Become Involved*

### *Vocabulary*

**1.** Suggest some guidelines for determining which words warrant direct instruction. Try your guidelines out on a colleague to see if additions or alterations are desirable. How closely does your actual day-to-day instruction meet your guidelines? Would you consider modifying your instruction now that you have thought through the guidelines?

**2.** Examine the vocabulary component of a basal series. In light of the mathematical limitations noted by Nagy and Herman, does the vocabulary component seem likely to enlarge a child's general vocabulary appreciably? Is it worth the effort and class time? Why or why not?

**3.** Consider the vocabulary subtest of a standardized test, perhaps one used at your school. Do you think the assessment format reflects word knowledge? Do you think that the sampling approach used to select words reflects the breadth of a child's vocabulary? How are these issues addressed by the test publisher?

# Chapter 10

# *National Standards*

The drive to establish national standards in literacy is best viewed in the context of a larger trend toward standards in virtually all academic areas (De Souza, 1994; Greene, 1994; Myers, 1994; Porter, 1994). The standards for the English language arts, developed jointly by the International Reading Association and the National Council of Teachers of English, are similar in many respects to those proposed by other national organizations in a variety of disciplines. In particular, the work of the National Council of Teachers of Mathematics has served as a model for the creation of standards.

At first blush, the notion of national standards has the innate appeal of educators striving for excellence. On the other hand, the political forces that have pushed for standards seem to be martialed around the assumption that the problems afflicting U.S. schools can be solved by clarifying our aims as educators. Opponents of standards argue that this logic is naive and ignores the complexity of the circumstances.

Certainly those involved in the creation of the IRA/NCTE national standards in literacy will attest to the complexity of the task they undertook. Barbara Kapinus, for example, recently outlined the four principal issues with which the committees wrestled:

1. *Diversity vs. Commonality* (Should the same standards apply to all or should they vary with respect to culture, language, disabilities, and so forth?)
2. *Specific vs. General* (Should the standards amount to broad general goals or should they be specific enough to permit clear measurement?)
3. *Historically Grounded vs. Future Oriented* (Should the standards reflect the conventional literacy values of the past or should they embody a vision of what the coming age is likely to demand of its literates?)
4. *Guidance vs. Initiative* (Is it better to prescribe the outcomes believed to be desirable for society or to encourage educators to find their own way?)

## As You Read

These issues and the questions they raise presuppose a desire to establish standards. The wisdom of establishing them at all, however, is questioned by Patrick Shannon. He contends that standards represent a target, ironically erected by the profession itself, that must inevitably draw criticism leveled at teachers when the standards are not met. Diane Ravitch, on the other hand, argues for standards as a means of creating consensus on what students should be learning and of thereby ensuring that schooling is on course.

As you examine their arguments, ask yourself these questions:

**1.** How might the establishment of standards affect the performance of individual teachers?
**2.** Should teachers cooperate in the establishment of standards, or should they actively oppose them?
**3.** What role should professional literacy groups, such as IRA and NCTE, have in the development and assessment of standards?
**4.** Can standards ever be truly voluntary? Is their very establishment apt to create pressure on educators and students?
**5.** Does the creation of standards imply that U.S. teachers have failed to perform up to acceptable levels?

## References

De Souza, A. R. (1994). Time for geography: The new national standards. *NASSP Bulletin, 78,* 1–6.
Greene, M. (1994). The arts and national standards. *Educational Forum, 58,* 391–400.
Myers, M. (1994). Issues facing the national standards project in English. *Education and Urban Society, 26,* 141–157.
Porter, A. C. (1994). National standards and school improvement in the 1990's: Issues and promise. *American Journal of Education, 102,* 421–429.

**Developing Democratic Voices**
Patrick Shannon
*The Reading Teacher, 47,* 1993, 86–94

1. According to Shannon, the media tend to attribute "America's Slide toward Third World status" to what?


2. Summarize Shannon's argument that blaming educators for economic problems is a literacy issue.


3. (T/F) Lengthening the school day, according to Shannon, is one suggestion that has real promise.

4. (T/F) Convincing evidence has linked school problems with those of the economy.

5. Write a sentence summarizing Shannon's view on the redistribution of American wealth.


6. (T/F) According to Shannon, federal grants may be the way for schools to prove that they are not responsible for economic problems.

7. (T/F) According to Shannon, the standards produced by IRA and NCTE are a step in the right direction.

8. Why does Shannon feel schools need to be reformed?


9. Describe how IRA and NCTE are, according to Shannon, working against the creation of democratic voices.

**10.** (T/F)   According to Shannon, basal readers are of great value in promoting democracy. Explain:

**11.** Summarize Shannon's idea of moving from object to subject.

**12.** Why does Shannon object to direct instruction?

**13.** In what way, according to Shannon, does whole language fail to create democratic voices?

**14.** Which of the examples given by Shannon do you think would work in your classroom?

# DEVELOPING
# DEMOCRATIC VOICES

PATRICK SHANNON

When I began teaching primary grades in Rochester, New York, during the early 1970s, 20% of Rochester children lived below the poverty line, and the genius of capitalism and corporate executives was credited for the strong American economy. Last summer while visiting my mother, I read in the *Rochester Times Union* that now over 50% of the city's children live on less than US$12,700 for a family of four and that schools are to blame for America's slide toward Third World status. What's happened during the last 20 years to bring about these changes, and why are they literacy issues?

Although I was startled by Rochester's dramatic statistics, I was aware that poverty is a fact of American life. In fact, I became an educator because I believed that schools could do something about poverty—at least for the next generation. But now I am told that poverty for this and the next generation is getting worse and educators, including me, are to blame.

The first part of what I'm told is true. According to the U.S. Bureau of Census, the national poverty rate has increased by 7% for all Americans and has grown by nearly 10% for children during the last 2 decades. The rate of increase accelerated dramatically during the last decade, and contrary to popular opinion, poverty is not limited to urban areas or ethnic minorities. For example, out of 100 poor children in America, 28 live in suburban areas, 27 in rural areas, and 45 in cities; 41 are European Americans, 35 are African Americans, 21 are Latin Americans, and 3 are Asian Americans, Pacific Islanders, Native Americans, or Alaskan Natives. The fastest growing group among the poor are children under the age of 6 (Children's Defense Fund, 1991). Clearly, the ranks of the poor are growing and are growing younger.

However, educators are not the cause of any decline or rise of poverty in the United States. Government officials, chief executive officers (CEOs), and media pundits use a curious logic to link the two. This logic and the human suffering that it attempts to hide are literacy issues because they require critical reading to expose the illusion they project, writing to set the record straight, and action to demonstrate that schools could be places where teachers and students develop democratic voices in order to struggle against the realities of poverty in America. This literacy involves a language of critique to demystify the complexities of modern living and a language of hope to reinject human agency into schools.

I recognize that this concern expands the typical scope of literacy considered in *The Reading Teacher.* Most often, *RT* authors ask elementary school educators to reconsider the immediacy of teaching reading and writing in classrooms or schools. This is understandable given that teachers face seemingly overwhelming opportunities and constraints as they carry out their daily work. Yet clearly the illusion that schooling is an economic anchor influences, if not directly affects, the immediate circumstances of schooling in profound ways. For example, extended school days, "smartened up" textbooks, intensified curricula, and new calls for national standards and assessments are direct consequences of the promotion and power of these advocates and their illusion. Teachers who ignore this connection between classroom and social life are likely to be at a disadvantage when trying to participate in the restructuring of schools.

## Reading the Illusion

A decade ago, the *A Nation at Risk* report used a war metaphor to describe schooling's negation of "our once unchallenged preeminence in commerce, industry, science, and technological innovation" (National Commission on Educational Excellence, 1985, p. 1). Just 2 years ago, the government's *America 2000* proposal suggested that national standards and tests in all subjects are the means to regain our competitive edge (Commission on Work Force Skills, 1990). Although the title and language for America 2000 may change during the Clinton administration, the purpose and emphasis should remain the same since Hillary and Bill Clinton were involved in the articulation of America 2000 through their association with the Center for Education and the Economy. In these and many other reports, government officials, CEOs, and media pundits assume a causal link between what's happening in schools, which they characterize as being in a downward slide, and what's happening to the American economy, which everyone considers (at least in the fall of 1993) as being in a free fall. I use the phrase "assumed a causal link" because no one seems able to offer convincing data for the supposed connection except for an occasional anecdote about some workers who seem to have difficulty learning to work differently when new conditions are forced upon them (Noble, 1992a).

Such evidence is offered as proof that schools have not prepared the American worker well enough to enable American business and industry to compete with the Japanese, Germans, and Swedes. According to this logic, the lack of adaptability among the work force has depressed corporate profits, caused businesses and plants to close, and created poverty among working-class families. However, one need look no further than the success of the Toyota, Honda, and Nissan automobile factories in the United States, which employ American-educated workers, to render this logic suspect. Although these companies fall short as workers' paradises, their workers have adapted to new working conditions and relations, plant profits are as high as their plants in other countries, and employees' families are doing well economically.

These examples, and there are others (see Weisman, 1991), suggest that it is not school policy and practices but rather American governmental and corporate mismanagement and poor policy that have caused economic decline and growing poverty. Relying on Phillips' (1990) and Bartlett and Steele's (1992) analyses, I'll offer a critical reading of tax policy to illustrate how the rich get richer while the poor get poorer.

We are rapidly approaching a two-class society within the United States—the rich and the rest. Although we can still divide annual salary and wages into three categories: the poor (39% of all 1990 tax filers earned below US$15,000), the middle class (57% earned between US$15,000 and $75,000), and the rich (4% filed above US$75,000), these economic categories no longer explain very much because the rich now receive as much in salary and wages as the bottom 50% of the taxpayers (all the poor and half of the middle class). By contrast in 1959, the top 4% of the filers made as much through salary and wages as the bottom 35%. Put another way, while the total income of the middle class increased on average of 4% a year during the 1980s, the income of the rich increased between 69 and 218% *annually,* depending on whether their salaries were closer to $75,000 or the $1,000,000 mark.

This redistribution of wealth from the poor and middle class to the rich didn't just happen by accident. It is the result of governmental policy. For example, the 1986 tax reform legislation was supposed to equalize the tax burden across classes and ensure that everyone would pay some taxes. In fact, it was a windfall for the wealthy, who received two or three times the percentage tax cut as the poor or the middle class. While the average teacher with a salary in the mid-$30,000 range received an 11% tax cut, putting approximately $456 annually in his or her bank account, CEOs with average salaries in the $750,000 range received a 34% tax cut putting approximately $86,000 at their disposal. Those among the rich making over a million dollars a year in salary received a 31% cut leaving them with $280,000 more in after-tax income. At best, the poor received a 9% tax cut and pocketed an extra $50 a year.

Corporations have also enjoyed tax cuts during the last decade. The cuts were not always direct, but they were substantial. For example, the loosening of regulations concerning loan interest deductions for corporations allowed corporations to reduce their tax bill by nearly 60% ($159.7 to $67.5 billion) during the 1980s. During the 1950s, corporations paid nearly 40% of U.S. taxes; now they pay only 17%.

During the 1980s, these same government officials, CEOs, and media pundits, who now criticize education, considered these tax breaks for the rich and corporations necessary in order to stimulate investment in the economy and to create jobs. Yet most of the jobs that were created are low paying. For example, 78% of the jobs created by the government, retail businesses, or service industries since the 1950s pay less than $6 an hour, which means poverty for a family unless coupled with another income. Over half of these jobs employ workers for less than 40 hours a week, allowing employers to escape paying benefits. During the last decade, manufacturing jobs which pay middle class wages have declined by 10%. In my home town, the Eastman Kodak Co. cut one third of its work force (20,000 jobs) during the 1980s, and Xerox reduced its payroll by over 5,000 employees. Ironically, Kodak's CEO Kay Whitmore and Xerox's former CEO David Kearns, who oversaw these reductions, sat on the board of the New American Schools Development Corporation which President Bush established to distribute money for "break the mold schools" to improve America's competitiveness, stimulate the economy, and create new jobs. Multinational corporations moved many manufacturing jobs to other countries. For example, 1,800 factories and 500,000 jobs have moved to

Mexico where they pay workers $1 an hour and are not subject to environmental and labor safety standards.

Where did all the money from these tax cuts go? The rich have used some of their tax savings to buy tax-free bonds. This means that government debt repayments are transfers of tax money to the rich, who in turn pay no taxes on this guaranteed return on their investment. At present, the federal government spends nearly as much on such debt relief ($184 billion) as it does on K–12 education ($199 billion). Corporations spent some on CEOs' salaries, which have more than tripled during the last decade to average over $750,000, nearly double the average of their counterparts in Japan, Germany, and Sweden. However, more of it went to initiate or defend against corporate takeovers during the 1980s, when corporations acquired substantial debt in order to extend or maintain their holdings without any effort to improve productivity or to create jobs (Pollin, 1992). In fact, the typical pattern for takeovers and buyouts was to sell assets of the acquired business, to fire employees, and to raid employee pension funds in order to service the new debt acquired from the entire process.

These are the net results of government tax policy: Individual wealth has been transferred from the poor and the middle class to the rich, the size of the middle class has decreased during the last decade, corporations are encouraged to acquire debt in order to decrease tax payments, most new jobs cannot support families above the poverty line, and workers' health and retirement are subject to corporate whim. In short, because of government and corporate policy, process, and product (which had little or nothing directly to do with American schools), the rich got richer, while the poor got poorer, and the American economy was sacrificed in the process.

As a substitute for an economic policy that would address these issues, government officials, CEOs, and media pundits have initiated and maintained a campaign of misinformation about American schools (see *The Nation* 1992 special issue on schools). Their claims that today's youth are not as smart as their predecessors, that SAT scores have decreased greatly, that student performance on standardized tests are low, that school funding doesn't matter, that American schools are too expensive, that schools don't graduate enough mathematicians, scientists, and engineers to enable us to compete economically with other countries, and that American schools pale in international competitions are all inaccurate, if not deliberate distortions (Berliner, 1992).

Perhaps the most telling example of misinformation is the claim that schools do not produce workers with the skills employers desire. Two recent surveys of work force skill requirements conducted by the Michigan Education Department and my old school district (Rochester, NY) suggest that employees' deportment (no drugs, respectful behavior, following directions, etc.) is the most important and sought-after quality and that disciplined knowledge (mathematics, natural science, and foreign language, etc.) is the least important (Carson, Huelskamp, & Woodall, 1991). In fact, less than 10% of U.S. corporations are organized according to the high technology and high performance structures that schools are now expected to emulate and that require the sophisticated skills schools are now supposed to produce in all students (Commission on Work Force Skills, 1990).

Despite repeated demonstrations to the contrary, government officials from the Clinton administration and the two preceding it call for higher national standards and tests in all subject areas and more businesslike schools as the answers to what ails the schools and the economy. To attract agreement from educators and to begin their project, they offer grant funding to anyone, any school, or any professional organization that will allow their school to be restructured or will sit down and write national standards and tests (Noble, 1992b). Perennially starved for funds, many schools have taken this bait, and the National Council of Teachers of English and the International Reading Association have engaged in a joint venture to develop English/Language Arts standards. Some appear willing to admit that schools have caused economic decline, perhaps in the hope that they can redirect the government's focus on technology, nationalization, and business principles.

Enough is enough. If teachers and local communities hope to retain some control over their teaching, classrooms, and curricula, then they must stop their silence and simple reactions to top-down initiatives and start to address the issues facing America. Schools and literacy programs do need reform, because they perpetuate an unequal political and economic status quo, but they do not need to follow the governmental or corporate policies or practices that got us into this fix in the first place. Clearly, we do not need new national standards or tests in schools to meet the expressed demand of 95% of employers. By anyone's account, traditional reading instruction in American elementary school requires students to follow untold numbers of verbal and written directions, to work independently and respectfully, and to be punctual and attentive at all times.

Rather, we need reform in schools and literacy education that will enable us to take the blindfolds off so we can read what's really happening in America and around the world and that will untie our hands so we can write a new more jut and equitable future for ourselves and others. We need to create the conditions under which we can develop democratic voices at all levels of schooling so that together we can engage in an active public life. But how can we develop democratic voices when the government and business, and apparently professional organizations as well, are working actively against us? We can start by defining what we mean by these terms separately and collectively and by looking for examples of educators already engaged in such projects.

## Writing a Human Essence

*Democratic* does not refer to party politics. Both Democrats and Republicans are responsible for the political and economic mess we're in—they voted for it. For me, democratic refers to meaningful participation in the decision making that affects our lives. In theory, citizens in a democracy control the government equally and collectively. However, the redistribution of wealth in the United States is an example of how this theory does not fit reality. The rich exert undue influence over governmental decisions, which affect all our lives.

This is not a conspiracy theory; it's a political fact. To be specific, is it a coincidence that Dan Rostenkowski, Chairman of the House of Representatives Ways and Means Committee (the one responsible for writing all tax legislation) received over $1.7 million in honoraria during the 1980s from businesses and organizations with a direct interest in tax legislation (Bartlett & Steele, 1992)? Is it mere chance that the Bush/Quayle reelection committee received $1.3 million in 1991 from five food companies at the same time that the government pulled back on nutrition guidelines and delayed nutritional labeling for a year ("Who bought," 1993)?

Of course, economic class is not the only factor that separates individuals and social groups from democratic participation. Conflicts surrounding race, gender, age, and sexual orientation also distribute power unequally. However, naming is not sufficient for being democratic; we must also theorize our understanding of bias and privilege in order to explain why we desire democracy, but cannot find it in our lives. We must push past our traditional civics lessons in order to discover the historic struggles that were necessary to wrestle even the right to vote away from the few and to see the struggles still ahead in order to make those votes count for something for the 96% of the U.S. population left behind during the 1980s.

Using these theories, we can expand our reading of texts and the symbols embedded in social practices and institutions in order to uncover how they are organized to protect privilege and to undermine democracy. Moreover, we can use these theories to write text and other social actions to promote equality and political and economic justice. Such literate work is underway concerning medicine (Illich, 1982), media news (Herman & Chomsky, 1988), law (Unger, 1985), popular arts (Giroux & Simon, 1989), cognitive psychology and technology (Noble, 1991), and schooling (Apple, 1982). I have attempted to bring such theories to reading instruction in order to name and challenge the inequalities of instructional practices (e.g., Shannon, 1985), to develop theories to explain why reading programs are organized around these inequalities (e.g., Shannon, 1989), and to make teacher and student decision making the center of literacy programs (e.g., Shannon, 1992).

Basal readers are of limited value in literacy programs designed to promote democracy. With prepared skills hierarchies, directive language in scripted lessons, set lesson and story sequences, prescribed and collated tests, basals are decidedly antidemocratic in their makeup for teachers (Goodman, Shannon, Freeman, & Murphy, 1988) and for students (Bloome & Nieto, 1989). Since changes in the science, the literature, and the layout of basals simply make the 70-year-old logic of basals more attractive, nothing short of scrapping the teachers' manuals and all that's in them could make basals a useful tool in a democratic classroom. Only then will teachers and students be free to make meaningful decisions about their literacy and learning.

*To develop* means literally to unfold potential for the attainment of perfection that is appropriate to a species or is possible for an individual. Although educators are interested in intellectual, social, and moral development, we must also give attention to political potential if we intend to be democratic. Toward that end, educators might find chess players' use of the term helpful. In chess, to develop a piece is to bring it from its original position to one offering greater play of force, that is, to increase its relative power. Of course, chess pieces are tools in a game and students are not tools nor are life and education a game. For me, the metaphor is useful because it speaks directly to the power of our location: original positions—which I called political and economic illiteracy, and positions of potential power—which I described as being democratic. In order to realize that potential, this change in position must be accompanied by a change in consciousness, attitude, and proclivity to act.

To develop democratically means to move ourselves and our students from our original position of seeing ourselves as *objects,* who believe that economics, politics, and schooling happen to us, to a new position of seeing ourselves as *subjects,* who have the right, ability, and responsibility to participate in the decision making that affects our lives.

Alone and together, *subjects* move from the dormancy of the straight rows in classrooms and the margins of society to active centers, offering us greater chances to be democratic and to work toward equality and justice.

Interest in developing democratic subjects limits the utility of direct instruction (Kameenui & Shannon, 1988). Within direct instruction, everything becomes objective, that is, out of the meaningful control of teachers and students. Knowledge of content and process is objectified for the purpose of teachers' and students' systematic consumption. Teachers are directed not only to serve an often-fixed meal, but also to ensure satisfactory digestion. Students are considered to be underfed, if not empty; they must clean their plates before being served the next item on the menu. (And of course, teachers are students during preservice and inservice teacher education and staff development programs.) Even when teachers can choose which menu to serve during direct instruction or whether to bring dessert before the appetizer or when students can swallow without chewing, neither students can decide whose garden this knowledge came from, what it means to consume such knowledge, who cooks and who cleans, or when they've consumed enough.

Despite later efforts to instruct students to be independent, a steady diet of direct instruction makes teachers and students dependent consumers, not organic producers of knowledge. At best, students and teachers are left with only what they have been taught during direct instruction, secure that deference to producers of knowledge will serve them well and with little desire to fend for themselves. At worst, teachers and students believe that this is the way it should be. These may be the best and the worst of times.

*Voice* is the tool with which we make ourselves known, name our experience, and participate in decisions that affect our lives. Most literacy educators associate voice with writing. A writer's choice is considered an extension of his or her ego, which drives his or her interest in writing and revision. Accordingly, I want my thoughts and needs known and invested with the traditional authority of text, so I write and revise. When I "find my voice" while writing, I have taken control over the topic, genre, and audience for my written work. Within this view, voice becomes the hub of an individual's language use connecting ownership, choice, authenticity, and intellectual autonomy. We rejoice in the emergence of a student's voice because we have increased the possibility of coming to know that student and we can now begin a student-centered literacy program for him or her.

However, we must be careful when thinking about voice in this way. A voice does not constitute a person, nor can a person be reduced to a single voice. Individuals have as many voices as they have group memberships, and they use these multiple voices (sometimes in contradictory ways) in a variety of social relations and settings when they believe the time and place to be correct. They acquire these voices through immersions in the daily life of socially significant groups which initiate them into approximate dress, values, and behaviors as well as the language of group membership. First voices come from family and neighbors. Because even these voices are complex amalgams of different ethnic groups, classes, races, religions, and cultures, our first voices are not singular whole constructions. Rather they, as well as the ones we add later, should be understood as historical, fragmented, and social artifacts.

Teachers must remember that students do not speak only for themselves; rather social groups also speak to one another through individual students. Conflict within and among voices in a classroom is a fact of life because we are not a homogeneous society with one set of values, mores, and interests. And we are better for our diversity. How teachers (and all of society) choose to handle these conflicts and our diversity makes all the difference in how we will live together in and out of schools. To assert privilege for one type of voice among all others in a classroom promotes and maintains a hierarchy among social groups based on nationality, gender, race, economic class, and ethnicity. Unless teachers and students are allowed and willing to listen to each other, to explore the variety and historical and social origins of their differences, and to use their multiplicity of voices in any classroom, there is little hope for democratic development in our society.

Voice, then, is a social, not a personal, matter for individuals. This is why constructivist approaches to literacy education (e.g., apprenticeships, process teaching, whole language), as most often theorized or practiced, are not adequate for developing democratic voices. Although most advocates of these positions encourage individuals' movement from object to subject status in terms of language use, they do not address explicitly the political nature of voice nor do they develop students' intellectual tools sufficiently to enable them to analyze historical and social origins of the values, attitudes, and opinions in what they say, write, or do.

Without this political understanding of voice and these intellectual tools, individuals and the social groups they represent must accept all that others have put in their heads and remain political objects unable to participate in meaningful decision making. Although many of the values and practices in students' and our voices should be affirmed, others are decidedly antidemocratic and problematic if we seek equality and justice. As political and economic illiterates, we are living proof of this. When we listen to the traditional teachers' and students' voices that tell us to shy away from politics, we are our own worst enemies.

## Action to Develop Democratic Voices

At present, few American institutions take the ideal of developing democratic voices as their mission; perhaps this is why the misinformation about schooling and poverty seems to convince so many of us. As with any ideal, developing democratic voices must be made concrete on a simplified level in order to prepare us for the larger possibilities of that ideal. Classrooms at any level of schooling offer the possibility for these concrete actions. When developing democratic voices, teachers and students place their experiences at the center of the curriculum and ask, "How do we wish to live together?" This question enables all to study the linguistic, historic, scientific, social, artistic, economic, technical, intellectual, emotional, spiritual, and political factors that affect their daily lives. Such a curriculum makes both teacher and students subjects in their education, subjects who are able to make decisions that affect their lives at school and who can explore their diversity and similarities as they consider common interests and possible actions based on commitment to justice, social equality, and expanded possibilities of difference.

We have many examples to guide us in our efforts. From teachers in Quincy, Massachusetts, during the 1870s, to those in Dewey's Lab School in Chicago at the turn of the century, to Marietta Johnson's Organic School in Alabama beginning in 1907, to Caroline

Pratt's City/Country School in New York City, which started in 1913 and later became the Bank Street School, to Elsie Clapp's Arthurdale School in Kentucky during the Depression, to Myles Horton's Highlander Folk School in Tennessee, which just celebrated its 60th anniversary, to Septima Clark's Citizenship Schools across the deep South in the late 1950s and early 1960s, America has a remarkable tradition of teachers and students developing democratic voices (Shannon, 1990).

More recently, Audrey Sturk in Nova Scotia helped her students and the elderly in their community come to a common understanding through students' exploration of what it means to be old in rural King's County (Sturk, 1992). In northern Minnesota, John Schmidt organized his primary classroom according to a student-written Bill of Rights for Learners so that his students would take a stake in the well-being of the school and develop an understanding of individual and collective rights (Schmidt, 1990). Linda Christensen, who teaches middle school English in Portland, Oregon, used poetry to help her students hear the voices of those who have struggled for equality and justice throughout history (Christensen, 1991). In Calexico, California, Elena Castro recorded and displayed the "collective knowledge" of her Hispanic first graders on long sheets of butcher paper so that they would understand their valuable contributions to their education (Edelsky, Altwerger, & Flores, 1990). And, Sandra Lawing in McDowell County, North Carolina, has her multiaged primary grade students planning and making the decisions about academic work while they run a working restaurant and flower shop from their classroom (Shannon & Clark, 1993).

Teacher groups such as Rethinking Schools in Milwaukee, The Boston Women's Teachers' Group, The Foxfire Groups across the country, The North Dakota Study Group, The Network of Educators on the Americas, and The National Coalition of Education Activists are organized to help teachers, parents, and often students come together to consider how schools and their practice can be reorganized to become more democratic, even liberatory.

Efforts to develop democratic voices have spilled over into teacher education programs. For example, Michael O'Laughlin (1992) and Janet Miller offer the Hofstra University Summer Institute for Teachers; Eleanor Kutz and Hephzibah Roskelly (1991) investigate what they call the unquiet pedagogy for English teachers in Boston; Jesse Goodman (1992) examined elementary schooling for critical democracy in Indiana; and I (Shannon, 1992) have explored the politics of literacy education at the Mount Saint Vincent University's Summer Institute. At Penn State we have just started to reorganize our teacher education programs according to the following mission statement:

> *Our faculty have chosen to revise and reconstruct the long tradition that connects the struggle to create a democratic society to the diverse practices of education and schooling . . . We plan to deepen and extend our commitments to social justice, equality and democracy by developing teachers and others who are prepared to address issues of multiculturalism, public service, and leadership in and out of schools.*

What connects these educators across time and space is their commitment to social forms of knowing and learning that enhance our chances to build a compassionate society, to level power relationships between and among students and teachers, and to explore the social realities and political possibilities of empowerment. What connects these educators are their abilities to overcome economic and political illiteracy in order to read the illusion that the government and businesses offer at the expense of schools in order to protect privilege in the United States and to write a more just and equal future first at school, and then hopefully in society. They have and are developing democratic voices.

## References

Apple, M. (1982). *Education and power.* Boston: Routledge & Kegan Paul.

Bartlett, D., & Steele, J. (1992). *America: What went wrong?* Kansas City, MO: Andrews & McNeal.

The battle for public schools, (1992). *The Nation, 255,* pp. 266–307.

Berliner, D. (1992, February). *Educational reform in an era of disinformation.* Paper presented at American Association of Colleges for Teacher Education, San Antonio, TX.

Bloome, D., & Nieto, S. (1989). Children's understanding of basal readers. *Theory Into Practice, 28,* 258–264.

Carson, C., Huelskamp, R., & Woodall, T. (1991). *Perspectives on education in America.* Albuquerque, NM: Sandia National Laboratories.

Children's Defense Fund. (1991). *The state of America's children.* Washington, DC: Author.

Christensen, L. (1991). Unlearning myths that bind us. In B. Bigelow, B. Miner, & B. Peterson (Eds.), *Rethinking Columbus* (pp. 53–55). Milwaukee, WI: Rethinking School.

Commission on Work Force Skills. (1990). *America's choice: High skills or low wages!* Rochester, NY: National Center of Education and the Economy.

Edelsky, C., Altwerger, B., & Flores, B. (1990). *Whole language: What's the difference?* Portsmouth, NH: Heinemann.

Giroux, H., & Simon, R. (1989). *Popular culture, schooling and everyday life.* Westport, CT: Bergin & Garvey.

Goodman, J. (1992). *Elementary schooling for critical democracy.* Albany, NY: State University of New York Press.

Goodman, K., Shannon, P., Freeman, Y., & Murphy, S. (1988). *Report card on basal readers.* Katonah, NY: Richard C. Owens.

Herman, E., & Chomsky, N. (1988). *Manufactured consent.* New York: Pantheon.

Illich, I. (1982). *Medical nemesis.* New York: Pantheon.

Kaneenui, E., & Shannon, P. (1988). Direct instruction reconsidered. In J. Readence & R. S. Baldwin (Eds.), *Dialogues in literacy research* (pp. 35–46). Chicago: National Reading Conference.

Kutz, E., & Roskelly, H. (1991). *An unquiet pedagogy: Transforming practice in the English classroom.* Portsmouth, NH: Boynton/Cook.

National Commission on Educational Excellence. (1983). *A nation at risk: The imperative for educational reform.* Washington, DC: Department of Education.

Noble, D. (1991). *The classroom arsenal: Military research, information, technology and public education.* Philadelphia, PA: Fulmer.

Noble, D. (1992a). Let them eat skills. *Rethinking Schools, 5,* 18–19.

Noble, D. (1992b, April). *New American schools and the new world order.* Paper presented at American Educational Research Association, San Francisco, CA.

O'Laughlin, M. (1992). Engaging teachers in emancipatory knowledge construction. *Journal of Teacher Education, 43,* 336–346.

Phillips, K. (1990). *The politics of rich and poor: Wealth and the American electorate in the Reagan aftermath.* New York: Random House.

Pollin, R. (1992). Rossonomics. *The Nation, 255,* pp. 456–457.

Schmidt, J. (1990). Start your year with a bill of rights. *The Whole Idea, 2,* 1–4.

Shannon, P. (1985). Reading instruction and social class. *Language Arts, 62,* 604–613.

Shannon, P. (1989). *Broken promises: Reading instruction in the 20th century.* Westport, CT: Bergin & Garvey.

Shannon, P. (1990). *The struggle to continue: Progressive reading instruction in the United States.* Portsmouth, NH: Heinemann.

Shannon, P. (1992). *Becoming political: Reading and writing in the politics of literacy education.* Portsmouth, NH: Heinemann.

Shannon, P., & Clarke, C. (1993). Whole language and active citizenship. *Curriculum Review, 32,* 3–8.

Sturk, A. (1992). Developing a community of learners inside and outside the classroom. In P. Shannon (Ed.), *Becoming political: Reading and writing in the politics of literacy education* (pp. 263–273). Portsmouth, NH: Heinemann.

Unger, R. (1985). *Critical legal studies movements.* Cambridge, MA: Harvard University Press.

Weisman, J. (1991, November 13). Some economists challenging view that schools hurt competitiveness. *Education Week,* pp. 14, 17.

Who bought what? (1993). *Mother Jones, 21,* p. 53.

## CONTENT LITERACY GUIDE

**Launching a Revolution in Standards and Assessments**
Diane Ravitch
*Phi Delta Kappan, 74, 1993, 767–772*

**1.** What does Ravitch mean by "educational *perestroika*" in relation to the federal government's role in education?

**2.** Summarize the three objectives of the America 2000 plan.

    a.

    b.

    c.

**3.** In what way do standards require assessment?

**4.** (T/F)  Surveys have shown that most Americans believe there are problems in the schools but that their own schools are fine.

**5.** (T/F)  The National Educational Goals Panel recommended that national standards be established but that they be voluntary.

**6.** (T/F)  The National Educational Goals Panel recommended that a single national examination be established to monitor the standards.

**7.** A model for the development of national standards was supplied by educators in the field of _____ .

**8.** In what way does Ravitch see the process of consensus building as valuable?

**9.** What has been the historical fear of a federal Department of Education?

**10.** What two extremes does Ravitch claim must be avoided in the creation of standards?

    a.

    b.

**11.** Do you think Ravitch's belief in both excellence and equity is reasonable? Why?

**12.** What distinction does Ravitch make between "national" and "federal" standards?

**13.** (T/F) Ravitch maintains that the next logical step after the creation of national standards is the creation of a national curriculum.

**14.** Define *state curriculum framework*.

**15.** Why did the U.S. Department of Education decide to encourage the development of state curriculum frameworks before the national standards were complete?

**16.** What three organizations were chosen to develop national standards in literacy?

a.

b.

c.

**17.** Why is the Department of Education prevented by law from controlling curriculum?

**18.** What are some of the reasons for the fact that ways to assess the standards have lagged behind their creation?

**19.** (T/F) The United States is one of the few countries to consider creating national standards.

# LAUNCHING A REVOLUTION
# IN STANDARDS AND ASSESSMENTS

DIANE RAVITCH

During the brief period that Lamar Alexander was U.S. secretary of education, his department began several initiatives that altered the federal role in education. Before Alexander, the Department of Education was essentially a dispenser of formula grant monies, and the secretary was the nation's scold. During Alexander's tenure, the department became an advocate for educational *perestroika,* providing a platform for reformers, teachers, principals, community leaders, and anyone else who was willing to try new ways to improve schools and communities.

Lamar Alexander holds a rather paradoxical view of the federal role in education. On the one hand, he is an activist and a strategic planner, and when he was secretary he lent his influence to a wide spectrum of efforts to shake up lethargic bureaucracies and to demonstrate that all children could reach high levels of learning. But on the other hand, he strongly believes that the federal government ought not to tell everyone else what to do; he is instinctively skeptical of those who want to use the federal government to impose their ideas on others.

I first met Lamar Alexander and David Kearns early in 1991 when they invited me to join them at the department. At first, I was not interested; I had never wanted to work in government, and I was in the middle of writing a book. But I changed my mind when Alexander said that I would have the lead in developing new national standards and assessments. The offer was one I could not refuse, knowing as I did that any federal activity in these areas would be historic and would have to be managed with extreme sensitivity to the principles of federalism.

Alexander explained to me that the purpose of everything he intended to do was to support the national education goals. The goals, forged in a bipartisan pact between the President and the nation's 50 governors, provided a unique sense of direction for American education. They also supplied the rationale for the America 2000 plan that Alexander and Kearns designed. America 2000 was not a federal program but a strategy to help the nation reach the national education goals.

*Source:* "Launching a Revolution in Standards and Assessments" by Diane Ravitch, 1993, *Phi Delta Kappan, 74,* 767–772. Reprinted by permission of Diane Ravitch.

The America 2000 plan had three fundamental objectives: 1) to encourage every community to adopt the national goals, develop its own local strategy, and prepare an annual community report card on its progress toward the goals; 2) to stimulate the creation of thousands of "break-the-mold schools" that would approach education in totally new ways to meet the needs of today's children and families; and 3) to develop voluntary "world-class" standards and American Achievement Tests.

Standards and assessments were critical because they would allow teachers, students, parents, and communities to determine whether they were aiming high enough and whether they were making progress. Without standards and assessments, the "new American schools" and the community-based reformers would not know whether their innovative efforts were making a difference.

It was clear to us that the nation could not make progress toward the goals unless there were high national standards and valid, reliable individual student assessments. Goals 3 and 4 specifically required new standards and assessments. As a nation, we were not likely to be "first in the world in math and science" unless we set standards that were at least as high as those in other leading industrialized nations and unless we had the means to find out whether our students measured up to those standards. Nor would we know whether students could "demonstrate mastery of challenging subject matter" in core subjects unless we were able to agree on standards for those subjects and on assessments that measured mastery.

We also knew from numerous surveys on education that most Americans, and especially parents, were misinformed and self-satisfied. They thought that there was a problem in the nation's schools, but they believed that their own schools were fine. Perhaps their own schools *were* fine, but they had no objective measures by which to reach that judgment. As Harold Stevenson has found in his studies of American and Asian parents, the complacency of American parents acts as an obstacle to education reform.

At the outset it was not clear whether there was an appropriate federal role in setting standards or developing national examinations. But it was very clear that these are subjects on which there is a great deal of disagreement among educators.

In 1991, shortly after taking office, Alexander persuaded Congress to establish the National Council on Educational Standards and Testing (NCEST), a 32-member bipartisan body, to consider whether and how to develop new standards and tests. Co-chaired by the leaders of the National Education Goals Panel, Gov. Carroll Campbell of South Carolina and Gov. Roy Romer of Colorado, NCEST was broadly representative of teachers, administrators, civic leaders, political leaders, policy makers, and people in higher education.

NCEST issued its report early in 1992, recommending the establishment of voluntary national standards in key subject areas and a national system of achievement tests. The panel opposed the development of a single national examination, suggesting instead that new assessments could be developed by individual states or groups of states working together. However these new assessments were created, they were to be based on common national standards.

Throughout the hearings held by NCEST, the work of the National Council of Teachers of Mathematics (NCTM) served as a model of the power of national standards to drive education reform in a coherent manner, while involving a broad array of participants. Several years earlier, the nation's math teachers had surveyed their field and decided that it was in dire need of change after the failure of the New Math and the ascendancy of the back-to-basics movement. Eager to raise students' expectations and achievement and to promote problem-solving activities as the core of teaching and learning mathematics, the NCTM sponsored the development of national standards. The process of reaching consensus eventually involved thousands of math teachers, who collaborated to determine what students should know and be able to do in mathematics.

Published in 1989, the NCTM standards quickly became a dynamic force in changing staff development, instructional practices, teacher education, textbooks, technology, and assessment. Every new commercial mathematics textbook or instructional program that entered the market since 1989 has claimed to incorporate the NCTM standards. According to the NCTM, 30% to 40% of the nation's mathematics teachers were using the new standards by 1992. Even the federally sponsored National Assessment of Educational Progress (NAEP) began to change in response to the NCTM standards.

The powerful advance of the NCTM standards demonstrated that standards could serve as both the starting point and the goal of education reform. Suddenly it seemed crystal clear that the reform of education begins with a consensus about what children should learn, and every other part of the system should work in concert to support that result. Textbooks should be based on a solid consensus about what children should learn— not on checklists prepared by textbook-adoption states. Staff development should help teachers understand and teach the new standards. Teacher education should prepare new teachers to teach what children should learn. Tests should measure what is worth learning, not just what is easy to measure. And the very process of developing standards is a valuable exercise that builds consensus within a given field by promoting discussion about what is most worth learning.

But what was to be the federal role in the growing movement for standards? This was not yet determined. As a historian of education, I knew that there had long been antagonism toward federal involvement in education because of widespread fear that a federal Department of Education might be too powerful and might try to usurp local control. I knew that any federal role in the creation of standards and assessments had to be shaped very thoughtfully, with great respect for the legitimate concerns of states and localities.

The principle of *federalism* does not mean the supremacy of the federal government, but rather a careful balancing of the interests of the different levels of government. In this case it meant steering a course between two extremes: the familiar pattern of complete local control—in which there are no standards or wildly different standards from district to district—and the imposition of a federal one-size-fits-all program. These are the Scylla and Charybdis of standards, both to be avoided.

I must confess that at the outset we knew what we wanted to accomplish but did not know how we would get there. We wanted to begin the process of setting national standards, but we did not want the federal government to have the power to impose standards on unwilling states and localities; we wanted to encourage the development of a national testing system, but we knew that the U.S. Department of Education did not have the authority to do this on its own. We quickly realized that the department must play a leadership role in helping the public understand the importance of a strong national system of standards and assessments.

As we were trying to figure out our strategy, a chance conversation in the summer of

1991 between Lamar Alexander and Frank Press of the National Academy of Sciences opened a new vista. They talked about how standards should be developed and who should do it. Shortly afterward, with the secretary's encouragement, the academy submitted a proposal to develop national standards in the sciences. It was generally recognized that the National Academy of Sciences was uniquely situated to convene the full complement of science organizations and to develop a consensus around what children should know and be able to do in the sciences. In September 1991 the department made a grant to the academy and launched the first of the federally funded standard-setting projects.

The science standards project defined the procedures and roles for subsequent efforts. The federal government would give funds to applicants who agreed to create a broad and inclusive process of arriving at consensus. The organizations involved in this process should be led by and include teachers, scholars, and other members of the public. The project would agree to examine the standards used in other nations and in leading states. The standards produced by these projects would be voluntary, not mandatory.

From the beginning, the department stressed the importance of both excellence and equity as outcomes for the standards projects. The object was not to create higher hurdles for students, but to demystify what was to be learned and to help all students reach higher levels of learning.

The National Center for History in the Schools submitted a proposal to develop national standards in history and won an award from the Department of Education in December 1991. The director of the center, Charlotte Crabtree, had gained the endorsement of every organization that was involved in the fields of history and social studies. In addition, the National Endowment for the Humanities agreed to join in providing financial support for the project.

As I have already noted, NCEST published its report, titled *Raising Standards in American Education,* in January 1992. The release of the report put the issues of standards and assessments in the public spotlight. NCEST recommended the development of high standards that were national, not federal (i.e., not controlled by the federal government); voluntary, not mandatory; and dynamic, not static. The standards should be developed through a participatory process, and they should be used to provide focus and direction, not to create a national curriculum. NCEST also recommended a national testing system that was fair and equitable, in which different tests would be linked to common standards.

In the year following the release of the NCEST report, the Department of Education moved forward in a deliberate fashion to implement the council's recommendations. In a 12-month period, the department launched national standards projects in the arts, civics, geography, English, and foreign languages. (Each of these projects also received funding from the National Endowment for the Humanities.)

Five years before, even two years before, almost no one had spoken seriously about the possibility of national standards or a national testing system for individual students. Now both prospects were part of the national debate.

But while it was crucial to establish national standards, we saw that as only the first step in a process that would depend on the active participation of the states. We concluded that the best way to preserve the principle of federalism was to encourage states to develop their own K–12 curriculum frameworks *at the same time that the national standards were under development.* Some people thought this was an odd approach and wondered why we did not insist on a linear progression: first national standards, then state curriculum frameworks based on the national standards.

The reason we rejected the linear approach was that we felt there were as many smart people in the states as there were at the national level (indeed, they were often the very same people). We wanted to encourage a synergy between the national projects and the creation of state curriculum frameworks, and this synergy was likeliest to occur if both were going on at the same time. Indeed, the "state systemic reform" awards from the National Science Foundation to nearly two dozen states meant that many of those states were already working on their curriculum frameworks in mathematics and science.

What is a state curriculum framework? It is a declaration of the state's standards for its children—a description of what it expects children to know and be able to do. State frameworks are usually more detailed than statements of national standards, and they usually serve as the basis for textbook adoptions or state assessments. A state curriculum framework should also be a strategic plan for education, starting with what children should know and using that as the basis for reforming teacher education, teacher certification, staff development, textbooks, assessments, and so on. (California, under Bill Honig's leadership, was the first state to develop this strategy of starting with the curriculum framework as a master plan for systemic reform.)

So, even as we were making awards to support national consensus projects, we launched competitions to fund the development of state curriculum frameworks in the same subject areas as those for which national standards were being established. To qualify for funding, the states had to demonstrate how they intended to use their own curriculum frameworks as the basis for reforming teacher education, teacher certification, staff development, and assessment.

Our strategy, you see, was not to put the federal government in the driver's seat, but to use federal funds to encourage the states to set their *own* standards and to use them to reform the other key parts of their own education systems. I never tired of reminding state officials that *they* controlled the marketplace in education. They had the power to shape teacher education by saying that they would not hire people who didn't know what the children were supposed to learn. They could shape teacher certification by saying that new teachers would be certified *only* if they knew what they were expected to teach. They could use staff development to help teachers learn what they needed to know to meet the state's own goals, and they could reform assessment by basing it on their own determination of what children needed to know and be able to do.

We also believed that the national standards would be widely accepted only if they were truly representative of the best thinking in the field and only if they were developed in a process that was open and broadly inclusive. If they succeeded in providing a vision for what should happen in the best of circumstances, then they could be incorporated as part of federal programs, such as Chapter 1 or the Dwight D. Eisenhower Mathematics and Science Programs.

After science and history, the next area funded was the arts. The arts were not mentioned in the national education goals—a source of considerable annoyance to arts educators. Because he believes that the arts should be part of everyone's education, Alexander decided that the subjects that are specifically named in the national goals (mathematics, science, history, geography, and English) are given as examples and are not meant to exclude other subjects. In June 1992 the Department of Education funded a standards proposal by the Music Educators National Conference, which joined in collaboration with the American Alliance for Theatre and Education, the National Art Education Association, and the National Dance Association.

On 1 July 1992 a press conference was held at the Supreme Court to announce the department's award to the Center for Civic Education to develop national standards in civics—another area not specifically mentioned in the goals. The center, headed by Charles Quigley, had contacts in every state and had assembled a broad umbrella coalition of organizations committed to civic education.

Three weeks later, at the National Geographic Society's headquarters, the department announced an award for a national standards project in geography. The award went to the National Council of Geographic Education, which represented a consortium of the Association of American Geographers, the National Geographic Society, and the American Geographical Society.

Then in September 1992 the department made an award to the Center for the Study of Reading (University of Illinois at Champaign), together with the National Council of Teachers of English and the International Reading Association, to create English standards.

Finally, in January 1993 an award was made to develop national standards in the teaching of foreign languages. The award went to the American Council of Teachers of Foreign Languages, in conjunction with organizations of teachers of German, Portuguese, and Spanish.

The law establishing the Department of Education states that the department shall not supervise, control, or direct the curriculum of the schools (this prohibition reflects the decades-old fear of a federal "takeover" of the schools). In funding the standards projects, the department made clear that its role was to provide the money and then to get out of the way. Although a member of the department's staff monitors the progress of each project, the department does not attempt to supervise, control, direct, or influence the deliberations of the projects in any way.

Each of the projects received funding to set high national standards and to lead a broadly inclusive participatory process. The department also provided a list of negatives—a description of what the projects are *not* to be. The projects are *not* to create standards for the elite, but to create them for *all* children. The projects are *not* to create a national curriculum, but to describe what children should know and be able to do in a particular field. Also, the projects are *not* to end the pedagogical disputes within each field; rather, the standards should leave to the wit and ingenuity of teachers decisions about *how* to teach (although there will probably be some emphases that blend the *what* and the *how,* such as problem-solving activities).

The standard-setting projects are well under way, and most expect to have a finished draft of national standards available by 1994–95. In addition, the work of creating state curriculum frameworks is moving steadily forward. My office sought funding from Congress to sponsor large competitions for state curriculum frameworks, but the money was not forthcoming. We were able to go forward on a limited basis through the Eisenhower National Program, which has made money available in math and science. Shortly before leaving office, I approved a competition for state frameworks in the other subject areas, to be supported by discretionary funds (which are quite limited).

My own view is that, in a time of fiscal stringency at all levels, it is a federal responsibility to help states reform their own standards in order to preserve federalism and promote both excellence and equity.

The issue of assessment has been far more complex than that of national standards. Until this time, the only meaningful federal role in assessment has been the department's sponsorship of the National Assessment of Educational Progress, which tests large national samples, not individual students. NCEST recommended tests for individual students, leaving the matter largely to the states or groups of states to manage.

This recommendation comes at a time of massive rethinking about testing. During the past several years, there has been much discussion about how to deemphasize the current reliance on tests that are standardized, machine scorable, and multiple choice. Many states, local districts, and individual schools are experimenting with ways to gauge student "performance" by "authentic assessment." At the leading edge of this reform have been the work and advocacy of Lauren Resnick and Marc Tucker of the New Standards Project, which is affiliated with a number of states and school districts.

Although the Alexander team had come into office calling for American Achievement Tests (and the Phi Delta Kappa/Gallup Poll shows that a majority of the American public favors a national examination), there was no way to make such tests happen. There was no money in the department's budget to fund a national testing system, and Congress repeatedly made plain its strong hostility to any federal involvement in testing. The only visible exception was Sen. Claiborne Pell (D-R.I.), who has long been an advocate of a national academic achievement test. The House Committee of Education and Labor passed a flat prohibition against the department's support for assessment development (as well as a prohibition against national standards and even against new research on assessment).

There was, we thought, a perfectly reasonable and appropriate way for the department to support the improvement of assessment, and that was to offer funds competitively to states that were building new student assessments based on higher standards. We asked Congress for money to help states that were taking the lead in assessment reform, and again we were turned down.

We also thought that it was an appropriate federal role to support new research and development efforts related to assessment. Despite the fact that the department maintains a research center on assessment at the University of California at Los Angeles, we believed that there was a need for much more investment in research and development on this complex issue. More research was needed to understand how to administer and score performance assessments. Certainly new research was needed to figure out how to equate, link, and calibrate different assessments—one of NCEST's key recommendations. And more research was needed to understand issues of test fairness.

Unfortunately, though we asked for "only" $5 million for new research on assessment (one senator told me not to waste his time with such small requests), Congress denied those funds also.

Obviously, we were not able to produce American Achievement Tests during our brief tenure in office; given the lack of consensus among educators as well as the outright opposition in Congress, that is not surprising. Nonetheless, I would say that we managed to change the national discussion and to put onto the table questions that no one was raising before we got there. Whenever possible, we lent moral support (and, when funds were available, financial backing) to those who were trying to develop new kinds of assessment. We gave full support to the introduction of performance items on the NAEP.

The point is that standards will be meaningless if students continue to be tested without regard to them. Unless current tests change, the standards will wither and die. Teachers know that they will be judged by test results, and they will continue to teach to the tests by which they are judged. That is why we as an Administration sided with such people as Lauren Resnick and the leaders of the NCTM, who contend that the tests must test knowledge and skills that are meaningful to students. The tests should be based on what children learn in class, and what they learn in class should be worth knowing and doing and using.

Standards are the starting point of education reform. You can't design an assessment unless you have agreement about what children should learn. In the absence of national standards, we have evolved a haphazard, accidental, disconnected national curriculum based on mass-market textbooks and standardized, multiple-choice tests.

Education reform must begin with broad agreement on what children should learn. Learning, after all, is the heart and soul of education. When there is no agreement regarding what students should learn, then each part of the education system pursues different, sometimes contradictory, goals. As a result, our education system is riddled with inequity, incoherence, and inefficiency.

In the summer of 1991 the department sponsored a meeting with education ministers from 15 Asian Pacific countries. The subject of the meeting was standards for the 21st century. The United States was one of the few participants that had not established national standards. When we asked the various ministers why their society had set national standards, they all gave the same dual answer: to promote equality of opportunity and to promote high achievement. As they explained it, without explicit standards some schools would set high standards and others would not (and without assessments, no one would know the difference). Moreover, explicit standards enabled students to judge their performance against clear goals, thus raising everyone's expectations.

One of the joys of the federal position that I held for 18 months was that I was able to visit many school districts. Occasionally, I saw truly exciting programs in which schools were teaching all children to reach for very high standards. For example, at the Mission High School in San Francisco, I witnessed the Interactive Mathematics Project, which engages inner-city youngsters in high-level problem solving that requires them to use algebra and geometry. At Portland Middle School in Portland, Michigan, I saw a mathematics program transformed by the hard work of the staff, and I saw children who understood what they were doing in math class and why.

I know full well that standards are not a panacea. I understand that there are children who are growing up in terrible situations, and no academic program alone will rescue them. I realize that there are school districts that have sustained devastating budget cuts. For dysfunctional families, social programs are needed. For financially strapped districts, more resources are needed. But if we are to attend to the learning that goes on in schools and if we are to take that responsibility seriously, then we must work to make national standards a reality. We must work together so that every state establishes curriculum frameworks that reflect the best thinking in the field, and we must continue to explore ways to improve student assessments.

I will always be grateful for the opportunity to have been part of these historic changes in American education.

## *Integrating Sources*

1. How do you suppose Shannon would respond to Ravitch's call for excellence and equity?

2. Has Ravitch addressed Shannon's concern about standards coming back to haunt the very educators who participate in establishing them? If not, how might she respond to his concern?

## *Classroom Implications*

1. Assume that a set of national literacy standards is in place. What steps can an individual teacher take to help ensure their achievement? Would you do anything differently?

2. Do you believe that national standards might eventually be used to evaluate your teaching? If so, would you regard this as a positive or negative development? Explain.

3. In your own teaching situation, do you regard the dual goals of excellence and equity as unattainable for all children? Explain.

4. Given the U.S. Department of Education's inability to establish a national curriculum, can national standards ever have any real "teeth"? Explain.

## *Annotated Bibliography*

### *National Standards*

Darling-Hammond, L. (1993). Reframing the school reform agenda: Developing capacity for school transformation. *Phi Delta Kappan, 74,* 752–761.

*The issue of standards in the larger context of school reform is discussed. It is argued that externally mandated standards and assessment are doomed to failure.*

Eisner, E. W. (1994). Do American schools need standards? *School Administrator, 51*(5), 8–11, 13.

*The usefulness of standards is questioned since they may oversimplify a very complex situation. Focus should be on nurturing children, not on measuring them.*

Flood, J., & Lapp, D. (1993). Clearing the confusion: A closer look at national goals and standards. *The Reading Teacher, 47,* 58–61.

*The pros and cons of standards are reviewed and the types of standards to be produced by IRA/NCTE are outlined.*

National Council on Educational Standards and Testing. (1992). *Raising standards in American Education.* Washington, DC: U.S. Department of Education.

*This gives recommendations for national standards that are not controlled by the federal government, that are voluntary, and that are subject to revision over time.*

O'Neil, J. (1993). On the new standards project: A conversation with Lauren Resnick and Warren Simmons. *Educational Leadership, 50*(5), 17–21.

*This is a good examination of the kinds of assessment planned to undergird the national standards. (Note: This article is part of a themed issue, February 1993.)*

Zancanella, D. (1994). Local conversations, national standards, and the future of English. *English Journal, 83*(3), 23–29.

*This article presents a good background discussion of the joint English language arts standards project undertaken by IRA/NCTE.*

## *You Become Involved*

### *National Standards*

**1.** Try your hand at drafting a single standard relating to any one of the other nine topics in this book. Were you able to produce one that was sufficiently specific for an educator to know if it had been achieved?

**2.** Examine recent issues of your local newspaper for articles dealing with standards. These may well be associated with state initiatives. What arguments are offered for and against their implementation? What groups tend to favor or oppose them?

**3.** Use the *Reader's Guide to Periodical Literature* to identify articles by syndicated columnists on the subject of educational standards. These writers tend to apply general political philosophies to educational issues, and so the arguments they make may differ from those of Shannon and Ravitch. Can you find any new arguments?

**4.** Compose a questionnaire on the desirability of national literacy standards. Administer it, perhaps as a class project, to a set of adults, including parents and teachers. Analyze your findings and present them to your classmates.

# Chapter *11*

# *Technology*

The early 1980s brought microcomputers into classrooms in large numbers. Enthusiasm and expectations were high, but hardware was expensive and software was often poorly designed. These difficulties, together with lukewarm research findings, led to a general decline in teacher interest. More recent developments, however, have resulted in a resurgence of micro use that brings with it important issues for literacy educators to resolve (McLaughlin, 1994; Reinking, 1994; Zuga, 1994).

## *The Two Sides of Continuing Development*

The emergence of newer, faster, more powerful hardware continues at breathtaking speed. Simultaneously, carefully designed software is now reflecting our enhanced understanding of literacy processes and how children acquire them. Here are some examples of both trends:

- A kindergarten child uses a portable, laptop computer to explore *Daisy Quest,* a program designed to develop phonemic awareness in prereaders.
- A middle-grade student uses a CD encyclopedia in writing a report. Entries on related topics can be easily assembled while the student travels among them and eventually integrates their content.
- A high school student uses a videodisk player to read a "hypermedia" version of a context textbook, containing (on demand) built-in glossaries, audible pronunciations, related readings, simplified versions, motion picture footage, and other accessories.
- An elementary class in the United States communicates with other students from countries throughout the world using E-mail.
- A middle school social studies class, using E-mail, makes use of library resources from throughout the country.

Such developments in hardware and software are not without drawbacks, however. Each new generation of microcomputers renders the previous generation disadvantaged, if not obsolete, in its ability to accommodate up-to-date software. Districts cannot possibly keep pace with the costs of maintaining current hardware and software. Thus, the end result for many schools is a technology inventory containing items that are dated and incompatible.

Other problems with the use of technology by schools include the following:

- Whether to maintain a separate lab or disperse computers to classrooms
- How to align software with curricular objectives
- How to provide adequate training to classroom teachers
- How to acquire information on the evaluation of new hardware and software prior to purchase

## As You Read

This chapter differs from all of the others in this book in that it was not drawn from a previously published source. Because of rapid changes in the field, we solicited an article that could be modified and adapted up to the time of publication. Jay S. Blanchard is a national authority on the applications of technology to literacy development. In the following article, he explores the future of such applications and the issues they raise for educators. As you read the article, consider these questions:

**1.** How can you contend with the reality of limited hardware in your classroom?
**2.** How can you keep up with rapid developments in literacy-related software?
**3.** What are ways you might effectively integrate such software into your instruction?

## References

McLaughlin, C. H. (1994). Developing environmental literacy through technology education. *Technology Teacher, 54,* 30–34.

Reinking, D. (1994). *Electronic literacy. Perspectives in reading research no. 4.* Athens, GA: National Reading Research Center.

Zuga, K. F. (1994). *Education: A review and synthesis of the research literature. Information series no. 356.* Columbus, OH: ERIC Clearinghouse on Adult, Career, and Vocational Education.

## CONTENT LITERACY GUIDE

**Issues in Technology and Literacy Education**
Jay S. Blanchard

1. What unusual agreement have various groups of educational stakeholders reached?

2. How would you relate Thoreau's quote to the issue technology in classrooms?

3. (T/F)  Some critics charge that technology has had no notable impact on teaching.

4. Summarize the five ways, suggested by Blanchard, that teachers will come to approach technology.

   a.

   b.

   c.

   d.

   e.

5. Define MPC applications.

6. Name the two varieties of MPC.

   a.

   b.

7. Explain the difference between the two varieties of MPC.

8. Why does Blanchard see the entertaining side of multimedia as a potential problem?

9. In what way can telecommunications be a substitute for transportation?

10. What is the current definition of *telecommunications?*

11. Describe how word processors facilitate student writing.

12. (T/F) The most common way for teachers to use microcomputers is for student writing through word processing.

13. (T/F) The research underlying the use of word processing software in classrooms has been positive.

14. (T/F) The research on the effects of multimedia in classrooms is not extensive at present.

15. (T/F) Research suggests that above-average students benefit the most from word processing.

# ISSUES IN TECHNOLOGY
# AND LITERACY EDUCATION

JAY S. BLANCHARD

## Introduction

One of the most fascinating and modern aspects of life today is technology. Regardless of the community or culture where it is used, technology has vitality, force, and attention-gathering effects. People like it. They respond to it. They expect it. They define themselves and the world around them by what they see and hear through technology. As a result, technology seems to have few limitations and almost magical strengths. Unfortunately, these magical strengths exist in few of today's classrooms, although teachers are increasingly expected to employ technology to help students learn more, faster, better, and cheaper. Technology, so far, has not provided a solution to the "learning more, faster, better and cheaper" problem! Despite this, technology is in the daily lives of everyone, including students and teachers.

Most of today's K–12 classrooms are filled with students "who have spent the greater portion of their lives staring at tubes of one kind or another, television, Nintendo, MTV, and computers are for this generation the primary medium of cultural transmission. From the playpen to early adulthood, the 13-inch screen, not the printed page, offers the dominant learning environment" (Winner, 1994, p. 66). Already by the beginning of 1995, 26 percent of homes in the United States have personal computers and most have TVs and VCRs. As a result, technology transformations have resulted in cultural ones. Technology has become not only a vehicle for the transmission of culture but a means by which people define themselves and the world around them. It has become so important that diverse and quarrelsome groups such as school boards, national, state, and local government officials, administrators, teachers, and parents have reached an unusual agreement: Technology needs to be incorporated into education. This is understandable. Historically, the response by societies to change so rapid and profound has been to teach the young about the change. Unfortunately, these diverse groups have yet to reach agree-

Portions of this article have appeared in *Computers in the Schools, 11*(3), 1995, and *The Journal of Technology of Information for Teacher Education, 3*(2), 1994, and will appear in *The Handbook of Research on Teacher Education* (1996).

316

ment on what is meant by the terms *technology* and *incorporated!* And, in fact, they have ignored more fundamental questions, such as: What kind of learning does it permit? What are the intellectual tendencies it encourages? What sort of culture does it produce? (see also Ellul, 1964; McLuhan, 1964; Postman, 1985.)

Many years ago, Thoreau warned that inventions are but an improved means to an unimproved end. Technology may be the educational innovation of the twentieth century, but in order for teachers to sort out some of the hyperbole and oversell associated with it, they must engage in the kind of critical reflection that enables them to make and express informed judgments about what aspects of the human condition known as "teaching reading" will be improved by using technology. As Bork (1985) noted, technology must demonstrate that it is educationally useful and can contribute in some way to the learning process. Perhaps a few lines from the science fiction short story "The Fun They Had" (Asimov, 1974) might point out the need for critical reflection and informed judgments about the use of technology in reading education. The year is 2157 and there are no schools—everyone is taught at home with mechanical teachers. Margie, a school-age youngster, speculates about how it must have been when people were teachers:

> *Margie went into the schoolroom. It was right next door to her bedroom, and the mechanical teacher was on and waiting for her. It was always on at the same time every day except Saturday and Sunday. The screen lit up, and it said: "Today's arithmetic lesson is on addition of proper fractions. Please insert yesterday's homework in the proper slot." Margie did so with a sigh. She was thinking about the old schools they had when her grandfather's grandfather was a little boy. All the kids from the whole neighborhood came, laughing and shouting in the schoolyard, sitting together in the schoolroom, going home together at the end of the day. They learned the same things, so they could help one another with the homework and talk about it. And the teachers were people. (p. 155)*

Like it or not, modern technology is seen by many as the new Prometheus: the creator of a new order for both education in general and more specifically for reading education. Technology, once in the background of classroom reading education, is now coming to the foreground. There seems to be a collective enthusiasm and belief among many that technology offers solutions not only to reading problems but to complex social and educational problems as well (i.e., single-parent families, child abuse, gangs, poverty, crime, the widening gap between the rich and the poor, racial inequity, guns, drugs, AIDS, and endangered environments, to name a few). But before technology can solve these problems and create a new order, it needs to accomplish a variety of simpler tasks under some very difficult conditions. Technobabble, chatter, and slogans will not suffice as solutions. Teachers already know that technology will not be a panacea for the problems faced by reading education. Nevertheless, some teachers are developing and beginning to articulate what they believe are technology's answers to the reading problems in their classrooms. The success of technology to help solve any problems, whether educational or social, requires that teachers clearly decide what they want technology to do and how they want it to do it! As noted earlier, this means that teachers must develop and articulate clear views of which technology experiences can help their students.

Today, modern technology is available in most K–12 classrooms and teacher education classrooms but only in the form of TVs, VCRs, and videotapes. Beyond these simple applications, technology is not having a widespread impact on reading education (Bennett & Bennett, 1994; Kline, 1994; Strudler, 1994; U.S. Congress, Office of Technology Assessment, 1988, 1995; Waxman & Huang, 1993). (Word processing and desktop publishing is having an impact but it is not as widespread as the influence of TVs and VCRs.) More than a few critics of technology have noted that technology has produced no notable or worthwhile changes in teaching or learning (Cuban, 1989; Hannafin & Savenye, 1993; Hill, 1994; La Frenz & Friedman, 1989; MacWorld, 1992; Papert, 1993; Perelman, 1992; Piller, 1992; Postman, 1992; Scrimshaw, 1993; Selby, 1993). These pundits, columnists, and commentators have noted that initial enthusiasm for technology (especially for computers) and the rosy predictions that accompanied the enthusiasm were naive (Cuban, 1986).

These critics aside, as teachers struggle to articulate and operationalize views of technology in reading education, they will notice little agreement among themselves in views or actions. Some will seek to implement instruction and learning anchored by technology. Others will see technology leading to "different forms of thinking [that] lead to different forms of meaning" (Eisner, 1993, p. 6). Some will use technology to minimize weaknesses of classroom practices—while hopefully maximizing the strengths. Others will use technology as an almost unnoticed tool incorporated naturally into teaching and learning much like paper, pencils, and erasers. Finally, some teachers will use technology to do the same things they have always done—perhaps more efficiently and effectively. Given the number and diversity of these approaches, this article will focus on three issues of importance to reading education—namely, multimedia, telecommunications, and word processing/desktop publishing.

## Multimedia in Reading Education

*Media* and *multimedia* refer to ways of exchanging or communicating information. At the beginning of the twentieth century, multimedia meant blackboards and white chalk and a limited variety of books, paper, and pencils. By the midpoint of the twentieth century, teachers had green boards and yellow chalk, television, radio, film projectors and films, filmstrip projectors and filmstrips, record players and records, overhead projectors and transparencies, audio tape recorders and audio tapes as well as books, paper, and pencils in a wide variety of sizes, shapes, and colors. Today, exchanging information includes white boards and colored markers, computers, cameras, videotape players and tapes, compact disc players and discs, videodisc (laserdisc) players and discs, as well as telecommunication networks, both ground and satellite based. What all this means is that the sprawl of information and the diversity of media that mark the pop culture of the twentieth century present colossal challenges for literacy education (see *WIRED Magazine,* Wired Ventures Ltd., for some of the best examples of multimedia in the pop culture).

## Definition

*Multimedia personal computer (MPC) applications* "can best be defined as various combinations of text, graphics, sound, video, and animation that are controlled, coordinated, and delivered by the computer" (Lynch, 1992, p. 2). These applications tie together any number of audio, video, and textual resources (e.g., compact disc, videodisc, films, records, microphones, audio tapes and recorders, videotapes and recorders, cameras, photographs television, radio, telephone, and printed text).

The MPC is powerful and fast. It has large internal and external storage. It has a high resolution color screen that displays graphic information in stills, full motion, and animation. It has stereo sound with the ability to add, subtract, or mix sound. And finally, it has a "plug and play" or "built-in" compact disc and/or videodisc (laserdisc) player. Internal computer programs provide the cohesiveness necessary to retrieve and guide video and audio information from its internal and external sources. The user can communicate with the MPC through a keyboard and mouse as well as optional touch screen or light pen.

## Examples

MPC applications come in two basic varieties: ready to use (or prepackaged) and construct your own. Both of these varieties illustrate the two major functions of MPC applications—namely, a drawing together of diverse media (e.g., animation, text, graphics, music, recorded voices, miscellaneous sounds) and a means to control or orchestrate the uses of these media. In ready-to-use applications, teachers and students do not draw together different media—as is done in construct-your-own applications—instead, that is done by a publisher.

## Ready-to-Use MPC Application

The ready-to-use MPC applications can be very complex and expensive or quite simple and inexpensive. A simple and inexpensive example of a middle school reading application is Discis Knowledge Research's *Tell Tale Heart*. This application is one of many "books" that are interactive, multimedia tales. Each title provides the original text, illustrations, voices (bilingual), sound effects, and music. Students can read the text or listen to the text being read to them. Unknown words can be selected and pronounced (by the computer), and in-context definitions are provided.

Probably the most complex, advanced, and powerful multimedia application commercially available is IBM's *Illustrated Books and Manuscripts* (including a related product entitled "Columbus: A Journey to Discovery"). Each of the current titles in this application (e.g., "Letter from Birmingham Jail," "Black Elk Speaks," "Hamlet," "Declaration of Independence," "Ulysses") allows teachers and students to read and research literary works supported by a number of educational resources that include dictionaries, film, animation, speeches, discussions, and still photographs. All of these media resources help students explore relationships between the literary works and other disciplines. *Illuminated Books and Manuscripts* has been described as a text augmentation system—with a variety of audio and video enhancements.

For reference applications, the World Book's *New Illustrated Information Finder,* New Grolier's *Multimedia Encyclopedia Release 6,* Compton's *Interactive Multimedia Encyclopedia Version 2,* and Microsoft's *Encarta 1994 Edition*[1] provide ready-to-use search and access resources. These multimedia dictionaries and encyclopedias provide opportunities for student to use greatly expanded electronic versions of common reference tools. For example, the Compton Encyclopedia (on compact disc) has nine million words in 33,700 articles, 7,000 photos, 33 video clips, 35 slide presentations, 26 animations, and 100 audio clips, and it costs $99.00. The Grolier Encyclopedia (on compact disc) has 10 million words in 33,000 articles, 4,000 photos, 15 animated maps, 13 audiovisual essays, 27 narrated animations, 53 video clips totaling 35 minutes, and 40 minutes of audio clips, and it also costs $99.00.[2]

### Construct-Your-Own MPC Application

The construct-your-own or do-it-yourself MPC applications have historically required specially trained teachers and technically literate students. These applications provide tools that allow teachers and students to manipulate video and audio information in a multimedia environment; in essence, teachers and students can create their own multimedia programs provided they have the hardware, software, the expertise, and the content. However, teacher and students have not embraced the necessary technologies (i.e., scanners, video/audio digitizers, CD-ROMs, videodiscs and cameras [still and videotape], printers, as well as software authoring programs needed for widespread use). That may be changing. Easy-to-use multimedia applications involving these technologies have begun to appear.[3] Today, many students and teachers are authoring their own multimedia programs and products that can be used in reading education (Peterson & Orde, 1995; Milone, 1994).

Despite all of this power, there are some problems. For instance, multimedia can become the message—and for many students the messages must be entertaining. It would seem almost a certainty that as the power and popularity of multimedia increase, so would the chances for misuse. In the near future, the dazzling array of multimedia sights and sounds that have been reserved for buying and selling, entertaining, and advertising will be available to reading education. What will this mean? As seems the case with many of the twentieth century's most innovative technologies, the uses of multimedia are as powerful as they are troubling.

## Telecommunications in Literacy Education

Telecommunication technologies are transforming the means, and perhaps the ways, by which teachers and students share information and ideas, and this is true in all academic disciplines, including reading education. These technologies permit teachers and students to create classrooms with windows on the world. They are no longer bound by the walls of their classrooms. They can expand their knowledge of others and influence those with whom they interact by changing perceptions and opinions. All of this can happen without teachers and students leaving their classrooms. Telecommunications can be a substitute for transportation. Instead of moving people to information and ideas, telecommunications moves information and ideas to people (Rogers, 1986). As a result, it is no longer hyperbole to suggest that telecommunications has the potential to change the way teachers and students interact, communicate, and learn from one another (National Research Council, 1994).

## Definition

*Telecommunications* has historically meant communication across distances, but more recently has come to mean electronic communication across distances. Telecommunications (also called the Information Super Highway and officially known as the National Information Infrastructure [NII]) involves groups of technologies such as telephone, radio, television, videotape, compact and laser discs, computers, and satellites. These technologies, individually or as a group, do not automatically allow teachers and students electronic communication rights and capabilities to be obtained. Once linked or networked, telecommunications technologies can involve such activities as use of electronic bulletin boards, electronic mail, or on-line data services and databases. Networked commercial and non commercial resources are now available for classroom use (e.g., Kidlink, Internet, eWorld, CompuServe, America-On-Line, Prodigy, At&T Learning Network, Scholastic Net, National Geographic KidsNet, as well as state-funded resources such as Mass Ed Online [Massachusetts], CORE [California], and TENET [Texas]).

## Examples

Virtually every magazine, newspaper, and journal, whether remotely concerned with education or not, has by now featured the possible impact of telecommunications (e.g., the Information Superhighway, Internet) on classroom education in at least one article. It is a reoccurring theme that criss-crosses the landscape of classroom education. Although it is true that telecommunications is one of the "hot buttons" of education in the 1990s, nevertheless, it is not clear exactly what impact telecommunications is currently having on classroom education—or what impact it will have (Harris, 1994–1995, 1994). Recent classroom surveys indicate that telecommunications use is growing but it is still relatively new (Ross, 1995).[4]

Here are two recent examples. Eighth-grade teachers in seven locations across the Untied States used the AT&T Learning Network to study nutrition. Students analyzed each other's eating habits. This involved both on-line and off-line tasks that featured preparing surveys, administrating surveys, gathering data, displaying the data, and interpreting the data (Gray, 1995). In another example, sixth grade students in Minnesota used the Internet (World Wide Web and Mosaic) to investigate a number of research subjects and then create reports. The students then posted their reports on the Internet as Mosaic pages and created links to other Internet resources in the Mosaic pages (Harris, 1994–1995).

Not all telecommunications is world wide or uses a commercial network. In Lexington, Massachusetts middle school teachers and students studied the metamorphosis of butterflies with a scientist from Boston's Museum of Science. They shared their knowledge with other middle and junior high schools by way of interactive teleconferencing via cordless speaker phones located in their school's media center.

Despite these examples, many questions remain about telecommunications in reading education. For instance, how can telecommunications lead to more learning and understanding? Can these opportunities be universal? Will the Information Highway also be the Education Highway? Will the much-heralded claims of "expanded areas of communication" and "easier flows of information" come true—and to whose benefit? What will the students learn? What will it mean? How will they use that information? Who will control the format and content of classroom telecommunications. What information will teachers and students have access to? At what costs? Will the rich schools get telecommunications and the poor schools TVs and videotapes?

As reading educators struggle to articulate and operationalize their views on telecommunications these and many more questions need answers. In the final analysis, the Information Highway may contain all the problems encountered by its metaphorical parent with cracks, holes, ruts, poor signs, wrecks, off-ramps, inconsiderate motorists—and drive-by shootings.

# Word Processing/Desktop Publishing in Literacy Education

Word processing/desktop publishing (WP/DP) technologies have changed the way people communicate. All aspects of society have felt the impact—and reading education is not an exception. As a result, teachers have increased their emphasis on writing and publishing. Not surprisingly, many students now write and publish more.

## Defined

Very simply put, *word processing programs* allow writers to create and manipulate language through additions and deletions, cutting and pasting of text, and any number of other text or graphic arrangements or formats. Many programs include editing aids such as spelling checkers, grammar checkers, and thesauruses. Once word processing documents have been created, *desktop publishing programs* allow the writers to become publishers—creating print and pictorial documents.

## Examples

Recent surveys seem to indicate that the most common way teachers are using technology for reading education is WP/DP (U.S. Department of Education, Office of Educational Research, 1993).[5] This is not a recent trend. For example, a 1991 United States study of 600, K–12 teachers who considered themselves technology users, reported that the teachers used an average of 14 to15 different applications in their classrooms. Word processing was the most common application and the most common uses of word processing revolved around student projects such as reports and newsletters (Brady, 1991).

Here are a few examples of middle school students and teachers using WP/DP. Students in Moundsville, West Virginia, are electronic pen pals (using fictitious names) with prisoners at a nearby state prison. The success of the idea has spread and now involves 10 other schools from Alaska to the Netherlands—all pen pals with the West Virginia inmates. The teacher responsible for all this (Burrall, 1994) reports that communication with prisoners allows the students "to see how wrong choices can lead to disastrous consequences" (p. 42).

Reissman (1994) uses WP/DP and newspaper cartoons to teach persuasive writing to middle school students. Using newspaper comic strips distributed by the teacher, small groups of students "write out" the story or the "ideas" in comic strips (e.g., Cathy, Donnesbury, Ziggy, Garfield). The commentaries were then printed and shared with the other groups and each group explained their own comments about the comic strips.

## Impact on Achievement

At present, there is little about the effects of multimedia and telecommunications on reading achievement (regarding multimedia, see Fletcher, 1990; for telecommunications see Honey & Henriquez, 1993). However, there is data about the impact of WP/DP on reading achievement. Unfortunately, there is a problem! Most early research studies, while supporting the positive effects of WP/DP on reading achievement (See Cochran-Smith, 1991; Hawisher, 1989; Kozma, 1991; MacArthur, 1988 for reviews of the literature), did not use graphic user interfaces (GUI) and instead used the now outdated character-based word processors. Suffice it to say while these early research studies reported generally positive results, recent GUI/windows research studies are taking a more "wait and see" attitude. For example, Laidley (1991) compared the editing skills of sixth-grade students in the paper-and-pencil (control) group with the word processing (experimental) group. A story with "built-in" errors was used for student editing. The study revealed no statistically significant differences in the mechanical, grammatical, or conceptual error scores between paper-and-pencil and word processing groups.

In another study, Joram, Woodruff, Bryson, and Lindsay (1992) used eighth-graders to examine the influence of word processing on creative, expository prose writing assignments. In a guided writing activity, one group of students used word processors while another group wrote the paper and pencil. The initial results indicated that students using paper and pencil were rated more creative than those using word processors. However, when the eighth-graders were further divided by writing ability (average versus above average), different results were obtained. The average writers gained the most from word processing, and the above-average writers showed little gains in creativity. The Laidley (1991) and Joram, Woodruff, Bryson, and Lindsay (1992) research as well as research covering students from other grade levels (e.g., Peterson, 1993; high school) are the latest in a growing body of data that point to many unanswered questions about the impact of WP/DP impact on reading and writing achievement.

## Conclusion

Modern technology is not the new Prometheus for classroom education. It is not the creator of a new order for reading education. However, it is increasingly a part of the daily lives of students and teachers and it does have the power to change the lives of some students and teachers. For instance, the following poem was written by a man identified only as Ed. He has ALS (amyptrophic lateral sclerosis, or Lou Gehrig's disease). He was bedridden and was able to move only his eyes. Just before he died, he wrote this poem. It was written with a computer that recorded the movement of his eyelids with infrared sensors. It was featured in an article by Bill Machrone in a 1994 issue of *PC Magazine*.

*Every morning in Africa, a gazelle wakes up.*
*It knows it must run faster than the fastest lion,*
*Or it will be killed.*

*Every morning in Africa, a lion wakes up,*
*It knows that it must outrun the slowest gazelle,*
*Or it will starve to death.*

*It doesn't matter whether you're a lion or a gazelle,*
*When the Sun come up in the morning, you'd better be running!*

## Endnotes

1. See also Microsoft's *Dinosaurs, Beethoven, Mozart, Schubert, Stravinsky, Musical Instruments, Bookshelf 94,* and *Art Gallery.*
2. Other advanced reference applications include *CNN Newsroom Global View,* National Geographic's *Picture Atlas of the World,* New Media Schoolhouse's *Time Traveler,* Software Tool's *Mammals,* Computer Curriculum's *Choosing Success* and *Amazonia,* and Putnam New Media's *Cartoon History of the World.*
3. Examples of easy-to-use class multimedia applications include Scholastic *Electronic Portfolio,* Roger Wagner's *Hyperstudio,* and Davidson's *Multimedia Workshop* (see also *Electronic Learning,* November/December 1994, *Technology and Learning,* January 1995, and *The Computing Teacher,* November 1994, for a review of the subject).
4. The best examples of telecommunications use in reading education are apt to be found in *The Computing Teacher* (ISTE), *Technology and Learning* (Peter Li Publications) or *Electronic Learning* (Scholastic).
5. The popularity of WP/DP in the schools is probably related to its popularity on the job. The *Digest of Education Statistics* (U.S. Department of Education, Office of Educational Research and Improvement, 1994) reported that the most common use of technology on the job was bookkeeping, invoicing, and word processing.

## References

Asimov, I. (1974). *The best of Issac Asimov.* New York: Doubleday.

Bennett, C., & Bennett, J. (1994). United we stand: A portrait of teachers and technology in rural America. In J. Willis, B. Robin & D. Willis (Eds.), *Technology and teacher education annual* (pp. 725–729). Charlottesville, VA: Association for the Advancement of Computing in Education.

Bork, A. (1985). *Personal computers in education.* New York: Harper and Row.

Brady, H. (1991). New survey summarizes what top technology teachers have learned. *Technology and Learning, 11*(4), 38.

Burrall, B. (1994). The prison project. *The Computing Teacher, 22*(2), 41–42.

Carey, D., Carey, R., Willis, D., & Willis, J. (Eds.). (1993). *Technology and teacher education annual.* Charlottesville, VA: Association for the Advancement of Computing in Education.

Cochran-Smith, M. (1991). Word-processing and writing. *Review of Educational Research, 61*(1), 107–155.

Collins, A. (1991). The role of computer technology in restructuring schools. *Phi Delta Kappan, 73*(1), 28–36.

Cuban, L. (1986). *Teachers and machines: The classroom use of technology since 1920.* New York: Teachers College Press.

Cuban, L. (1989). Neoprogressive visions and organizational realities. *Harvard Educational Review, 59*(2), 217–222.

Cuban, L. (1993, January). The truth about technology. *Teacher,* pp. 30–32.

Eisner, E. (1993). Forms of understanding and the future of educational research. *Educational Researcher, 22,* 5–11.

Ellul, J. (1964). *The technological society.* New York: Knopf.

Fletcher, D. (1990). *Effectiveness and cost of interactive videodisc instruction in defense training and education.* Alexandria, VA: Institute for Defense Analyses.

Gray, T. (1995). Dynamic connections at the junior high. *The Computing Teacher, 22*(5), 23–27.

Hancock, V., & Betts, F. (1994). From the lagging edge to the leading edge. *Educational Leadership, 51*(7), 24–32.

Hannafin, R., & Savenye, W. (1993). Technology in the classroom: The teacher's new role and resistance to it. *Educational Technology, 33*(6), 26–31.

Harris, J. (1994). *Way of the ferret: Finding educational resources on the Internet.* Eugene, OR: ISTE.

Harris, J. (1994–1995). Mining the Internet. *The Computing Teacher, 22*(4), 36–38.

Hawisher, G. (1989). Research and recommendations for computers and composition. In G. Hawisher and C. Selfe (Eds.), *Critical perspectives on computers and composition instruction* (pp. 44–69). New York: Teachers College Press.

Hill, D. (1994, January). Professor Papert and his learning machine. *Teacher,* pp. 16–19.

Holland, H. (1994). Technology & tradition. *Electronic Learning, 14*(2), 24–26.

Honey, M., & Henriquez, A. (1993). *Telecommunications and K–12 educators: Findings from a national survey.* New York: Center for Technology in Education, Bank Street College of Education.

Joram, E., Woodruff, E., Bryson, M., & Lindsay, P. (1992). The effects of revising with a word processor on written composition. *Research in the Teaching of English, 26*(2), 167–193.

Kean, D. M., & Kean, D. K. (1992). Using model technology. *Middle School Journal, 23*(5), 44–45.

Kline, F. (1994). Multimedia in teacher education: Coping with the human element. In J. Willis, B. Robin & D. Willis (Eds.), *Technology and teacher education annual* (pp. 759–763). Charlottesville, VA: Association for the Advancement of Computing in Education.

Kozma, R. (1991). Learning with media. *Review of Educational Research, 61*(2), 179–211.

La Frenz, D., & Friedman, J. (1989). Computers don't change education, teachers do! *Harvard Educational Review, 59*(2), 222–225.

Laidley, J. (1991). A study of students' writing abilities with microcomputers (word-processing). *Dissertation Abstracts International, 51/10A,* 3393-A.

Lapp, D., Flood, J., & Lungren, L. (1995). Strategies for gaining access to the information superhighway: Off the side street and on to the main road. *The Reading Teacher, 48*(5), 432–436.

Lepper, M., & Gurtner, J. (1989). Children and computers. *American Psychologist, 44*(2), 1701–1708.

Levin, J. (1991). You can't just plug it in: Integrating the computer into the curriculum (CAI). *Dissertation Abstracts International, 51/12A,* 4096-A.

Lewis, P. H. (1991). The technology of tomorrow. *Principal, 71*(2), 6–7.

Lynch, P. (1992). Teaching with multimedia. *Syllabus, 22,* 2–5. (Syllabus, P.O. Box 2716, Sunnyvale, CA, 94087-0716).

MacArthur, C. (1988). The impact of computers on the writing process. *Exceptional Children, 54*(6), 536–542.

MacWorld. (1992). *America's shame: Personal computers in education, 9*(9), 225–239.

Machrone, B. (1994, June 28). Eyes on the Prize. *PC Magazine,* pp. 87–88.

Mathew, N. (1994). The Mary Butterworth School experience. *The Computing Teacher, 22*(2), 20–22.

McLuhan, M. (1964). *Understanding media.* New York: McGraw-Hill.

Milone, M. (1994). Multimedia authors, one and all. *Technology and Learning, 5*(2), 25-31.

Moursund, D. (1992). Crossroads. *The Computing Teacher, 20*(3), 5.

National Research Council. (1994). *Realizing the information future.* National Research Council, National Academy of Sciences. New York: National Academy Press.

Ornstein, A. (1992). Making effective use of computer technology. *NASSP Bulletin: The Journal for Middle Level and High School Administrators, 76*(524), 27–33.

Papert, S. (1993). *The children's machine.* New York: Basic Books.

Perelman, L. (1992). *School's out: Hyperlearning, the new technology, and the end of education.* New York: William Morrow.

Peterson, N., & Orde, B. (1995). Implementing multimedia in the middle school curriculum: Pros, cons and lesson learned. *T.H.E. Journal, 22*(7), 70–75.

Peterson, S. (1993). A comparison of student revisions when composing with pen and paper versus word-processing. *Computers in the Schools, 9*(4), 55–69.

Pillar, C. (1992). Separate realities. *MacWorld, 9*(9), 218–239.

Postman, N. (1985). *Amusing ourselves to death: Public discourse in the age of show business.* New York: Penguin.

Postman, N. (1992). *Technology.* New York: Knopf.

Reissman, R. (1994). Computer carton commentaries. *The Computing Teacher, 21*(5), 23–25.

Reissman, R. (1994-1995). Multimedia memoirs. *The Computing Teacher, 22*(4), 33–35.

Rogers, E. (1986). *Communication technology: The new media in society.* New York: Free Press.

Ross, P. (1995). Relevant telecomputing activities. *The Computing Teacher, 22*(5), 28–30.

Scrimshaw, P. (Ed.). (1993). *Language, classrooms & computers.* London: Routledge.

Selby, C. (1993). Technology: from myths to realities. *Phi Delta Kappan, 74*(9), 684–689.

Sheingold, K. (1991). Restructuring for learning with technology: The potential for synergy. *Phi Delta Kappan, 73*(1), 17–27.

Siegel, J. (1994). Walking the new walk. *Electronic Learning, 14*(1), 34–38.

Strudler, N. (1994). A tale of computer use at three elementary schools: Implications for teacher educators. In J. Willis, B. Robin, & D. Willis (Eds.), *Technology and teacher education annual* (pp. 756–758). Charlottesville, VA: Association for the Advancement of Computing in Education.

U.S. Congress, Office of Technology Assessment. (1988). *Power on!* Washington, DC: U.S. Government Printing Office.

U.S. Congress, Office of Technology Assessment. (1995). *Untitled.* (Report to be released in 1995). Washington, DC: U.S. Government Printing Office.

U.S. Department of Education, Office of Educational Research and Improvement. (1993). *Using technology to support education reform.* Washington, DC: U.S. Government Printing.

U.S. Department of Education, Office of Educational Research and Improvement (1994). *Digest of Education Statistics.* Washington, DC: U.S. Government Printing.

Waxman, H., & Huang, S. (1993). Investigating computer use in elementary and middle school inner-city classrooms. In D. Carey, R. Carey, D. Willis, & J. Willis (Eds.), *Technology and teacher education annual* (pp. 524–527). Charlottesville, VA: Association for the Advancement of Computing in Education.

Willis, J., Robin, B., & Willis, D. (Eds.). (1994). *Technology and teacher education annual.* Charlottesville, VA: Association for the Advancement of Computing in Education.

Winner, L. (1994, May/June). The virtually educated. *Technology Review,* p. 66.

Yoder, S. (1991, October 21). Readin', writin' and multimedia. *The Wall Street Journal,* p. R-12.

Zorfass, J., Remz, A., & Persky, S. (1991). A technology integration model for middle schools. *T.H.H. Journal, 19*(2), 69–71.

## *Classroom Implications*

**1.** Reexamine the uses Blanchard mentions in his three subsections labeled "Examples." Select one example per section and list its strengths and limitations as you see them.

| Area | Strengths | Limitations |
|---|---|---|
| 1. Multimedia | | |
|    a. Ready to Use | | |
|    b. Construct Your Own | | |
| 2. Telecommunications | | |
| 3. Word Processing/ Desktop Publishing | | |

**2.** Suggest ways that a classroom teacher might integrate technology effectively even though hardware might be limited.

**3.** Blanchard suggests three limitations of, or warnings about, computerized multimedia. Two other limitations are cost and the time a teacher needs to acquire the necessary expertise to make computerized multimedia work. Can you suggest possible ways of overcoming these limitations?

a. *Ways of conserving costs:*

b. *Ways of contending with the need for teacher expertise:*

## *Annotated Bibliography*

### *Technology*

#### *Historical References*

McLuhan, M. (1962). *The Gutenberg galaxy: The making of typographic man.* Toronto: University of Toronto Press.

*This is a classic discussion of how print defines humanity and the implications of literacy for human growth and functioning (see Provenzo, below).*

Turkle, S. (1984). *The second self: Computers and the human spirit.* New York: Simon and Schuster.

*Reflections are given on how computers may transform the ways in which people develop and view themselves and their culture.*

#### *Current References*

Bangert-Drowns, R. L. (1993). The word processor as an instructional tool: A meta-analysis of word processing in writing instruction. *Review of Educational Research, 63,* 69–93.

*The encouraging research underlying the use of computers to improve writing ability is reviewed.*

Bolter, J. D. (1991). *Writing space: The computer, hypertext, and the history of writing.* Hillsdale, NJ: Erlbaum.

*This book examines ways in which technology fundamentally alters the way writing must be viewed (and taught).*

Bruce, B. C., & Rubin, A. (1993). *Electronic quills: A situated evaluation of using computers for writing in classrooms.* Hillsdale, NJ: Lawrence Erlbaum.

*Alternative means of assessing writing based on the use of word processing software are explored.*

Delaney, P., & Landow, G. P. (Eds.). (1991). *Hypermedia and literary studies.* Cambridge, MA: MIT Press.

*This book is a discussion of how hypermedia can transform children's conceptions of literature.*

Duffy, T. M., & Jonassen, D. H. (Eds.). (1992). *Constructivism and the technology of instruction: A conversation.* Hillsdale, NJ: Lawrence Erlbaum.

*This book strives to describe the implications of two current movements in education: technology and constructivism. It also examines how the latter is helped by technological advances.*

Edwards, B. L. (1991). How computers change things: Literacy and the digitized word. *Writing Instructor, 10*(2), 68–76.

*This is a good introduction to how literacy is being redefined by technology.*

Hawisher, G. E., & Selfe, C. L. (1991). *Evolving perspectives on computers and composition studies: Questions for the 1990s.* Urbana, IL: National Council of Teachers of English.

*This examines issues in writing instruction raised for the first time due to the availability of technology.*

Jonassen, D. H., & Mandl, H. (Eds.). (1990). *Designing hypermedia for learning.* Berlin, Germany: Springer-Verlag.

*The potential of hypermedia as a mode of instruction is described.*

Kaufer, D. S., & Carley, K. M. (1993). *Communication at a distance: The influence of print on sociocultural organization and change.* Hillsdale, NJ: Lawrence Erlbaum.

*This explores the dynamic ways in which print media—including computer-media print—affects the functioning of society.*

Landow, G. (1992). *Hypertext: The convergence of contemporary critical theory and technology.* Baltimore, MD: The Johns Hopkins University Press.

*This discusses how hypertext can actually succeed in fulfilling the potential of literacy development, as advocated by critical theorists.*

Lanham, R. A. (1993). *The electronic word: Democracy, technology, and the arts.* Chicago, IL: University of Chicago Press.

*A wide range of issues are explored, many of which touch on literacy instruction and development, as technology becomes more sophisticated and pervasive.*

McArthur, T. (1986). *Worlds of reference: Lexicography, learning and language from the clay tablet to the computer.* Cambridge: Cambridge University Press.

*This is an excellent overview of many of the issues raised by technology as it affects literacy. Issues are placed in a useful historical perspective.*

Means, B. (Ed.). (1994). *Technology and education reform.* San Francisco, CA: Jossey-Bass.

*This collection of essays focuses on the need to integrate technology into present-day instruction.*

Provenzo, E., Jr. (1986). *Beyond the Gutenberg Galaxy: Microcomputers and the emergence of post-typographic culture.* New York: Teachers College Press.

*McLuhan's classic work is used as a springboard for discussing how computer-mediated print further transforms the nature of society.*

Reinking, D., & Bridwell-Bowles, L. (1991). Computers in reading and writing. In R. Barr, M. Kamil, P. B. Mosenthal, & P. D. Pearson (Eds.), *Handbook of reading research* (Vol. II, pp. 310–340). White Plains, NY: Longman.

*This extensive review of research into the effectiveness of microcomputers in the development of literacy includes a section on issues and trends.*

Rheingold, H. (1993). *The virtual community: Homesteading on the electronic frontier.* Reading, MA: Addison-Wesley.

*This discusses the transformation of culture and society that is now resulting from the development of telecommunications.*

Selfe, C. L., & Hilligoss, S. (Eds.). (1994). *Literacy and computers: The complications of teaching and learning with technology.* New York: The Modern Language Association.

*This excellent discussion of how technology presents teachers both with breathtaking potential in developing literacy and with an entirely new set of problems to be overcome in making it happen.*

Tuman, M. (1992). *Word perfect: Literacy in the computer age.* London, UK: Falmer Press.

*This is a good discussion of issues raised for educators and others as computer-mediated print becomes more the rule than the exception.*

Tuman, M. C. (Ed.). (1992). *Literacy online: The promise (and peril) of reading and writing with computers.* Pittsburgh, PA: University of Pittsburgh Press.

*This extends discussion of how computers affect literacy development and use by examining the issues raised related to computers networked together.*

## You Become Involved

**1.** Conduct an ERIC search to determine the number of articles published under the joint subjects "Reading" and "Computers" over the past 10 years. What trend do you uncover?

**2.** Choose one of the other topics discussed in this book (phonics, spelling, etc.) and describe an *ideal* program to develop students' abilities in that area. Do you know of existing software with a similar format?

**3.** See if you can identify sources of reviews of software targeting literacy. Check the major journals listed in Chapter 1. Which sources seem most useful to you? (Did you find any promising software in your sojourn?)

# Index